SURPRISE!

YOU MAY BE READING THE WRONG WAY!

It's true: In keeping with the original Japanese comic format, this book reads from right to left—so action, sound effects, and word balloons are completely reversed. This preserves the orientation of the original artwork—plus, it's fun! Check out the diagram shown here to get the hang of things, and then turn to the other side of the book to get started!

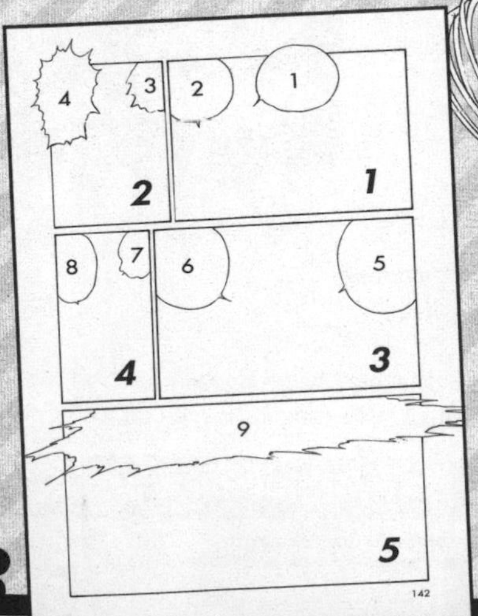
1
2
3
4
5
6
7
8
9
142

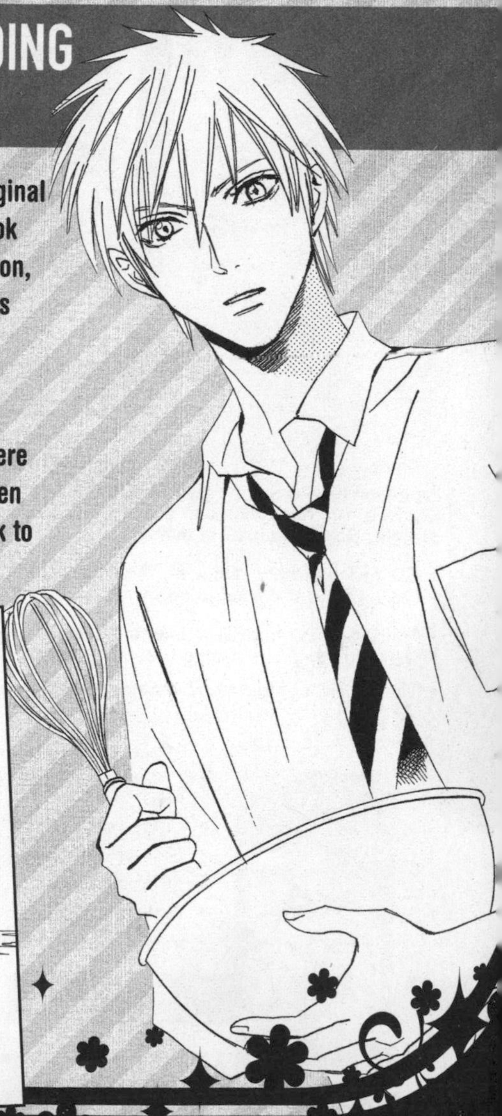

⊓IZMΛⁿGΛ

Read manga anytime, anywhere!

From our newest hit series to the classics you know and love, the best manga in the world is now available digitally. Buy a volume* of digital manga for your:

- iOS device (**iPad®**, **iPhone®**, **iPod® touch**) through the **VIZ Manga app**

- Android-powered device (**phone or tablet**) with a browser by visiting VIZManga.com

- **Mac or PC computer** by visiting VIZManga.com

VIZ Digital has loads to offer:

- 500+ ready-to-read volumes
- New volumes each week
- FREE previews
- Access on multiple devices! Create a log-in through the app so you buy a book once, and read it on your device of choice!*

To learn more, visit www.viz.com/apps

* Some series may not be available for multiple devices.
Check the app on your device to find out what's available.

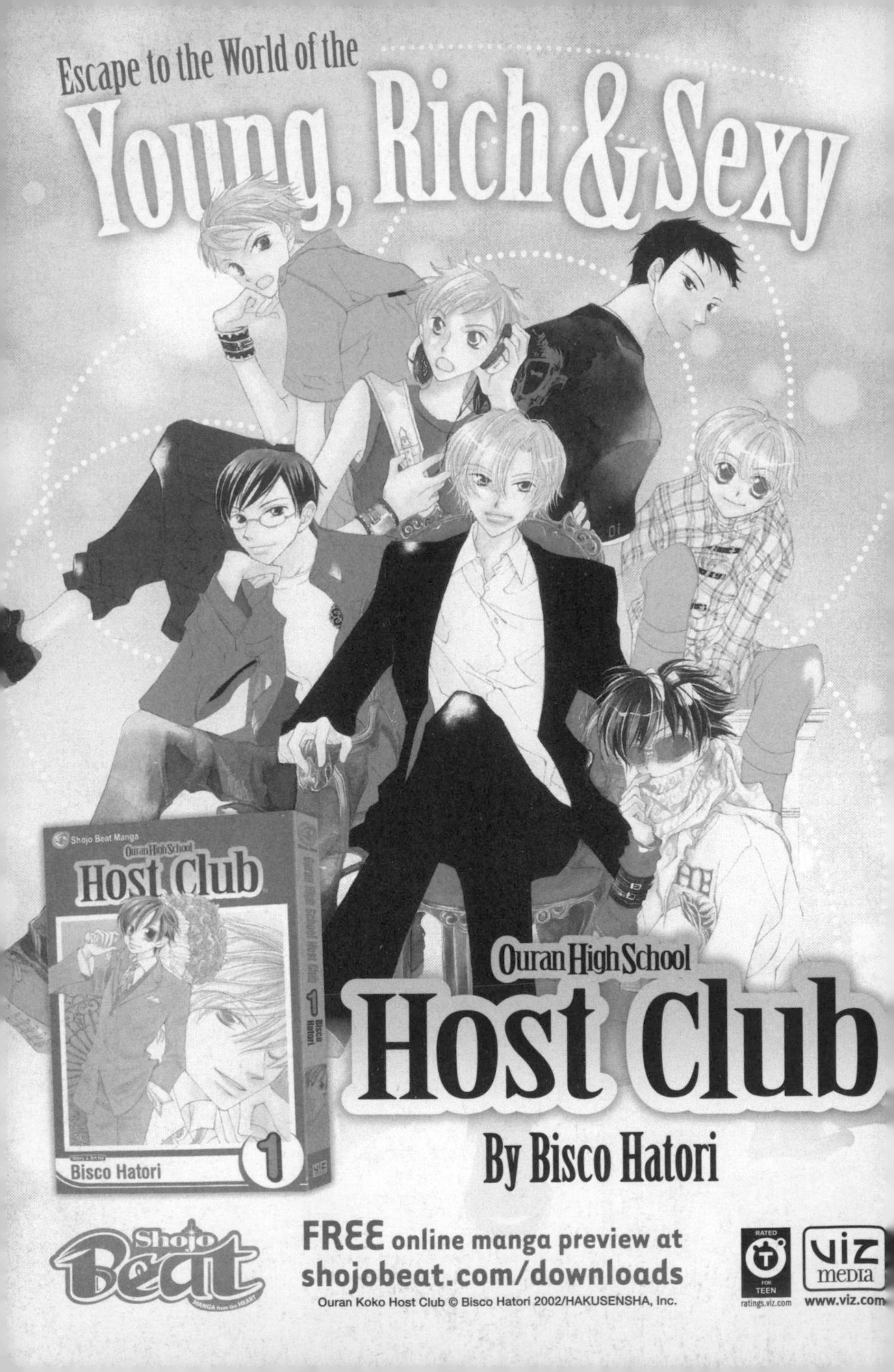
Escape to the World of the
Young, Rich & Sexy
Shojo Beat Manga
Ouran High School
Host Club
1
Bisco Hatori
Ouran High School
Host Club
By Bisco Hatori
Shojo Beat
FREE online manga preview at
shojobeat.com/downloads
Ouran Koko Host Club © Bisco Hatori 2002/HAKUSENSHA, Inc.
RATED
T
FOR TEEN
ratings.viz.com
VIZ media
www.viz.com

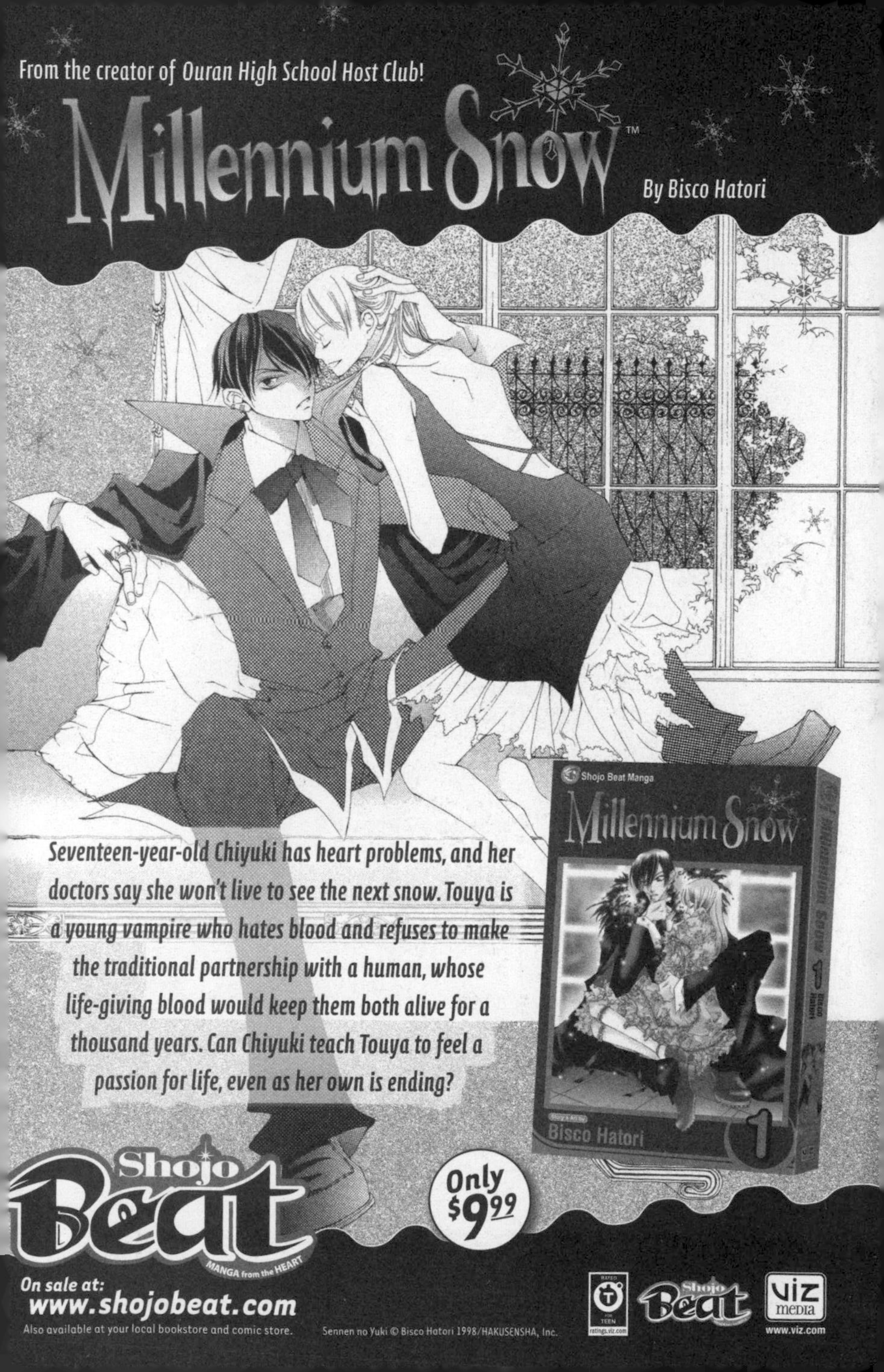
From the creator of Ouran High School Host Club!
Millennium Snow™
By Bisco Hatori
Shojo Beat Manga
Millennium Snow
Bisco Hatori
1
Seventeen-year-old Chiyuki has heart problems, and her doctors say she won't live to see the next snow. Touya is a young vampire who hates blood and refuses to make the traditional partnership with a human, whose life-giving blood would keep them both alive for a thousand years. Can Chiyuki teach Touya to feel a passion for life, even as her own is ending?
Shojo Beat
MANGA from the HEART
Only $9.99
On sale at:
www.shojobeat.com
Also available at your local bookstore and comic store.
Sennen no Yuki © Bisco Hatori 1998/HAKUSENSHA, Inc.
TEEN
ratings.viz.com
Shojo Beat
VIZ media
www.viz.com

OTOMEN

Vol. 18
Shojo Beat Edition

Story and Art by | **AYA KANNO**

Translation & Adaptation | **JN Productions**
Touch-up Art & Lettering | **Mark McMurray**
Design | **Fawn Lau**
Editor | **Amy Yu**

Otomen by Aya Kanno © Aya Kanno 2013
All rights reserved. First published in Japan in 2013 by HAKUSENSHA, Inc., Tokyo.
English language translation rights arranged with HAKUSENSHA, Inc., Tokyo.

The stories, characters and incidents mentioned
in this publication are entirely fictional.

Printed in the U.S.A.

Published by VIZ Media, LLC
P.O. Box 77010
San Francisco, CA 94107

10 9 8 7 6 5 4 3 2 1
First printing, May 2014

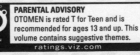

PARENTAL ADVISORY
OTOMEN is rated T for Teen and is
recommended for ages 13 and up. This
volume contains suggestive themes.
ratings.viz.com

Aya Kanno was born in Tokyo, Japan.
She is the creator of *Soul Rescue* and
Blank Slate (originally published as *Akusaga*
in Japan's *BetsuHana* magazine).

NOTES

Page 27, panel 1 | **Mira Jonouchi**
A shojo manga artist who inspired Juta to become a shojo manga artist himself. For more information, see *Otomen* volume 5.

Page 58, panel 1 | **Beauty Samurai**
Asuka and Hajime get roped into secretly masquerading as the Beauty Samurai, a duo who are famous for their mastery of makeup and fashion. For more information, see *Otomen* volumes 3 and 5.

Page 119, sidebar | **Kiyomi Masamune**
The character draft of the younger sister Kiyomi Masamune actually has the kanji "将棟" for "Masamune" rather than "正宗."

Page 122, panel 1 | **Hana to Mame**
The name *Hana to Mame* (Flowers and Beans) is a play on the real shojo manga magazine *Hana to Yume* (Flowers and Dreams) published by Hakusensha.

Page 153, panel 3 | **Pukkanabona**
Pukkanabona is the name of the place Kitora, Asuka, Ryo, and Kuriko visited when Kitora won a lottery to go overseas. For more information, see *Otomen* volume 14.

Confused by some of the terms, but too MANLY to ask for help?

Here are some **cultural notes** to assist you!

HONORIFICS

Chan – an informal honorific used to address children and females. *Chan* can also be used toward animals, lovers, intimate friends and people whom one has known since childhood.

San – the most common honorific title. It is used to address people outside one's immediate family and close circle of friends.

Senpai – used to address one's senior colleagues or mentor figures; it is used when students refer to or address more senior students in their school.

Sensei – honorific title used to address teachers as well as professionals such as doctors, lawyers and artists.

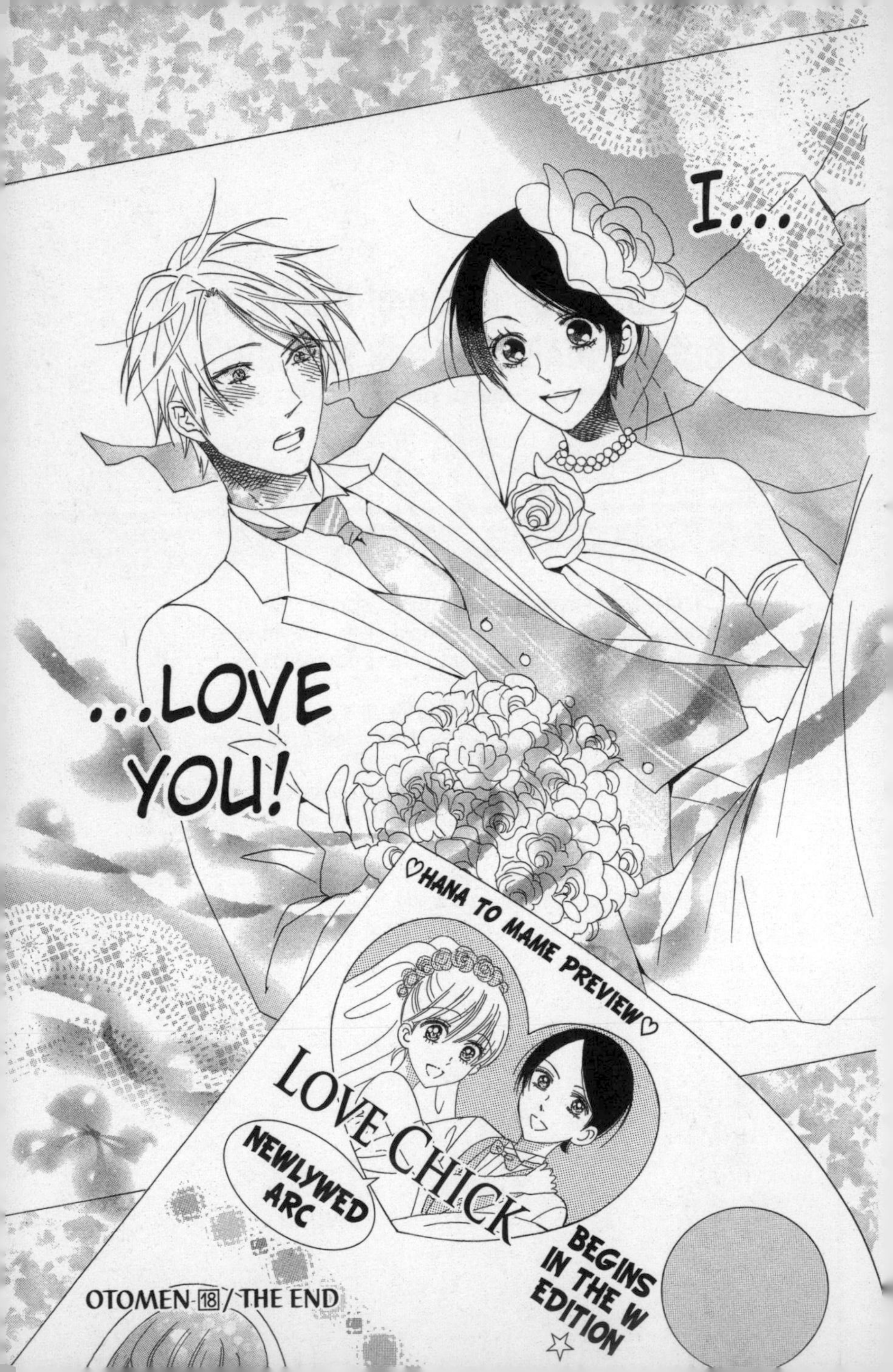
I...
...LOVE YOU!
♡HANA TO MAME PREVIEW♡
LOVE CHICK
NEWLYWED ARC
BEGINS IN THE W EDITION ☆
OTOMEN 18 / THE END

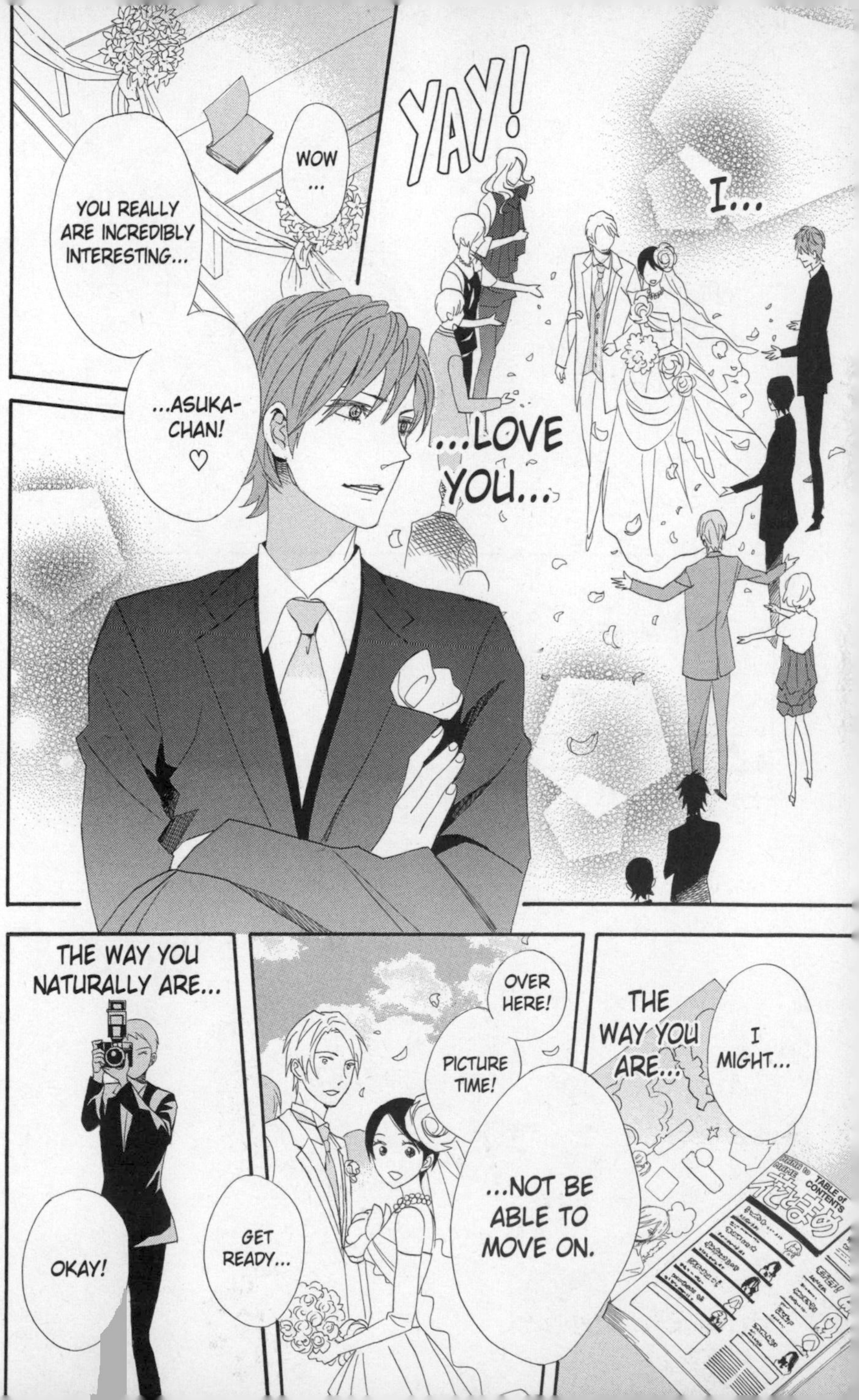
YAY!
I...
...LOVE YOU...
WOW...
YOU REALLY ARE INCREDIBLY INTERESTING...
...ASUKA-CHAN! ♡
I MIGHT...
THE WAY YOU ARE...
...NOT BE ABLE TO MOVE ON.
TABLE of CONTENTS
OVER HERE!
PICTURE TIME!
GET READY...
THE WAY YOU NATURALLY ARE...
OKAY!

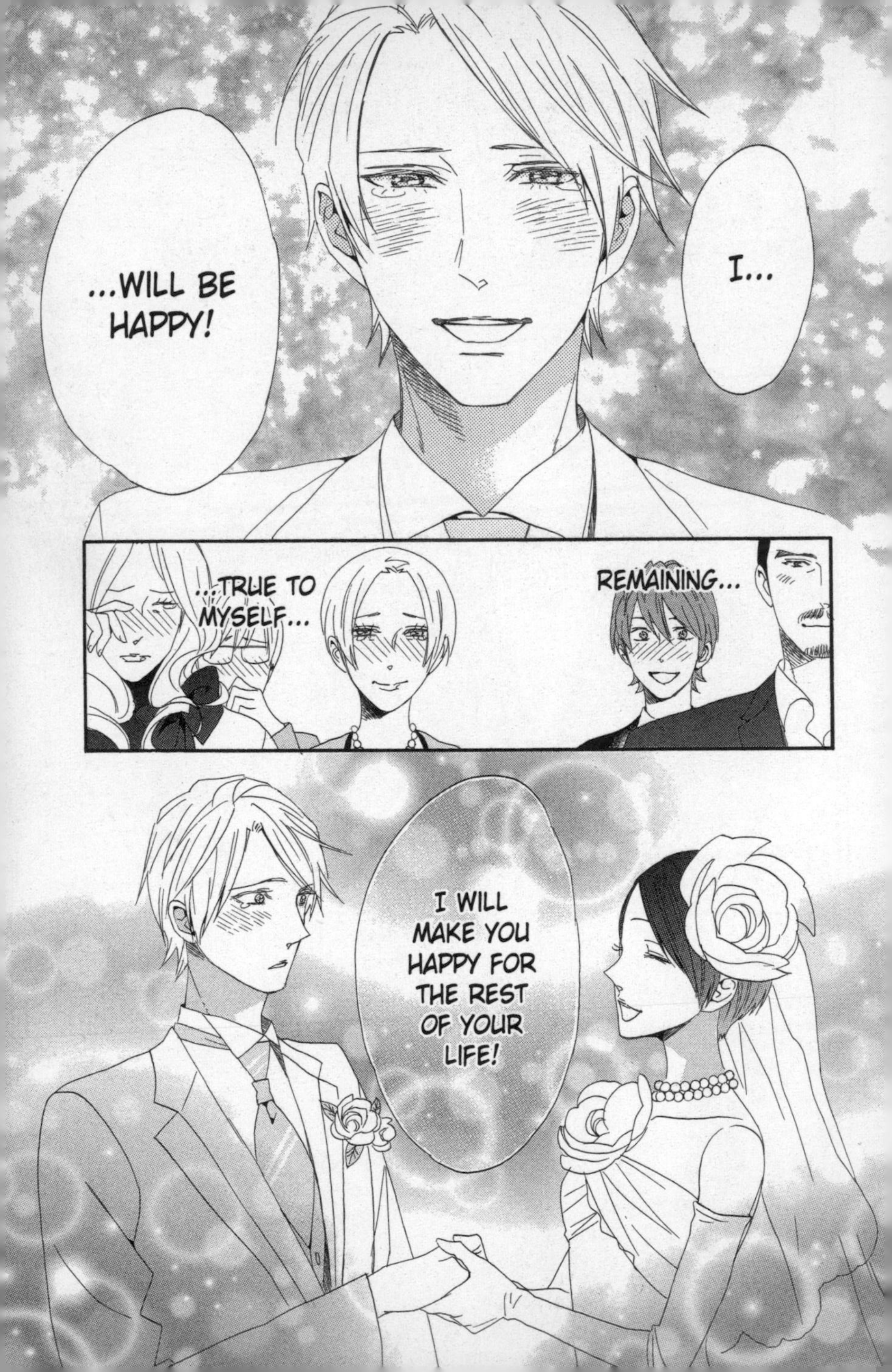
I...
...WILL BE HAPPY!
REMAINING...
...TRUE TO MYSELF...
I WILL MAKE YOU HAPPY FOR THE REST OF YOUR LIFE!

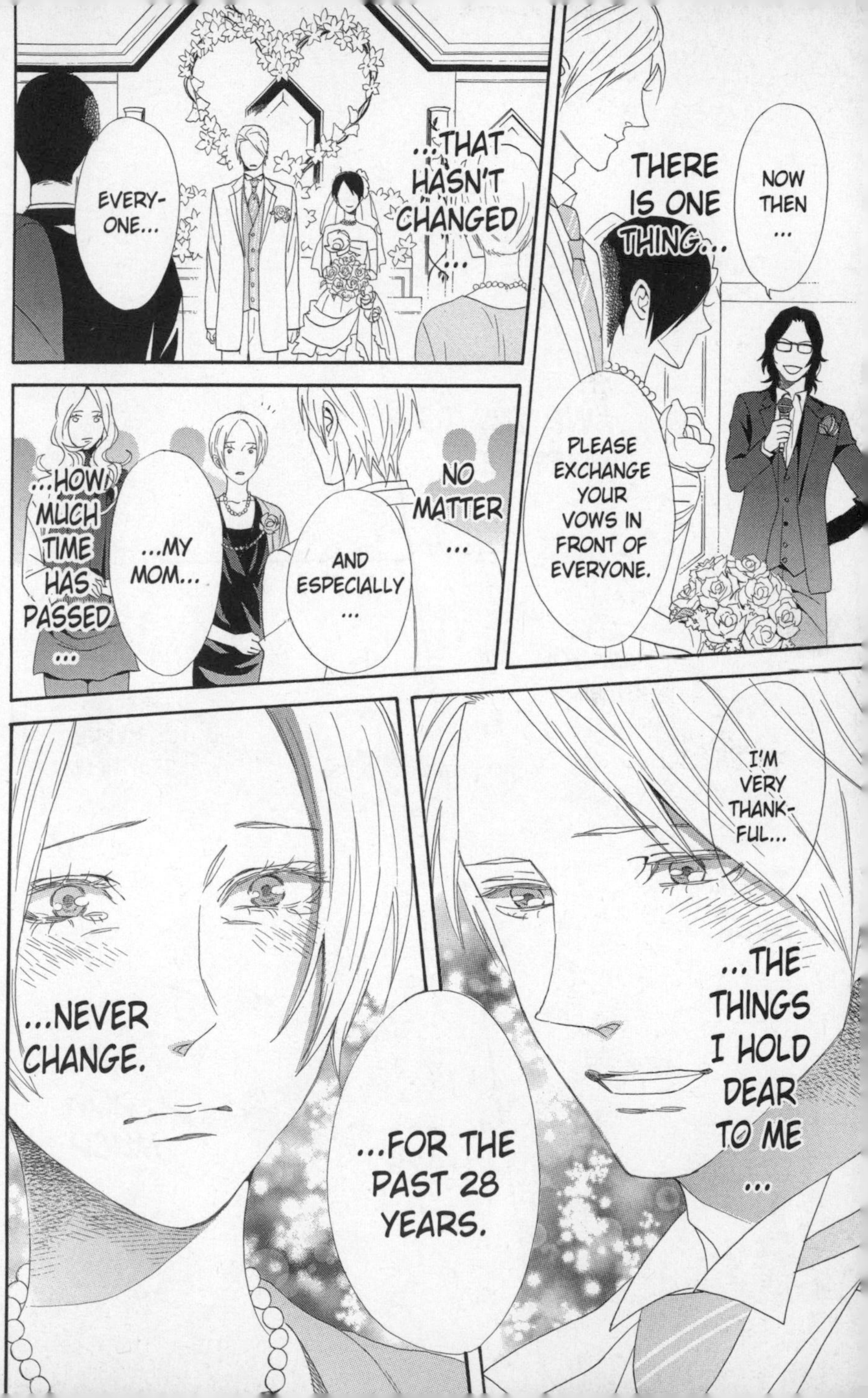
NOW THEN ...
THERE IS ONE THING...
PLEASE EXCHANGE YOUR VOWS IN FRONT OF EVERYONE.
...THAT HASN'T CHANGED ...
EVERY-ONE...
NO MATTER ...
AND ESPECIALLY ...
...MY MOM...
...HOW MUCH TIME HAS PASSED ...
I'M VERY THANK-FUL...
...THE THINGS I HOLD DEAR TO ME ...
...FOR THE PAST 28 YEARS.
...NEVER CHANGE.

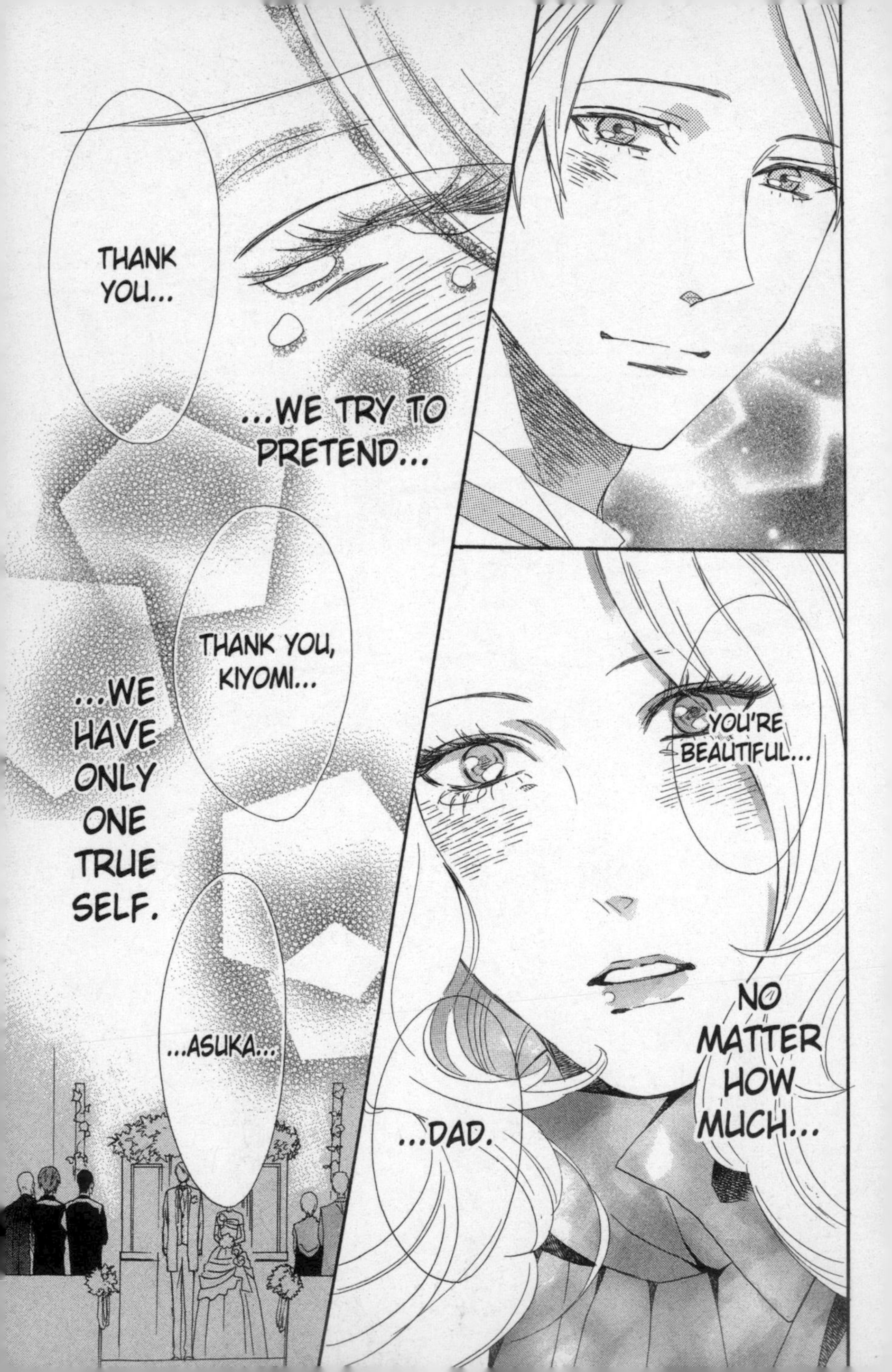
YOU'RE BEAUTIFUL...
NO MATTER HOW MUCH...
...DAD.
THANK YOU...
...WE TRY TO PRETEND...
THANK YOU, KIYOMI...
...WE HAVE ONLY ONE TRUE SELF.
...ASUKA...

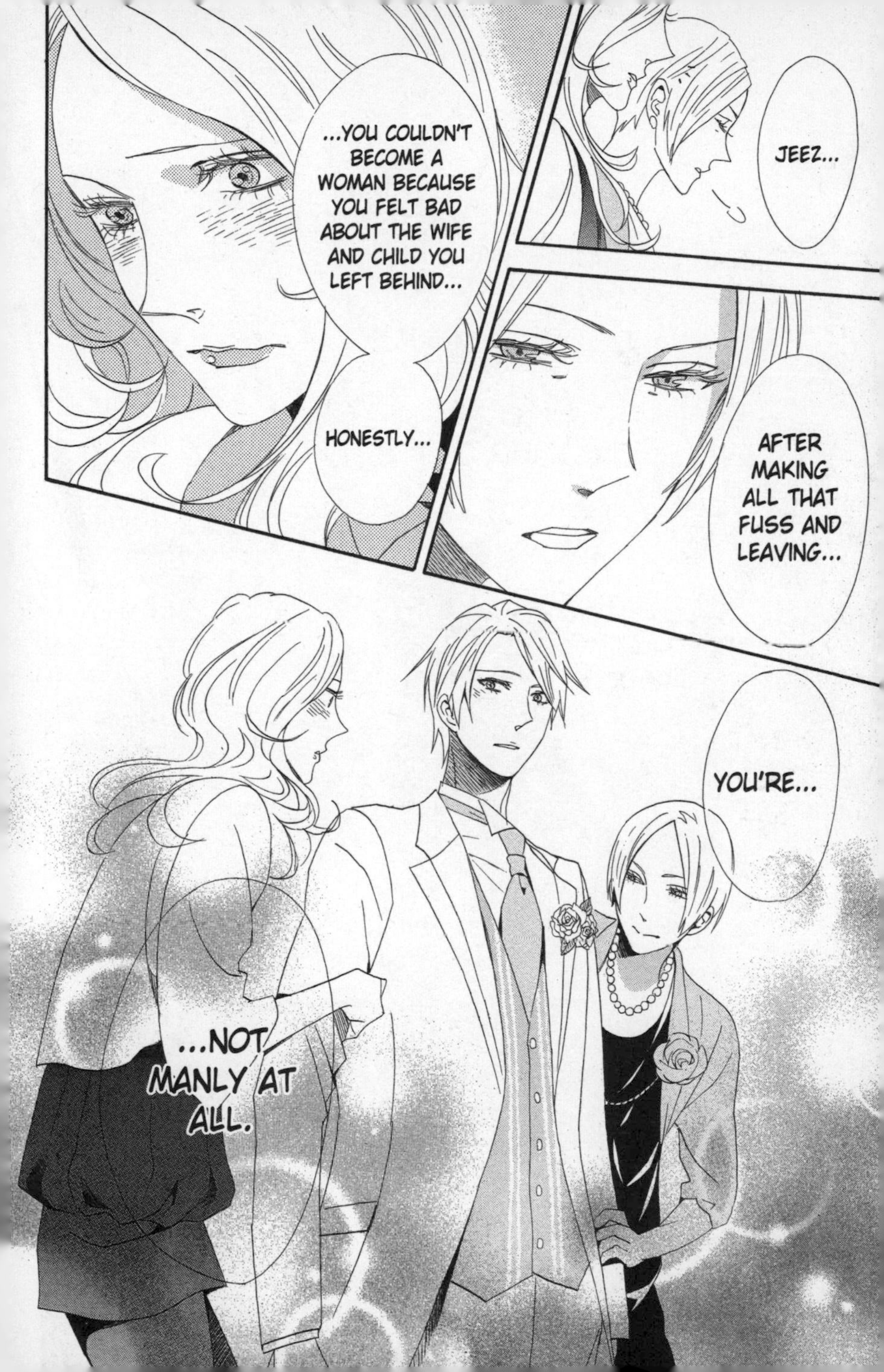
JEEZ...
AFTER MAKING ALL THAT FUSS AND LEAVING...
...YOU COULDN'T BECOME A WOMAN BECAUSE YOU FELT BAD ABOUT THE WIFE AND CHILD YOU LEFT BEHIND...
HONESTLY...
YOU'RE...
...NOT MANLY AT ALL.

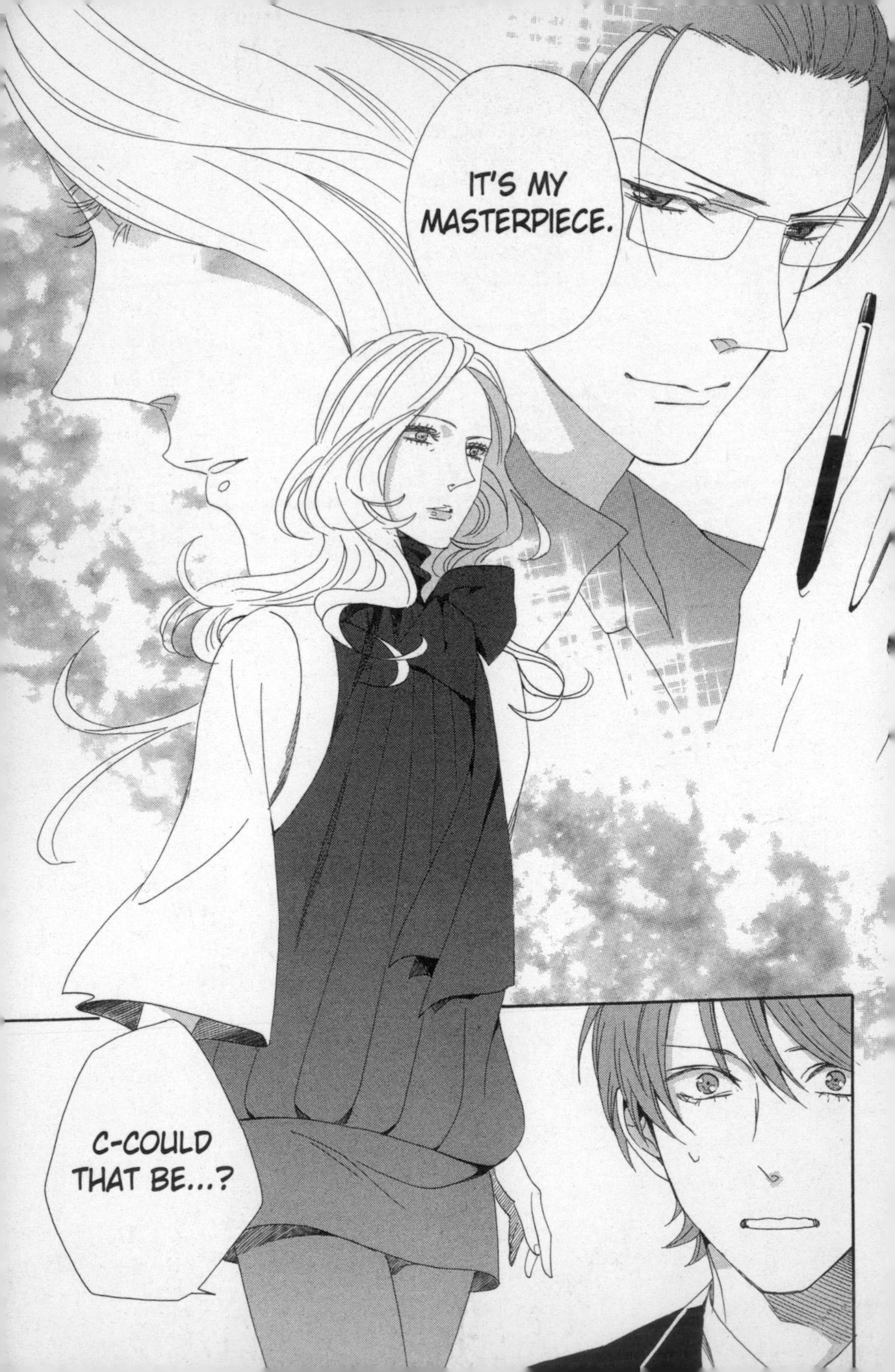
IT'S MY MASTERPIECE.
C-COULD THAT BE...?

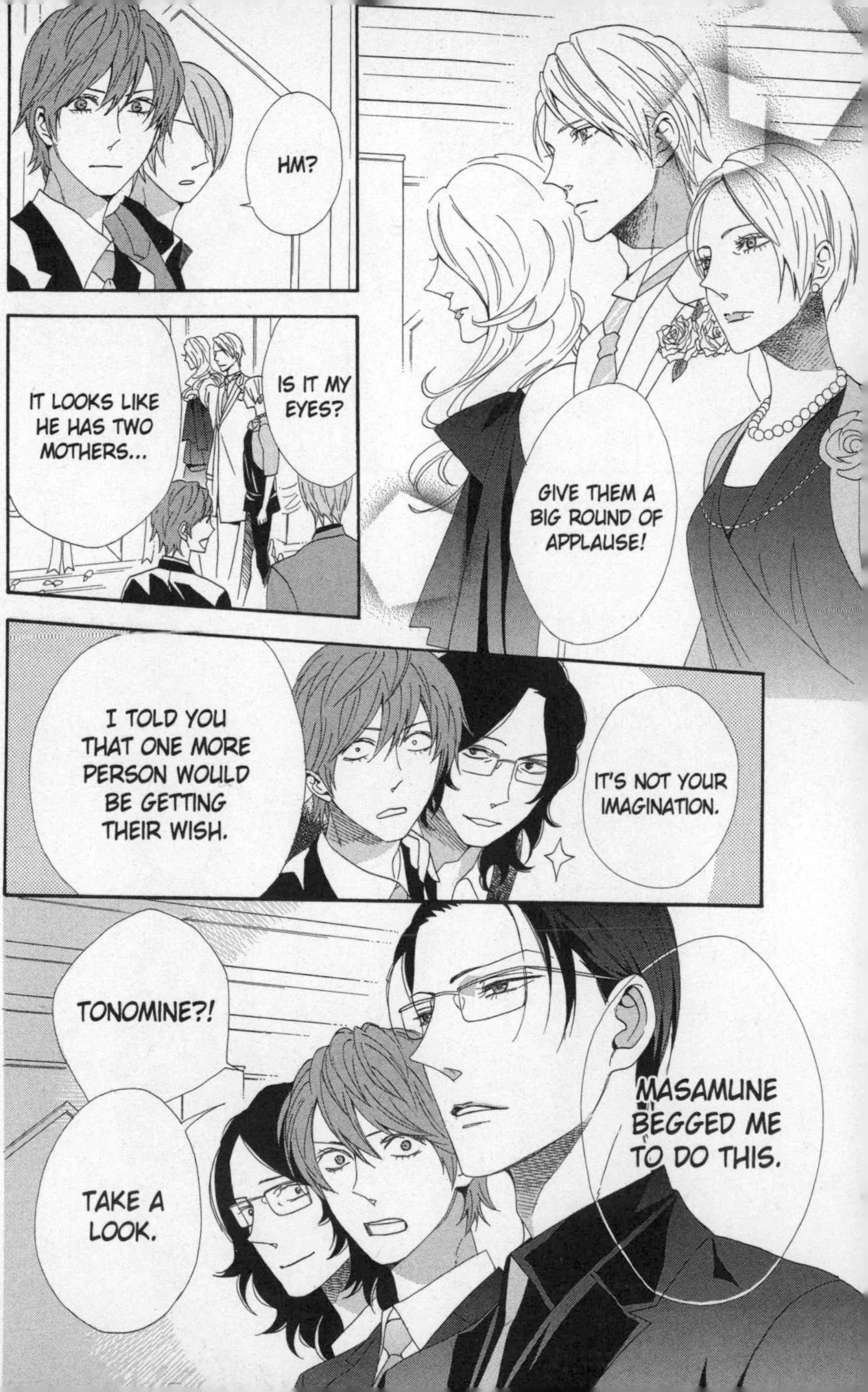
GIVE THEM A BIG ROUND OF APPLAUSE!
HM?
IS IT MY EYES?
IT LOOKS LIKE HE HAS TWO MOTHERS...
IT'S NOT YOUR IMAGINATION.
I TOLD YOU THAT ONE MORE PERSON WOULD BE GETTING THEIR WISH.
MASAMUNE BEGGED ME TO DO THIS.
TONOMINE?!
TAKE A LOOK.

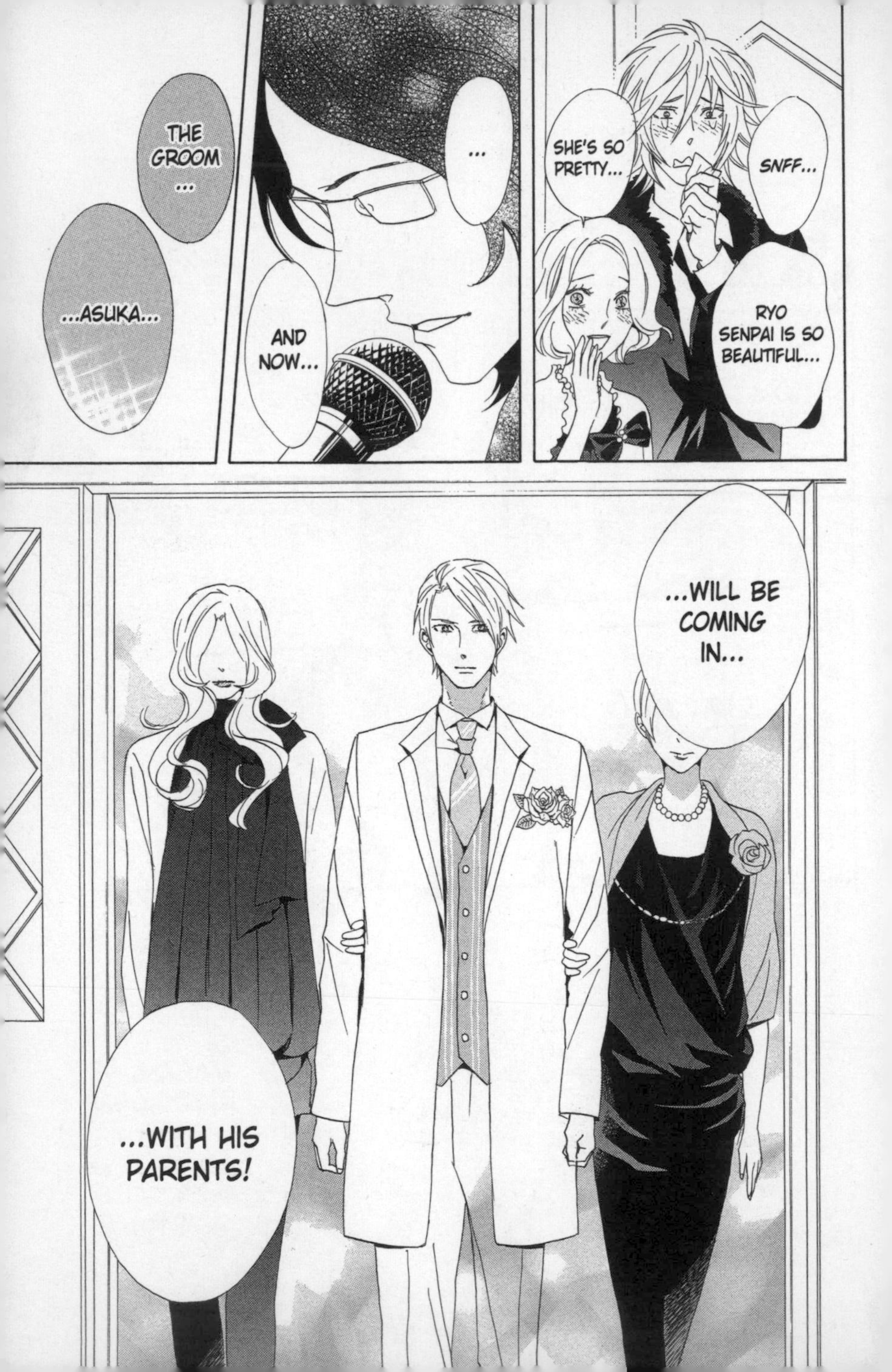
SNFF...
SHE'S SO PRETTY...
RYO SENPAI IS SO BEAUTIFUL...
...
AND NOW...
THE GROOM ...
...ASUKA...
...WILL BE COMING IN...
...WITH HIS PARENTS!

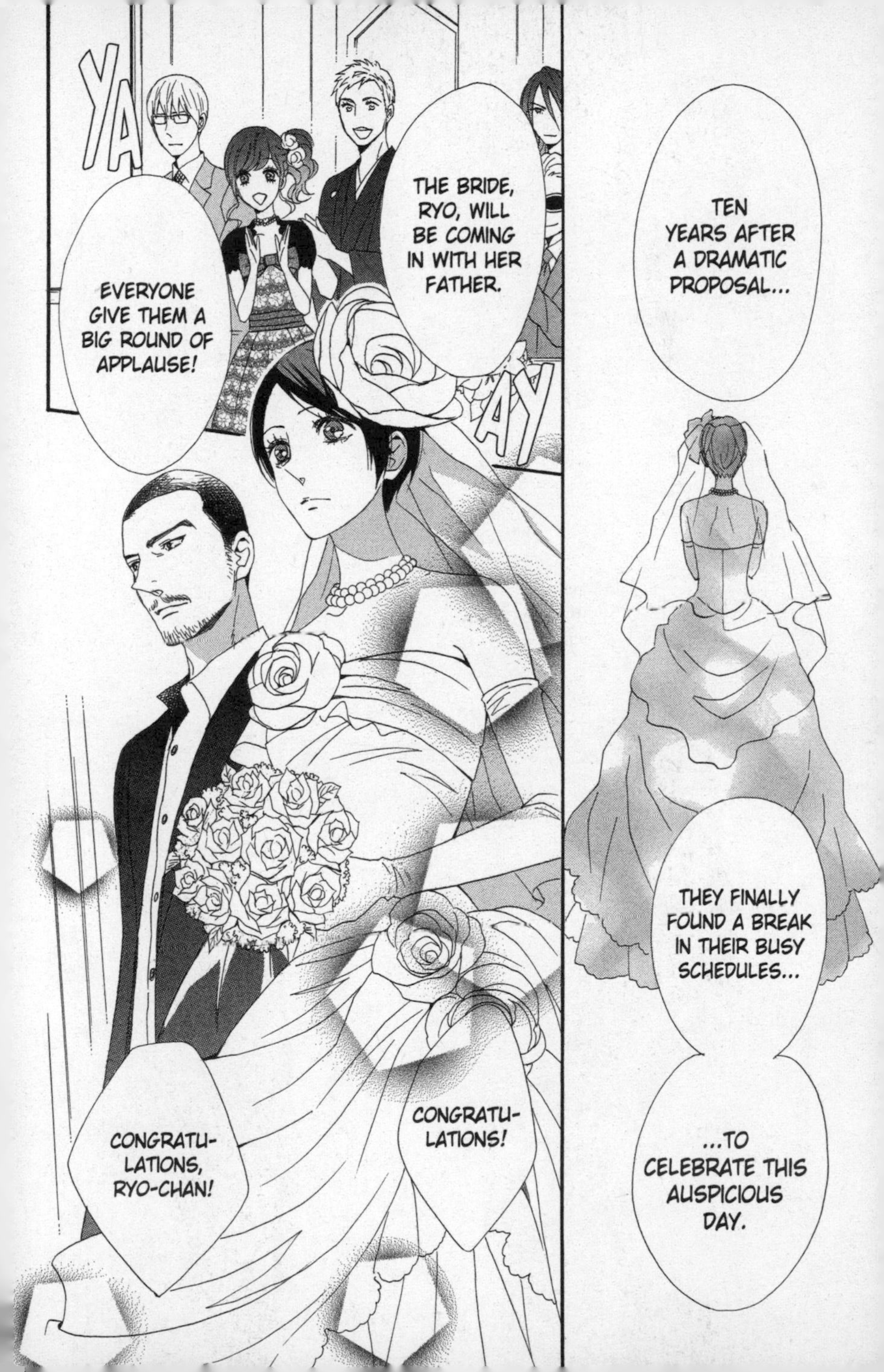
TEN YEARS AFTER A DRAMATIC PROPOSAL...
THEY FINALLY FOUND A BREAK IN THEIR BUSY SCHEDULES...
...TO CELEBRATE THIS AUSPICIOUS DAY.
THE BRIDE, RYO, WILL BE COMING IN WITH HER FATHER.
YA
EVERYONE GIVE THEM A BIG ROUND OF APPLAUSE!
AY
CONGRATU-LATIONS!
CONGRATU-LATIONS, RYO-CHAN!

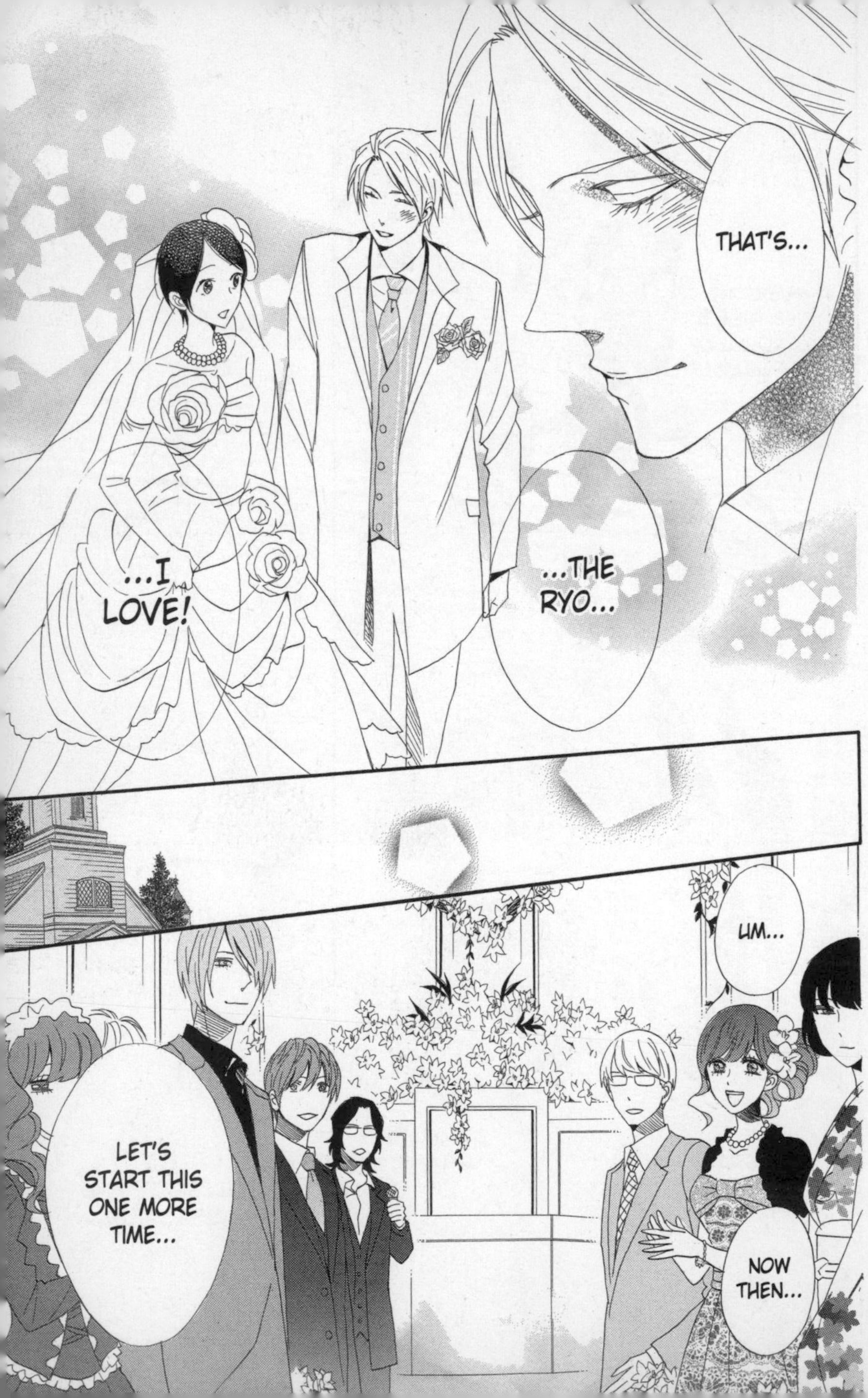
THAT'S...
...THE RYO...
...I LOVE!
UM...
NOW THEN...
LET'S START THIS ONE MORE TIME...

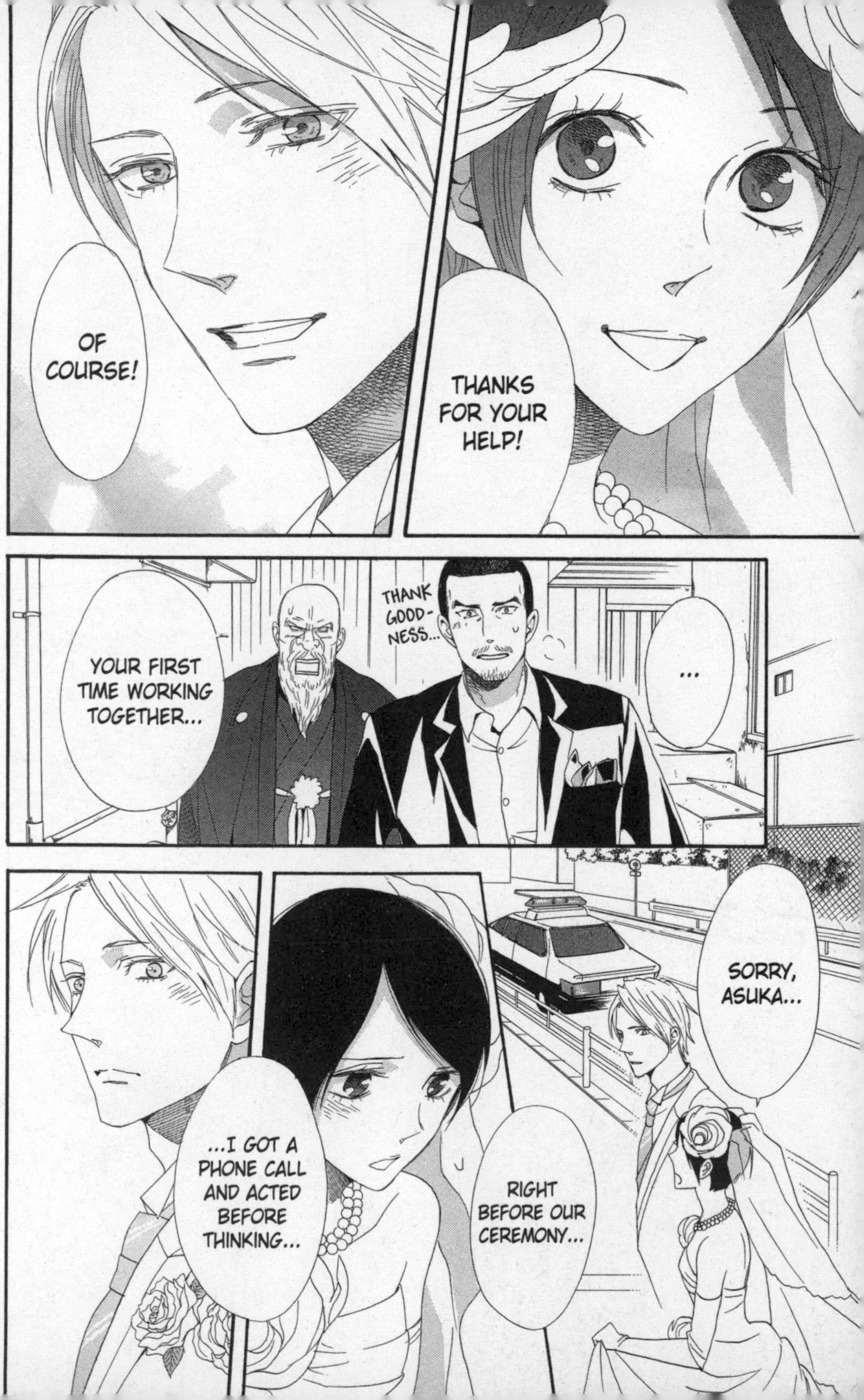
THANKS FOR YOUR HELP!
OF COURSE!
...
THANK GOOD-NESS...
YOUR FIRST TIME WORKING TOGETHER...
SORRY, ASUKA...
RIGHT BEFORE OUR CEREMONY...
...I GOT A PHONE CALL AND ACTED BEFORE THINKING...

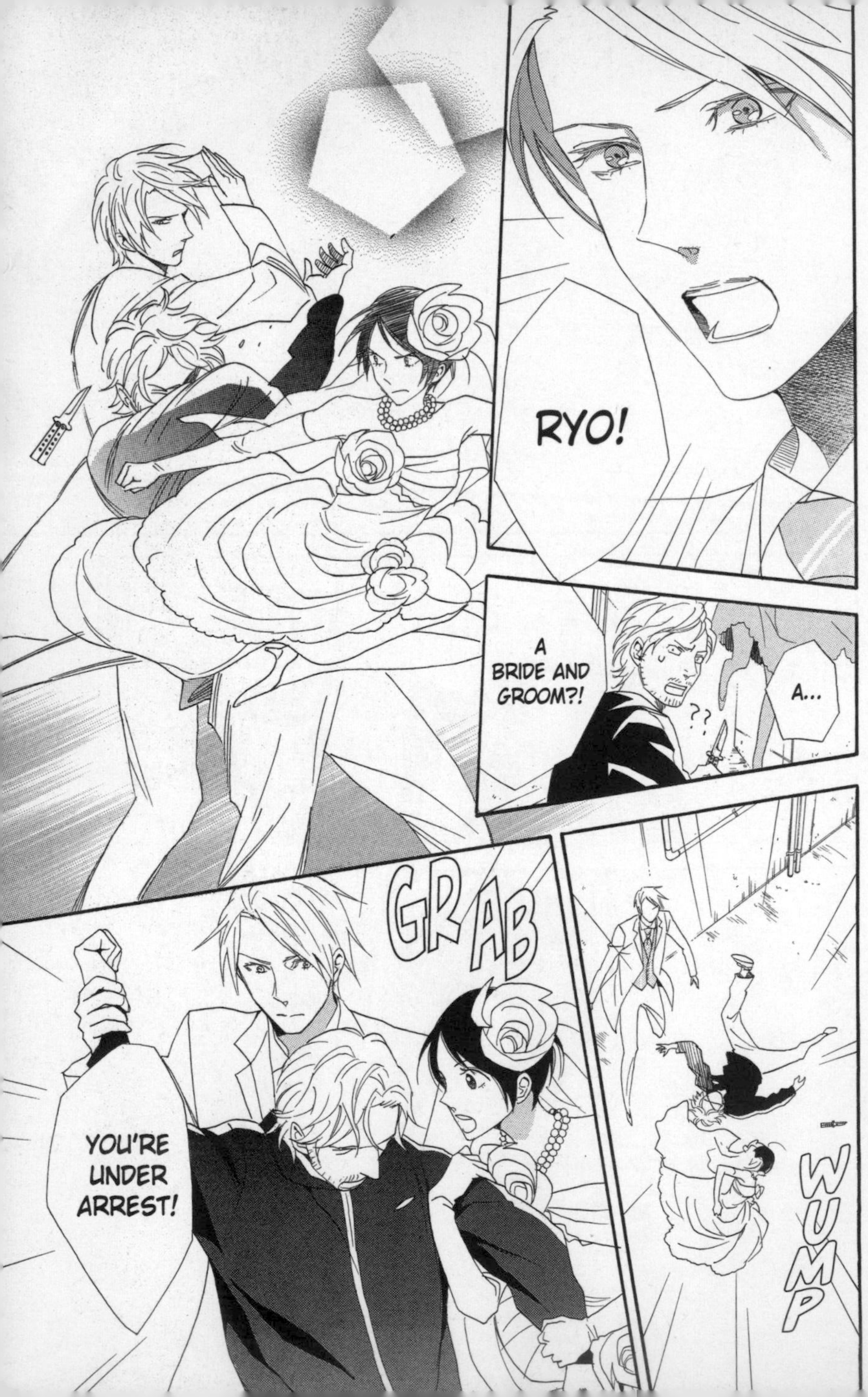
RYO!
A...
A BRIDE AND GROOM?!
??
WUMP
GRAB
YOU'RE UNDER ARREST!

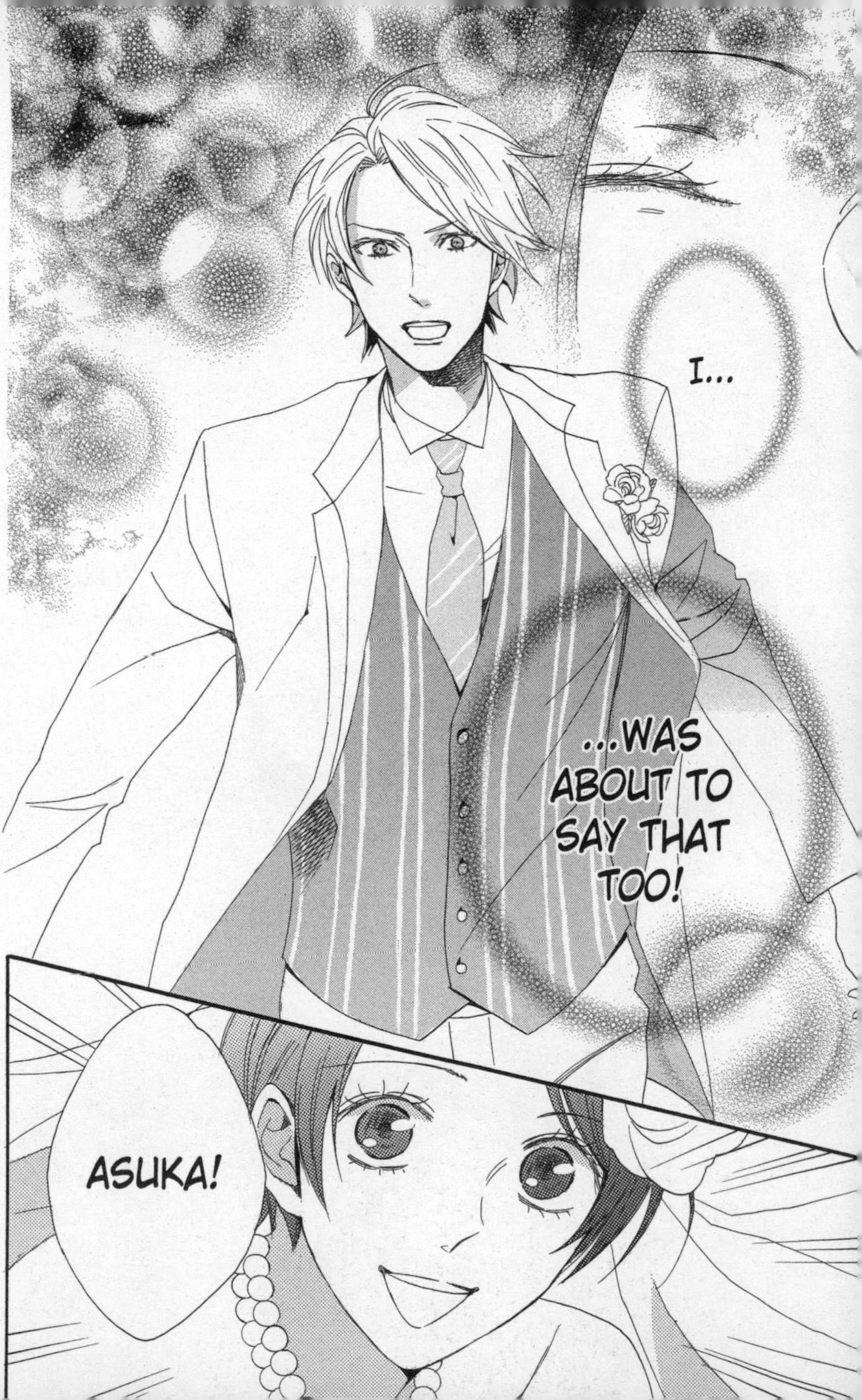
I...
...WAS ABOUT TO SAY THAT TOO!
ASUKA!

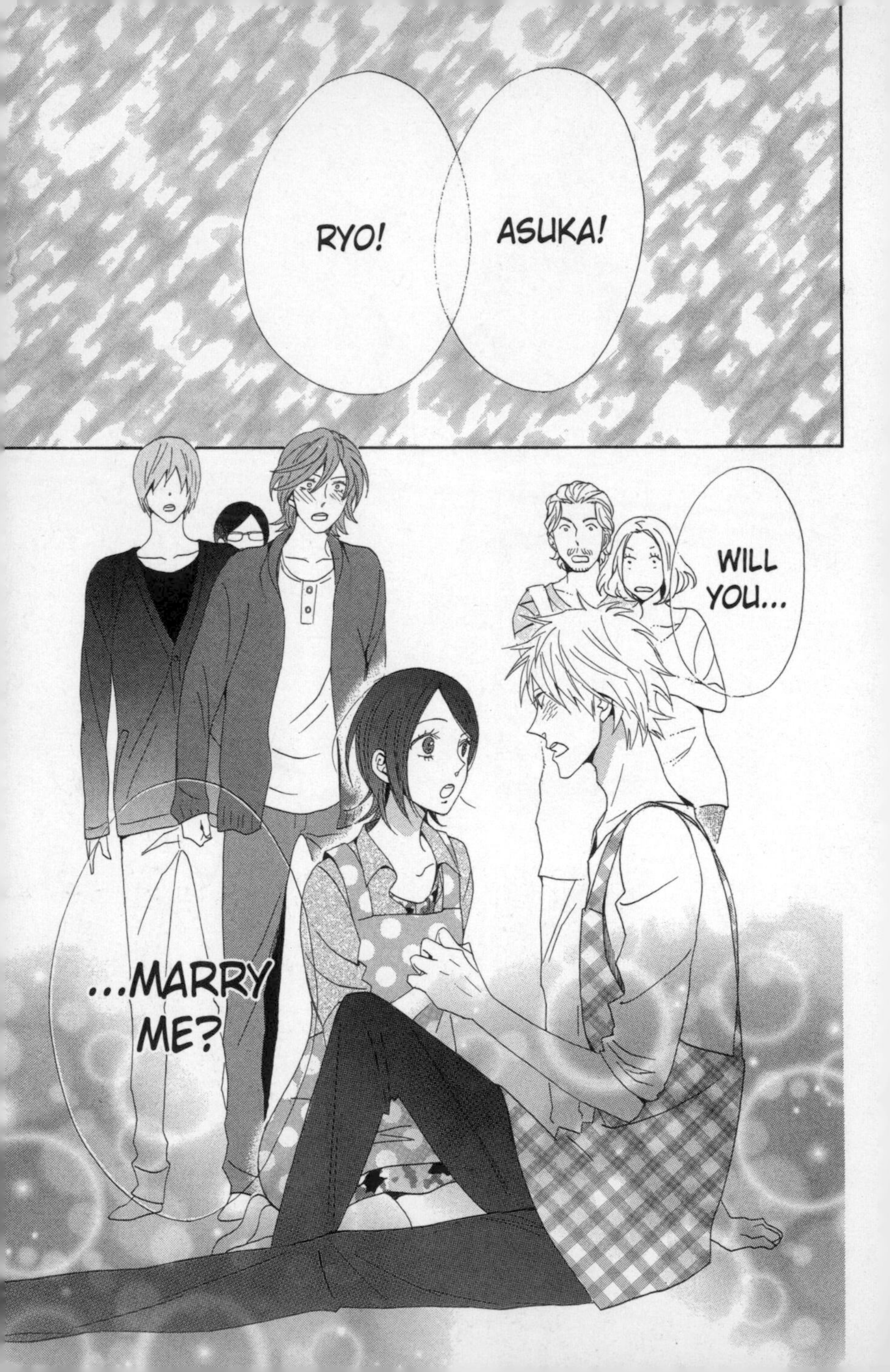
ASUKA!
RYO!
WILL YOU...
...MARRY ME?

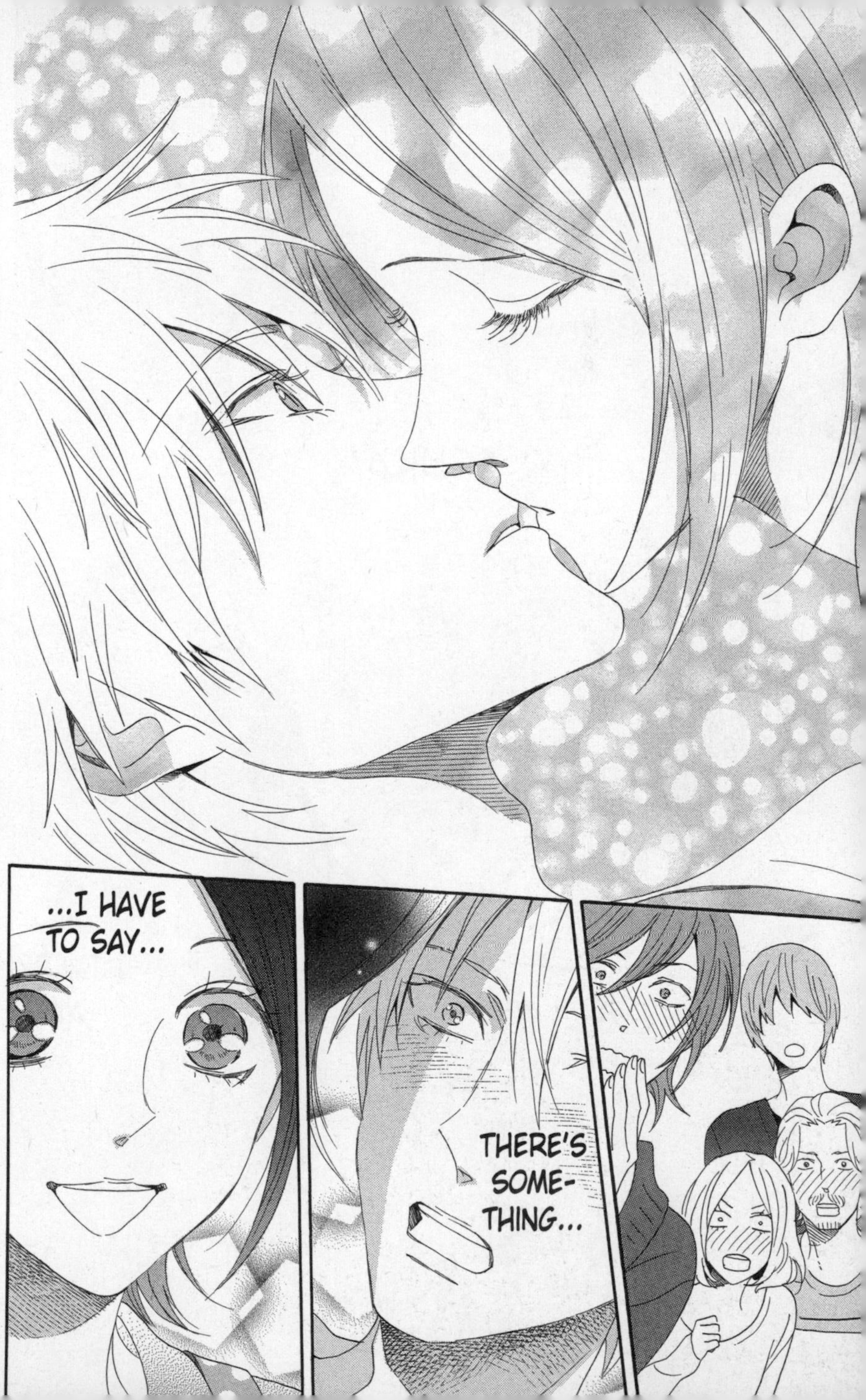
THERE'S SOME-THING...
...I HAVE TO SAY...

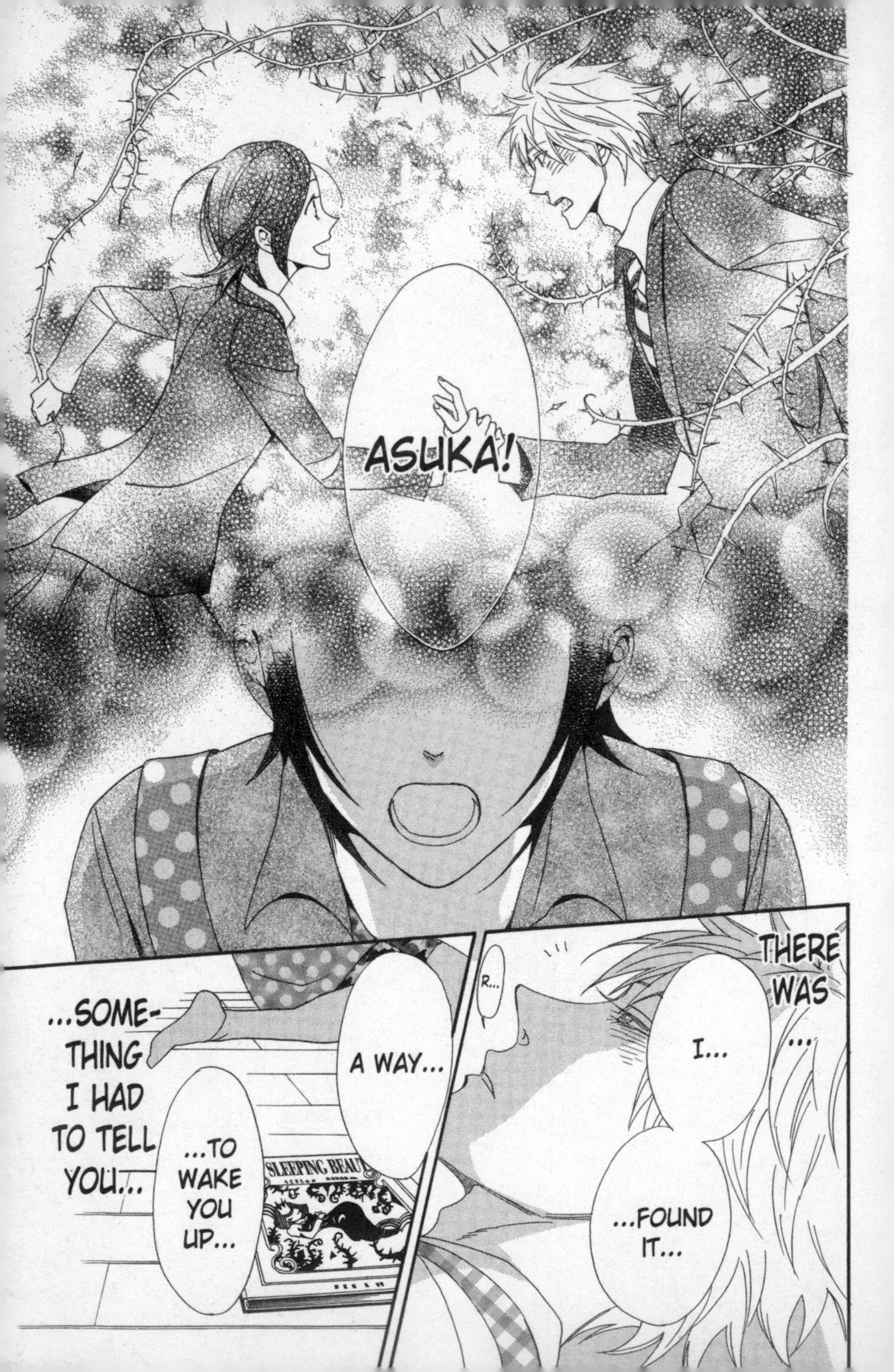
ASUKA!
THERE WAS ...
R...
I...
...FOUND IT...
A WAY...
...TO WAKE YOU UP...
...SOME-THING I HAD TO TELL YOU...
SLEEPING BEAU

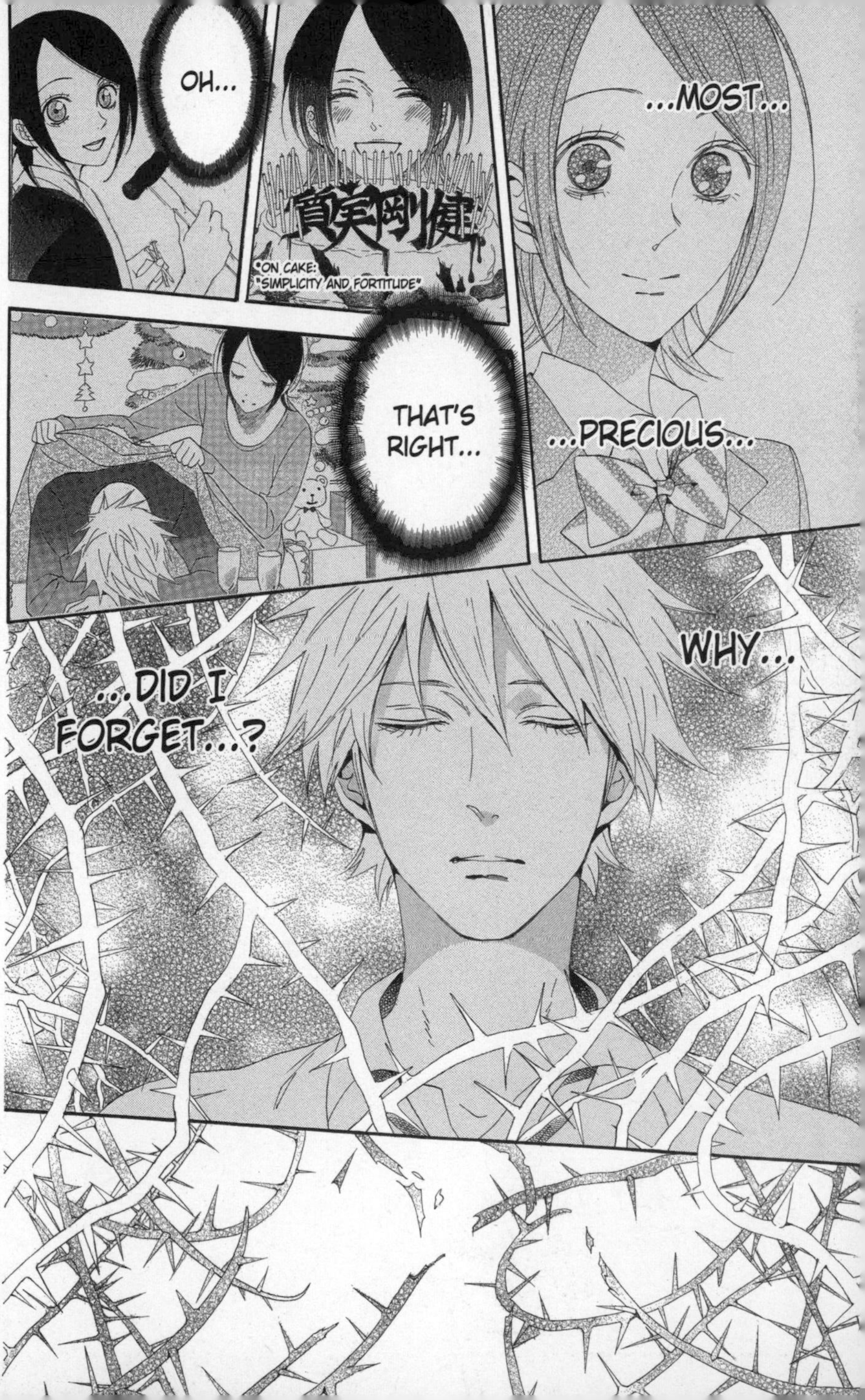
...MOST...
...PRECIOUS...
質実剛健
*ON CAKE: "SIMPLICITY AND FORTITUDE"
OH...
THAT'S RIGHT...
WHY...
...DID I FORGET...?

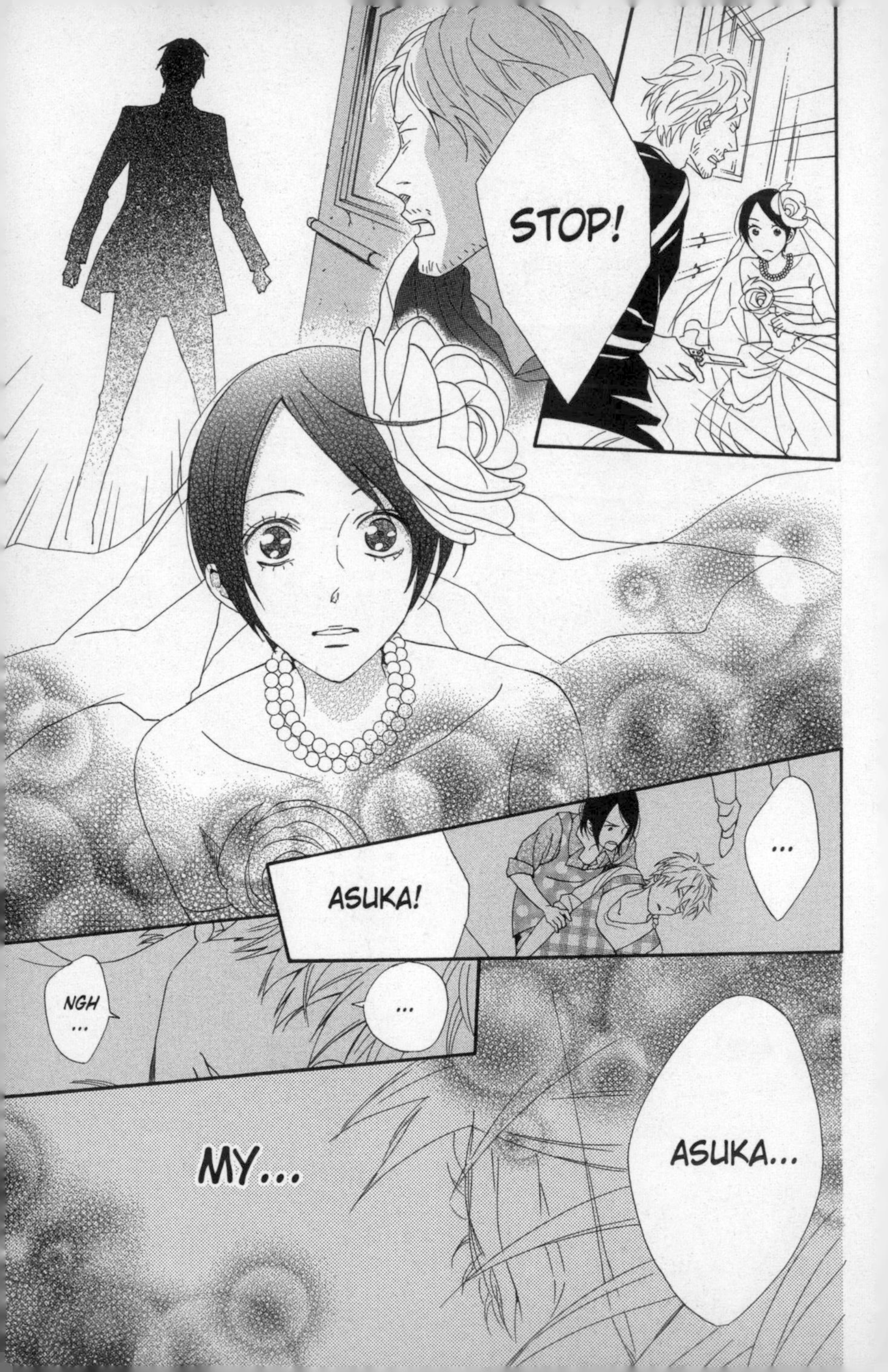
STOP!
...
ASUKA!
...
NGH ...
ASUKA...
MY...

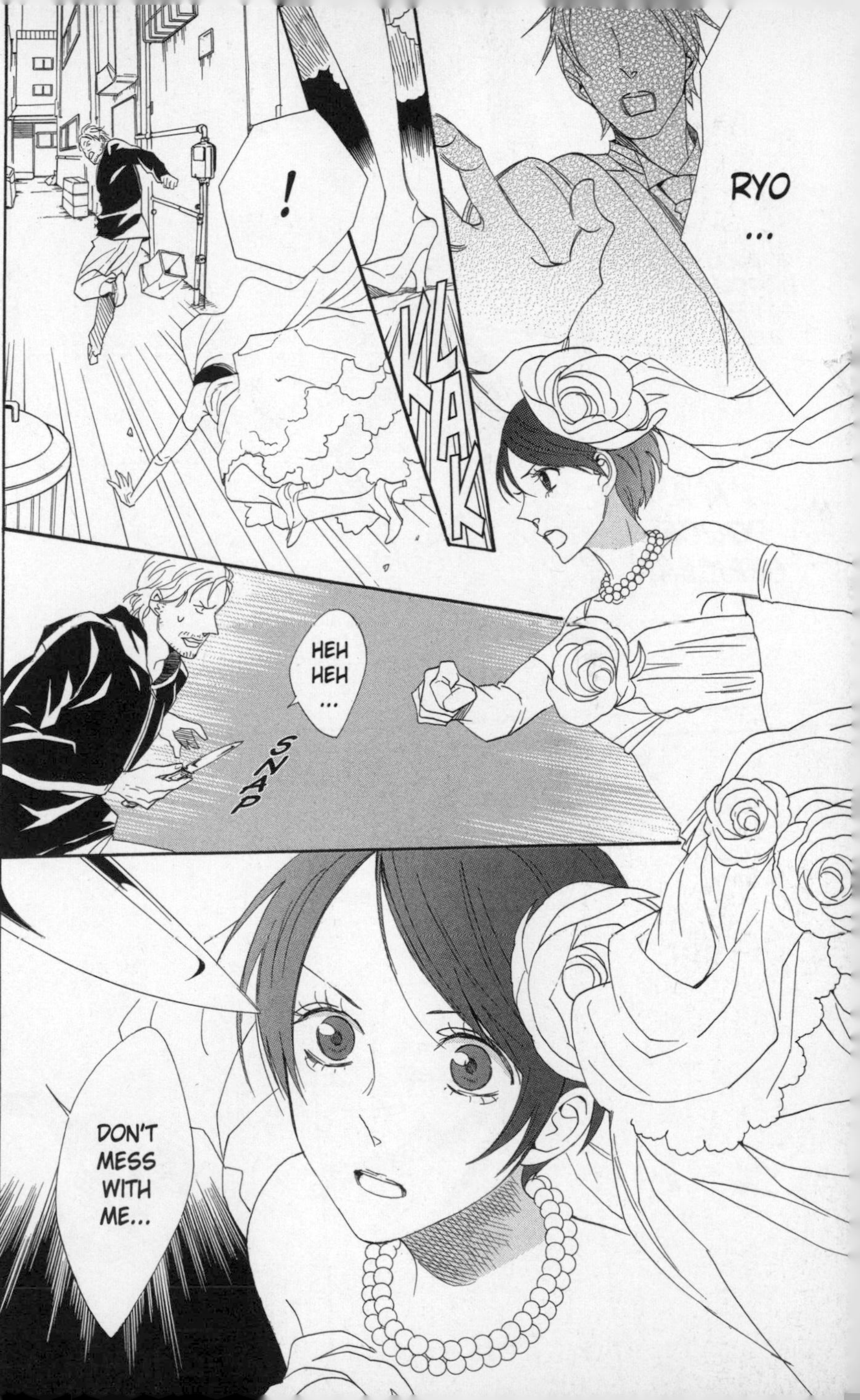
RYO ...
!
KLAK
HEH HEH ...
SNAP
DON'T MESS WITH ME...

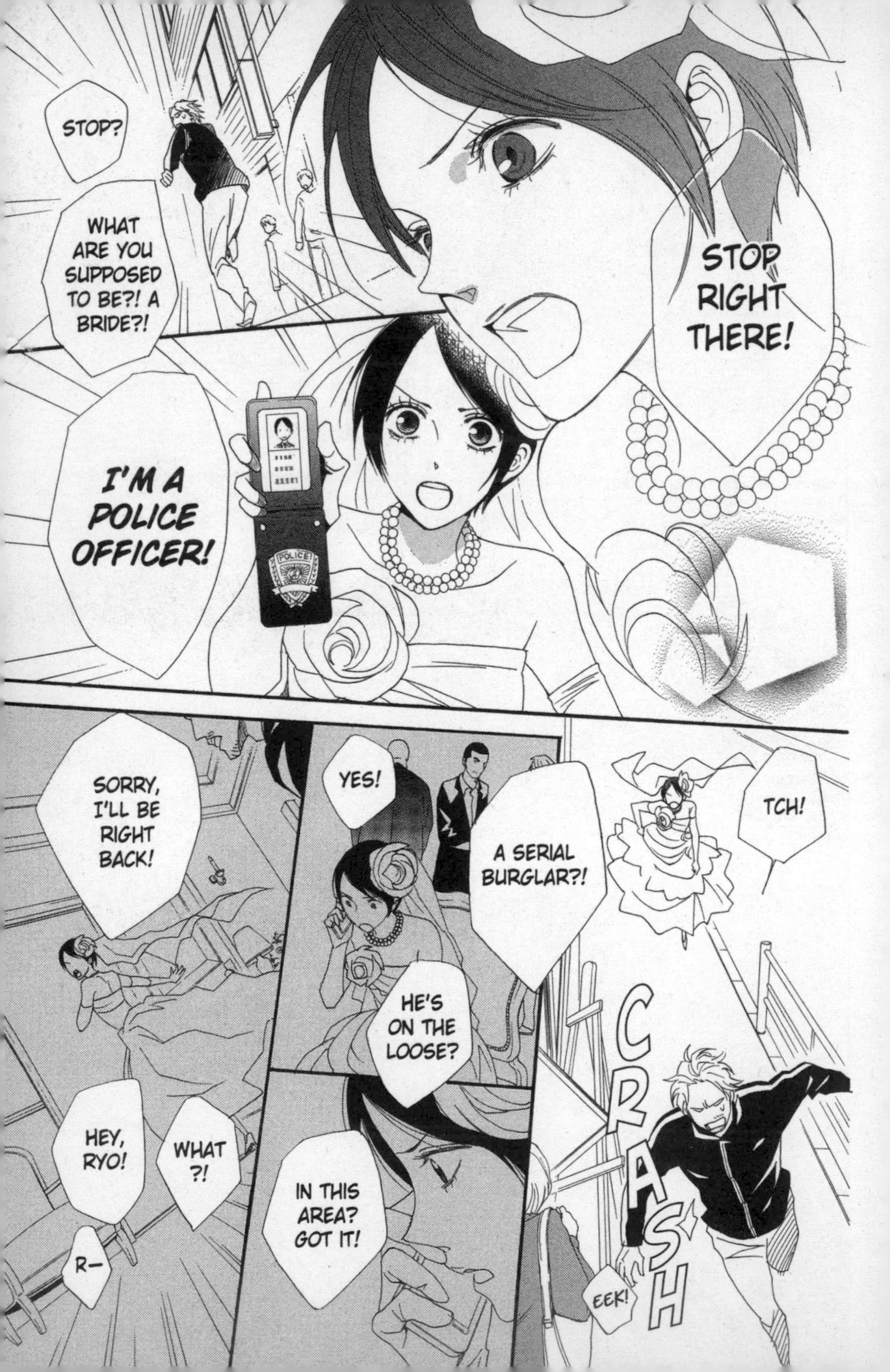
STOP RIGHT THERE!
STOP?
WHAT ARE YOU SUPPOSED TO BE?! A BRIDE?!
I'M A POLICE OFFICER!
POLICE
TCH!
CRASH
EEK!
A SERIAL BURGLAR?!
YES!
HE'S ON THE LOOSE?
IN THIS AREA? GOT IT!
SORRY, I'LL BE RIGHT BACK!
WHAT?!
HEY, RYO!
R—

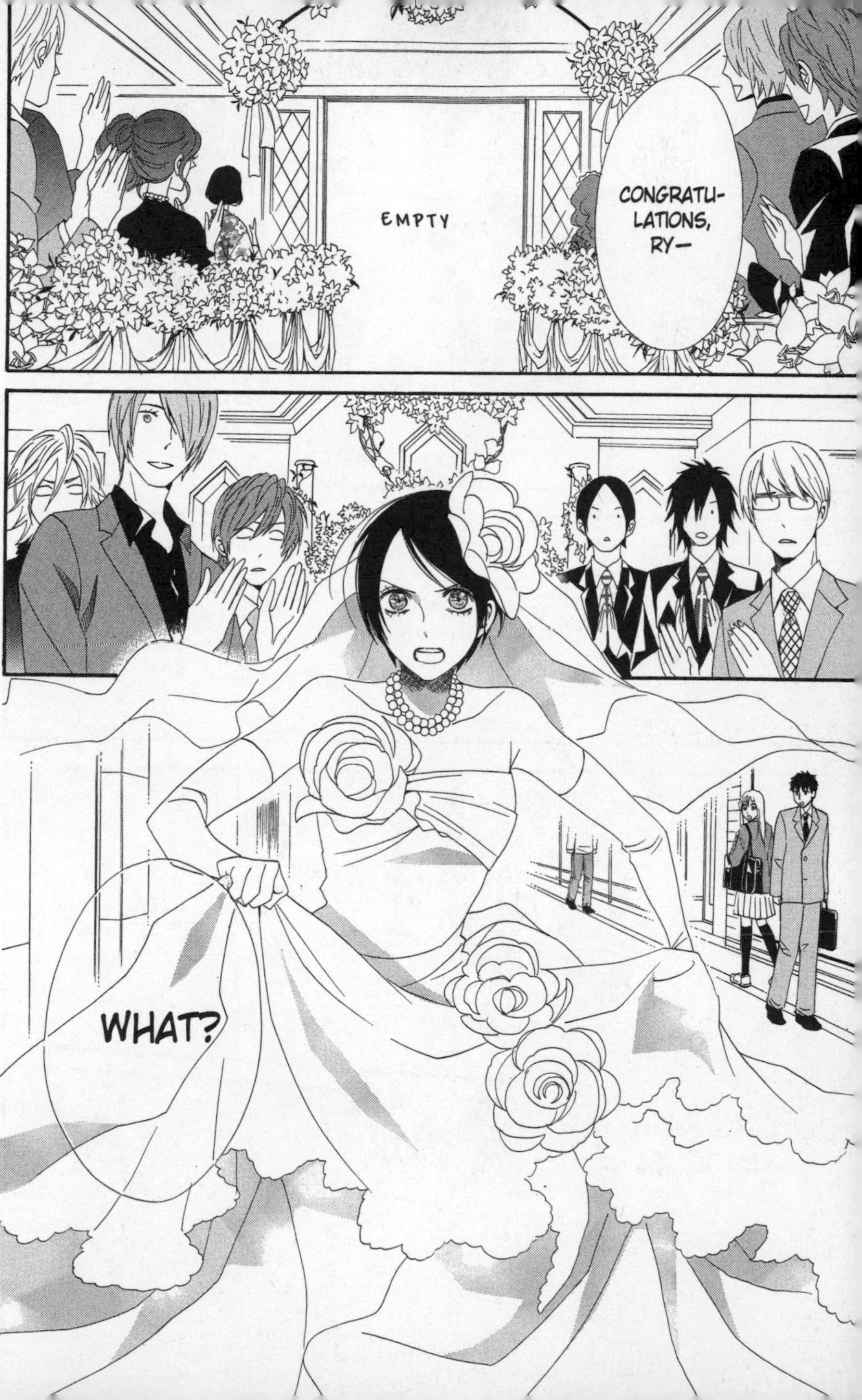
CONGRATULATIONS, RY—
EMPTY
WHAT?

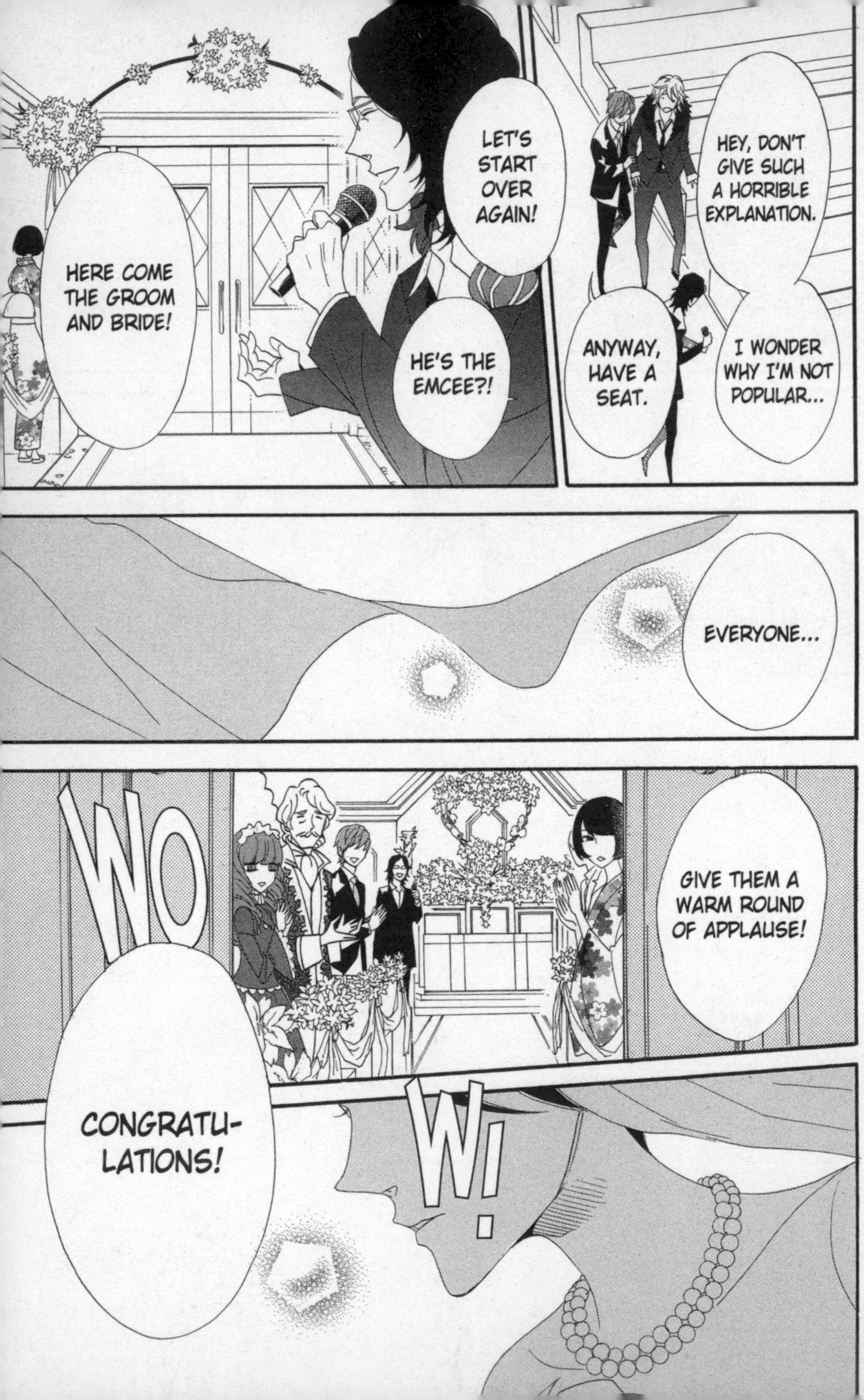
HEY, DON'T GIVE SUCH A HORRIBLE EXPLANATION.
I WONDER WHY I'M NOT POPULAR...
ANYWAY, HAVE A SEAT.
LET'S START OVER AGAIN!
HE'S THE EMCEE?!
HERE COME THE GROOM AND BRIDE!
EVERYONE...
GIVE THEM A WARM ROUND OF APPLAUSE!
WO
CONGRATU-LATIONS!
W!

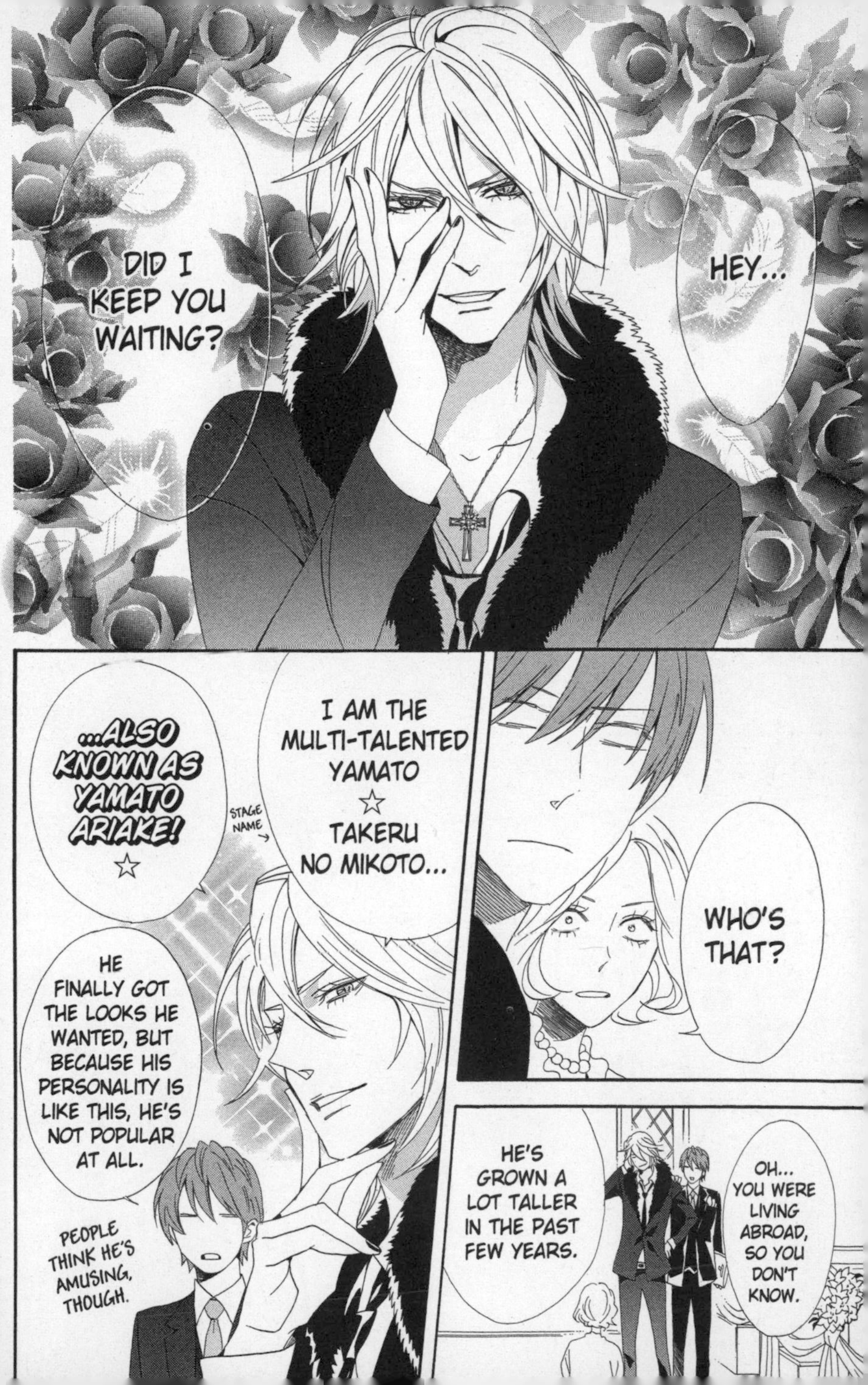
HEY...
DID I KEEP YOU WAITING?
WHO'S THAT?
OH... YOU WERE LIVING ABROAD, SO YOU DON'T KNOW.
HE'S GROWN A LOT TALLER IN THE PAST FEW YEARS.
I AM THE MULTI-TALENTED YAMATO ☆ TAKERU NO MIKOTO...
STAGE NAME
...ALSO KNOWN AS YAMATO ARIAKE! ☆
HE FINALLY GOT THE LOOKS HE WANTED, BUT BECAUSE HIS PERSONALITY IS LIKE THIS, HE'S NOT POPULAR AT ALL.
PEOPLE THINK HE'S AMUSING, THOUGH.

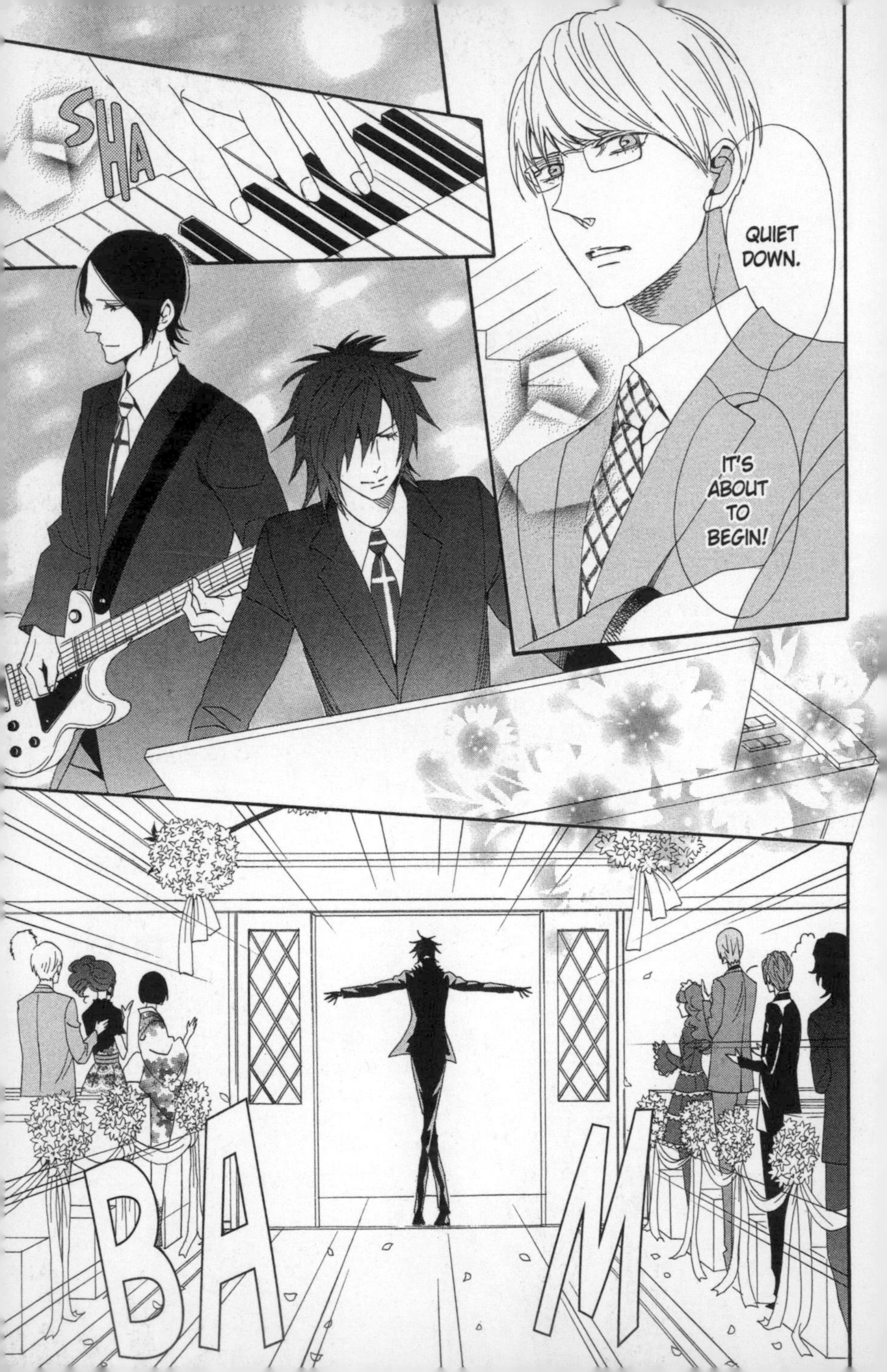
QUIET DOWN.
IT'S ABOUT TO BEGIN!
SHA
BAM

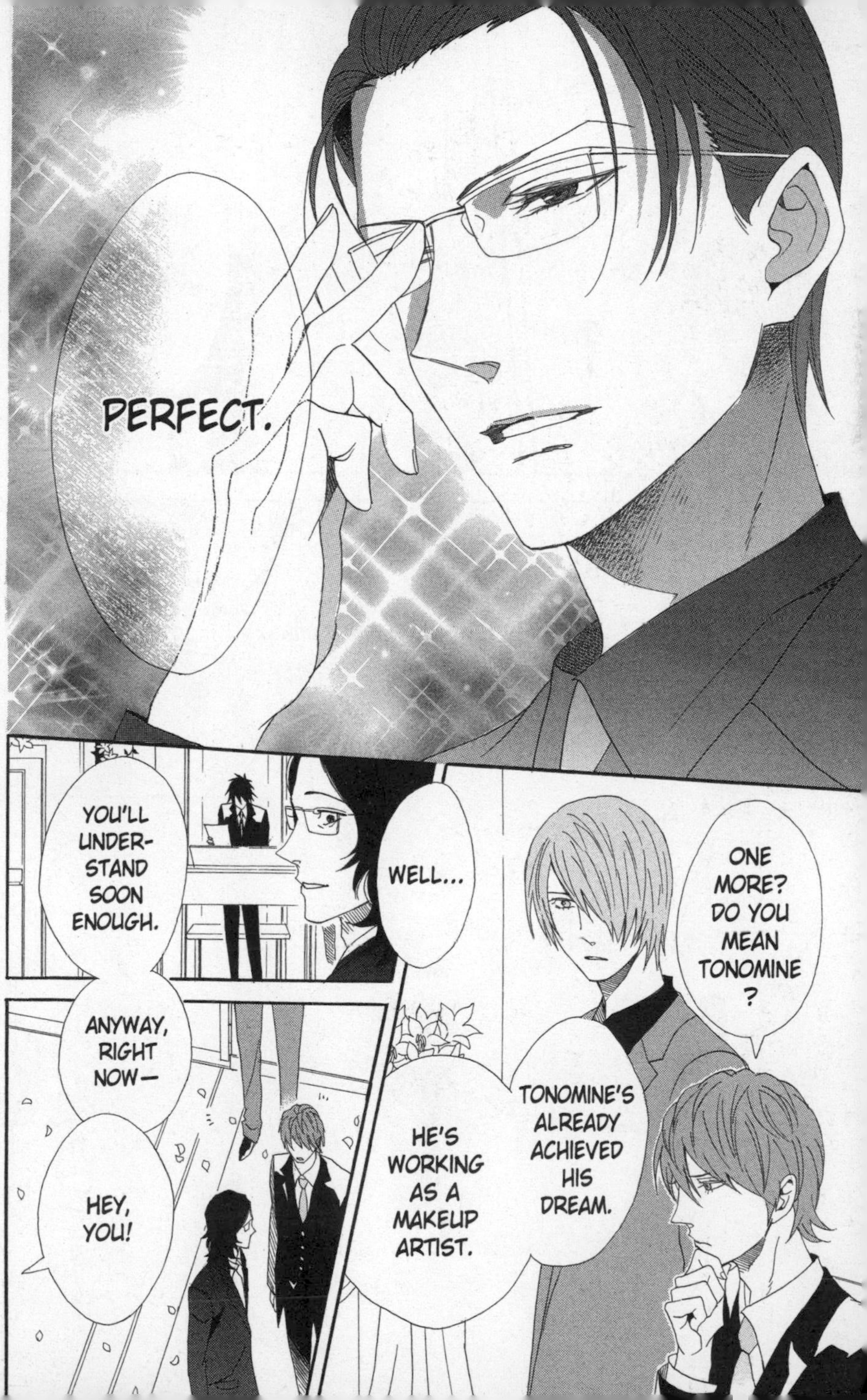
PERFECT.
ONE MORE? DO YOU MEAN TONOMINE?
TONOMINE'S ALREADY ACHIEVED HIS DREAM.
HE'S WORKING AS A MAKEUP ARTIST.
WELL...
YOU'LL UNDER-STAND SOON ENOUGH.
ANYWAY, RIGHT NOW—
HEY, YOU!

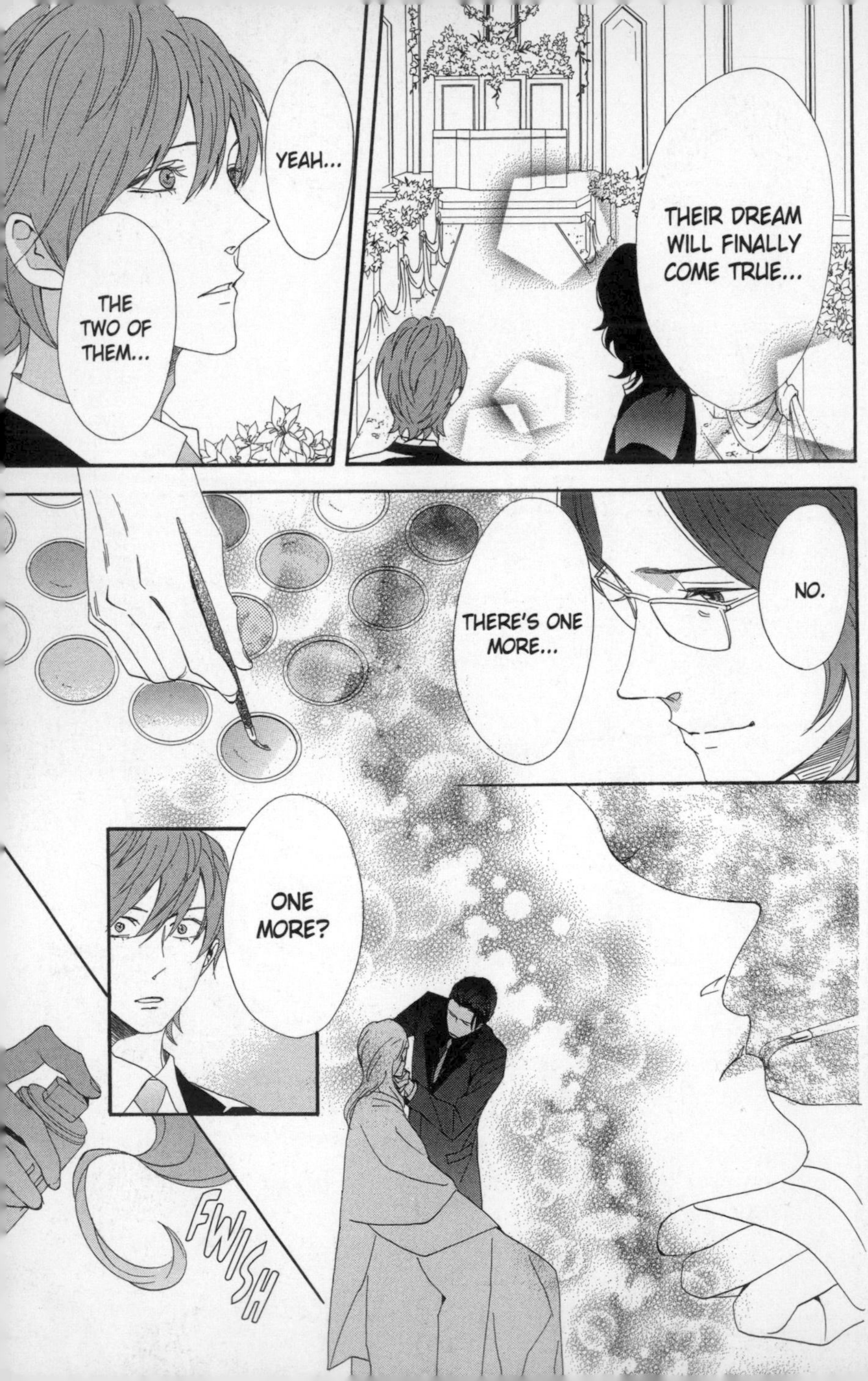
THEIR DREAM WILL FINALLY COME TRUE...
YEAH...
THE TWO OF THEM...
NO.
THERE'S ONE MORE...
ONE MORE?
FWISH

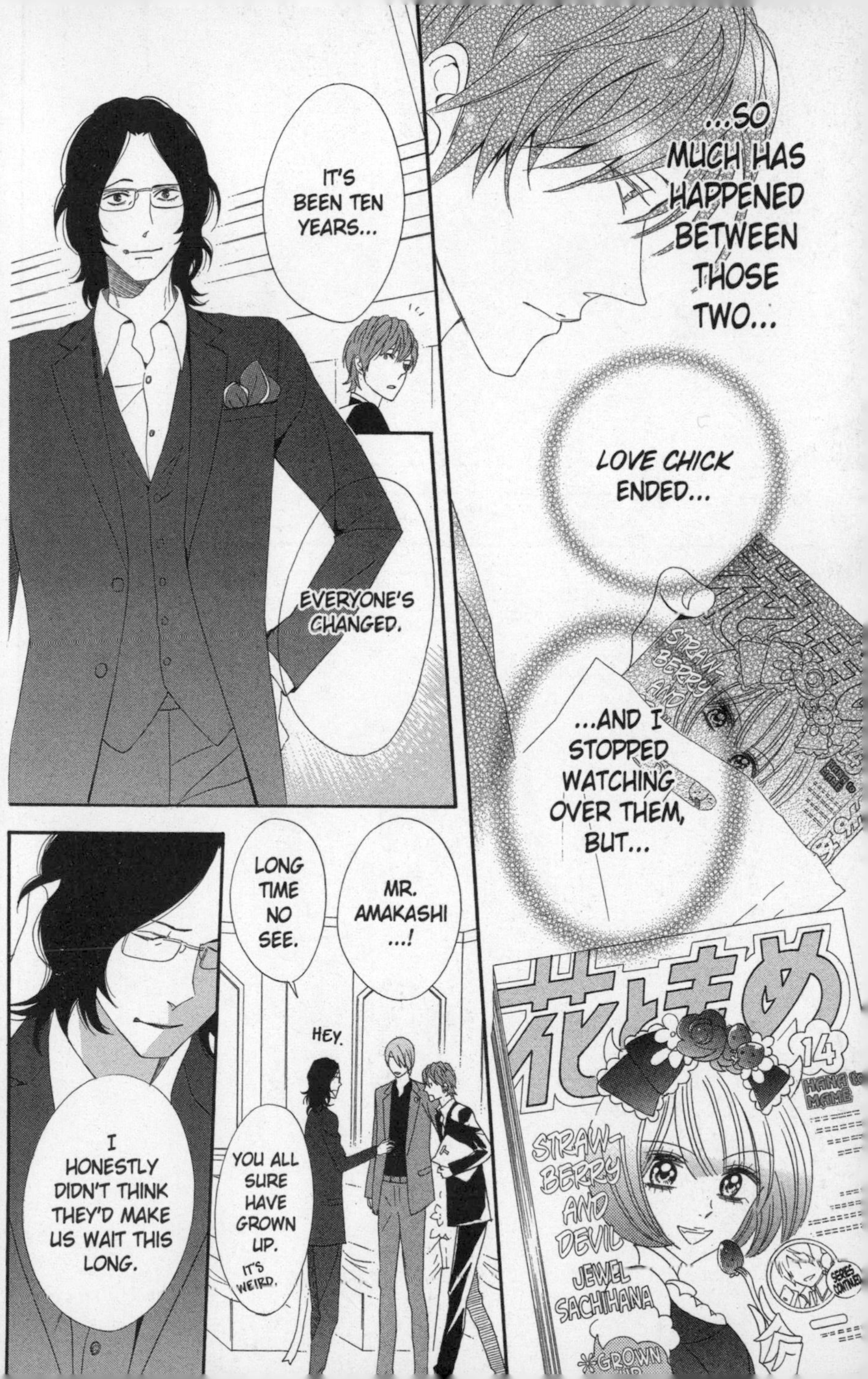
...SO MUCH HAS HAPPENED BETWEEN THOSE TWO...
LOVE CHICK ENDED...
...AND I STOPPED WATCHING OVER THEM, BUT...
STRAW-BERRY AND
花とまめ
14
STRAW-BERRY AND DEVIL
JEWEL SACHIHANA
SERIES CONTINUED
IT'S BEEN TEN YEARS...
EVERYONE'S CHANGED.
MR. AMAKASHI ...!
LONG TIME NO SEE.
HEY.
YOU ALL SURE HAVE GROWN UP.
IT'S WEIRD.
I HONESTLY DIDN'T THINK THEY'D MAKE US WAIT THIS LONG.

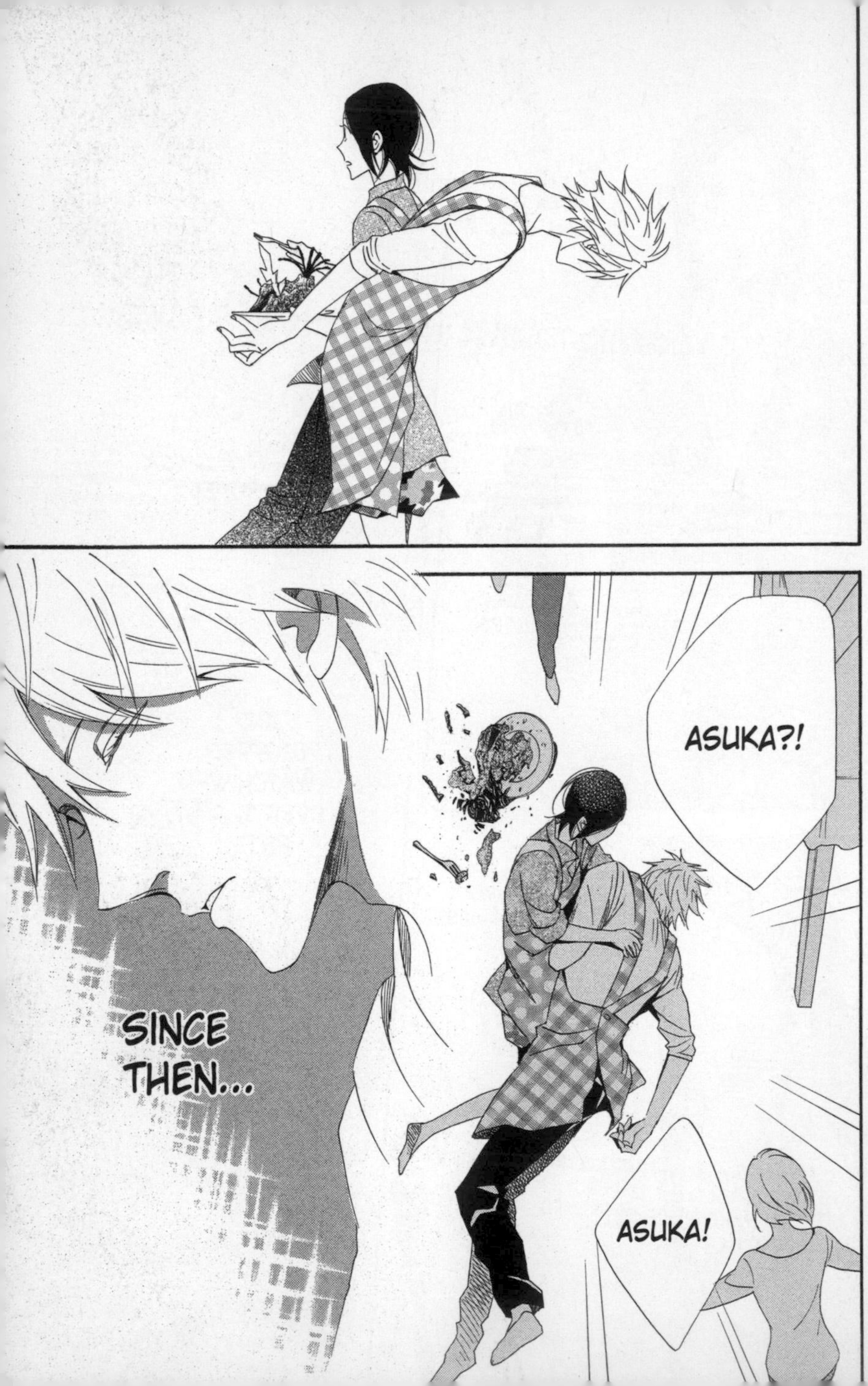
ASUKA?!
ASUKA!
SINCE THEN...

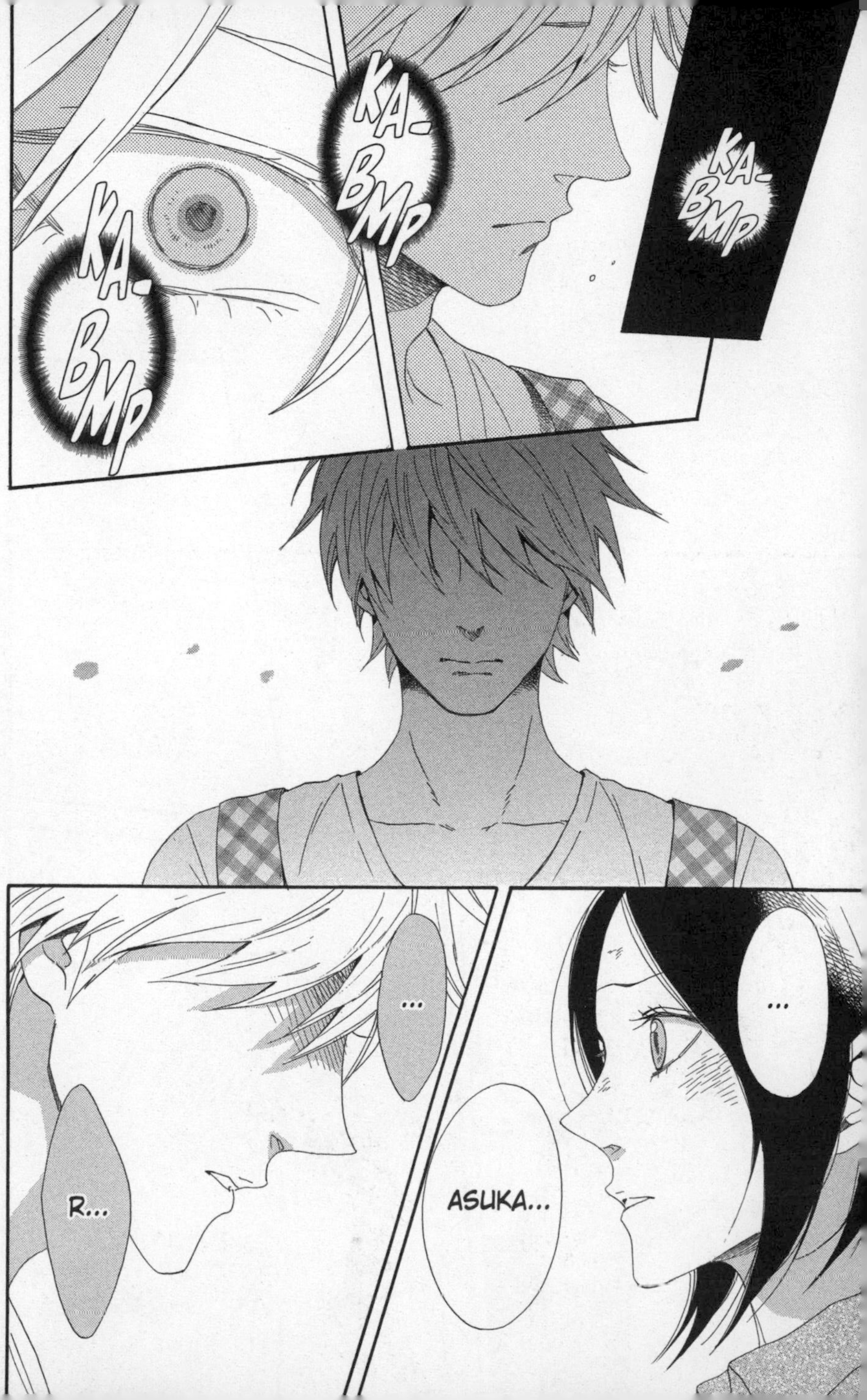
KA-BMP
KA-BMP
KA-BMP
...
ASUKA...
...
R...

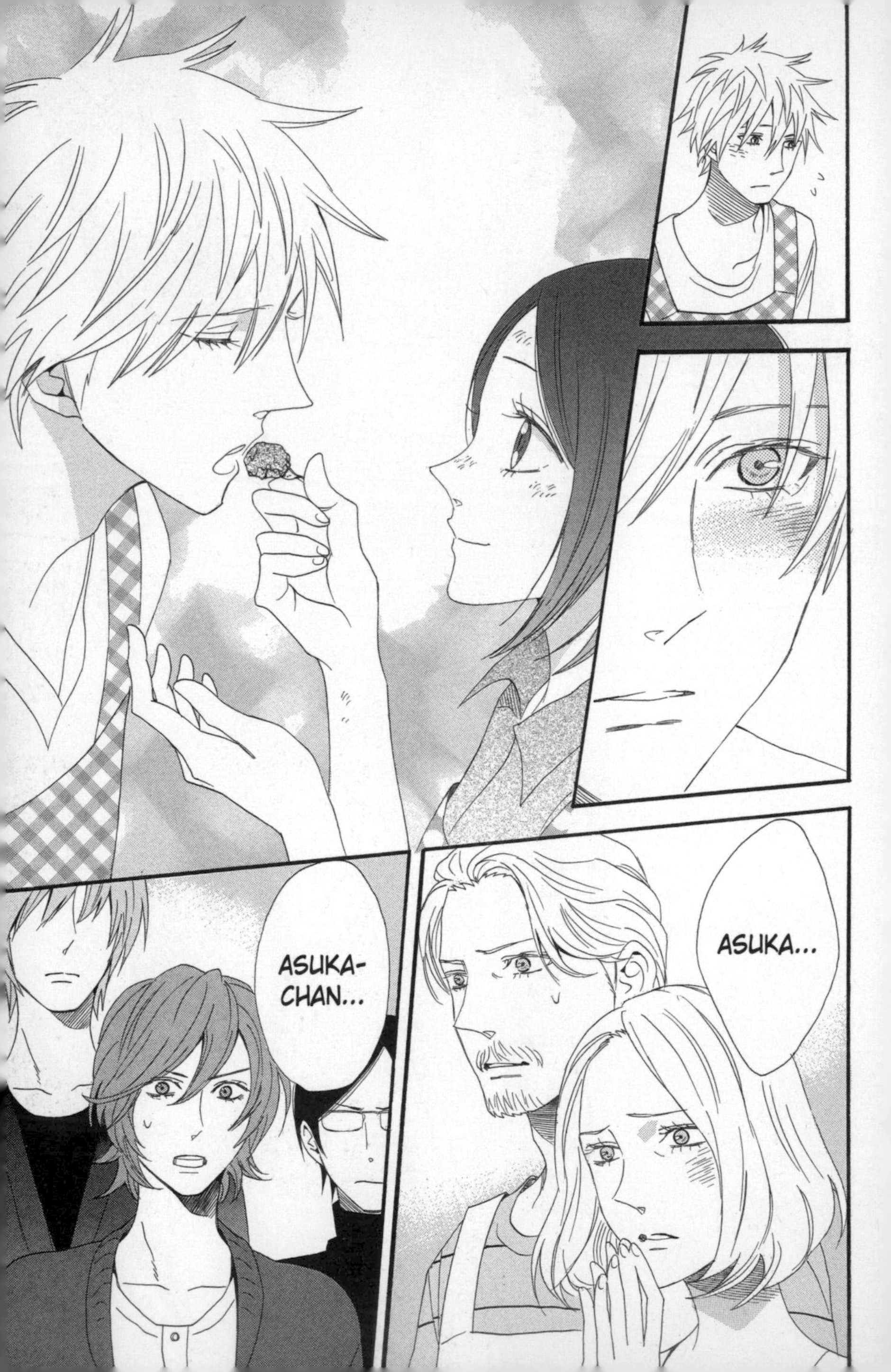
ASUKA...
ASUKA-CHAN...

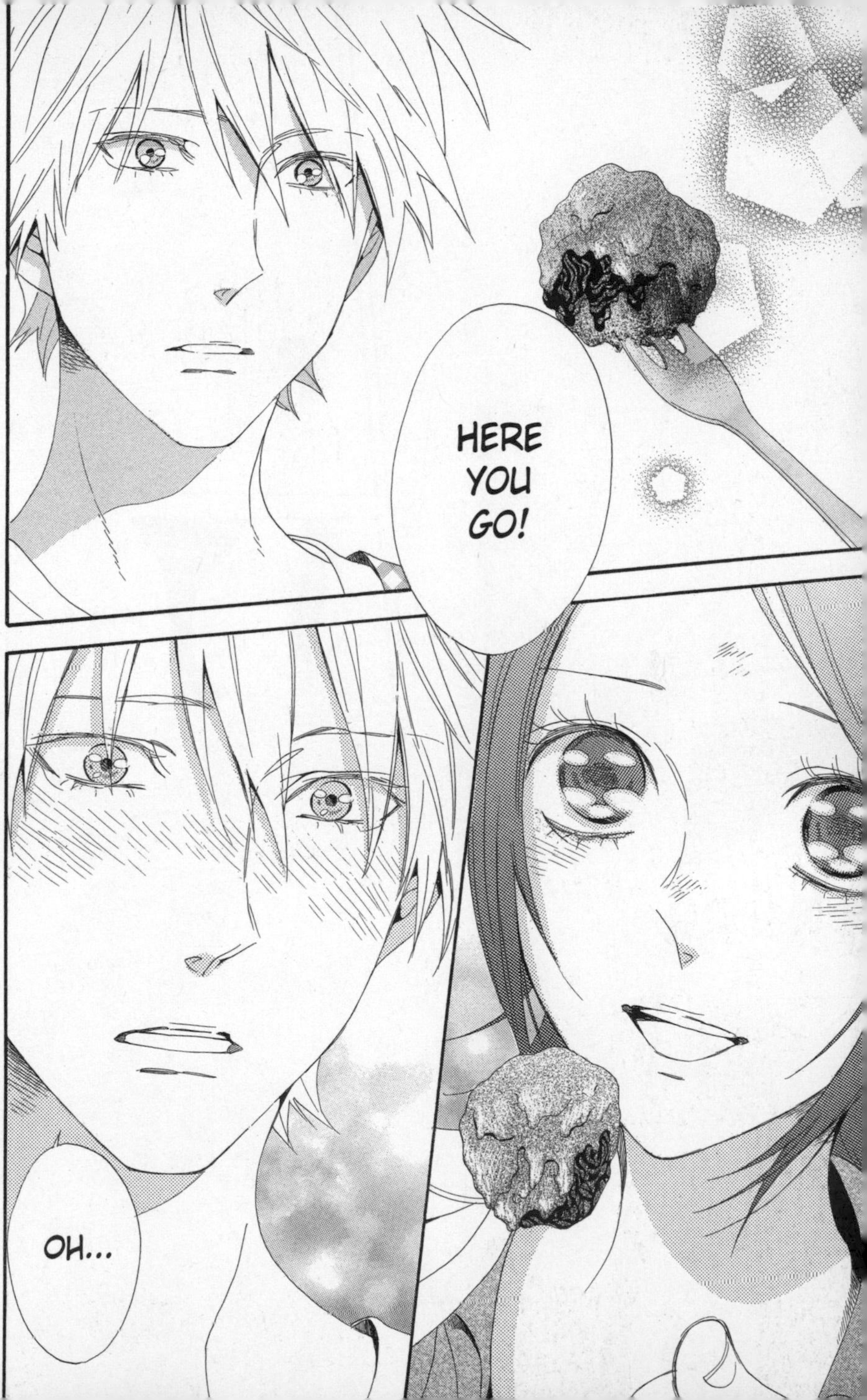
HERE YOU GO!
OH...

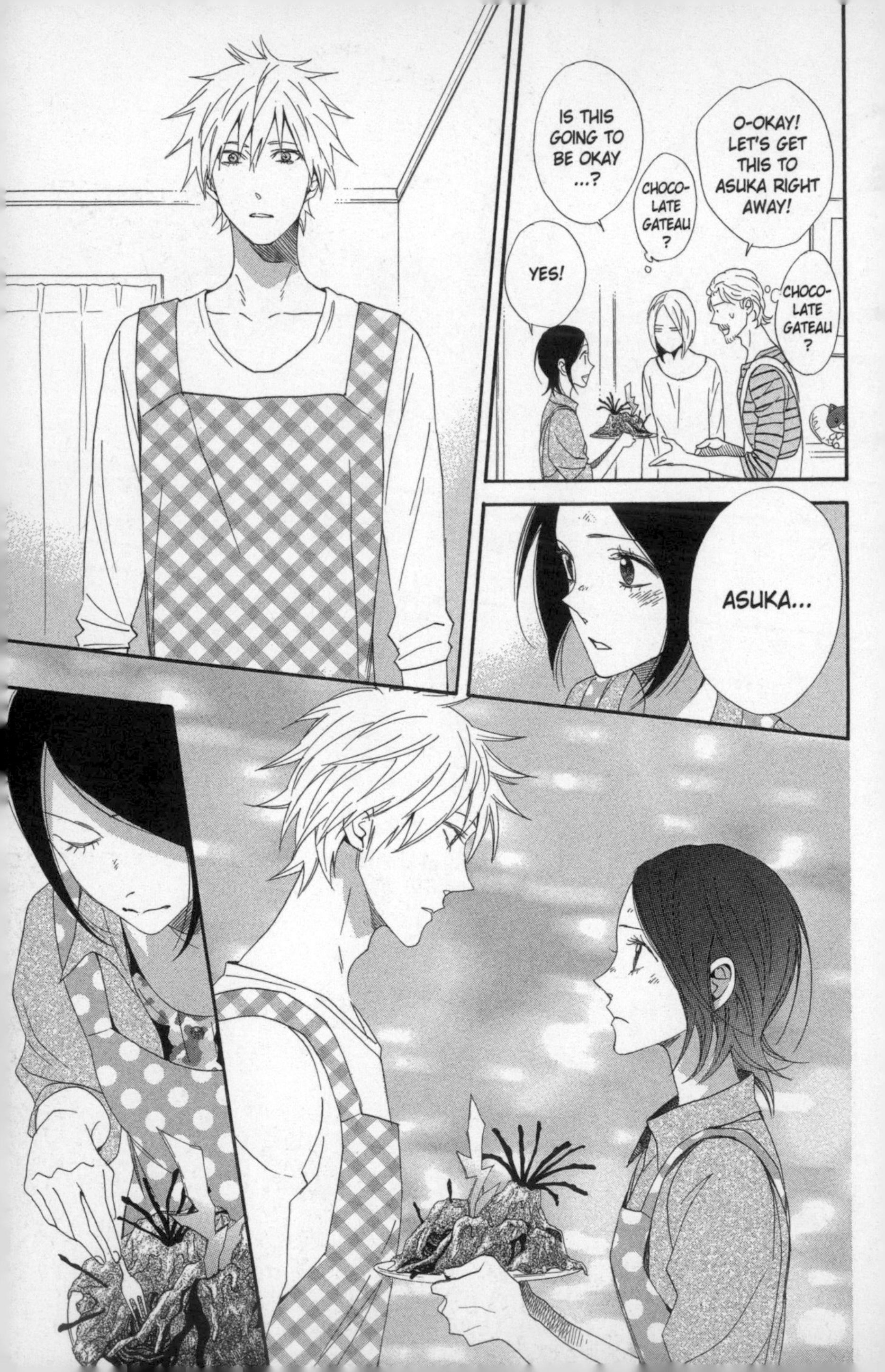
O-OKAY! LET'S GET THIS TO ASUKA RIGHT AWAY!
IS THIS GOING TO BE OKAY ...?
CHOCO-LATE GATEAU?
CHOCO-LATE GATEAU?
YES!
ASUKA...

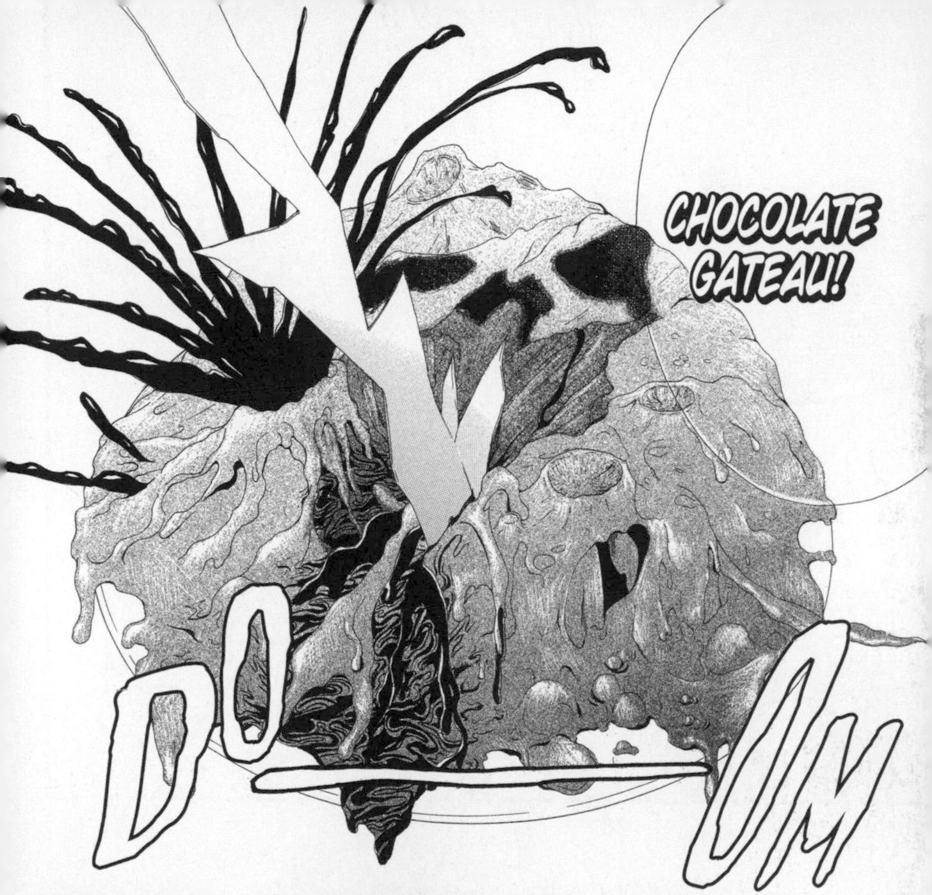
CHOCOLATE GATEAU!
DOOM
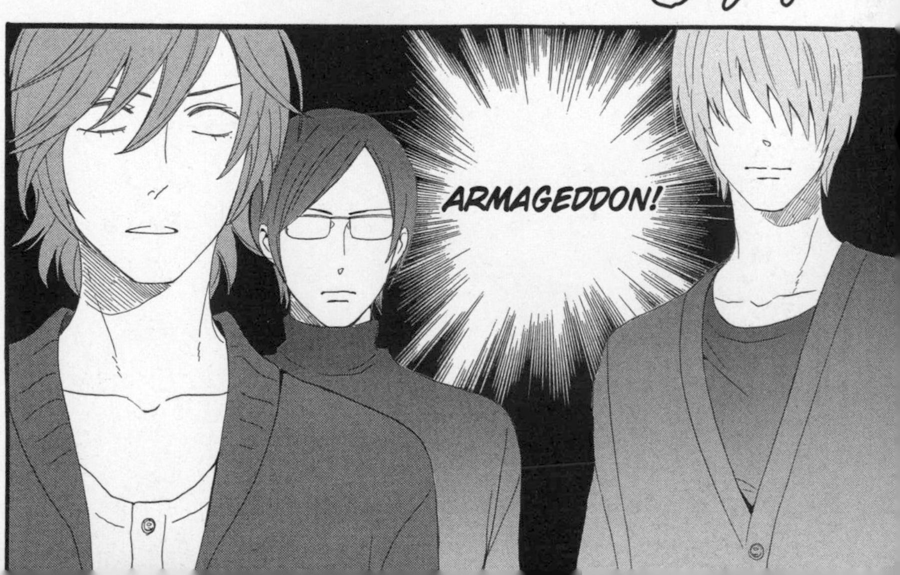
ARMAGEDDON!

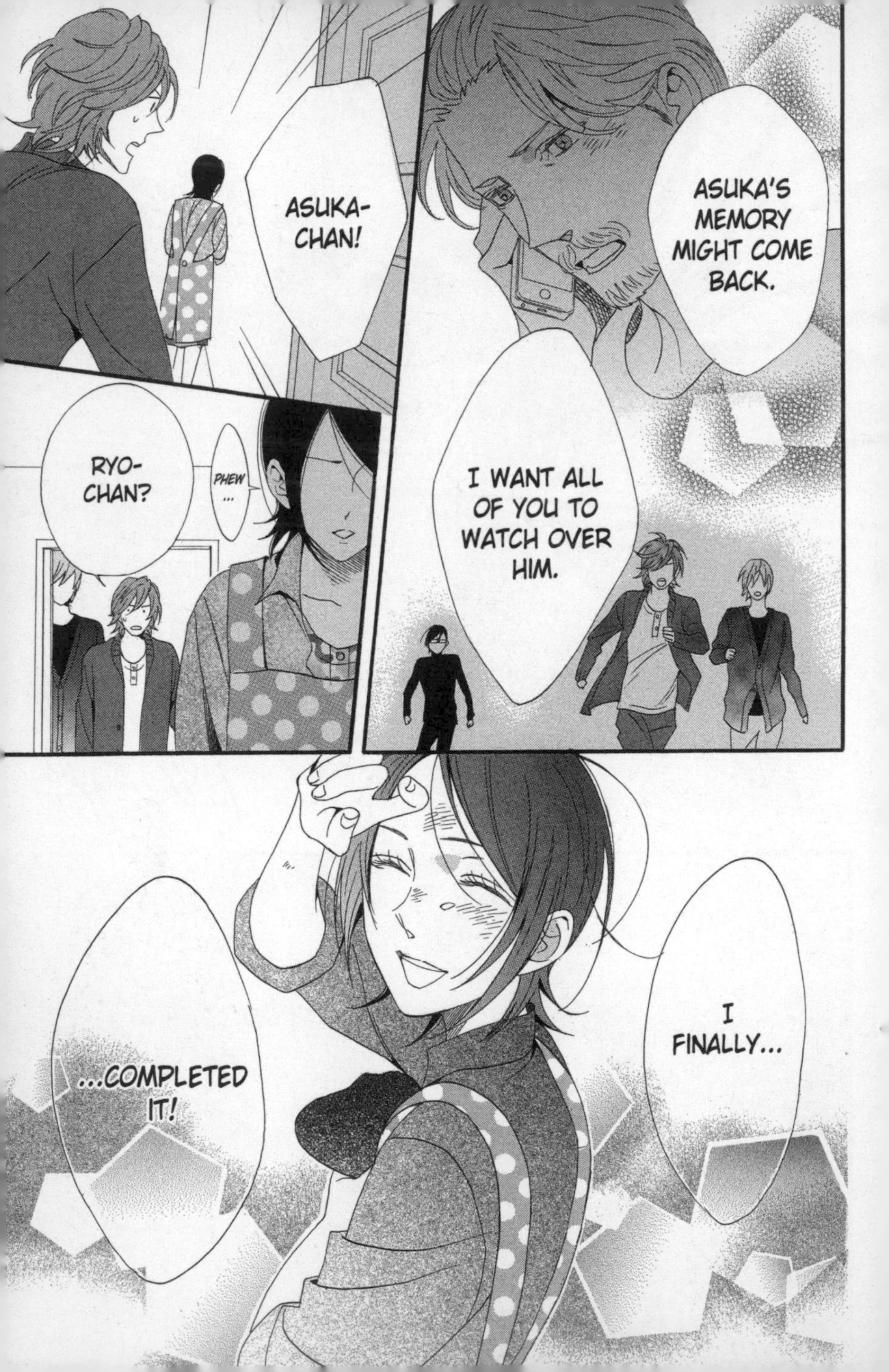
ASUKA'S MEMORY MIGHT COME BACK.
I WANT ALL OF YOU TO WATCH OVER HIM.
ASUKA-CHAN!
PHEW...
RYO-CHAN?
I FINALLY...
...COMPLETED IT!

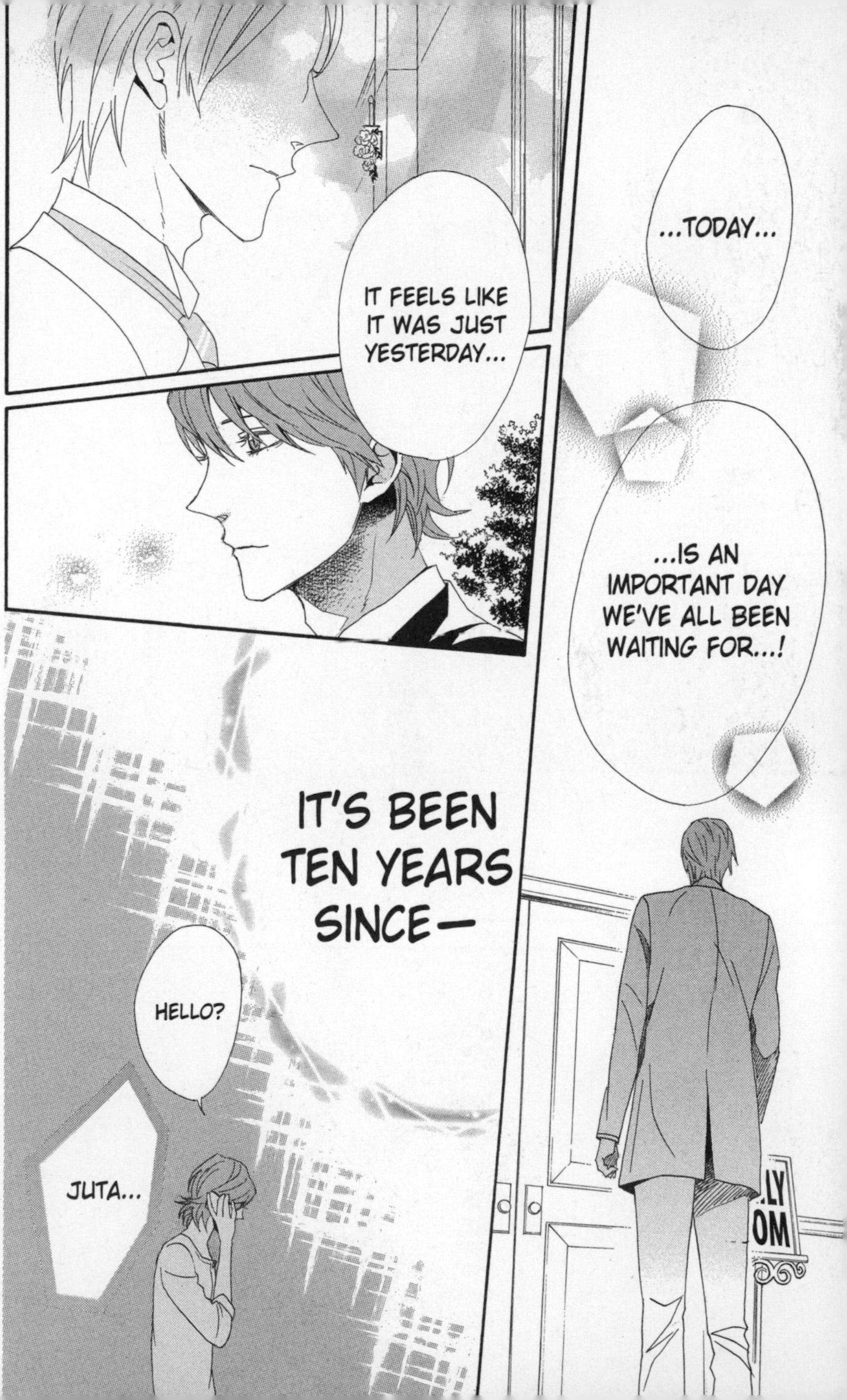
...TODAY...
...IS AN IMPORTANT DAY WE'VE ALL BEEN WAITING FOR...!
IT FEELS LIKE IT WAS JUST YESTERDAY...
IT'S BEEN TEN YEARS SINCE—
HELLO?
JUTA...

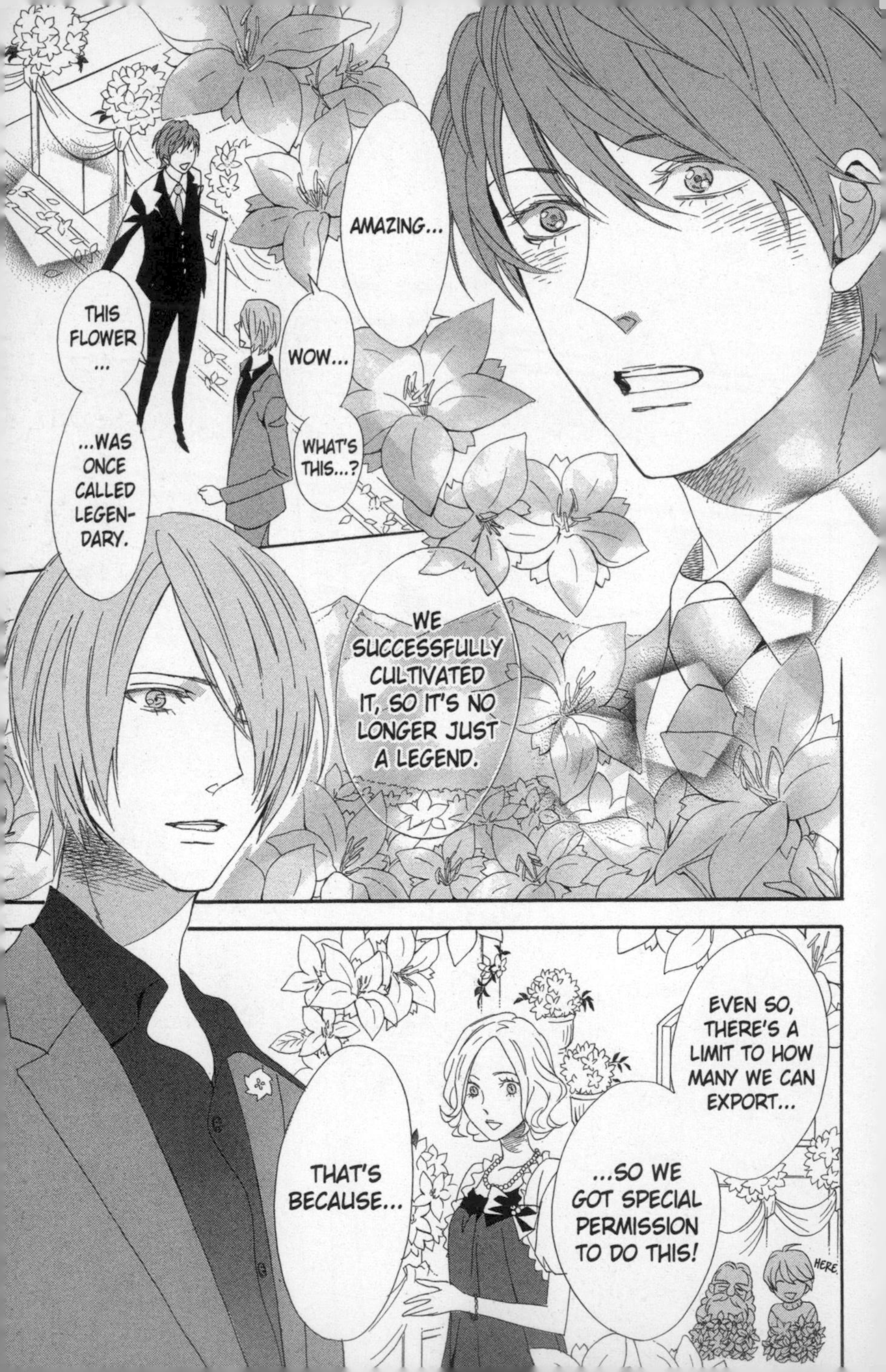
AMAZING...
WOW...
WHAT'S THIS...?
THIS FLOWER ...
...WAS ONCE CALLED LEGEN-DARY.
WE SUCCESSFULLY CULTIVATED IT, SO IT'S NO LONGER JUST A LEGEND.
EVEN SO, THERE'S A LIMIT TO HOW MANY WE CAN EXPORT...
...SO WE GOT SPECIAL PERMISSION TO DO THIS!
HERE.
THAT'S BECAUSE...

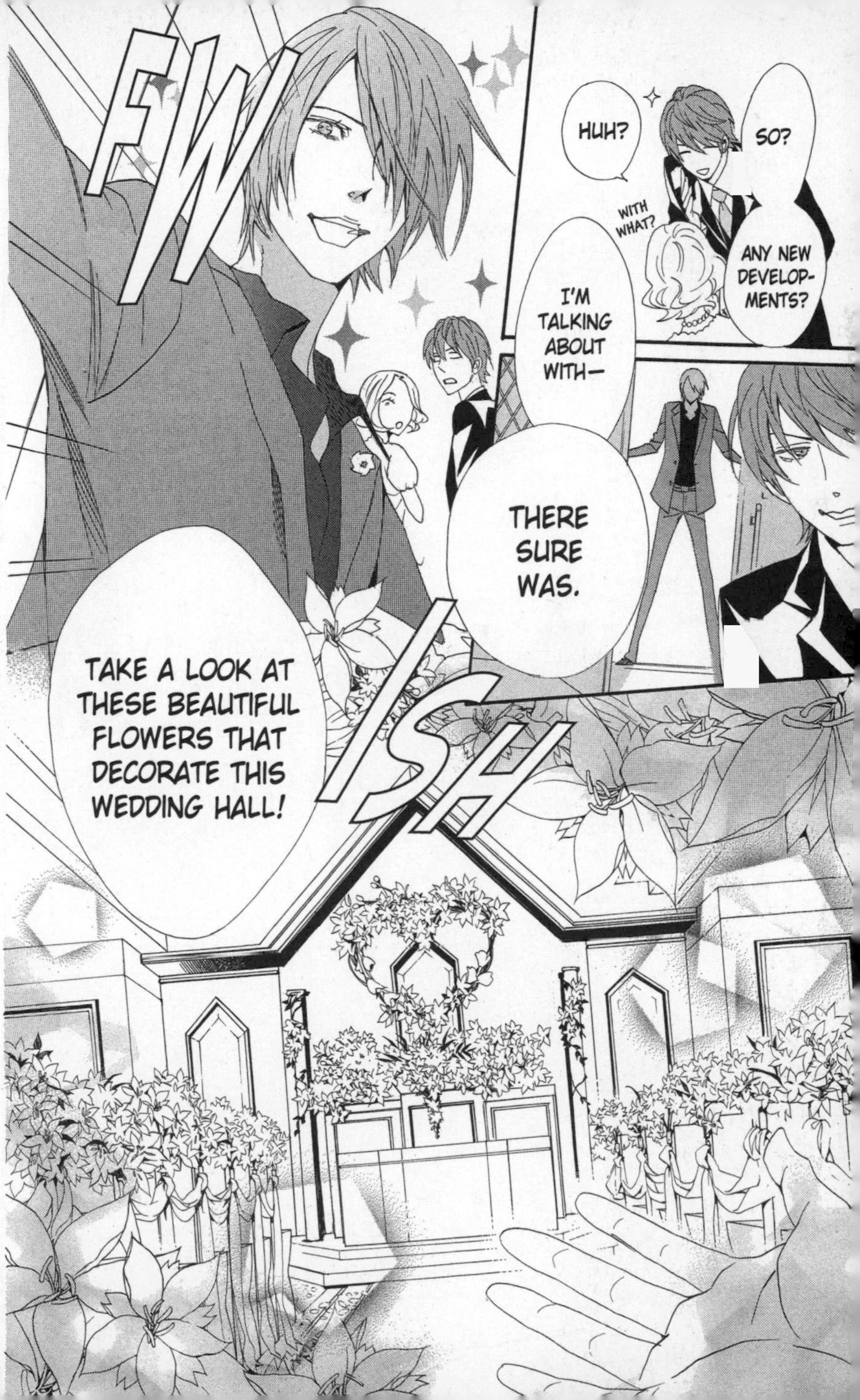
SO?
ANY NEW DEVELOPMENTS?
HUH?
WITH WHAT?
I'M TALKING ABOUT WITH—
THERE SURE WAS.
FWISH
TAKE A LOOK AT THESE BEAUTIFUL FLOWERS THAT DECORATE THIS WEDDING HALL!

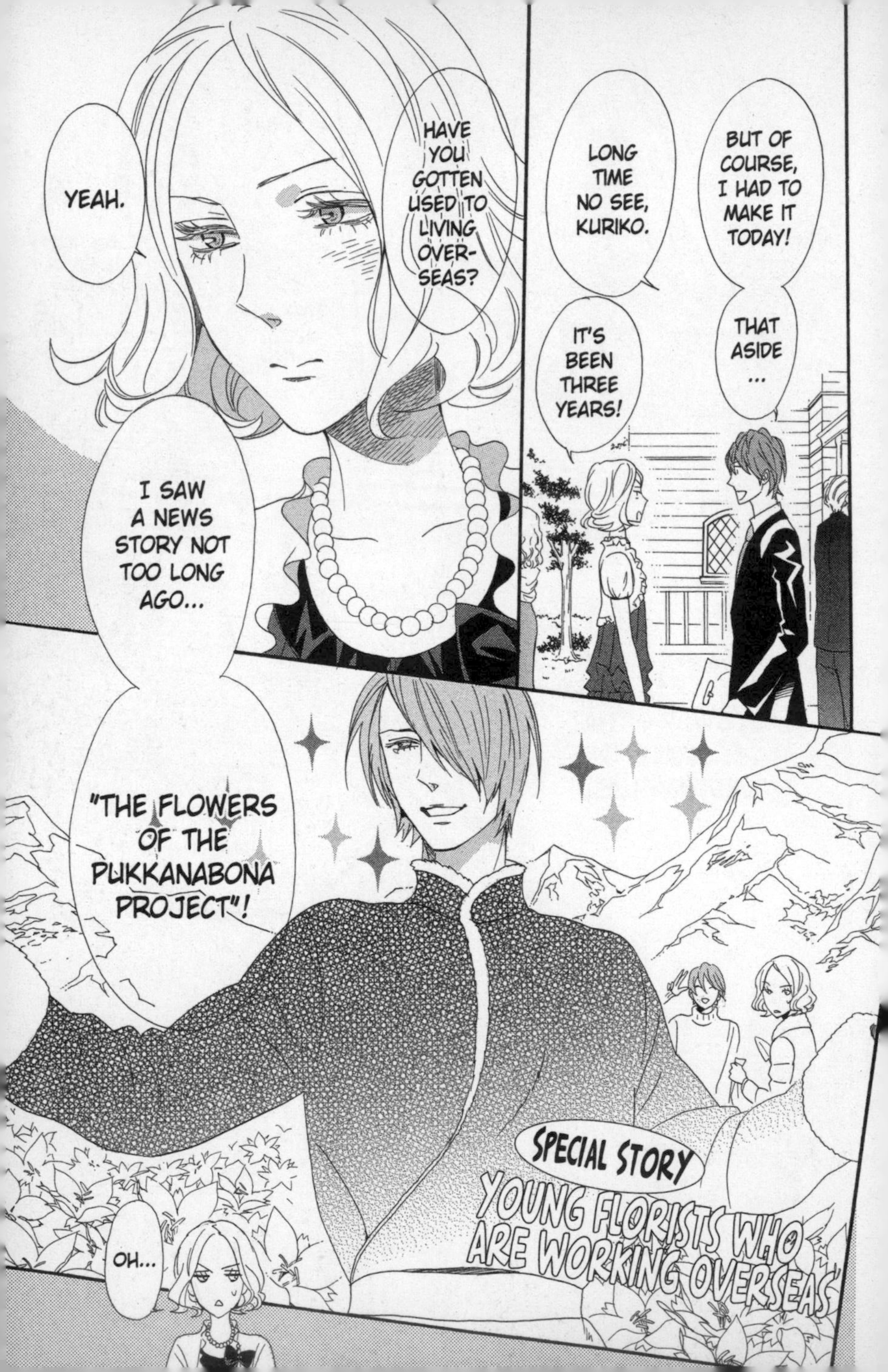
BUT OF COURSE, I HAD TO MAKE IT TODAY!
THAT ASIDE ...
LONG TIME NO SEE, KURIKO.
IT'S BEEN THREE YEARS!
HAVE YOU GOTTEN USED TO LIVING OVER-SEAS?
YEAH.
I SAW A NEWS STORY NOT TOO LONG AGO...
"THE FLOWERS OF THE PUKKANABONA PROJECT"!
SPECIAL STORY
YOUNG FLORISTS WHO ARE WORKING OVERSEAS
OH...

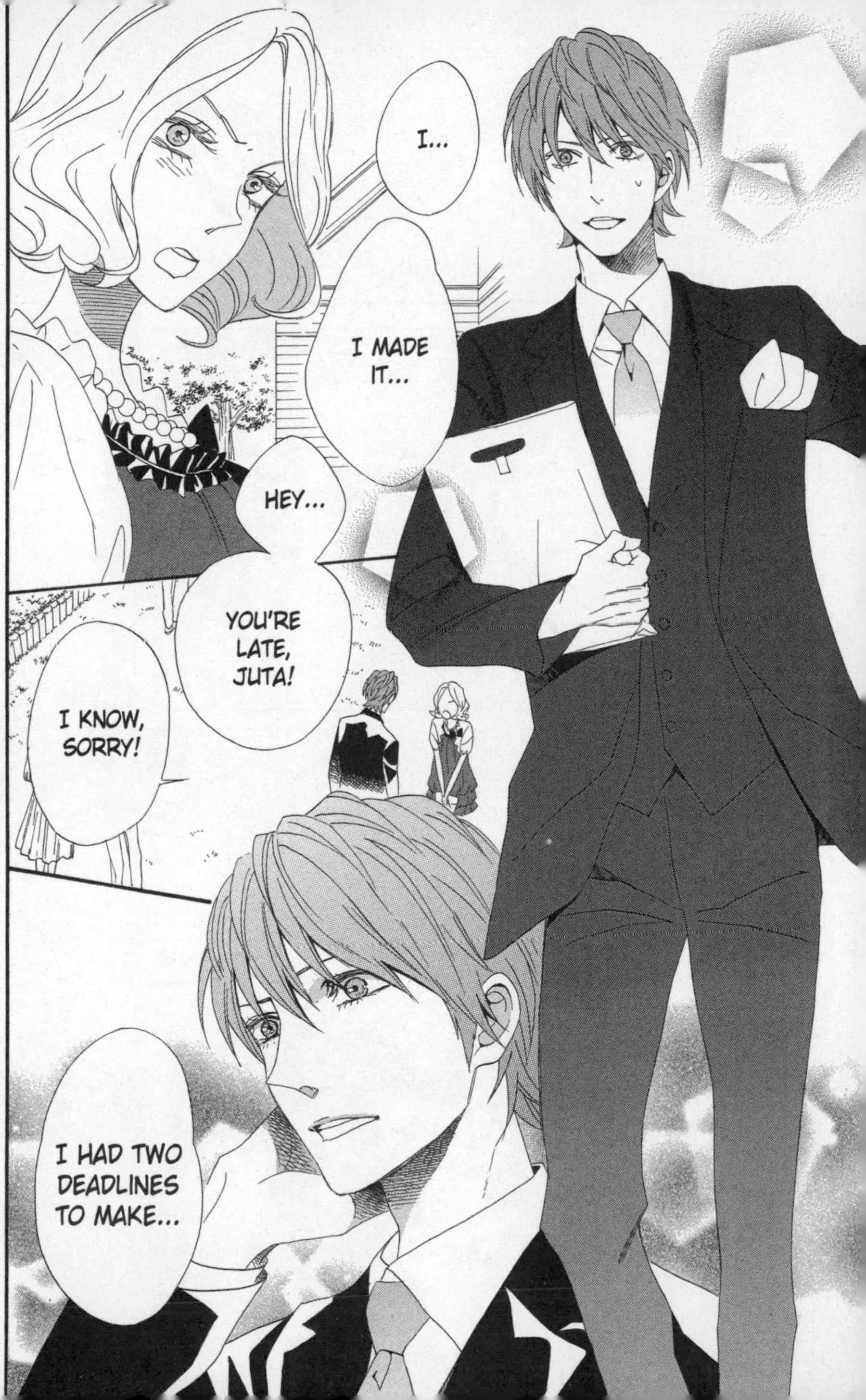
I...
I MADE IT...
HEY...
YOU'RE LATE, JUTA!
I KNOW, SORRY!
I HAD TWO DEADLINES TO MAKE...

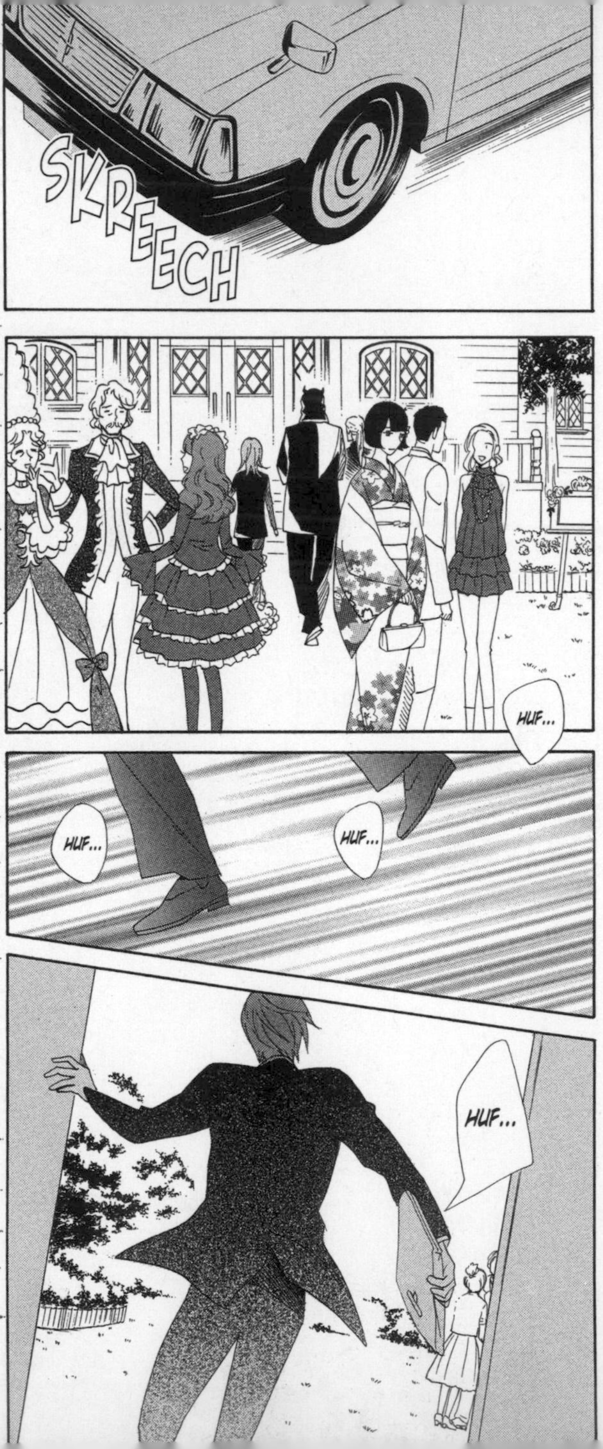
SKREECH
HUF...
HUF...
HUF...
HUF...

Production Assistance:

Shimada-san
Kuwana-san
Kaneko-san
Sakurai-san
Nakazawa-san
Tanaka-san
Kawashima-san
Sayaka-san
Yone-yan
Takowa-san

Special Thanks:

Abe-san
My Family
My Friends
Houen Kikaku

and

All My Readers

THANK YOU VERY MUCH!

菅野文
Aya Kanno

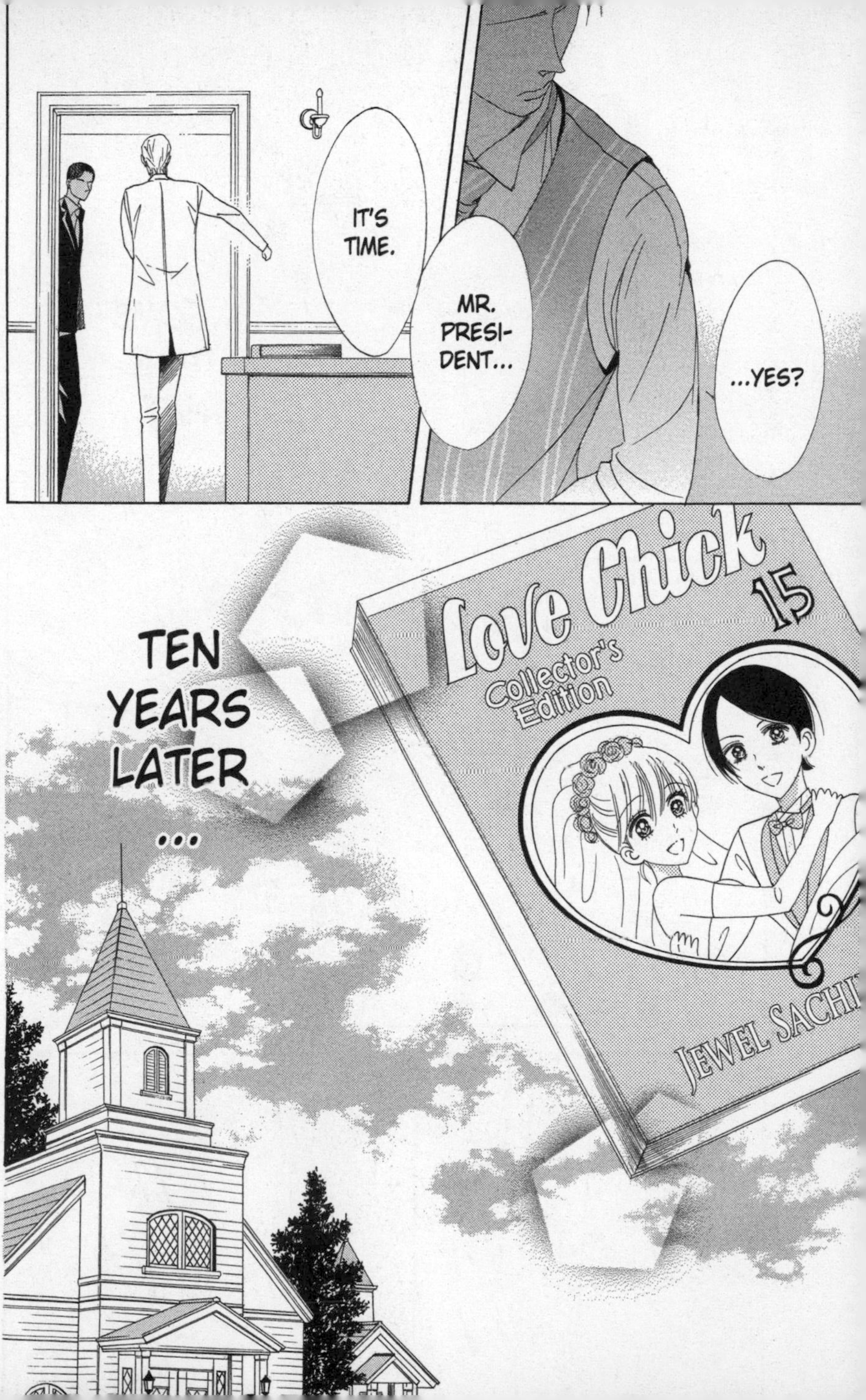
IT'S TIME.
MR. PRESIDENT...
...YES?
Love Chick
15
Collector's Edition
JEWEL SACHI
TEN YEARS LATER...

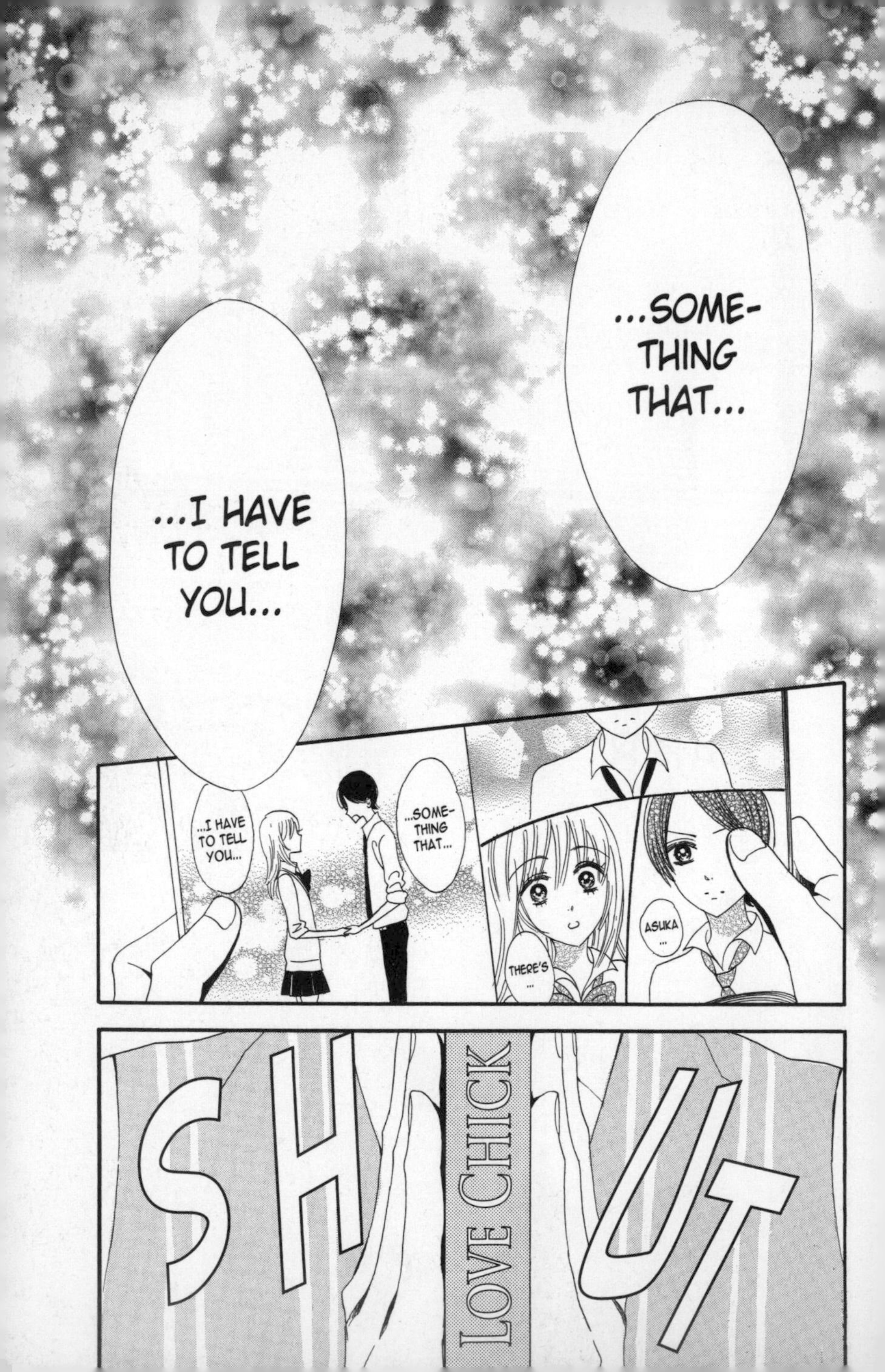
...SOME-THING THAT...
...I HAVE TO TELL YOU...
ASUKA ...
THERE'S ...
...SOME-THING THAT...
...I HAVE TO TELL YOU...
SHUT
LOVE CHICK

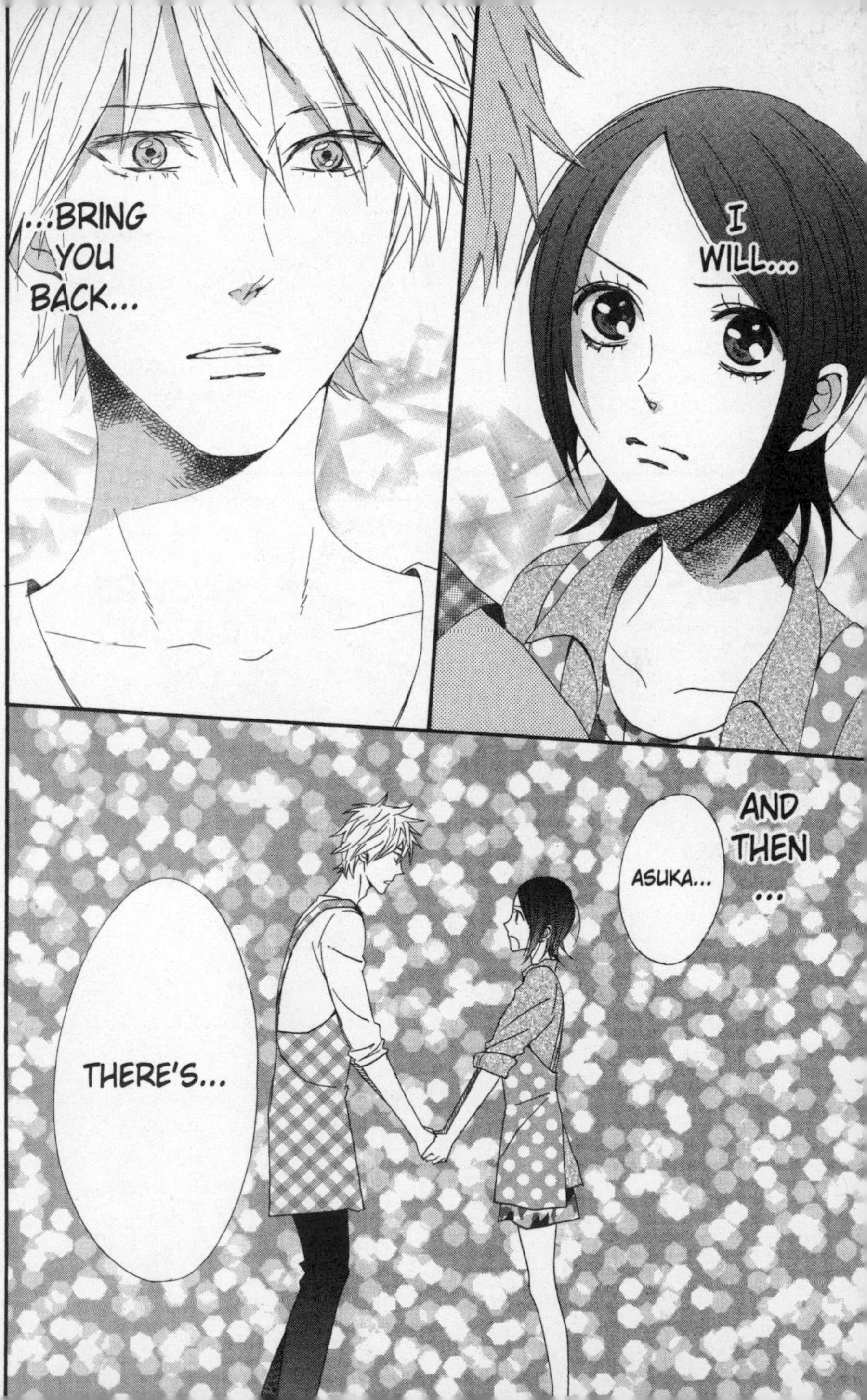
I WILL...
...BRING YOU BACK...
AND THEN ...
ASUKA...
THERE'S...

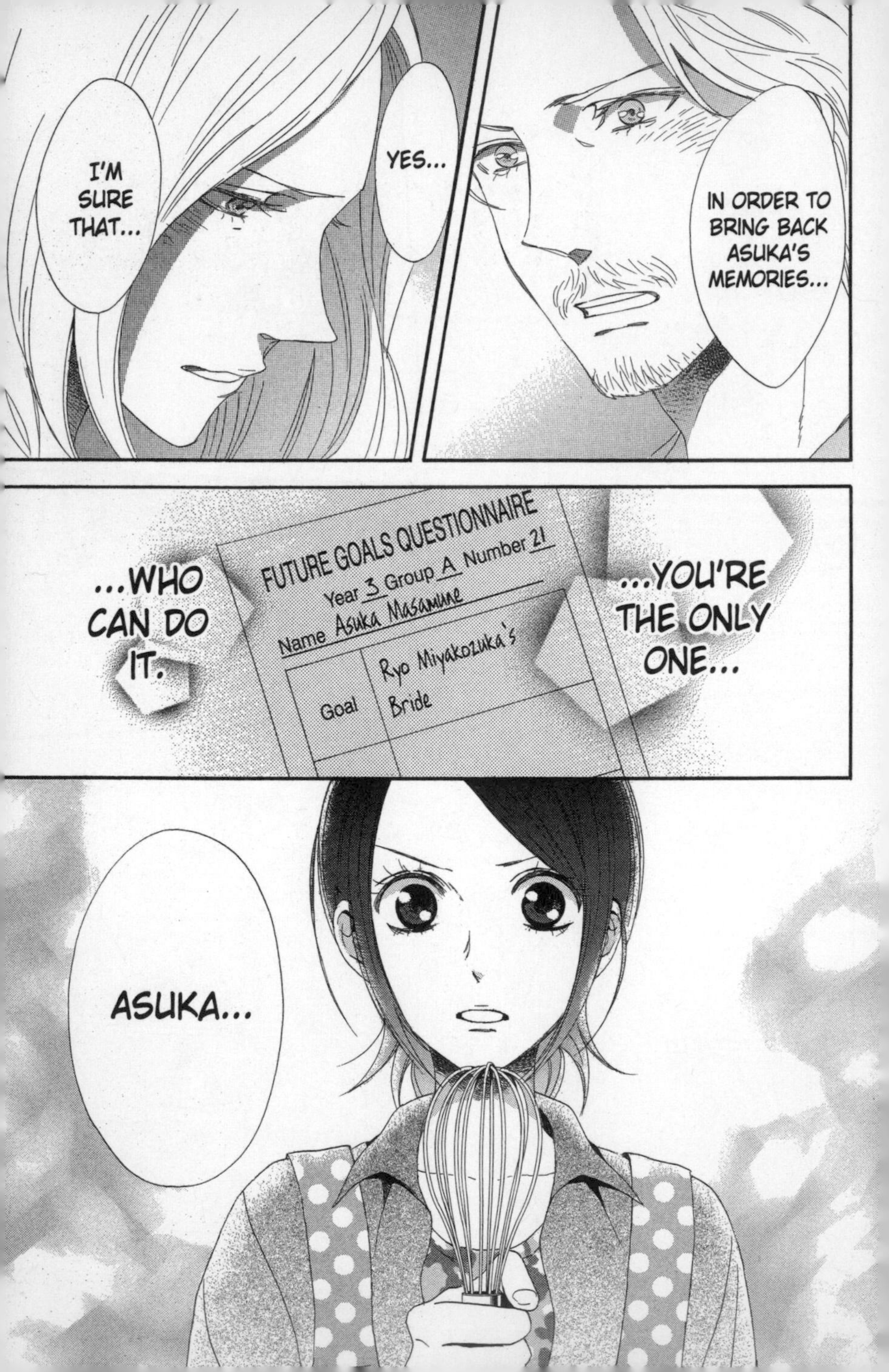
IN ORDER TO BRING BACK ASUKA'S MEMORIES...
YES...
I'M SURE THAT...
...YOU'RE THE ONLY ONE...
FUTURE GOALS QUESTIONNAIRE
Year 3 Group A Number 21
Name Asuka Masamune
Goal Ryo Miyakozuka's Bride
...WHO CAN DO IT.
ASUKA...

OTOMEN

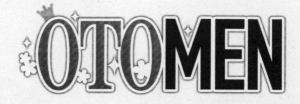

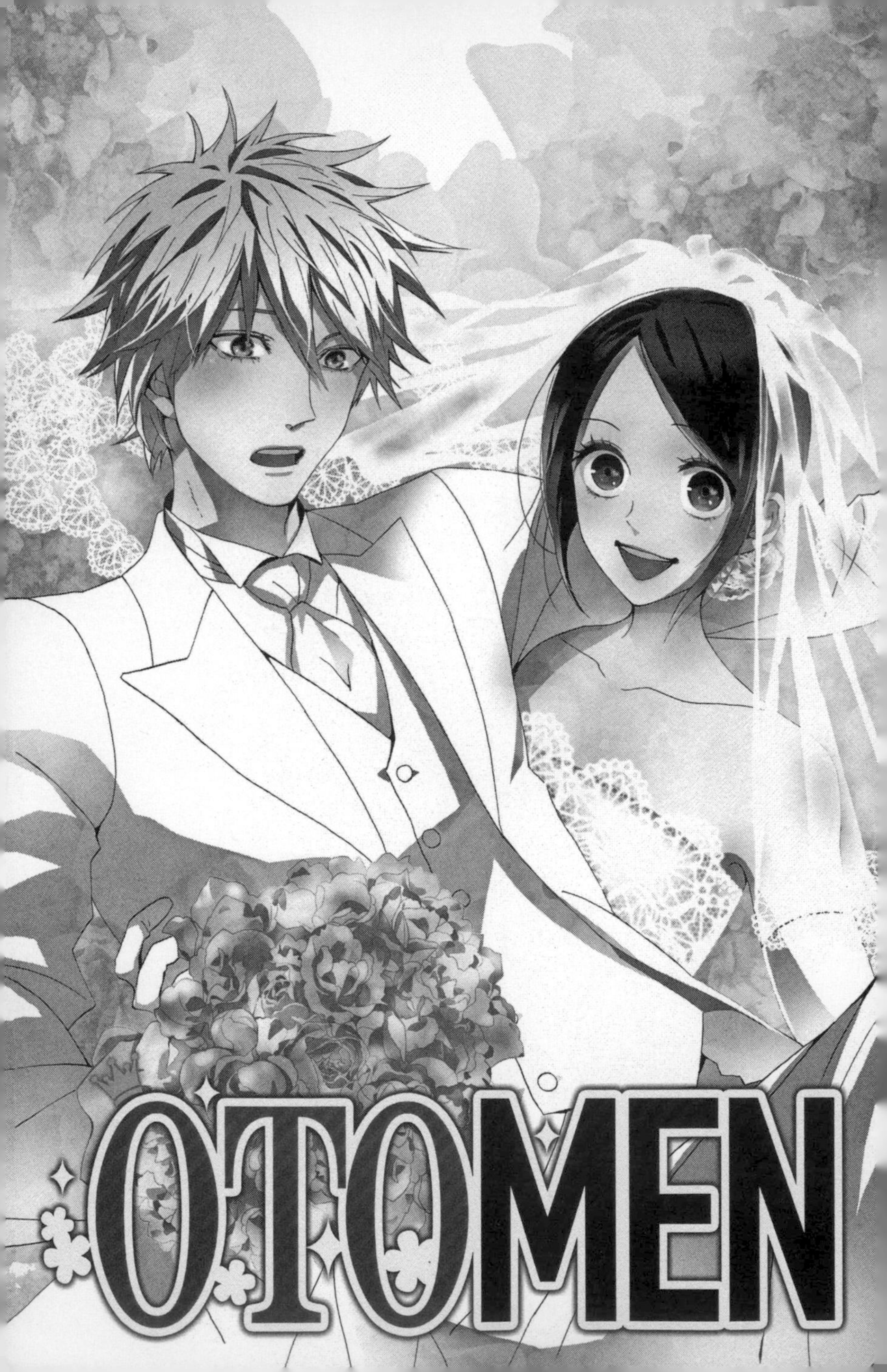
OTOMEN

OTOMEN

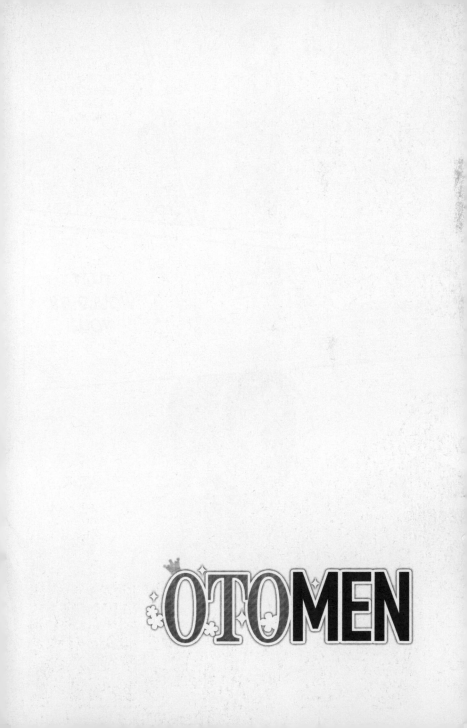

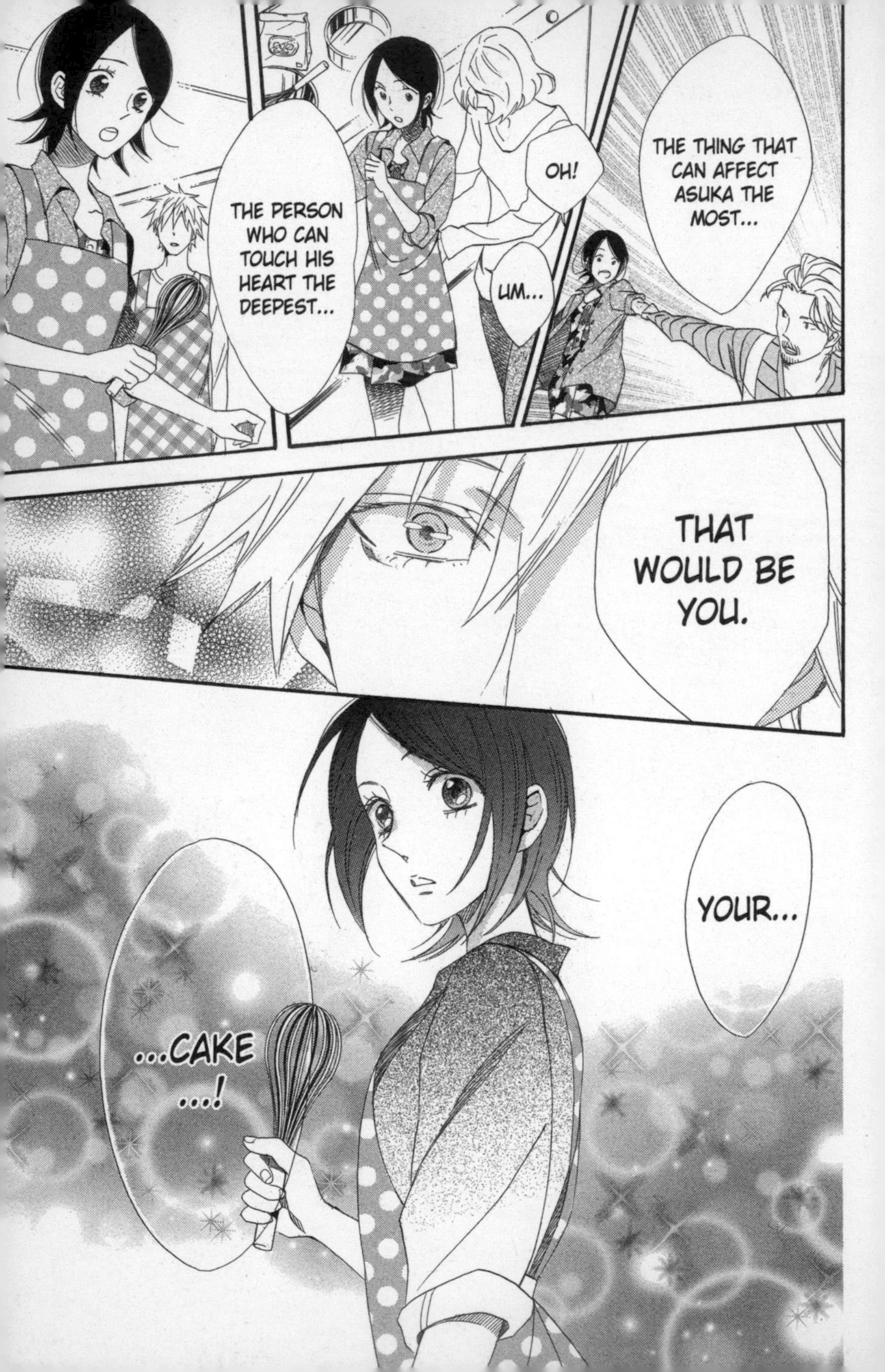
THE THING THAT CAN AFFECT ASUKA THE MOST...
OH!
UM...
THE PERSON WHO CAN TOUCH HIS HEART THE DEEPEST...
THAT WOULD BE YOU.
YOUR...
...CAKE ...!

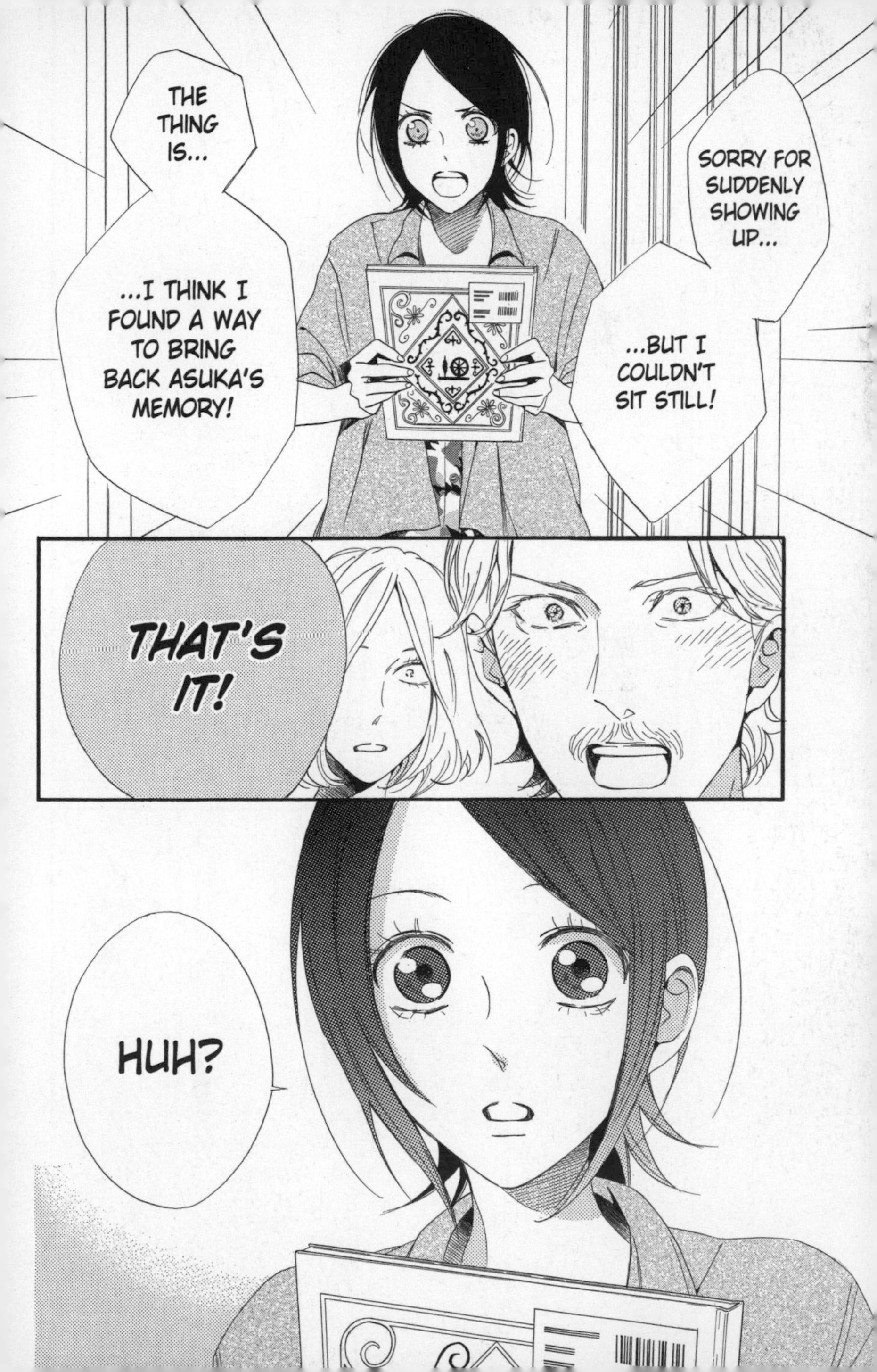
SORRY FOR SUDDENLY SHOWING UP...
...BUT I COULDN'T SIT STILL!
THE THING IS...
...I THINK I FOUND A WAY TO BRING BACK ASUKA'S MEMORY!
THAT'S IT!
HUH?

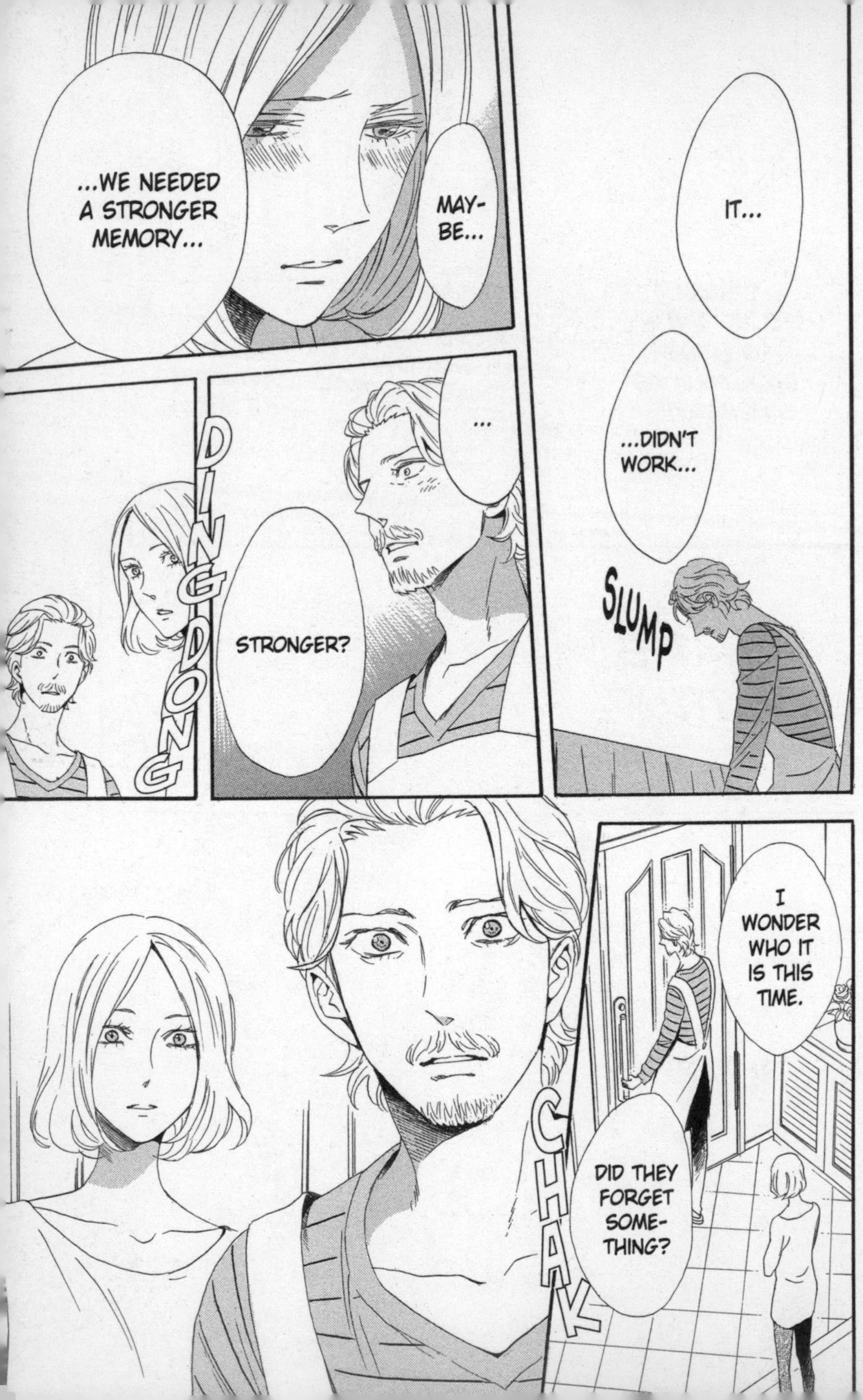
IT...
...DIDN'T WORK...
SLUMP
MAY-BE...
...WE NEEDED A STRONGER MEMORY...
...
STRONGER?
DING DONG
I WONDER WHO IT IS THIS TIME.
DID THEY FORGET SOME-THING?
CHAK

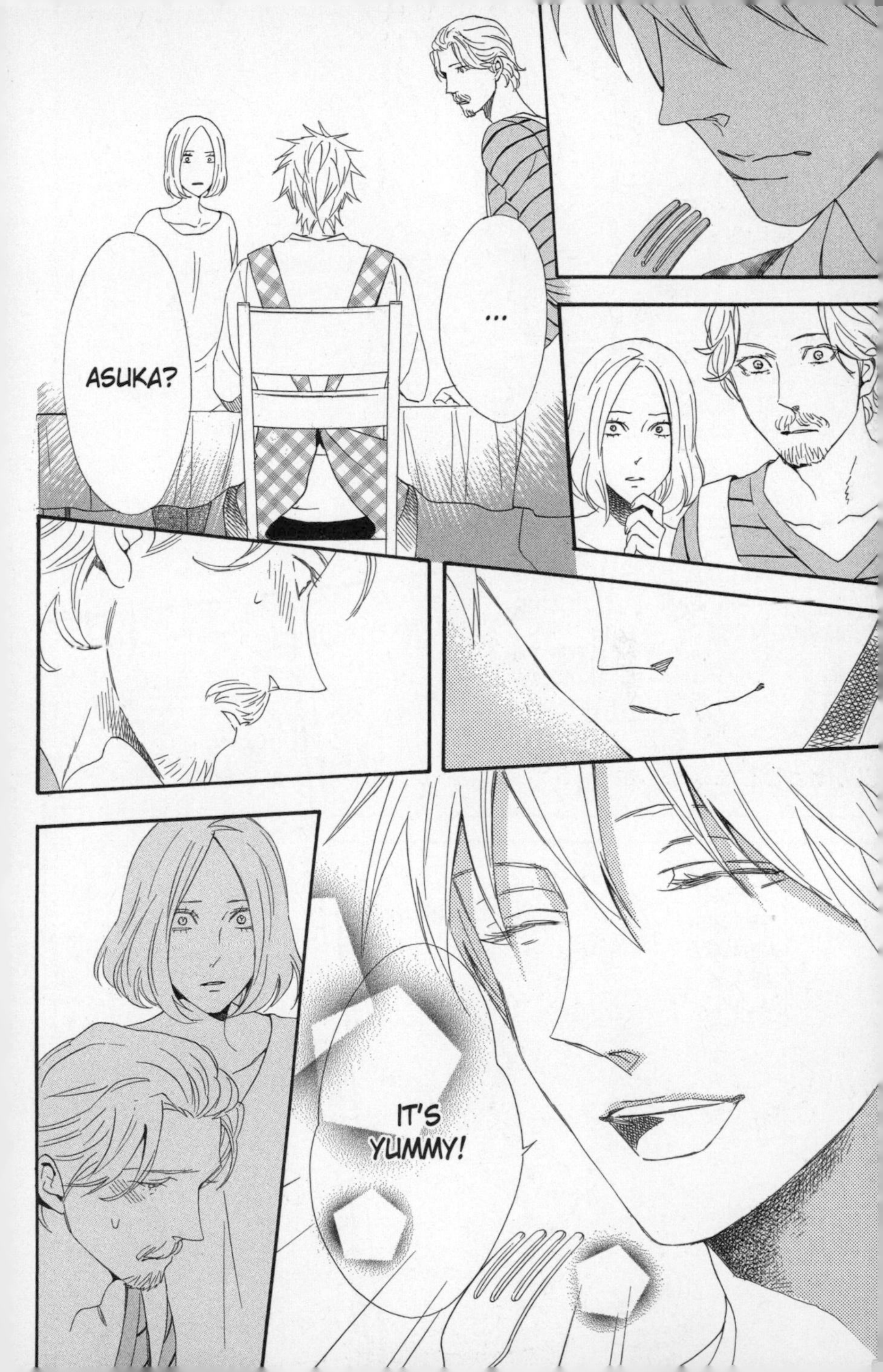
...
ASUKA?
IT'S YUMMY!

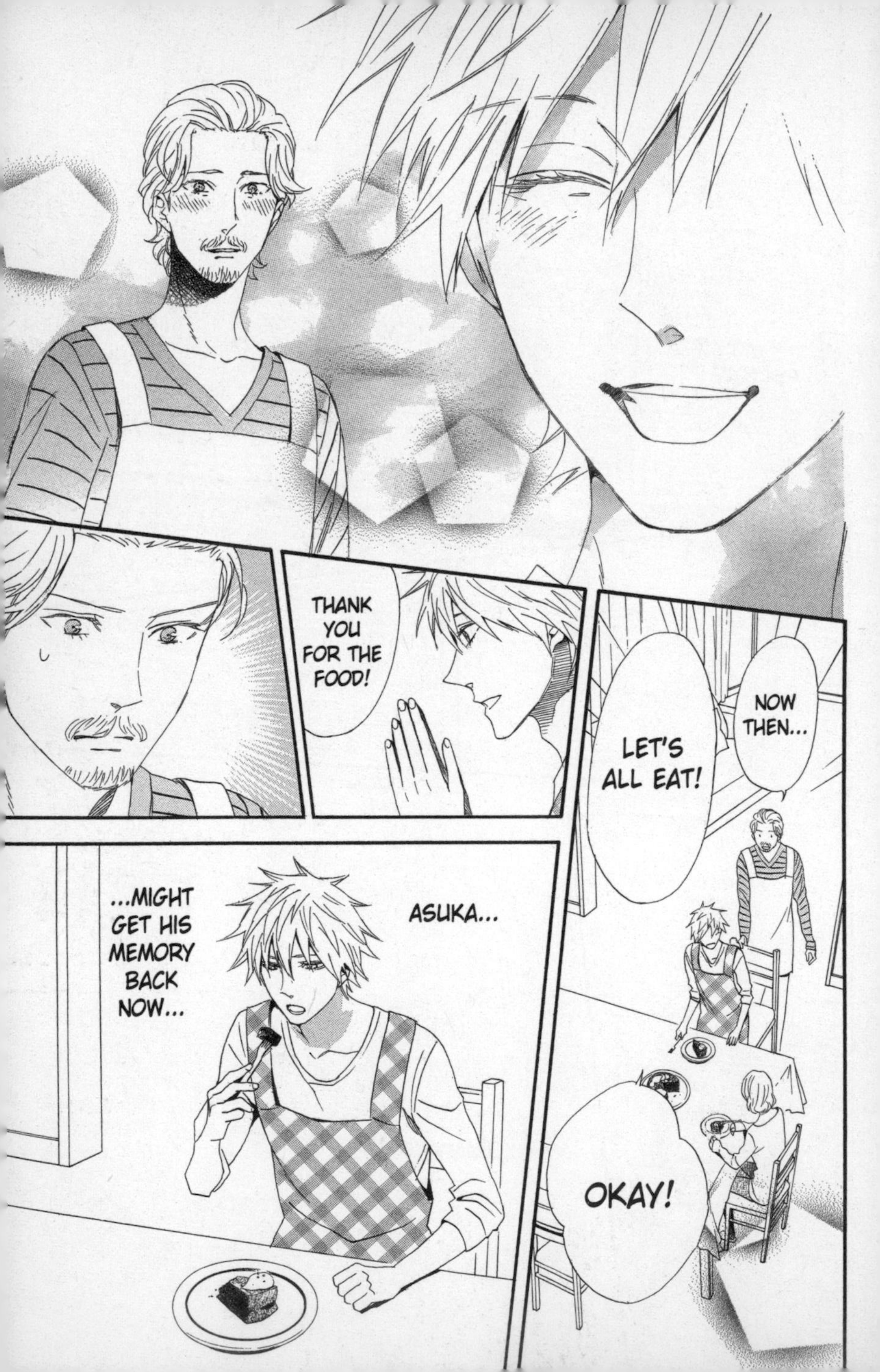
NOW THEN...
LET'S ALL EAT!
OKAY!
THANK YOU FOR THE FOOD!
ASUKA...
...MIGHT GET HIS MEMORY BACK NOW...

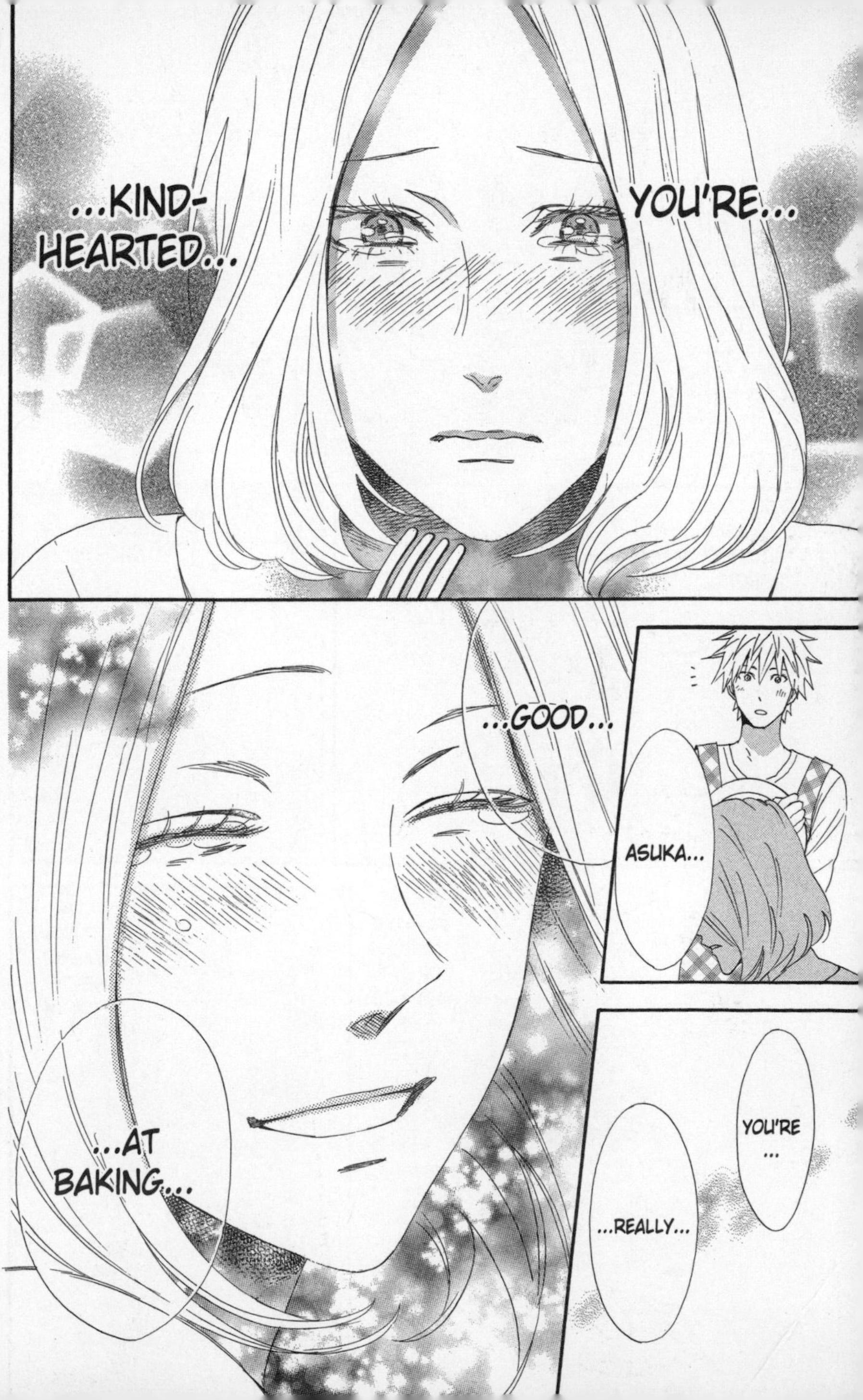
YOU'RE...
...KIND-HEARTED...
ASUKA...
YOU'RE...
...REALLY...
...GOOD...
...AT BAKING...

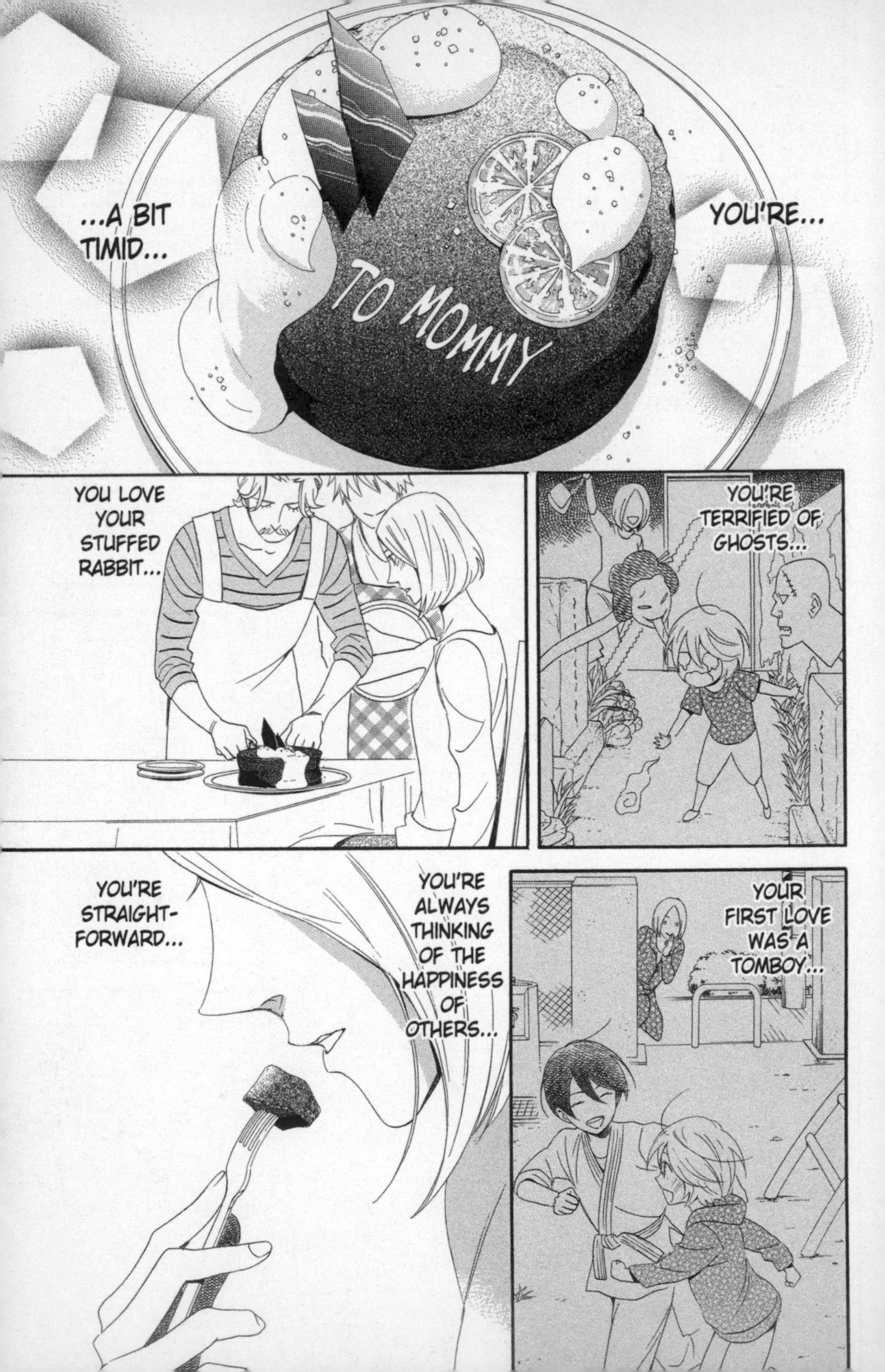
YOU'RE...
TO MOMMY
...A BIT TIMID...
YOU'RE TERRIFIED OF GHOSTS...
YOU LOVE YOUR STUFFED RABBIT...
YOUR FIRST LOVE WAS A TOMBOY...
YOU'RE ALWAYS THINKING OF THE HAPPINESS OF OTHERS...
YOU'RE STRAIGHT-FORWARD...

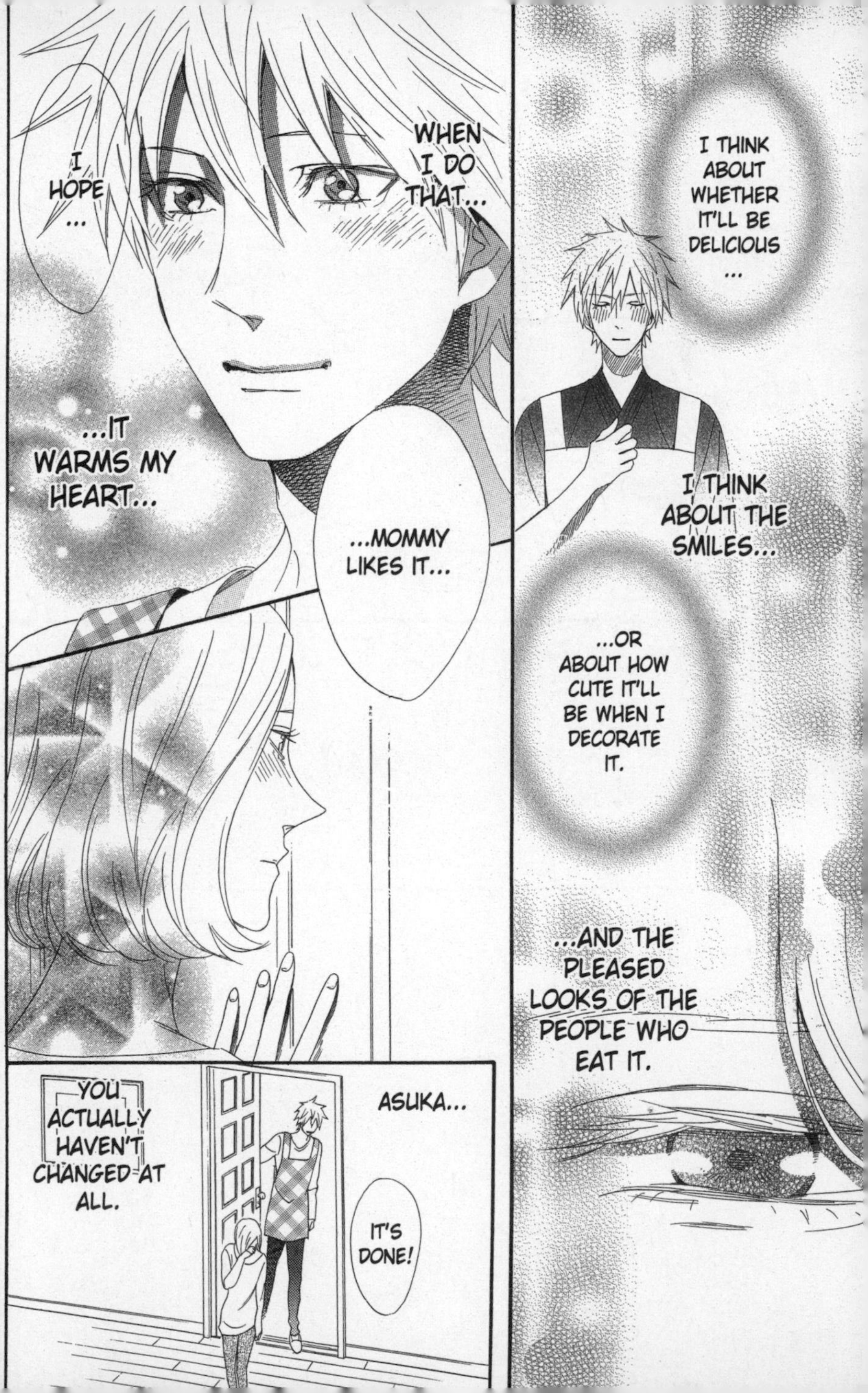
I THINK ABOUT WHETHER IT'LL BE DELICIOUS...
I THINK ABOUT THE SMILES...
...OR ABOUT HOW CUTE IT'LL BE WHEN I DECORATE IT.
...AND THE PLEASED LOOKS OF THE PEOPLE WHO EAT IT.
WHEN I DO THAT...
I HOPE...
...MOMMY LIKES IT...
...IT WARMS MY HEART...
ASUKA...
IT'S DONE!
YOU ACTUALLY HAVEN'T CHANGED AT ALL.

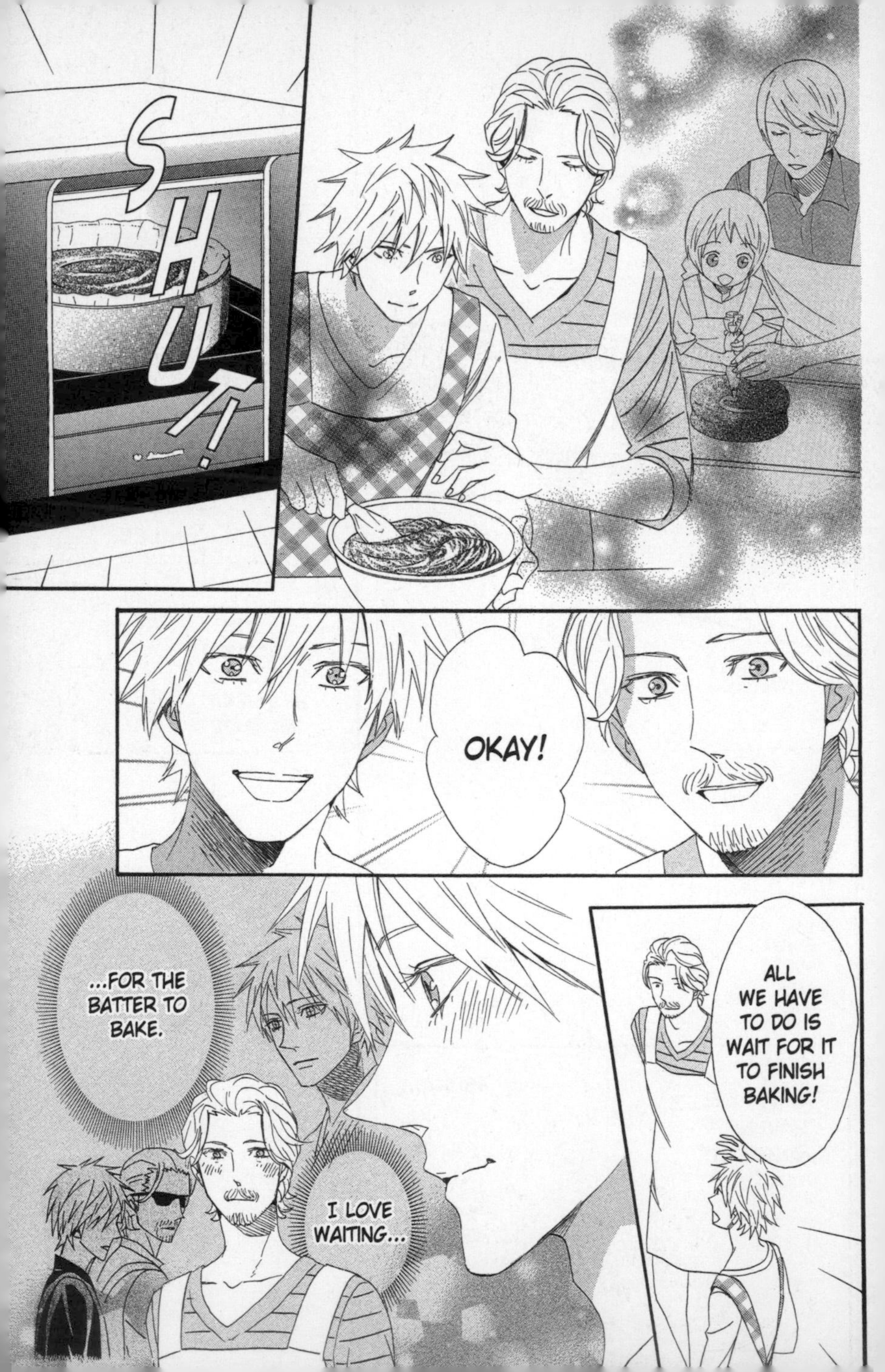
SHUT!
OKAY!
ALL WE HAVE TO DO IS WAIT FOR IT TO FINISH BAKING!
I LOVE WAITING...
...FOR THE BATTER TO BAKE.

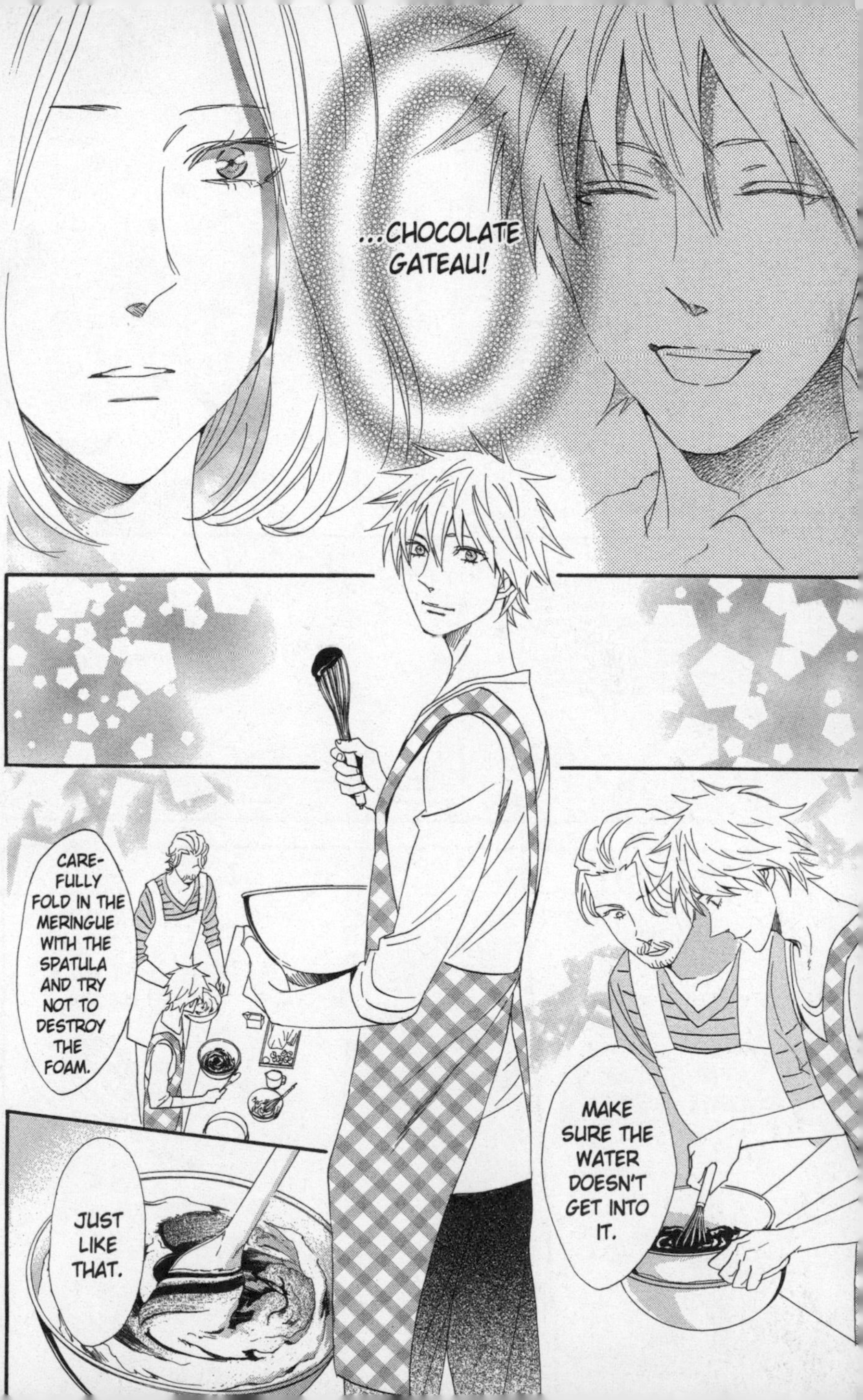
...CHOCOLATE GATEAU!
MAKE SURE THE WATER DOESN'T GET INTO IT.
CARE-FULLY FOLD IN THE MERINGUE WITH THE SPATULA AND TRY NOT TO DESTROY THE FOAM.
JUST LIKE THAT.

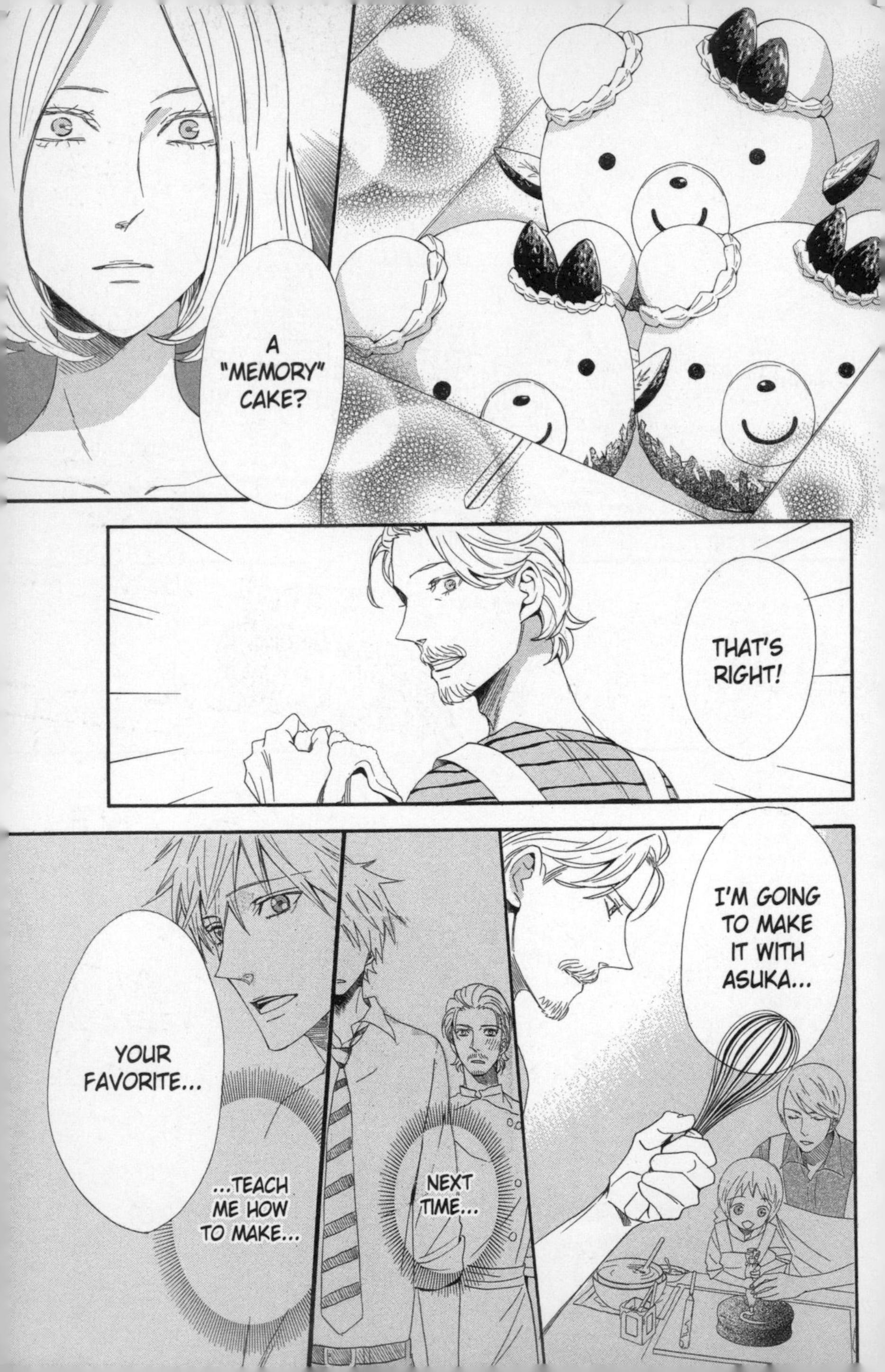
A "MEMORY" CAKE?
THAT'S RIGHT!
I'M GOING TO MAKE IT WITH ASUKA...
NEXT TIME...
...TEACH ME HOW TO MAKE...
YOUR FAVORITE...

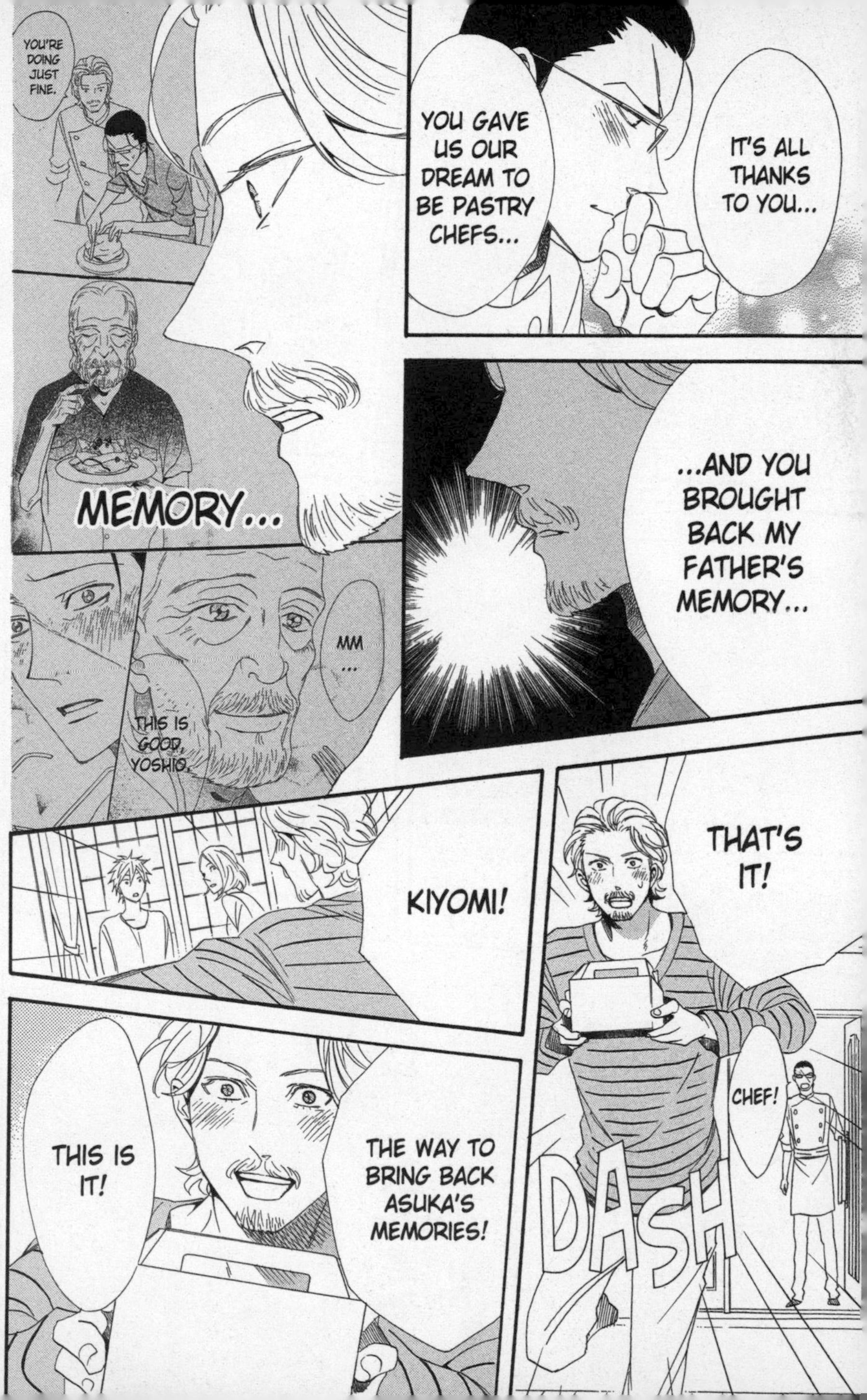
IT'S ALL THANKS TO YOU...
YOU GAVE US OUR DREAM TO BE PASTRY CHEFS...
...AND YOU BROUGHT BACK MY FATHER'S MEMORY...
YOU'RE DOING JUST FINE.
MEMORY...
MM...
THIS IS GOOD, YOSHIO.
THAT'S IT!
CHEF!
DASH
KIYOMI!
THE WAY TO BRING BACK ASUKA'S MEMORIES!
THIS IS IT!

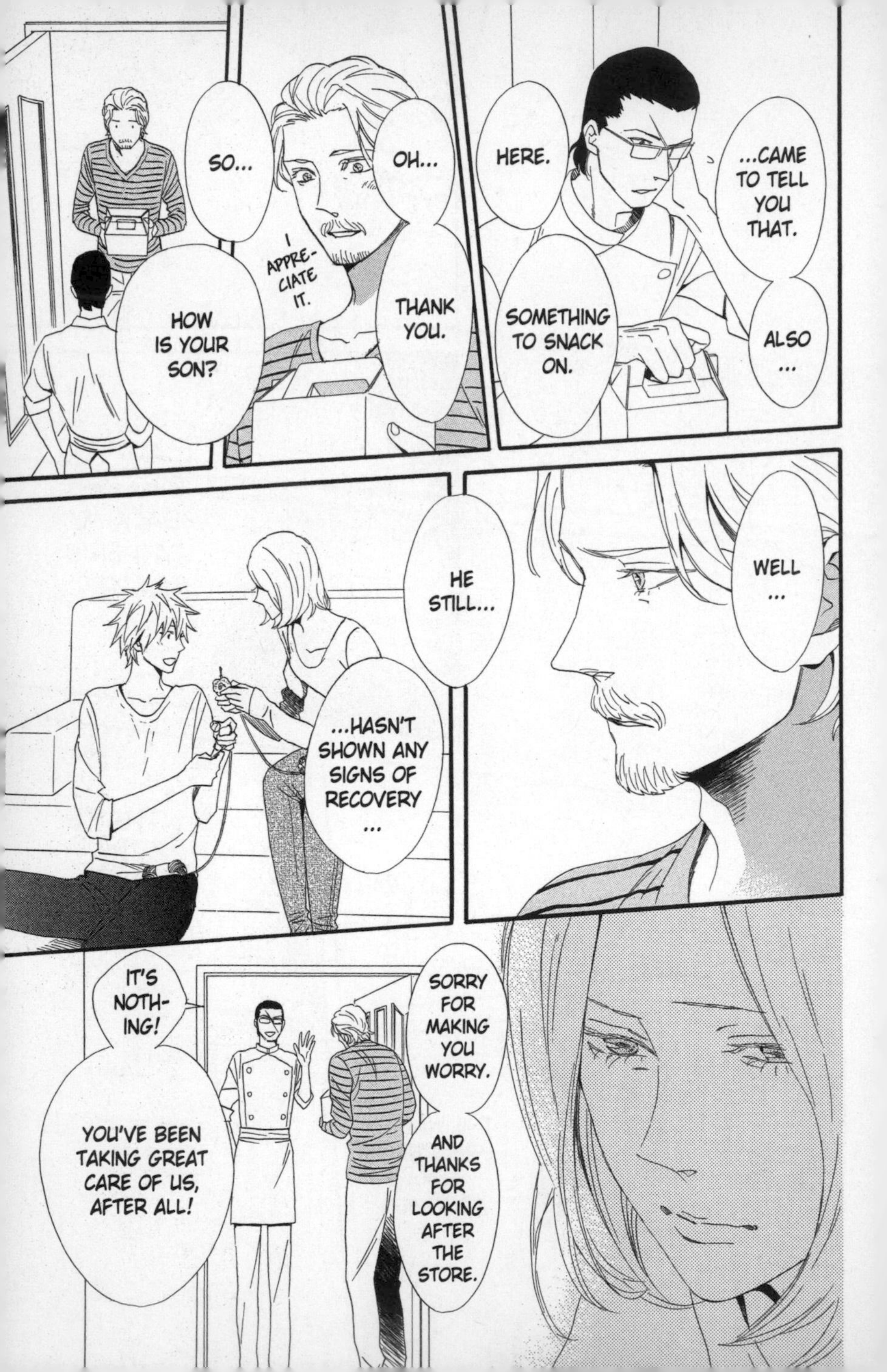
...CAME TO TELL YOU THAT.
ALSO ...
SOMETHING TO SNACK ON.
HERE.
OH...
THANK YOU.
I APPRE-CIATE IT.
SO...
HOW IS YOUR SON?
WELL ...
HE STILL...
...HASN'T SHOWN ANY SIGNS OF RECOVERY ...
SORRY FOR MAKING YOU WORRY.
AND THANKS FOR LOOKING AFTER THE STORE.
IT'S NOTH-ING!
YOU'VE BEEN TAKING GREAT CARE OF US, AFTER ALL!

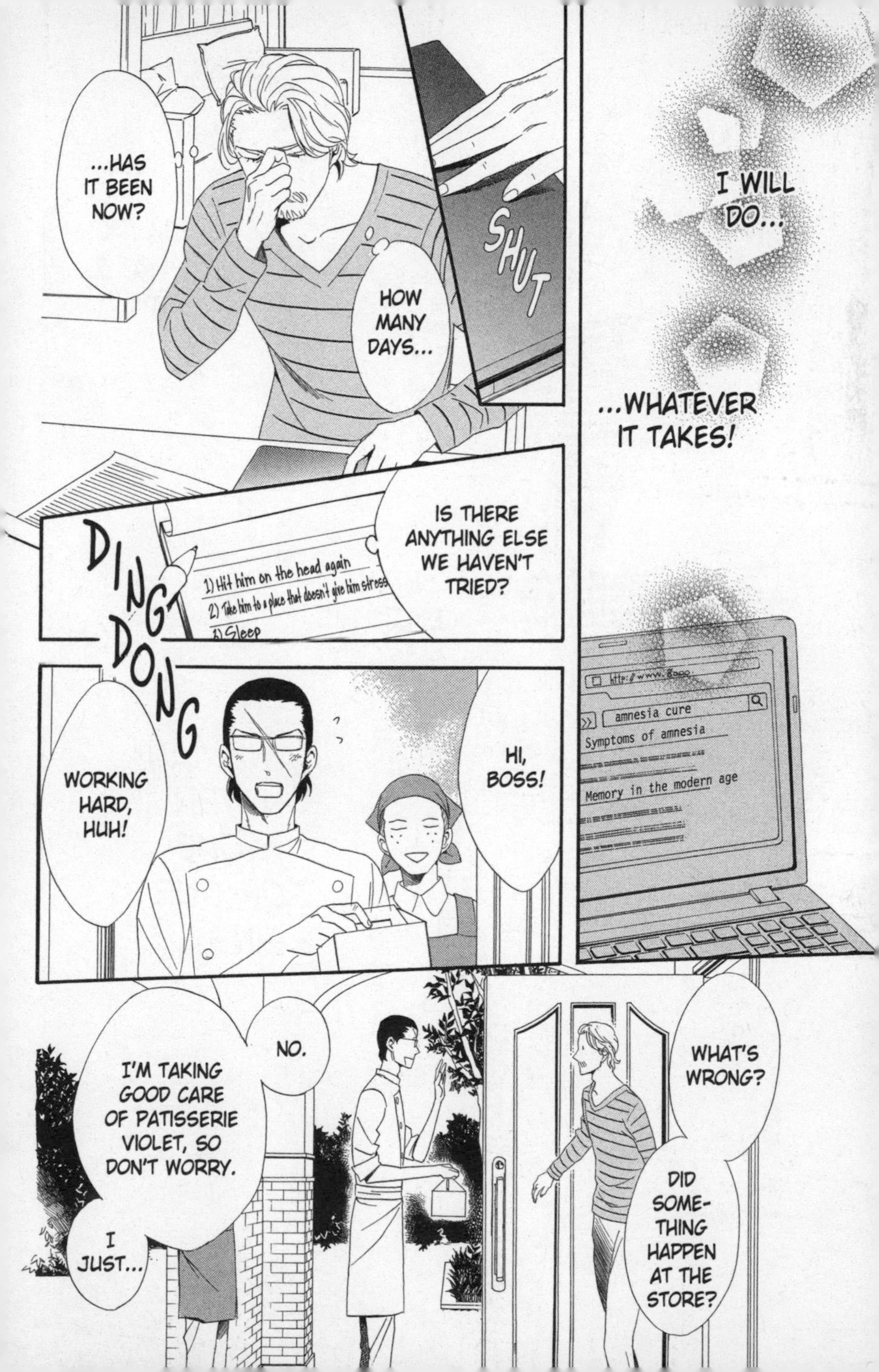
I WILL DO...
...WHATEVER IT TAKES!
amnesia cure
Symptoms of amnesia
Memory in the modern age
SHUT
HOW MANY DAYS...
...HAS IT BEEN NOW?
IS THERE ANYTHING ELSE WE HAVEN'T TRIED?
1) Hit him on the head again
2) Take him to a place that doesn't give him stress
3) Sleep
DING DONG
HI, BOSS!
WORKING HARD, HUH!
WHAT'S WRONG?
DID SOME-THING HAPPEN AT THE STORE?
NO.
I'M TAKING GOOD CARE OF PATISSERIE VIOLET, SO DON'T WORRY.
I JUST...

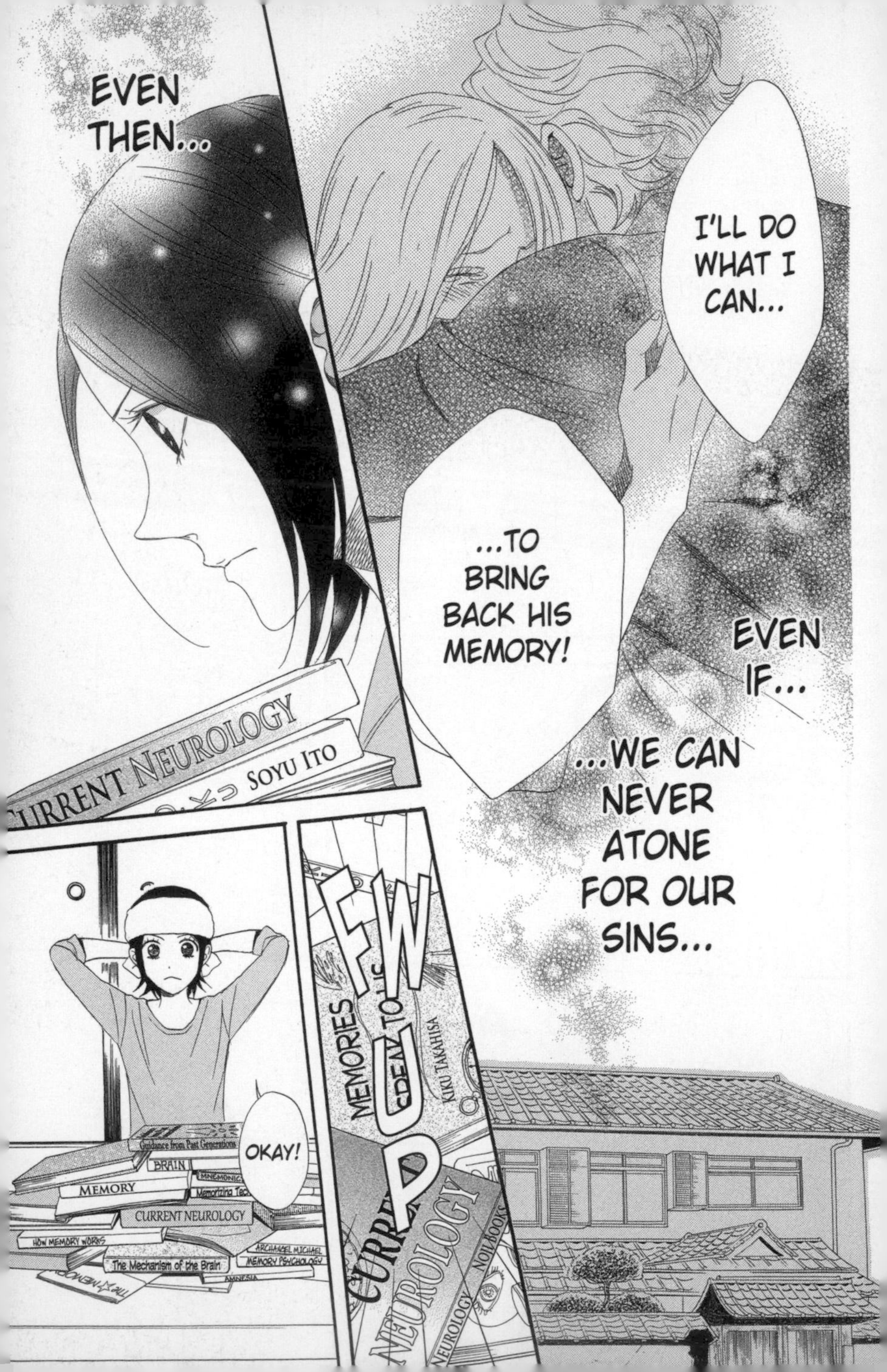
I'LL DO WHAT I CAN...
...TO BRING BACK HIS MEMORY!
EVEN IF...
...WE CAN NEVER ATONE FOR OUR SINS...
EVEN THEN...
CURRENT NEUROLOGY
SOYU ITO
FWUP
MEMORIES
KIKU TAKAHISA
CURRENT NEUROLOGY
NEUROLOGY
OKAY!
Guidance from Past Generations
BRAIN
MNEMONICS
MEMORY
CURRENT NEUROLOGY
HOW MEMORY WORKS
ARCHANGEL MICHAEL
The Mechanism of the Brain
MEMORY PSYCHOLOGY
AMNESIA

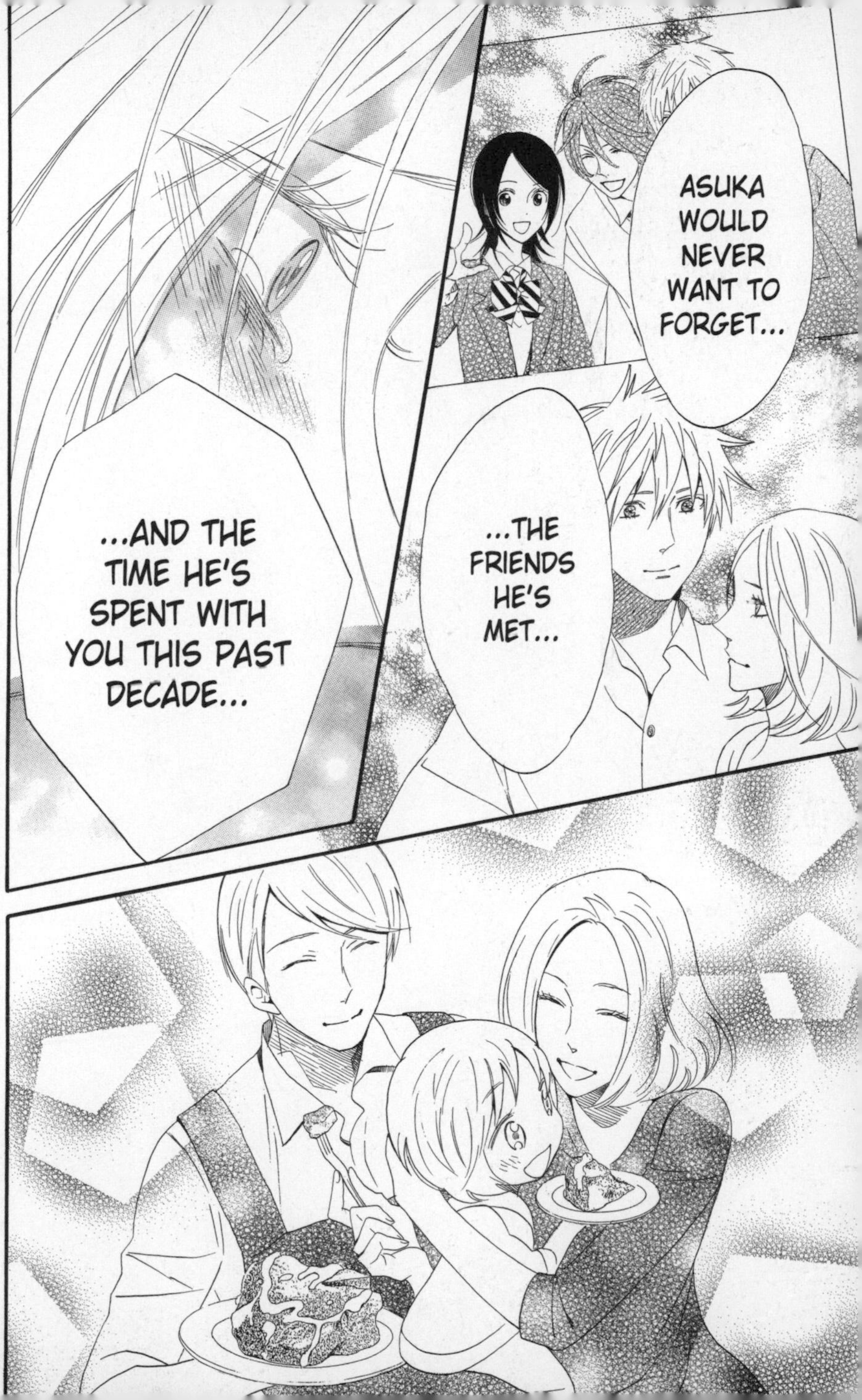
ASUKA WOULD NEVER WANT TO FORGET...
...THE FRIENDS HE'S MET...
...AND THE TIME HE'S SPENT WITH YOU THIS PAST DECADE...

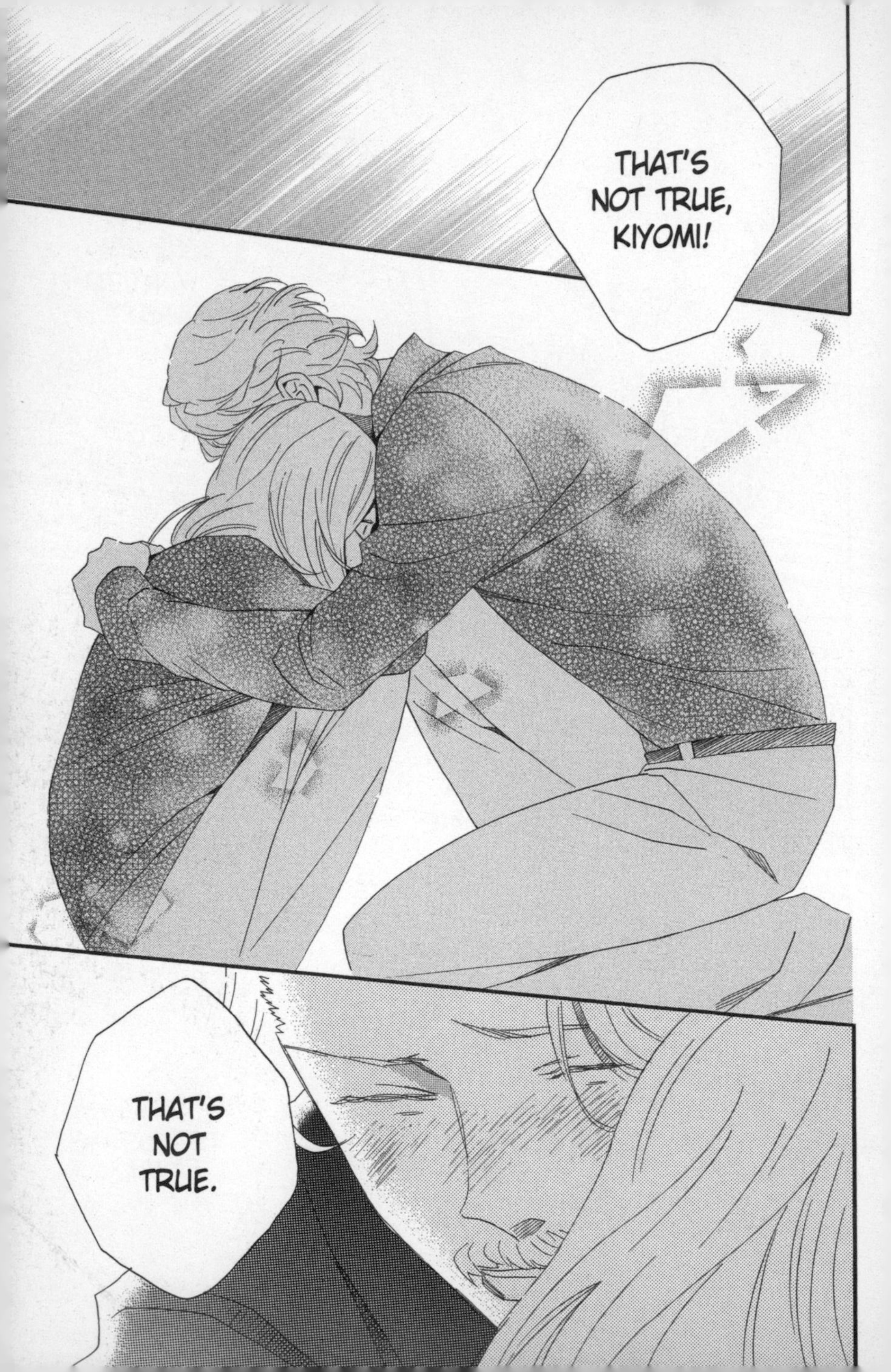
THAT'S NOT TRUE, KIYOMI!
THAT'S NOT TRUE.

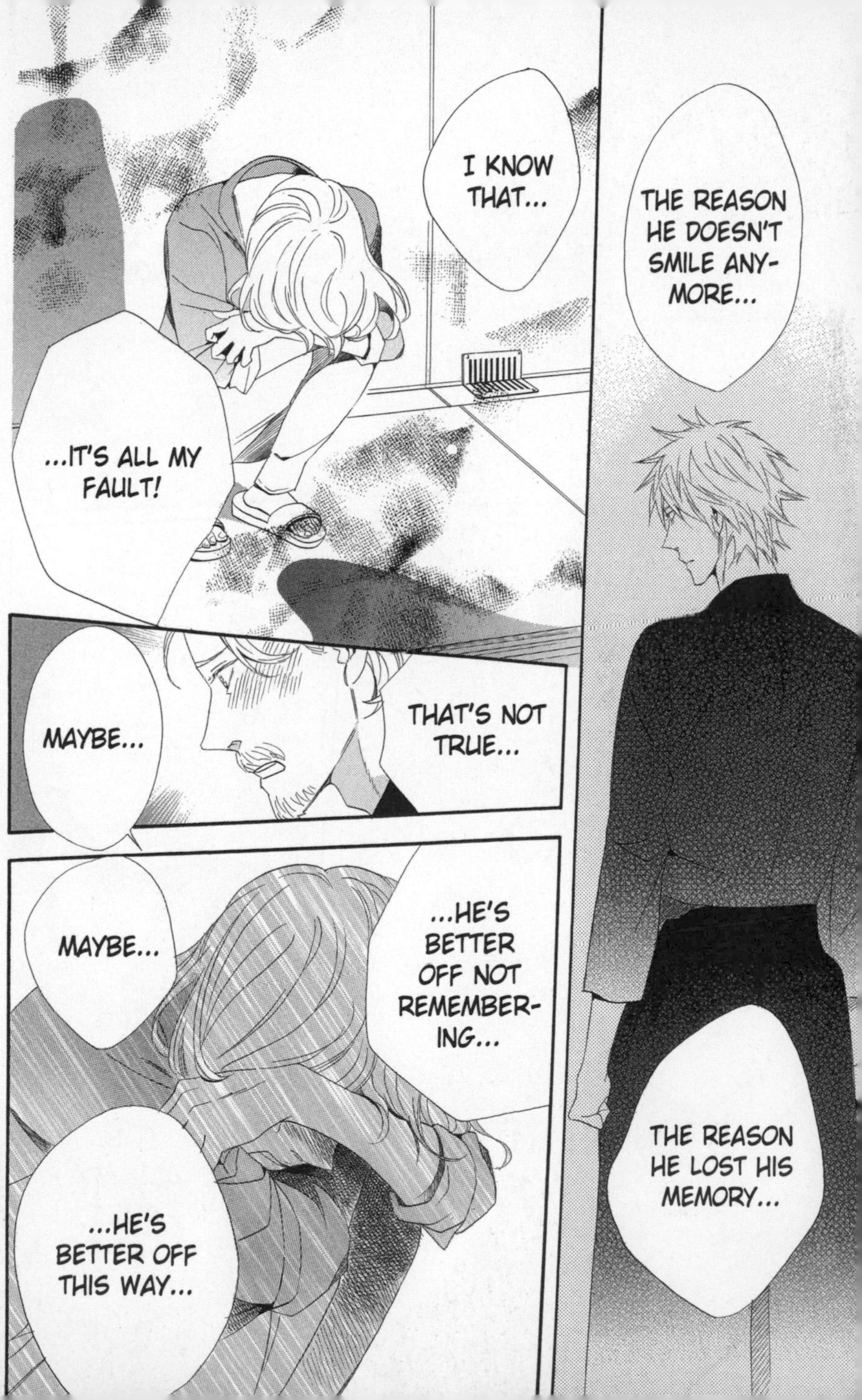
THE REASON HE DOESN'T SMILE ANY-MORE...
THE REASON HE LOST HIS MEMORY...
I KNOW THAT...
...IT'S ALL MY FAULT!
THAT'S NOT TRUE...
MAYBE...
...HE'S BETTER OFF NOT REMEMBER-ING...
MAYBE...
...HE'S BETTER OFF THIS WAY...

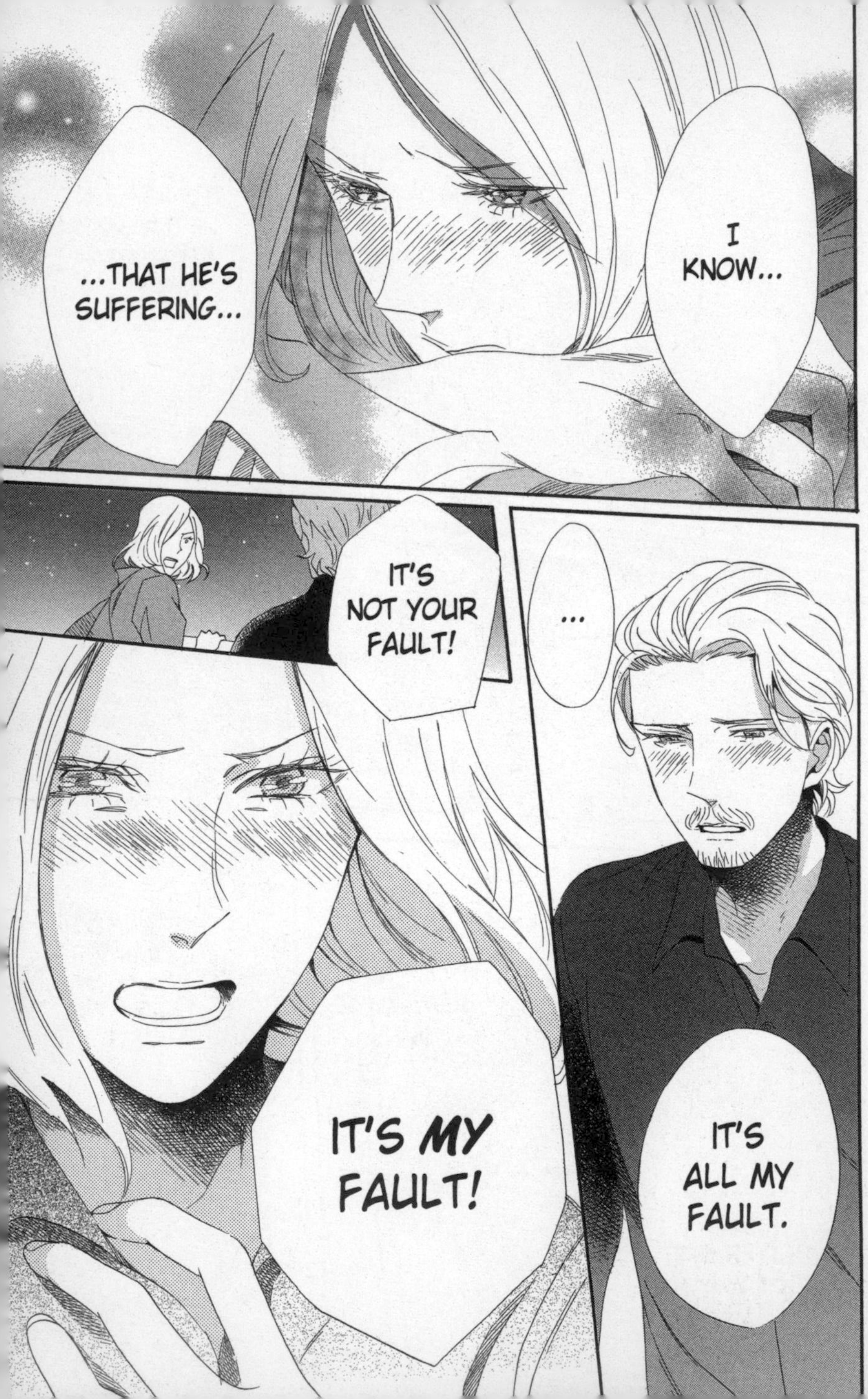
I KNOW...
...THAT HE'S SUFFERING...
...
IT'S ALL MY FAULT.
IT'S NOT YOUR FAULT!
IT'S *MY* FAULT!

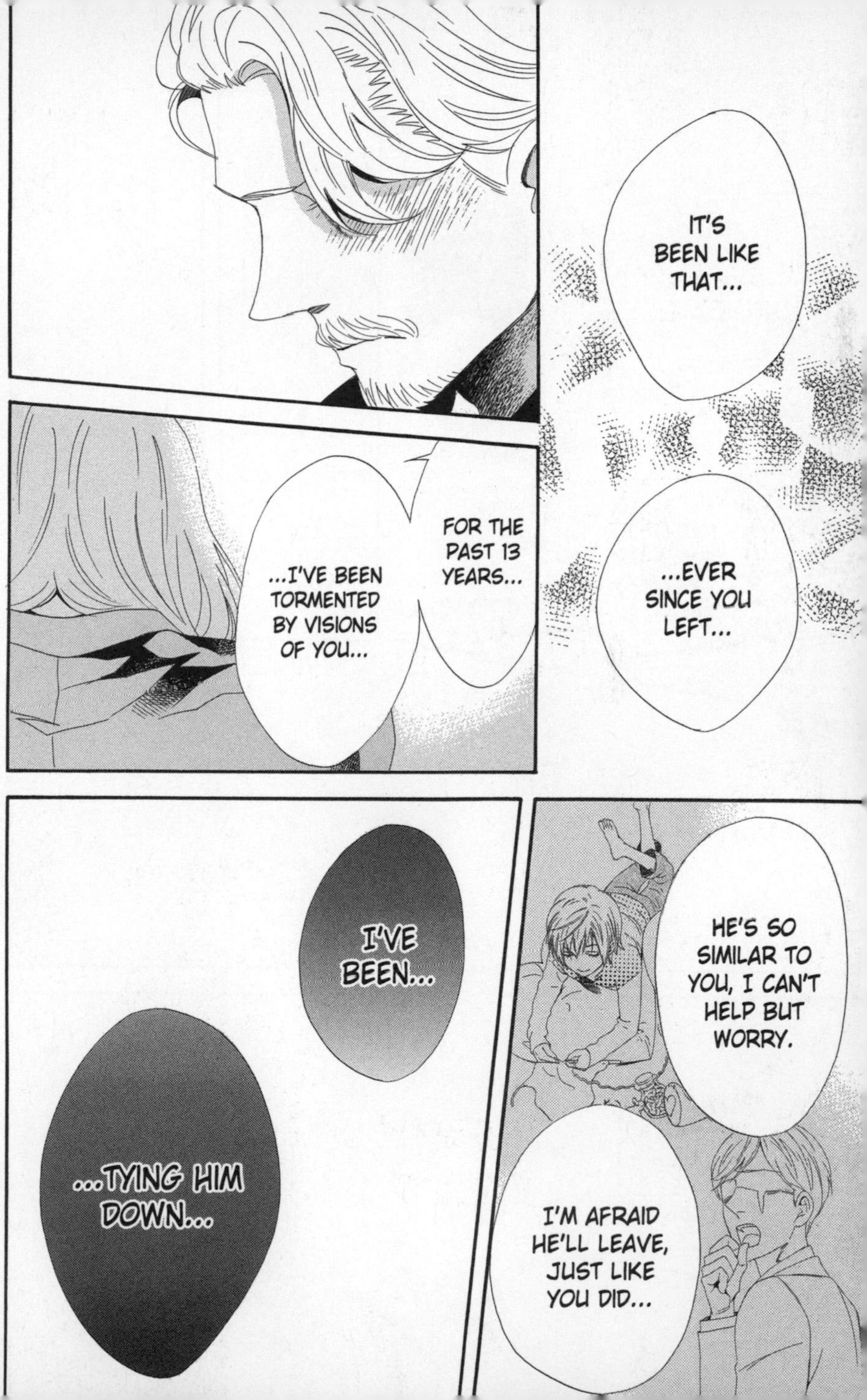
IT'S BEEN LIKE THAT...
...EVER SINCE YOU LEFT...
FOR THE PAST 13 YEARS...
...I'VE BEEN TORMENTED BY VISIONS OF YOU...
HE'S SO SIMILAR TO YOU, I CAN'T HELP BUT WORRY.
I'M AFRAID HE'LL LEAVE, JUST LIKE YOU DID...
I'VE BEEN...
...TYING HIM DOWN...

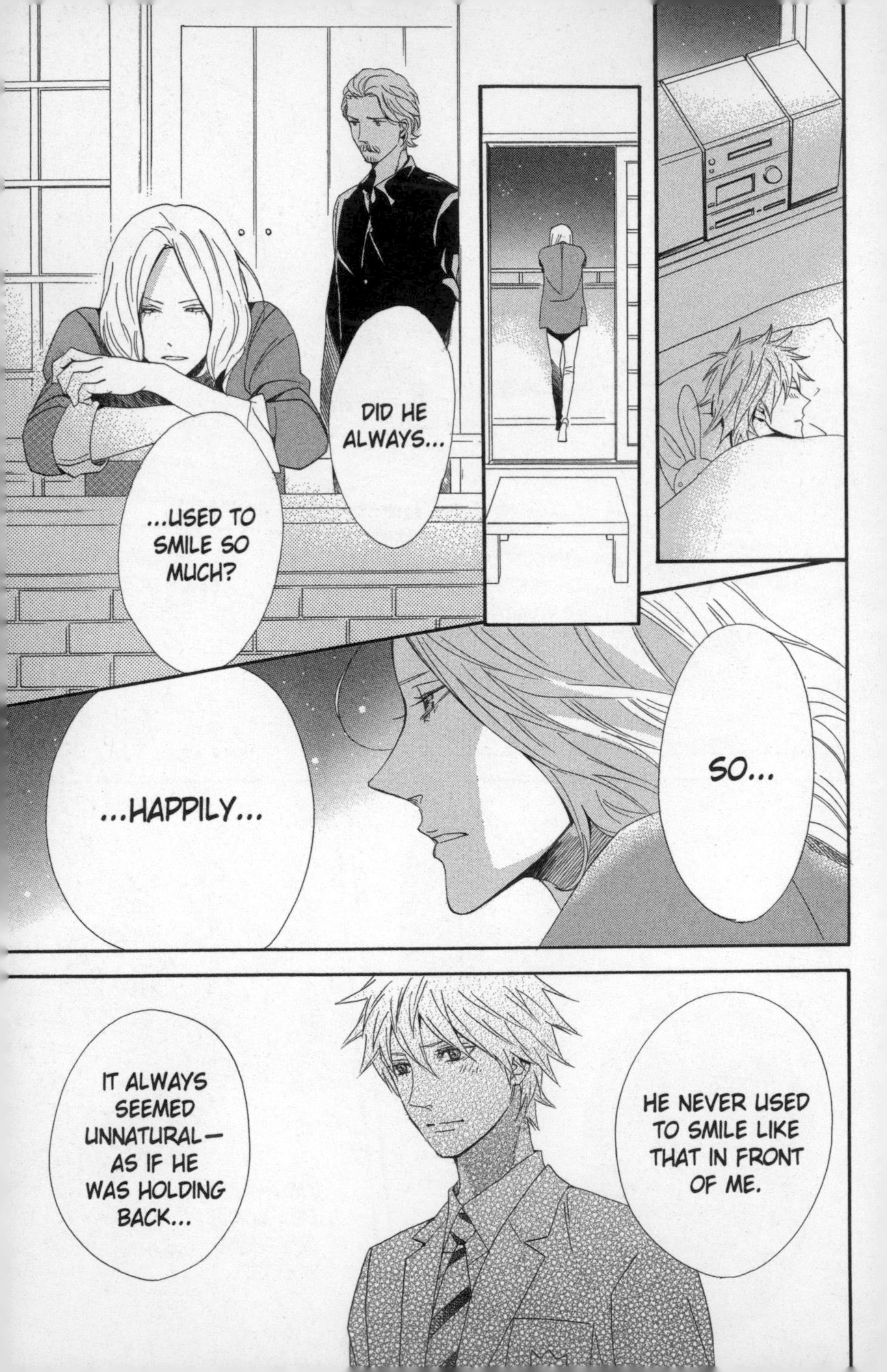
DID HE ALWAYS...
...USED TO SMILE SO MUCH?
SO...
...HAPPILY...
HE NEVER USED TO SMILE LIKE THAT IN FRONT OF ME.
IT ALWAYS SEEMED UNNATURAL— AS IF HE WAS HOLDING BACK...

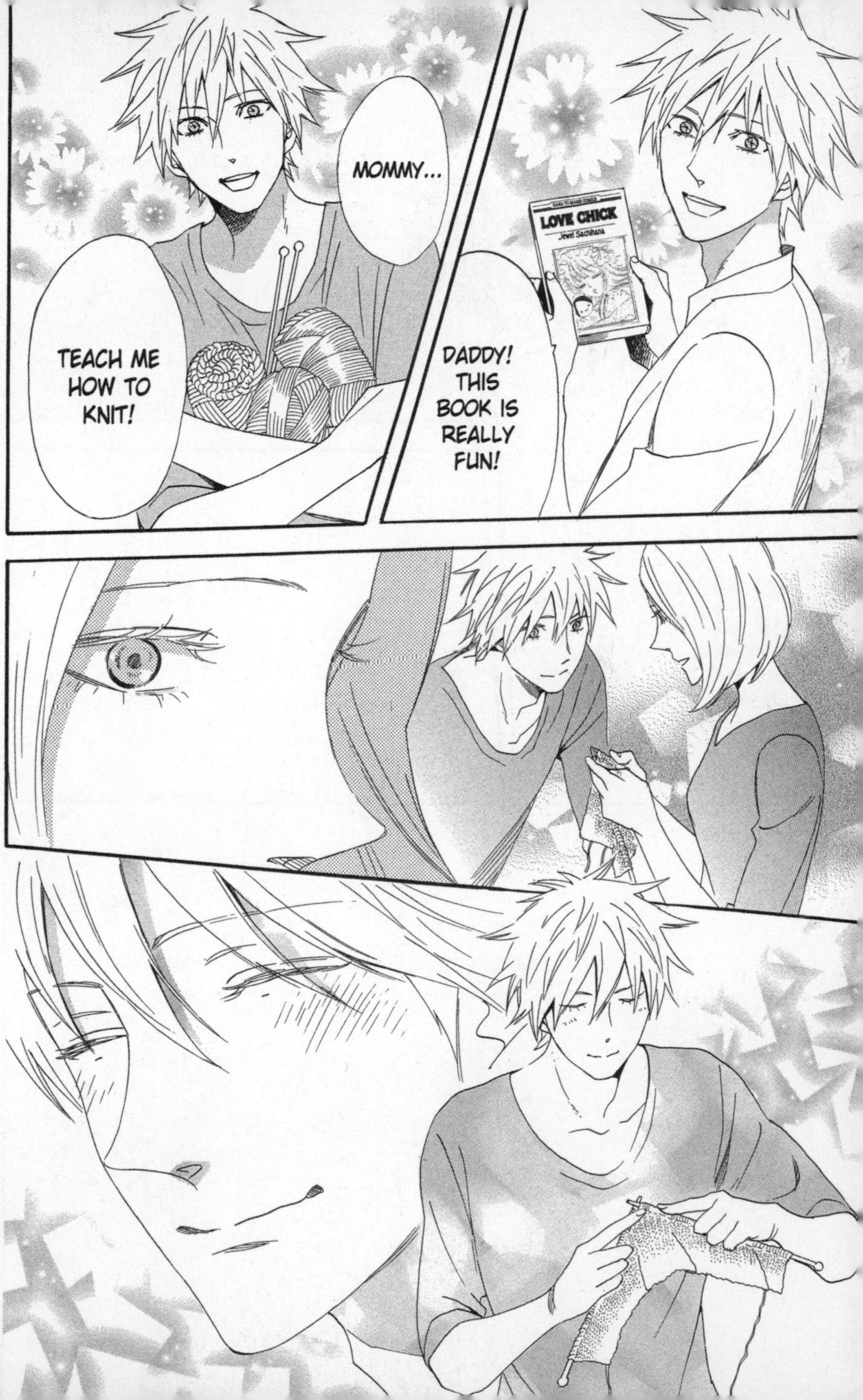
LOVE CHICK
Jewel Sachihana
DADDY! THIS BOOK IS REALLY FUN!
MOMMY...
TEACH ME HOW TO KNIT!

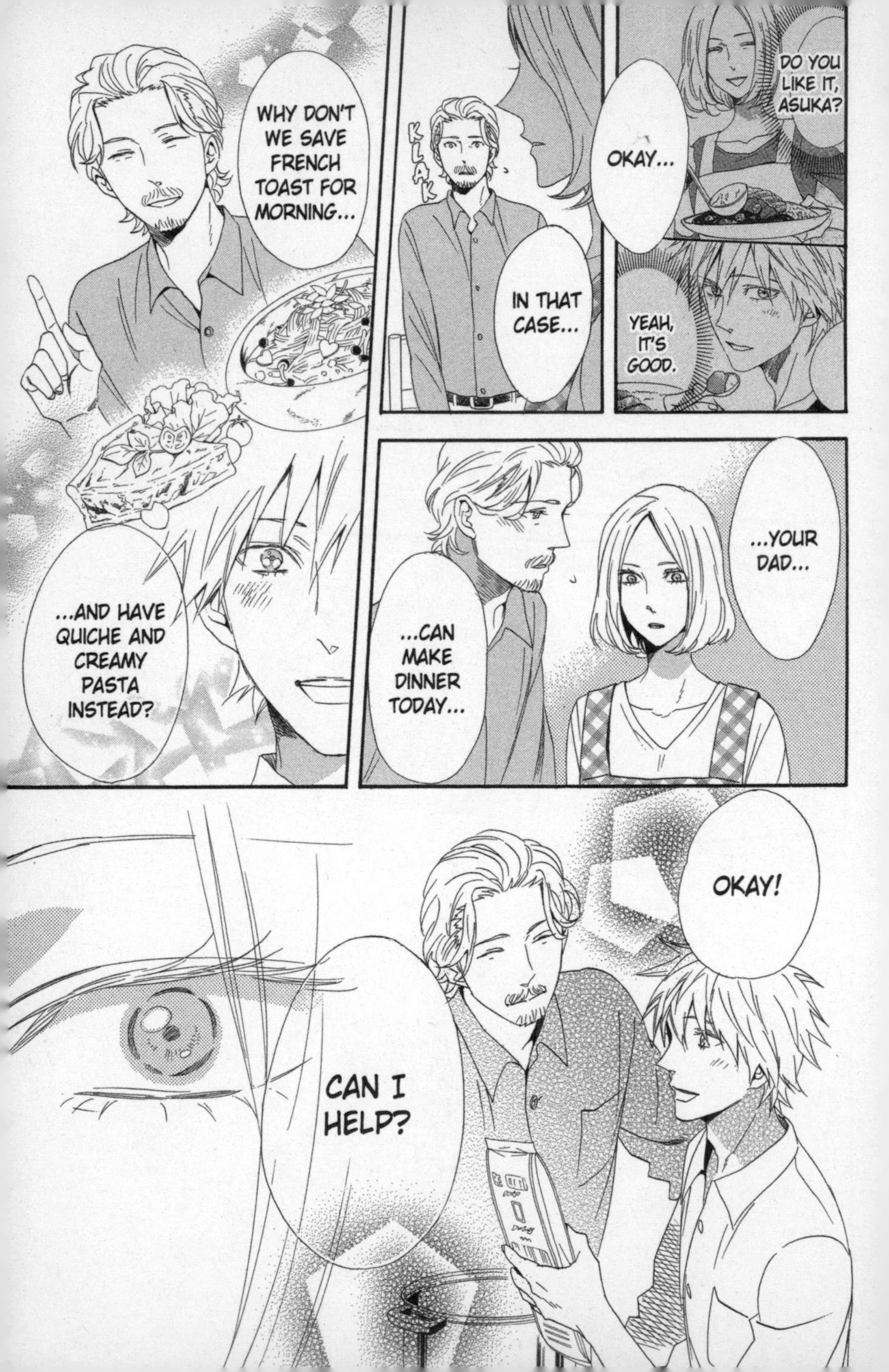

DO YOU LIKE IT, ASUKA?
YEAH, IT'S GOOD.
KLAK
OKAY...
IN THAT CASE...
...YOUR DAD...
...CAN MAKE DINNER TODAY...
WHY DON'T WE SAVE FRENCH TOAST FOR MORNING...
...AND HAVE QUICHE AND CREAMY PASTA INSTEAD?
OKAY!
CAN I HELP?

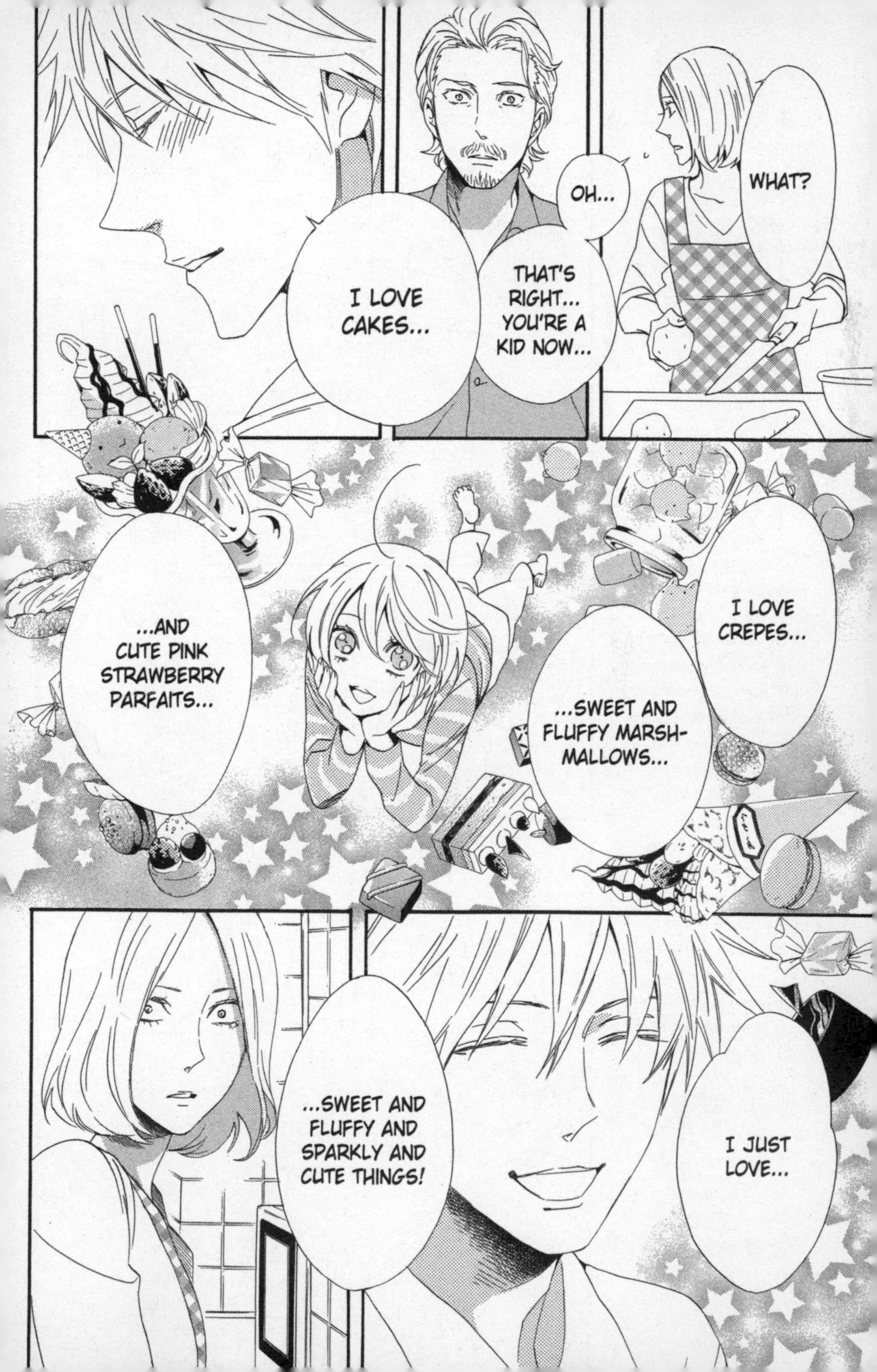
WHAT?
OH...
THAT'S RIGHT... YOU'RE A KID NOW...
I LOVE CAKES...
I LOVE CREPES...
...SWEET AND FLUFFY MARSH-MALLOWS...
...AND CUTE PINK STRAWBERRY PARFAITS...
I JUST LOVE...
...SWEET AND FLUFFY AND SPARKLY AND CUTE THINGS!

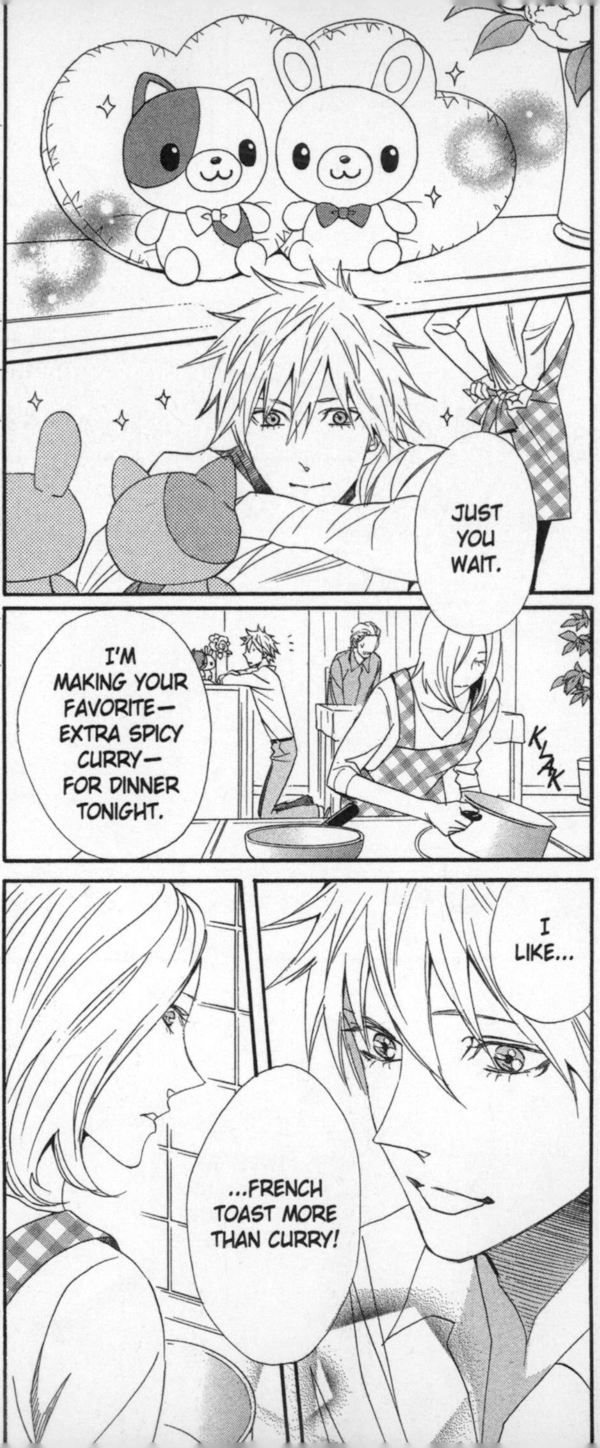
JUST YOU WAIT.
I'M MAKING YOUR FAVORITE—EXTRA SPICY CURRY—FOR DINNER TONIGHT.
KLAK
I LIKE...
...FRENCH TOAST MORE THAN CURRY!

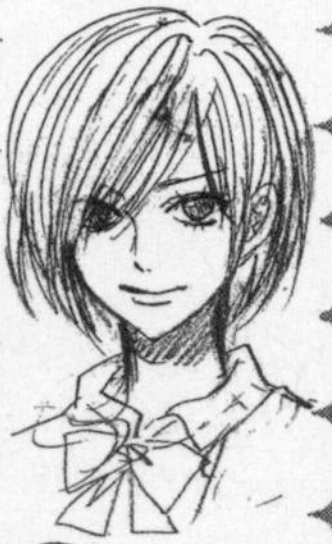

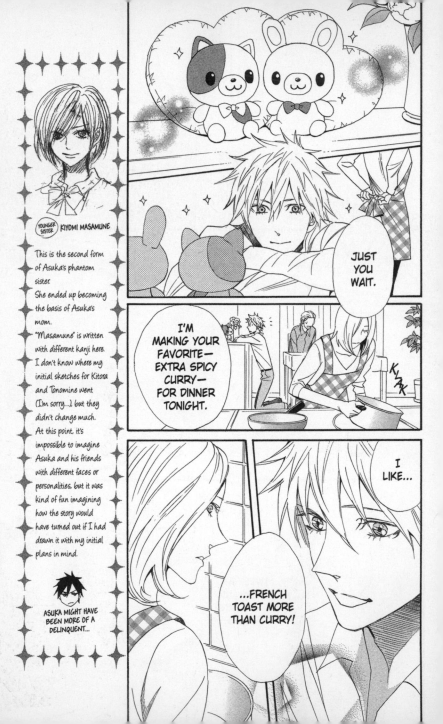

YOUNGER SISTER KIYOMI MASAMUNE

This is the second form of Asuka's phantom sister.
She ended up becoming the basis of Asuka's mom.
"Masamune" is written with different kanji here.
I don't know where my initial sketches for Kitora and Tonomine went (I'm sorry...), but they didn't change much.
At this point, it's impossible to imagine Asuka and his friends with different faces or personalities, but it was kind of fun imagining how the story would have turned out if I had drawn it with my initial plans in mind.

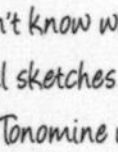

ASUKA MIGHT HAVE BEEN MORE OF A DELINQUENT...

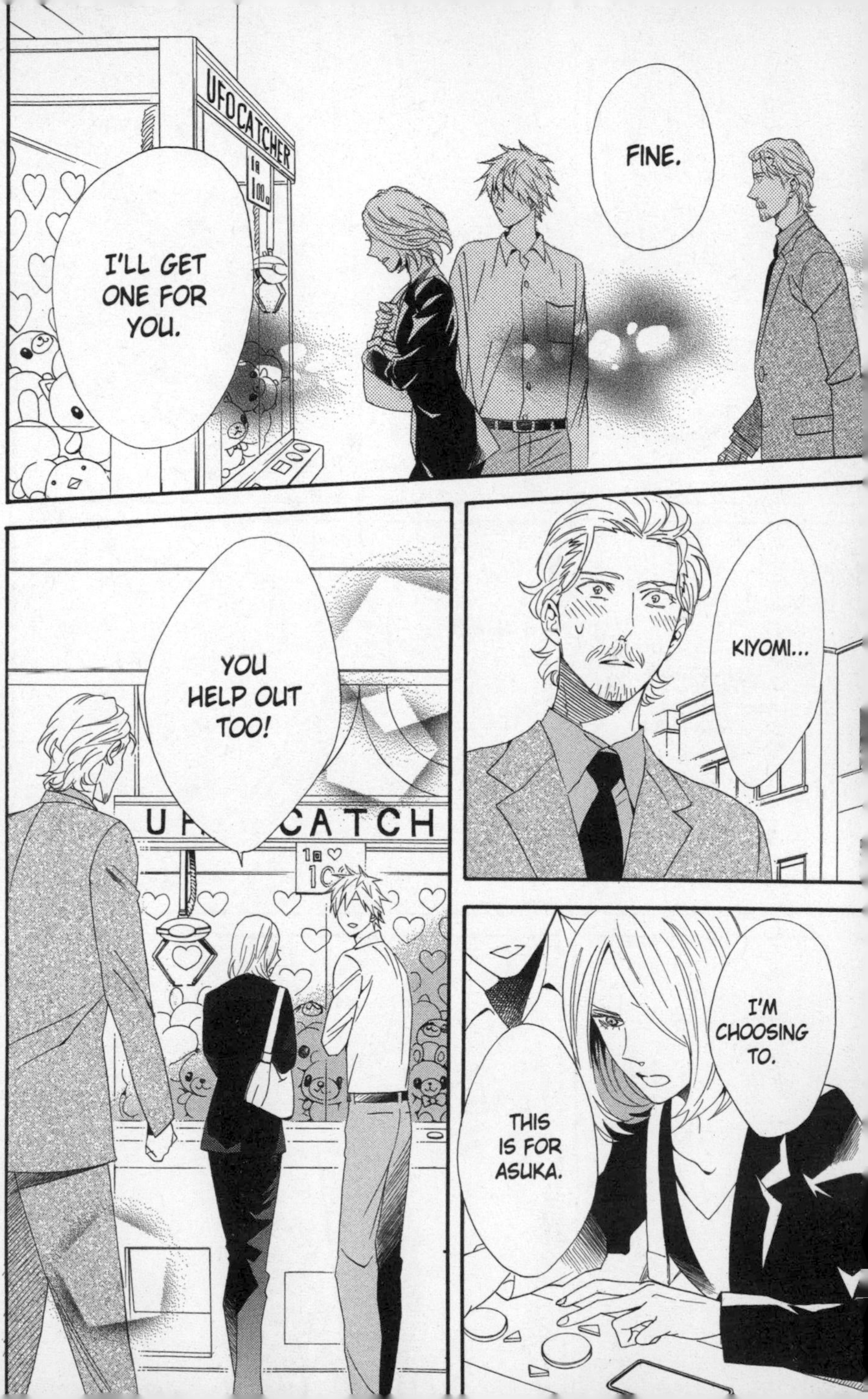
FINE.
UFOCATCHER
I'LL GET ONE FOR YOU.
KIYOMI...
I'M CHOOSING TO.
THIS IS FOR ASUKA.
YOU HELP OUT TOO!

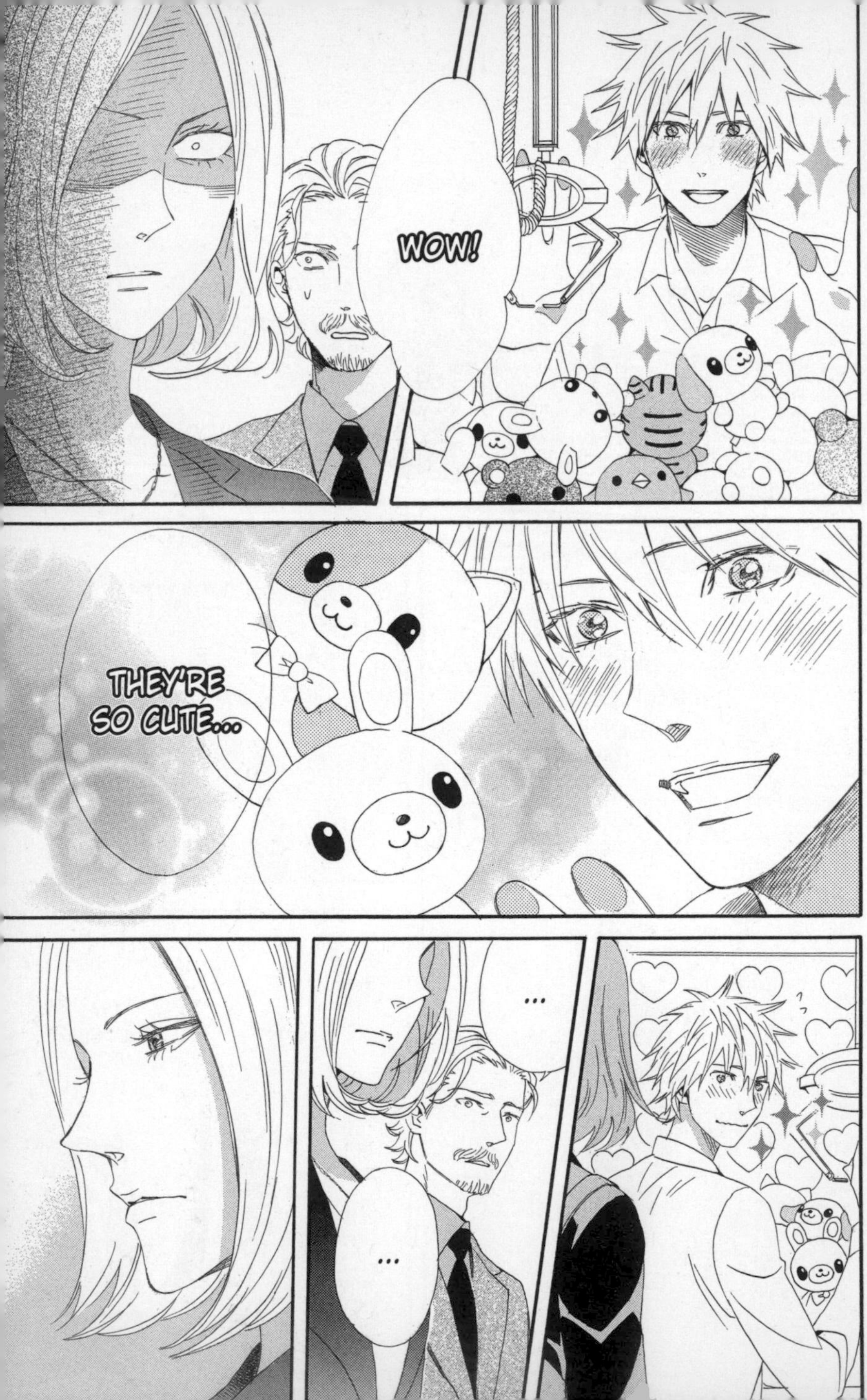
WOW!
THEY'RE SO CUTE...
...
...

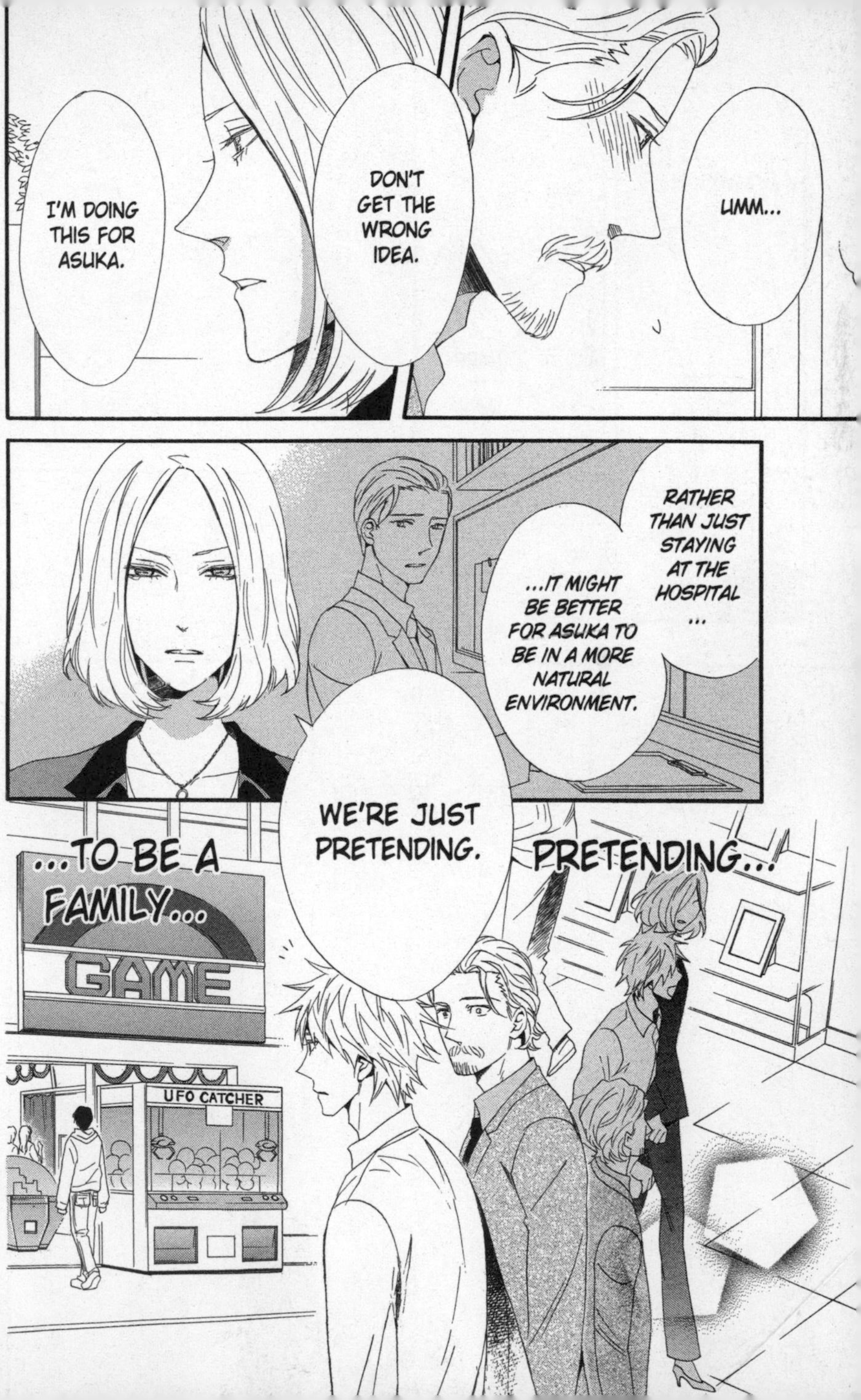
UMM...
DON'T GET THE WRONG IDEA.
I'M DOING THIS FOR ASUKA.
RATHER THAN JUST STAYING AT THE HOSPITAL...
...IT MIGHT BE BETTER FOR ASUKA TO BE IN A MORE NATURAL ENVIRONMENT.
WE'RE JUST PRETENDING.
PRETENDING...
...TO BE A FAMILY...
GAME
UFO CATCHER

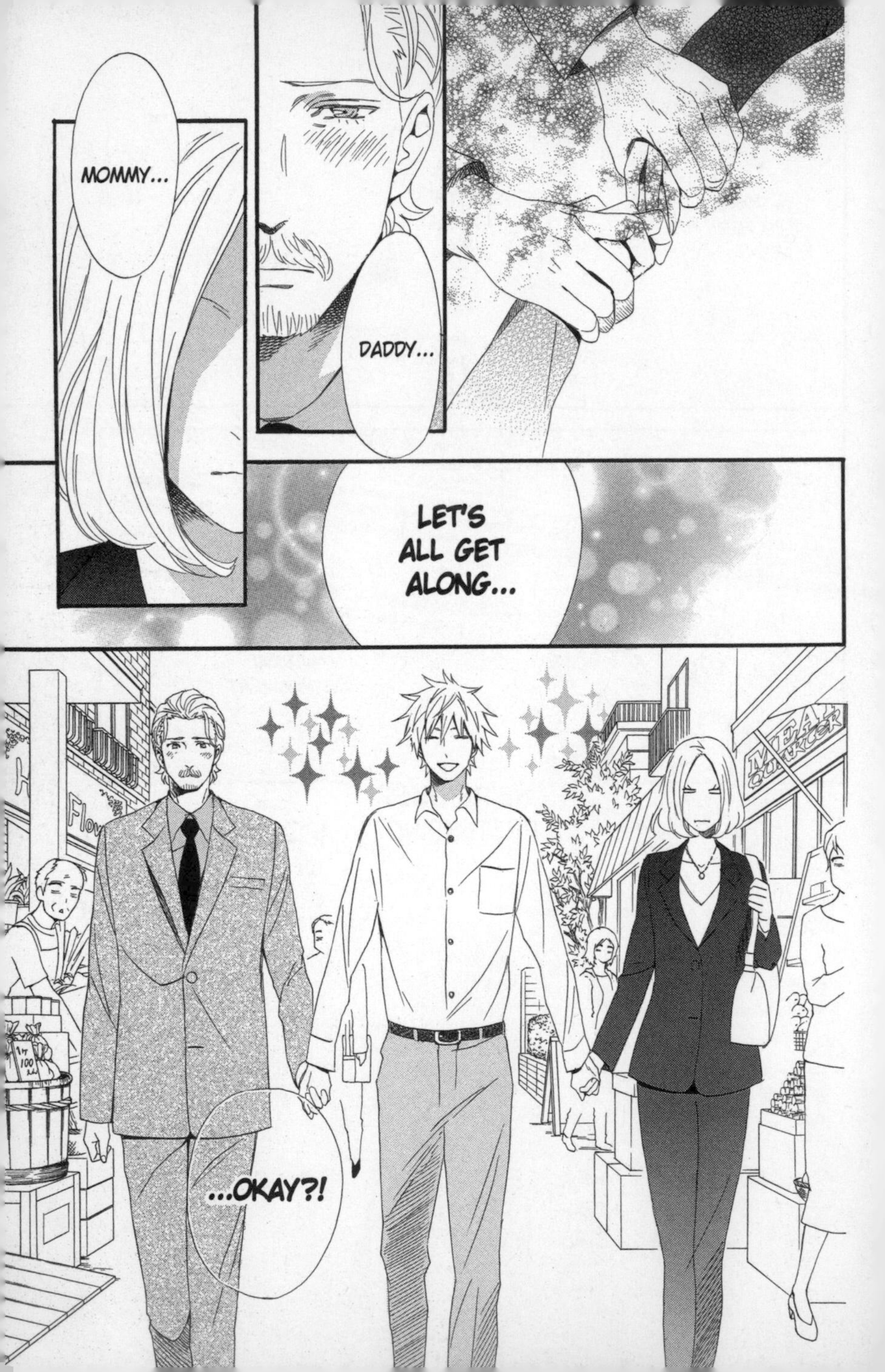
DADDY...
MOMMY...
LET'S ALL GET ALONG...
...OKAY?!

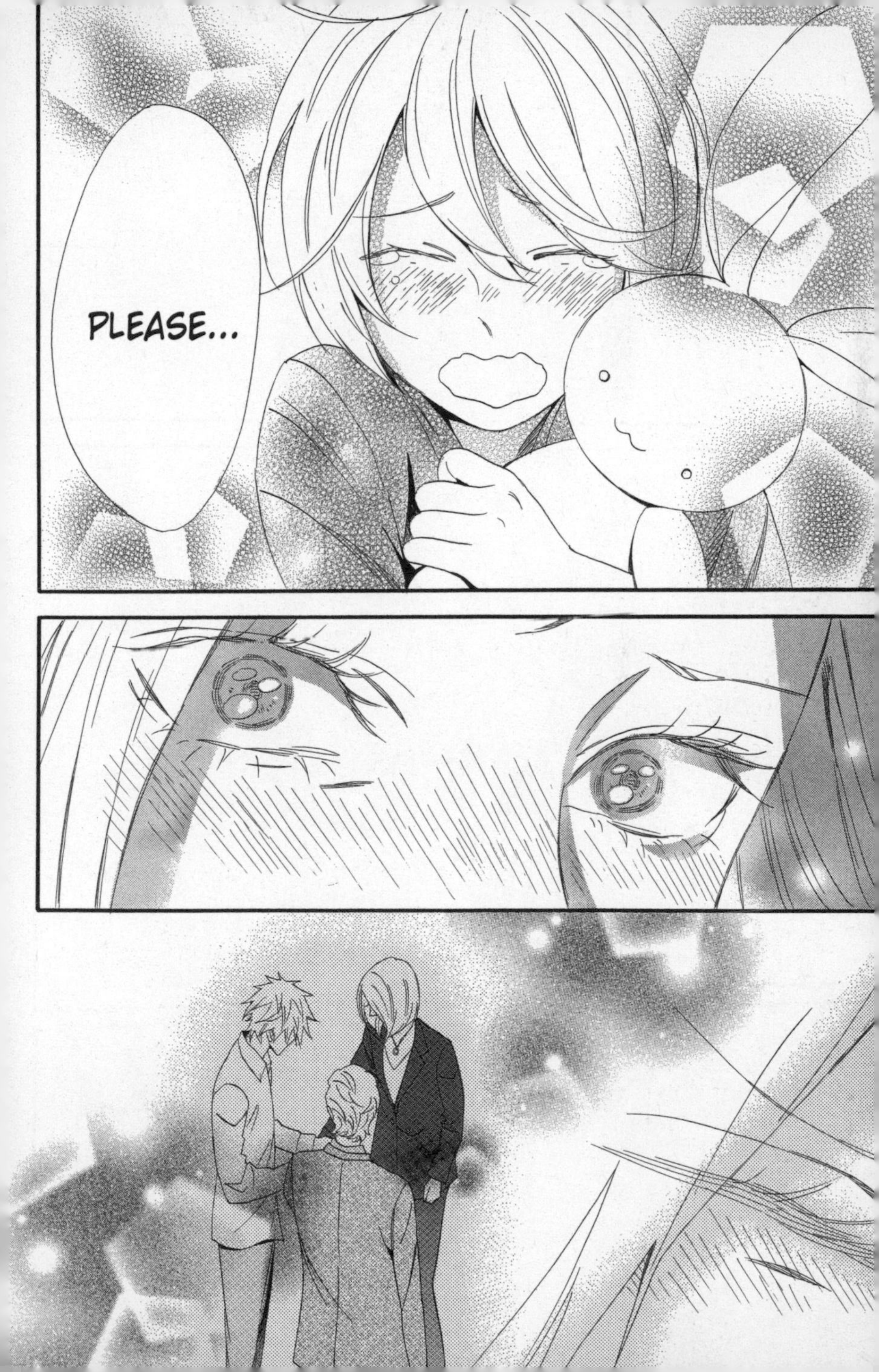
PLEASE...

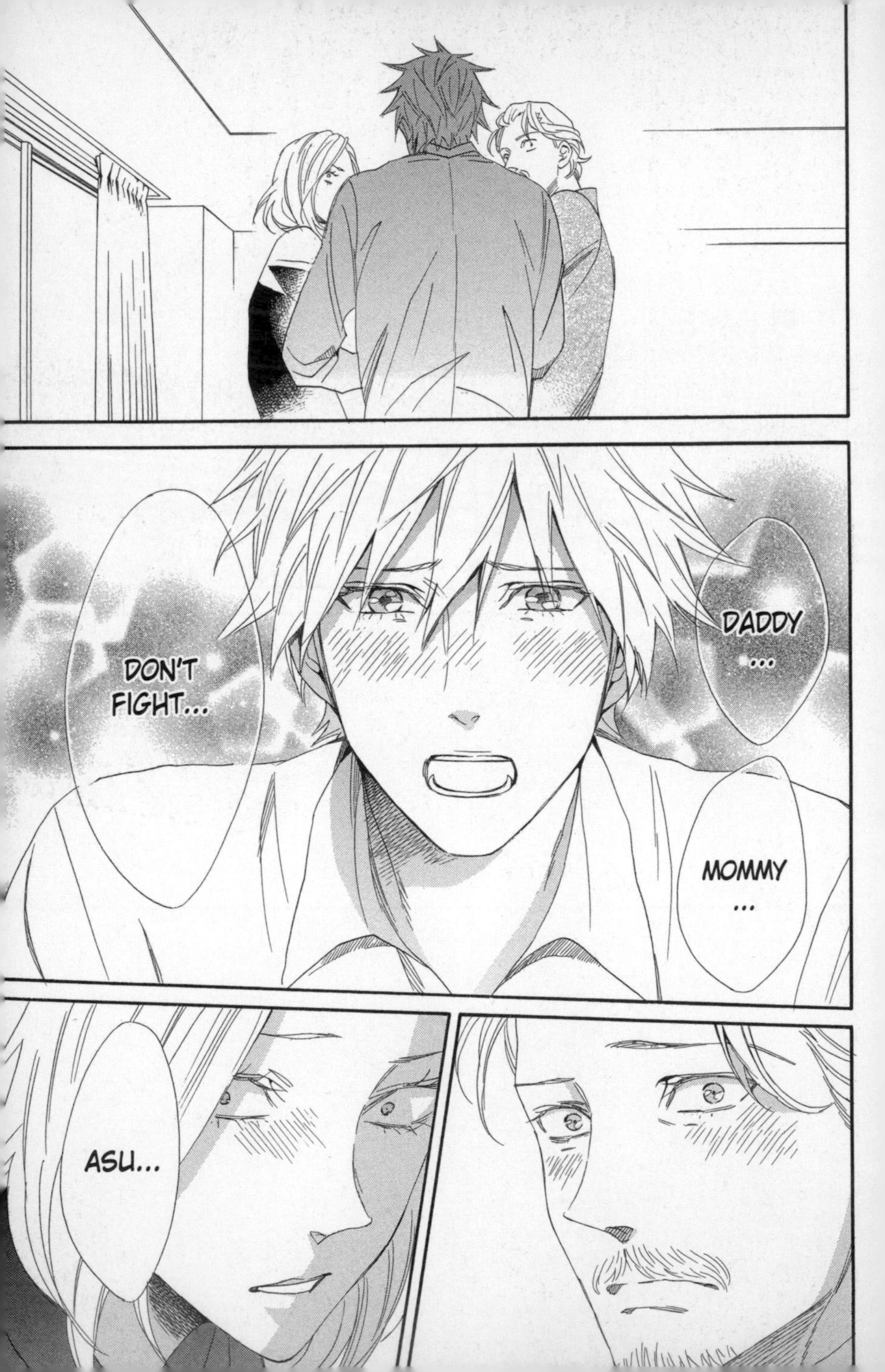
DADDY...
MOMMY...
DON'T FIGHT...
ASU...

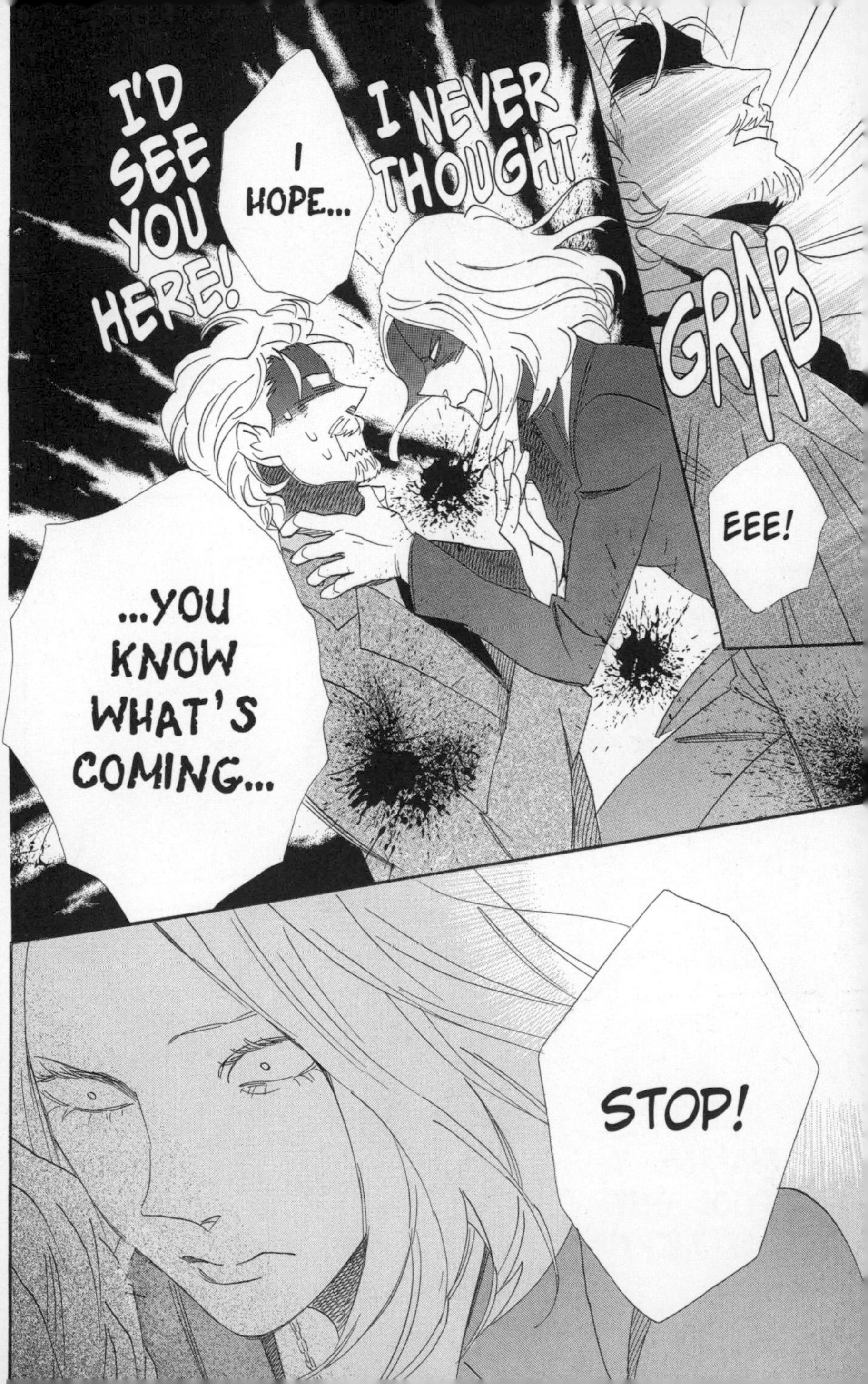
GRAB
EEE!
I NEVER THOUGHT
I HOPE...
I'D SEE YOU HERE!
...YOU KNOW WHAT'S COMING...
STOP!

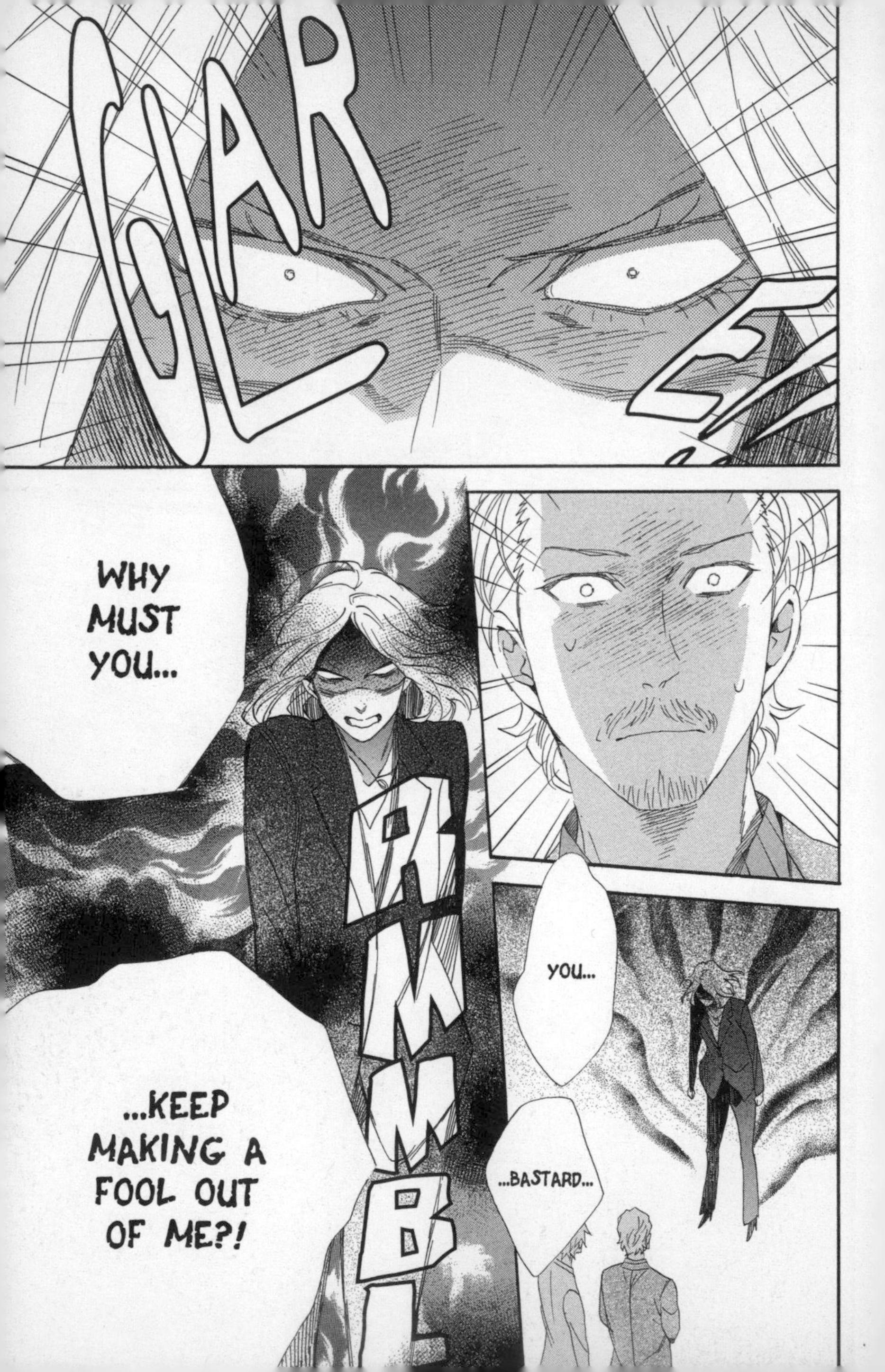
GLAR
YOU...
...BASTARD...
WHY MUST YOU...
...KEEP MAKING A FOOL OUT OF ME?!

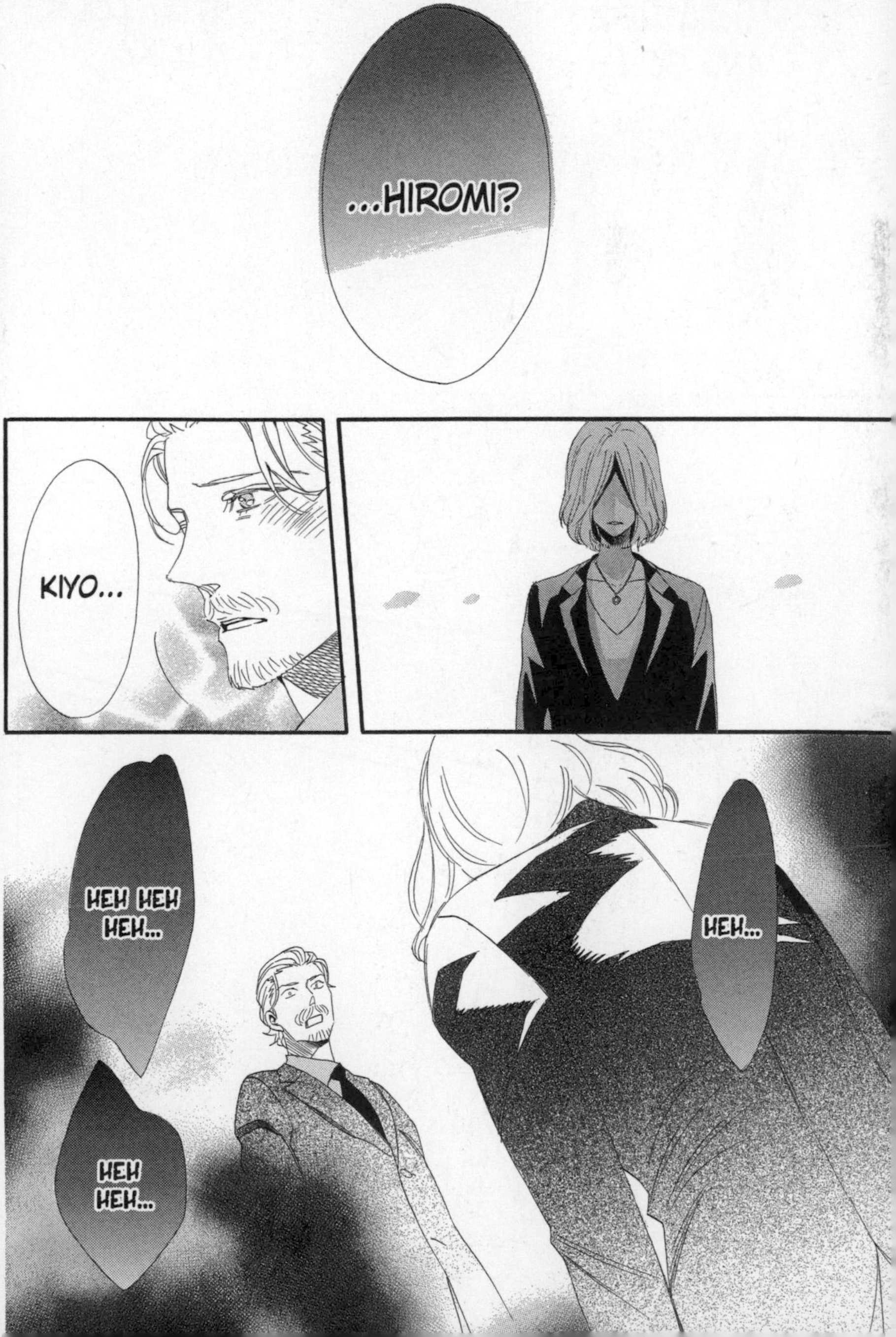
...HIROMI?
KIYO...
HEH...
HEH HEH HEH...
HEH HEH...

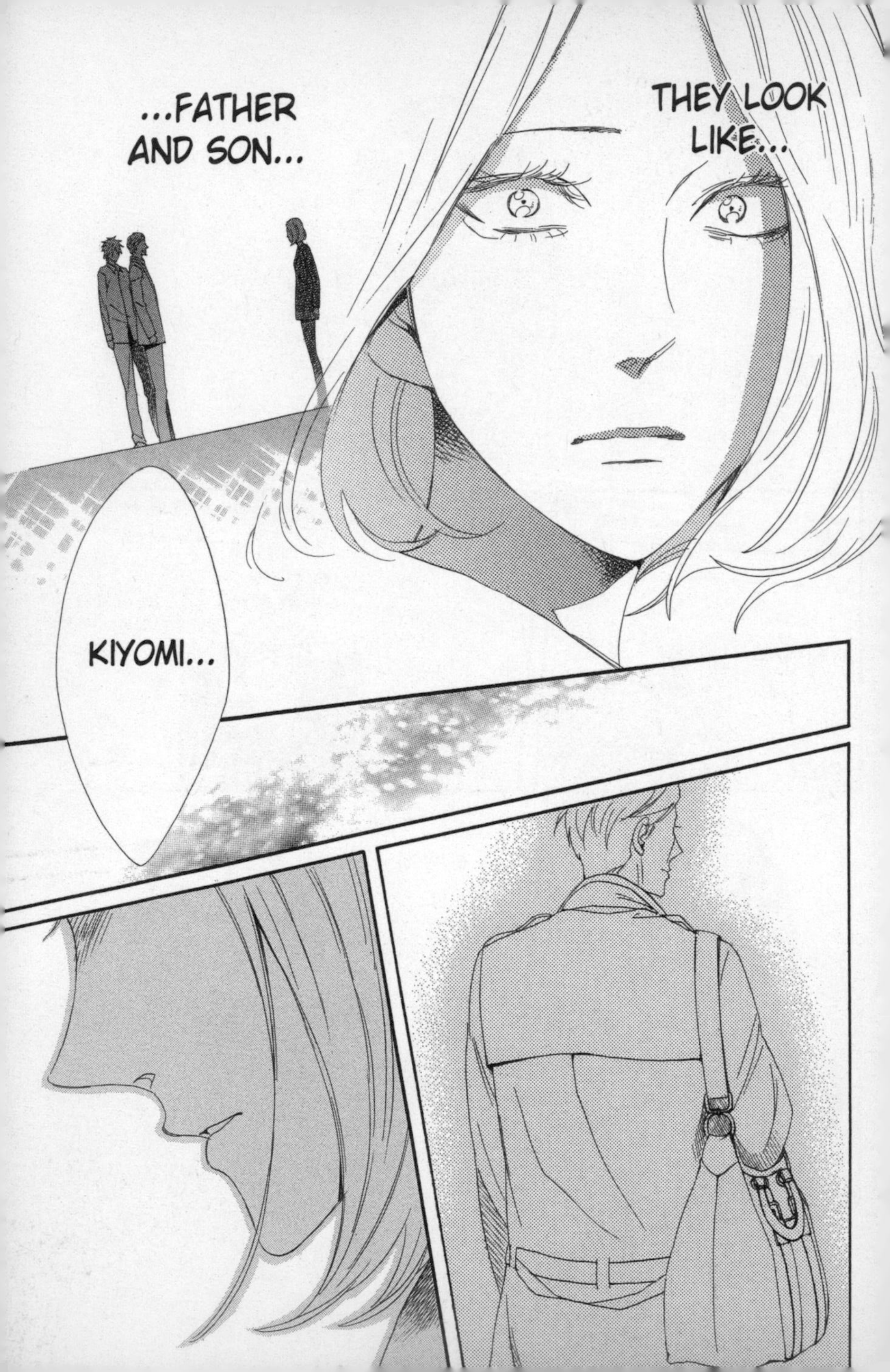
THEY LOOK LIKE...
...FATHER AND SON...
KIYOMI...

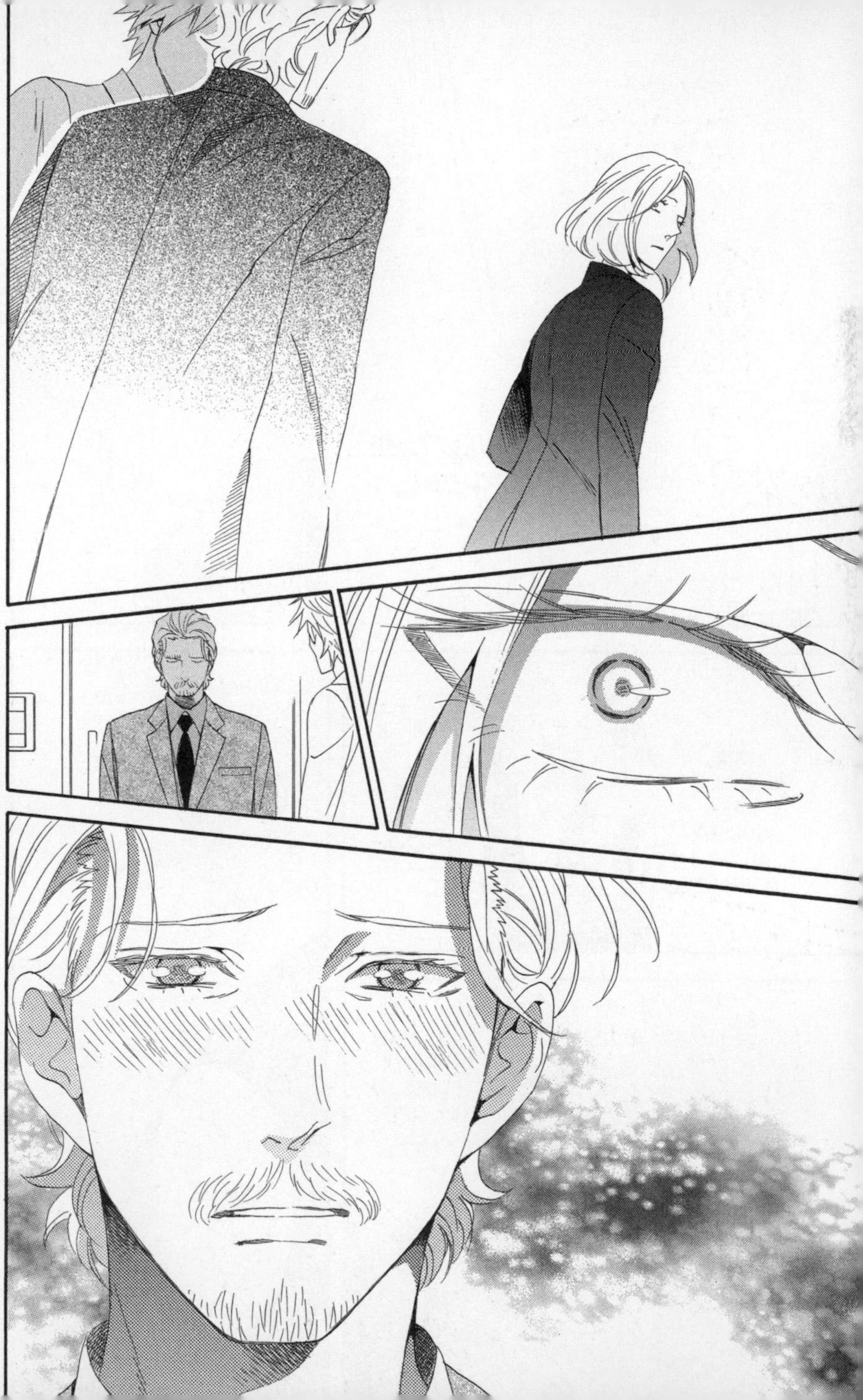

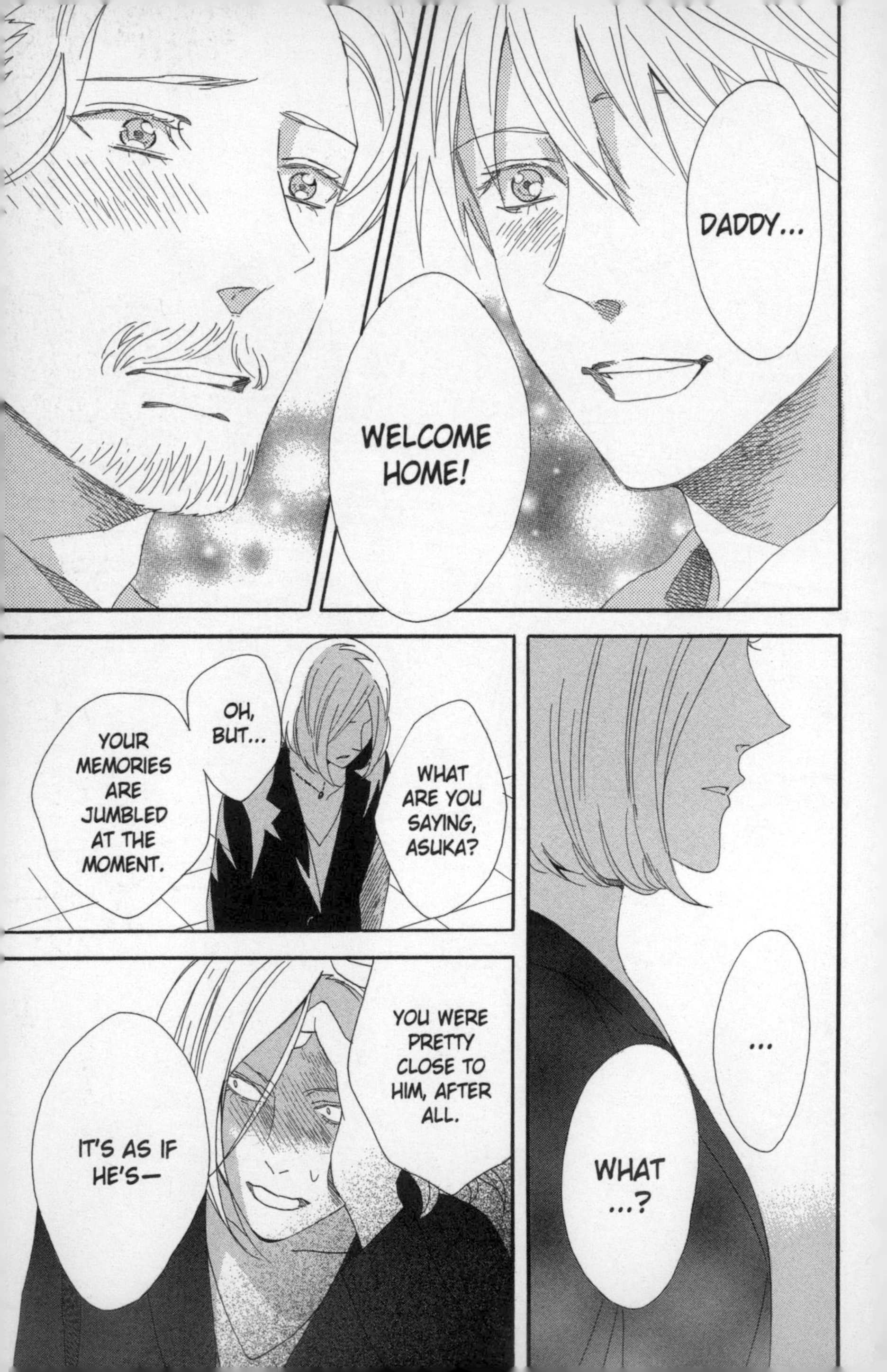
DADDY...
WELCOME HOME!
...
WHAT ...?
WHAT ARE YOU SAYING, ASUKA?
OH, BUT...
YOUR MEMORIES ARE JUMBLED AT THE MOMENT.
YOU WERE PRETTY CLOSE TO HIM, AFTER ALL.
IT'S AS IF HE'S—

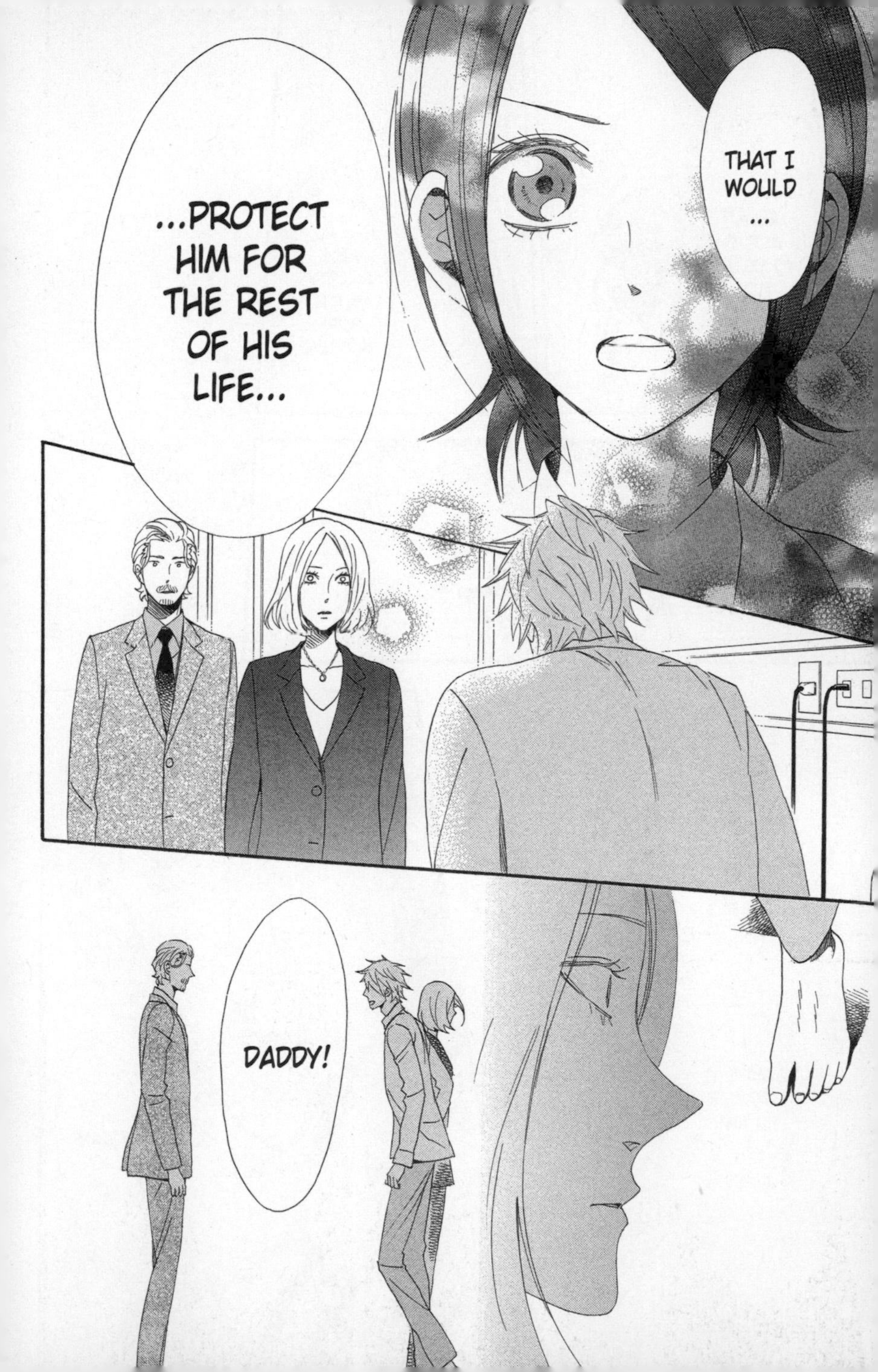
THAT I WOULD ...
...PROTECT HIM FOR THE REST OF HIS LIFE...
DADDY!

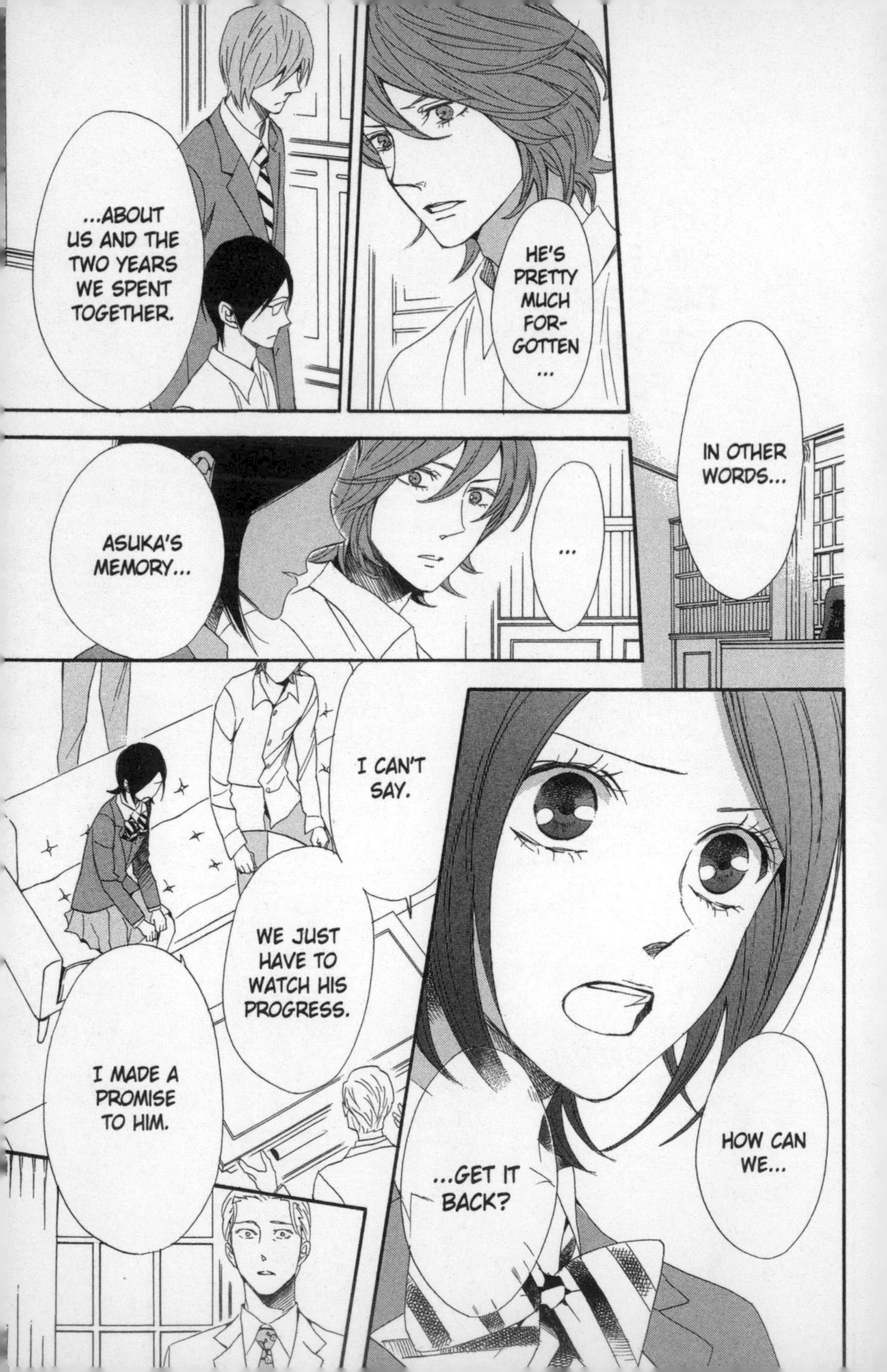
HE'S PRETTY MUCH FOR-GOTTEN...
...ABOUT US AND THE TWO YEARS WE SPENT TOGETHER.
IN OTHER WORDS...
...
ASUKA'S MEMORY...
HOW CAN WE...
...GET IT BACK?
I CAN'T SAY.
WE JUST HAVE TO WATCH HIS PROGRESS.
I MADE A PROMISE TO HIM.

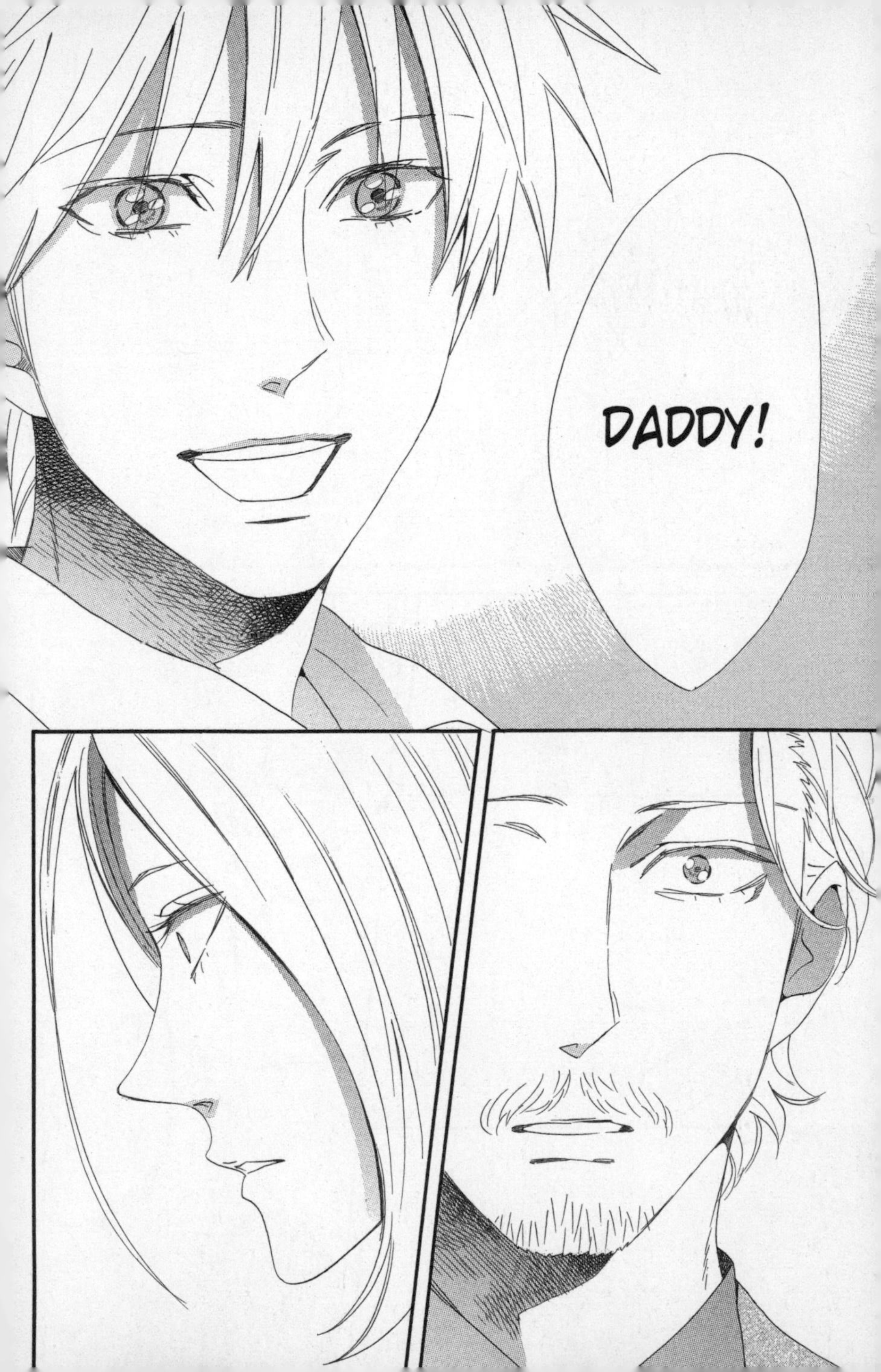
DADDY!

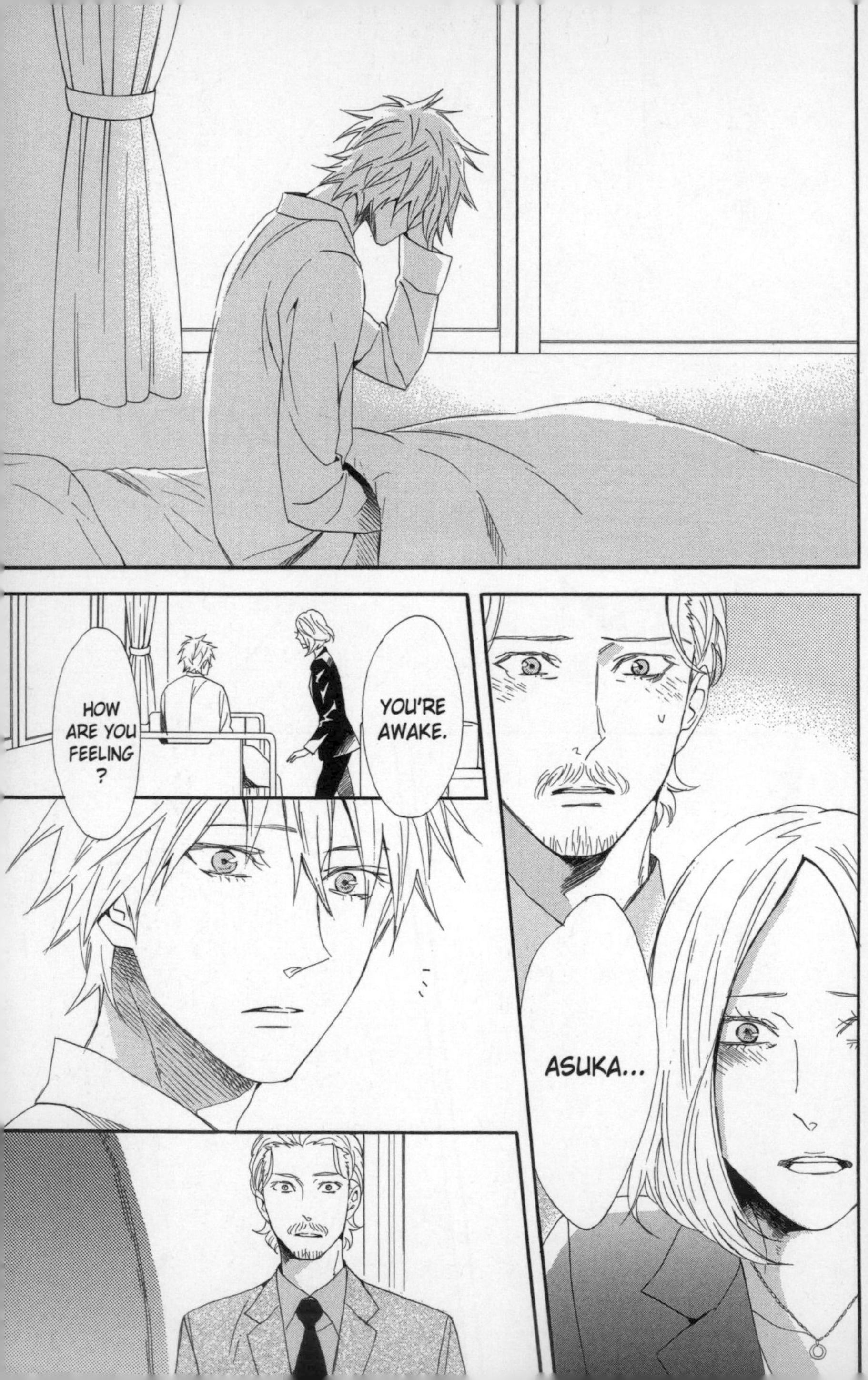
ASUKA...
YOU'RE AWAKE.
HOW ARE YOU FEELING ?

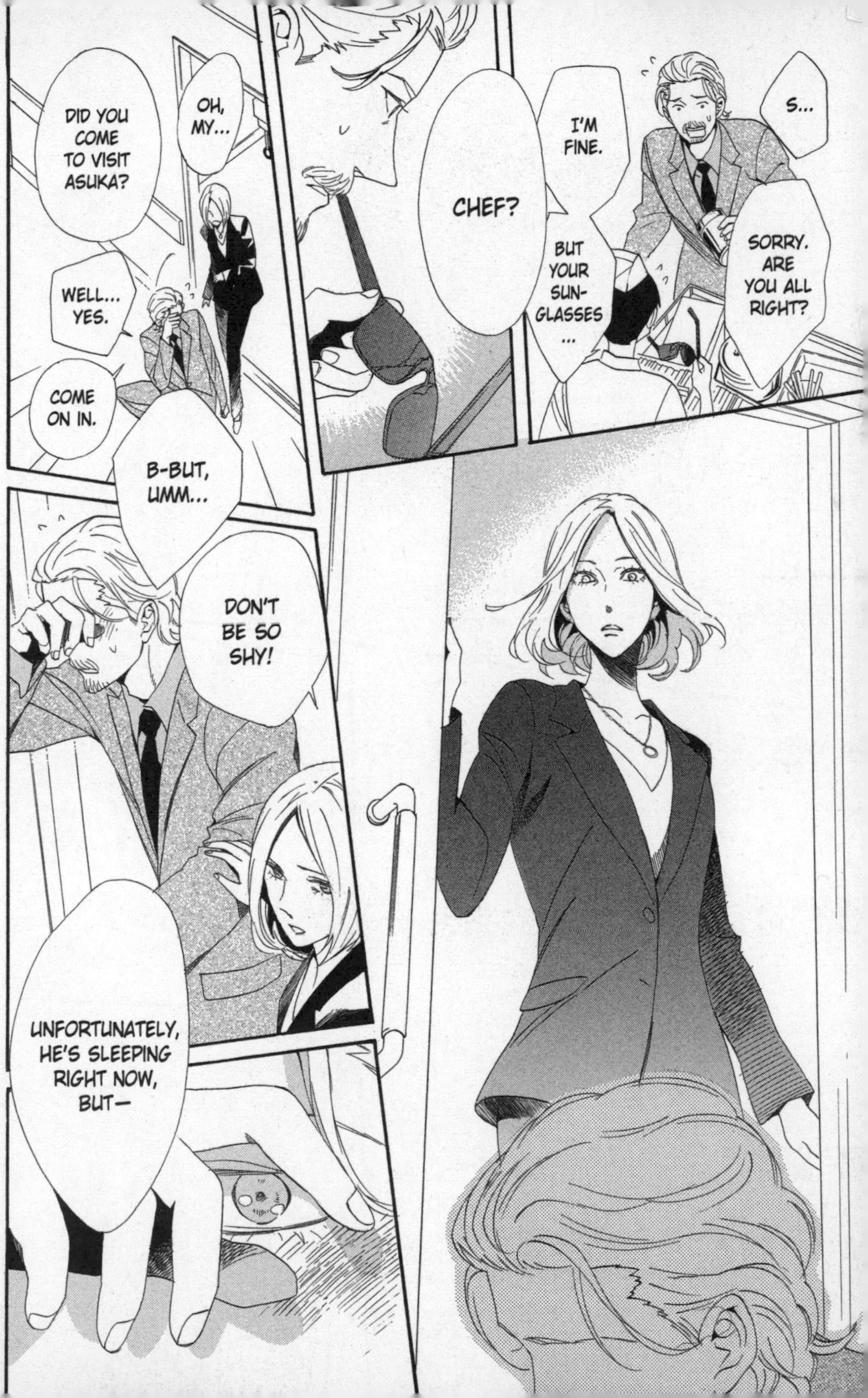
S...
SORRY. ARE YOU ALL RIGHT?
I'M FINE.
BUT YOUR SUN-GLASSES ...
CHEF?
OH, MY...
DID YOU COME TO VISIT ASUKA?
WELL... YES.
COME ON IN.
B-BUT, UMM...
DON'T BE SO SHY!
UNFORTUNATELY, HE'S SLEEPING RIGHT NOW, BUT—

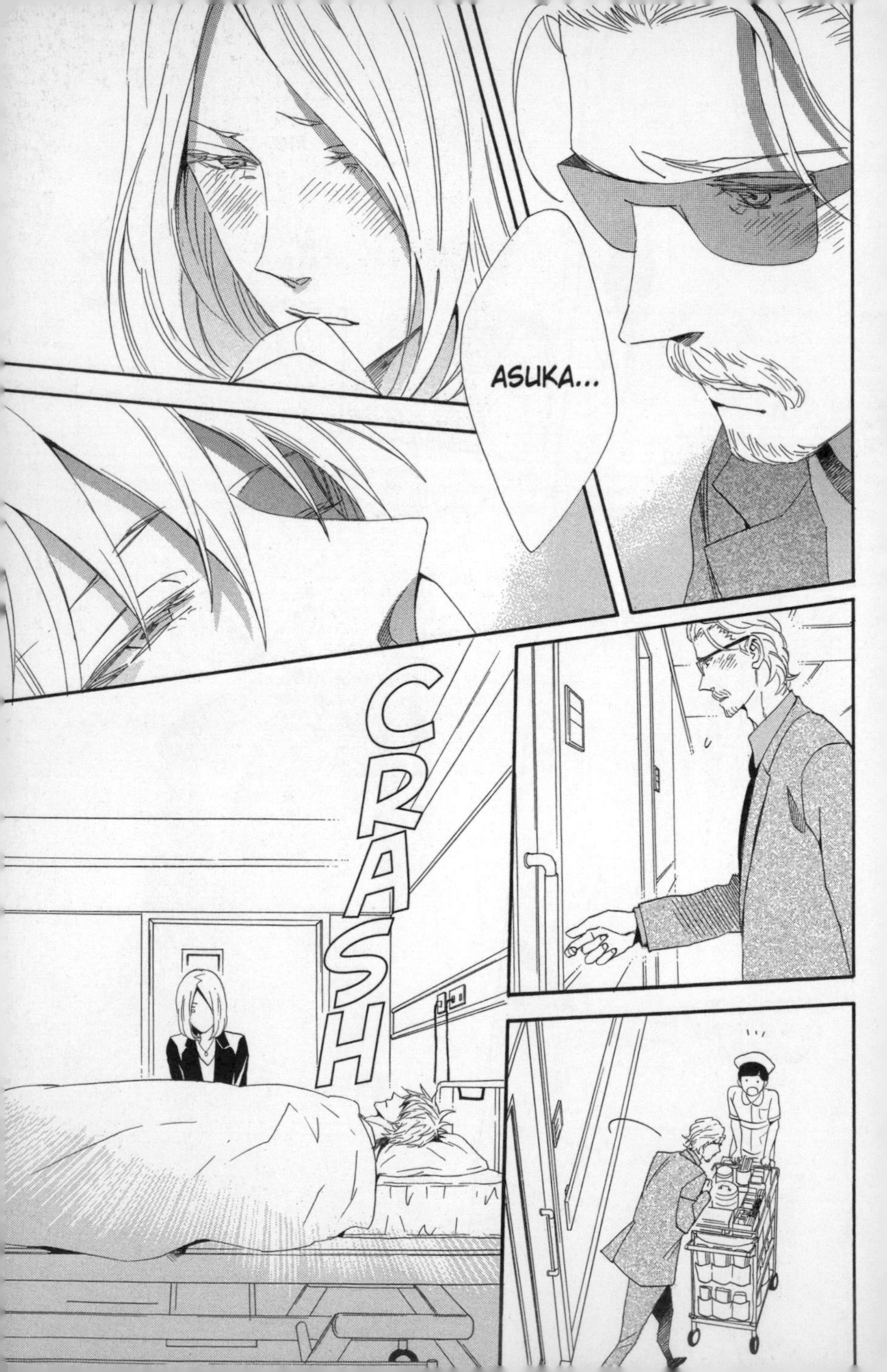
ASUKA...
CRASH

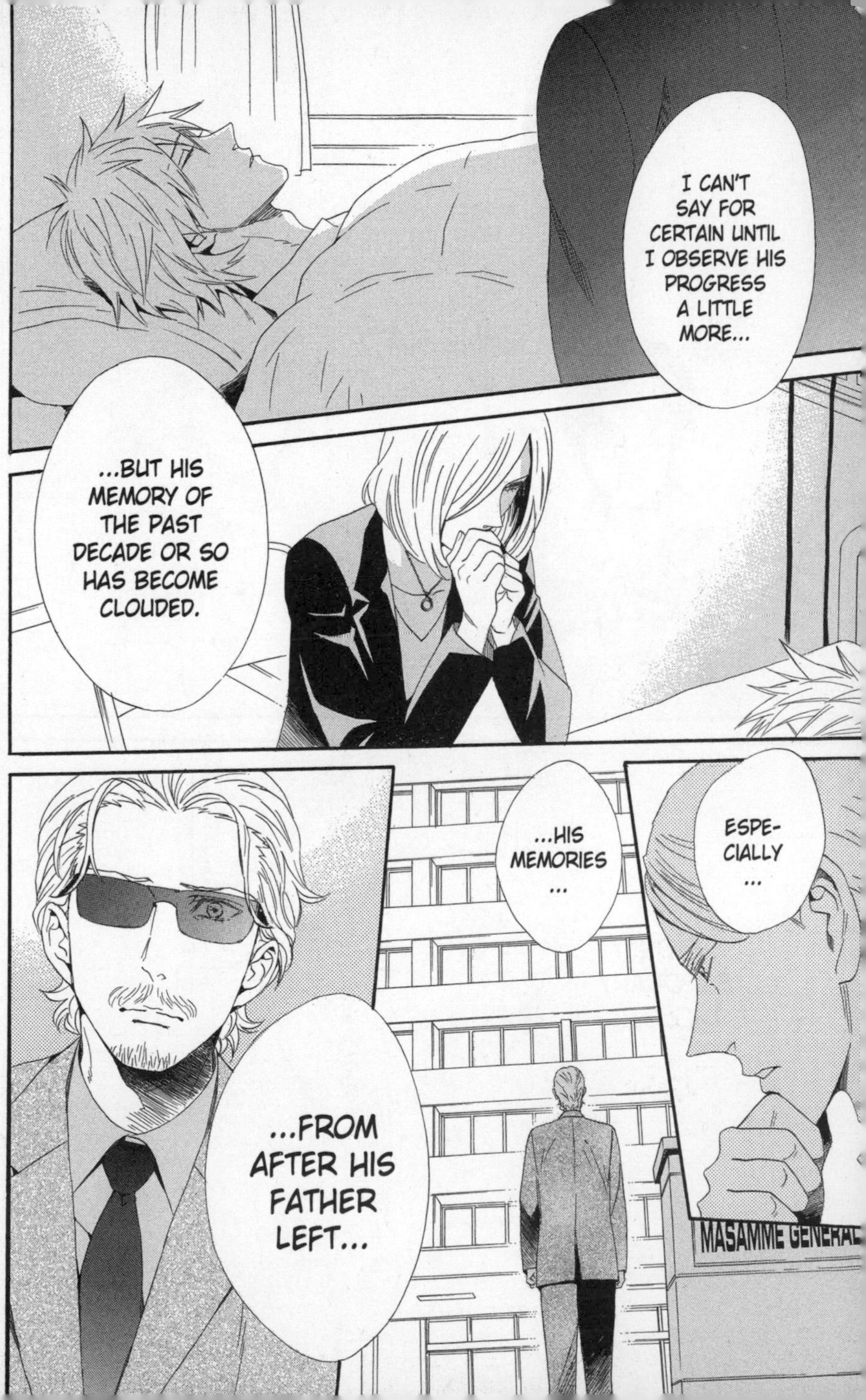
I CAN'T SAY FOR CERTAIN UNTIL I OBSERVE HIS PROGRESS A LITTLE MORE...
...BUT HIS MEMORY OF THE PAST DECADE OR SO HAS BECOME CLOUDED.
ESPE- CIALLY ...
...HIS MEMORIES ...
MASAMME GENERAL
...FROM AFTER HIS FATHER LEFT...

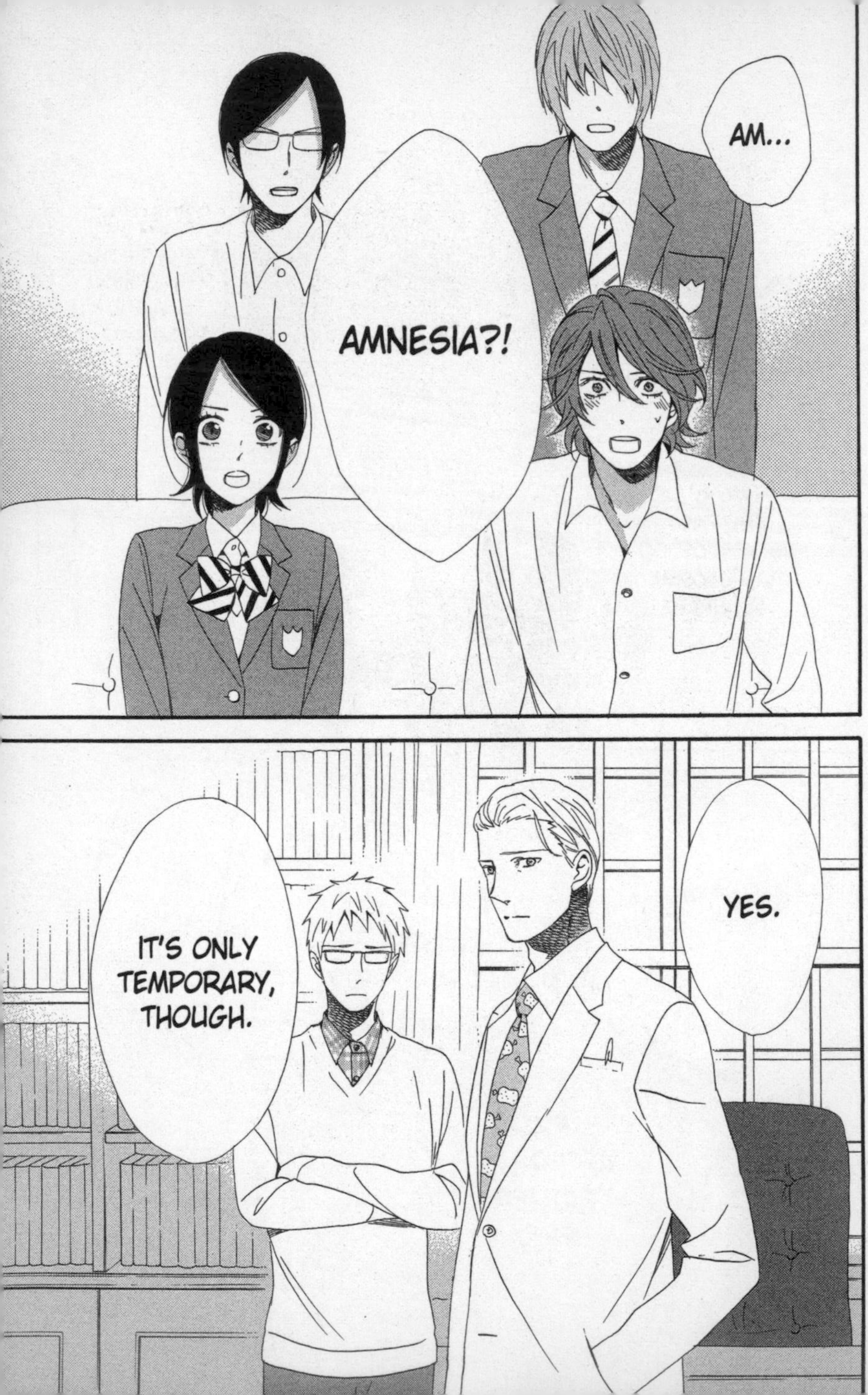
AM...
AMNESIA?!
YES.
IT'S ONLY TEMPORARY, THOUGH.

OTOMEN

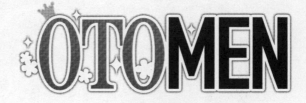

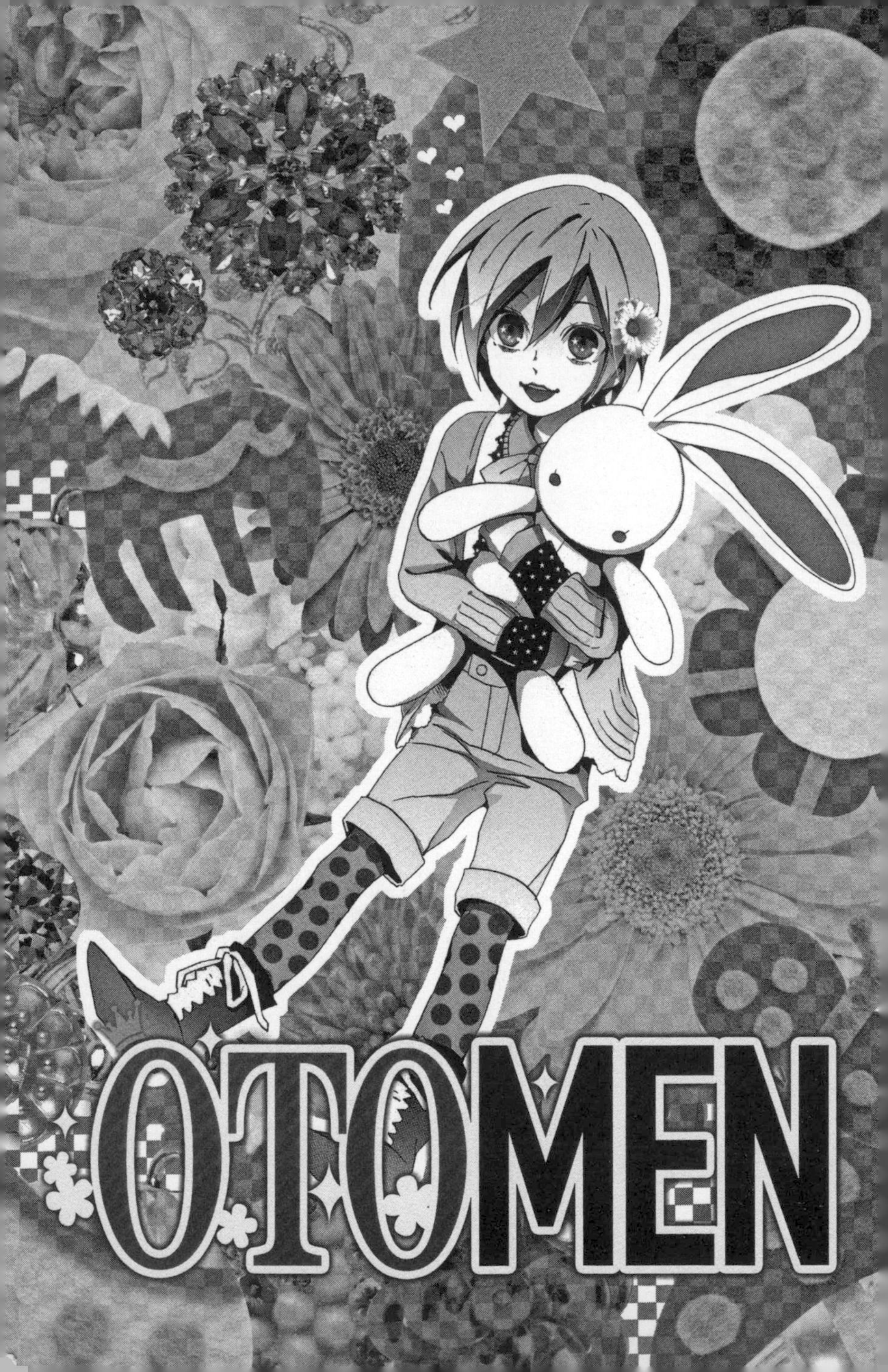
OTOMEN

OTOMEN

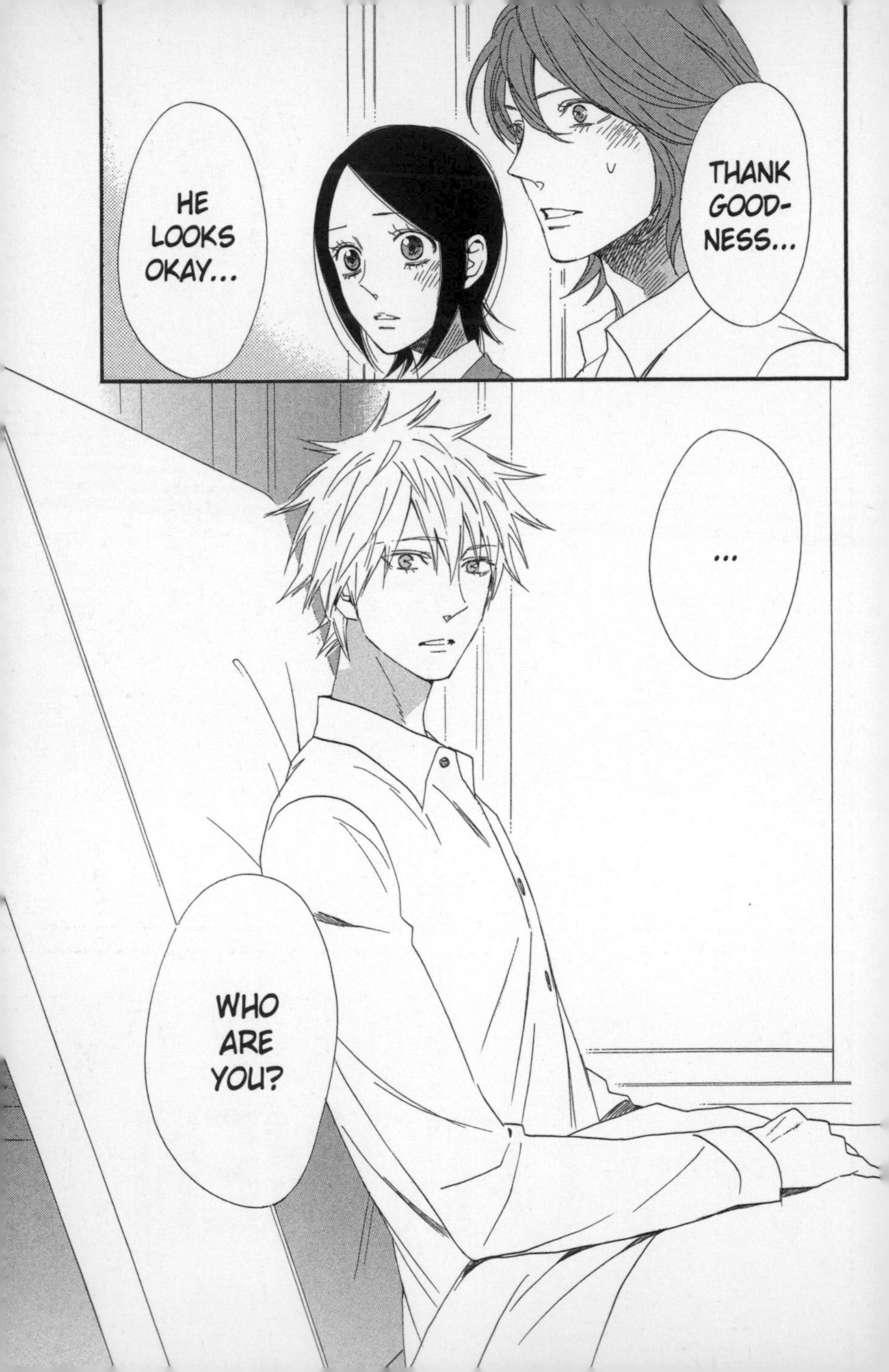
THANK GOODNESS...
HE LOOKS OKAY...
...
WHO ARE YOU?

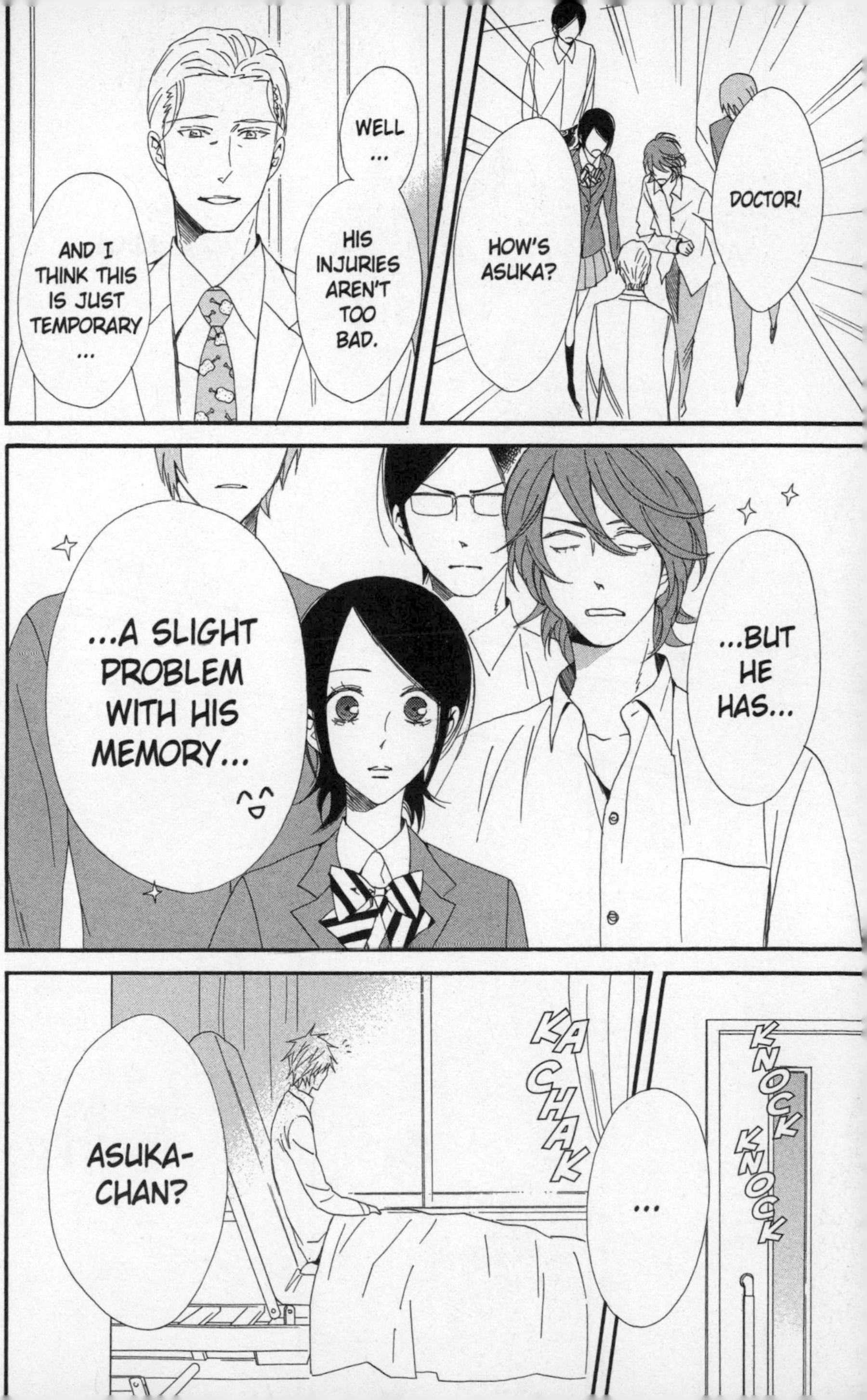
DOCTOR!
HOW'S ASUKA?
WELL ...
HIS INJURIES AREN'T TOO BAD.
AND I THINK THIS IS JUST TEMPORARY ...
...BUT HE HAS...
...A SLIGHT PROBLEM WITH HIS MEMORY...
KNOCK KNOCK
KACHAK
...
ASUKA-CHAN?

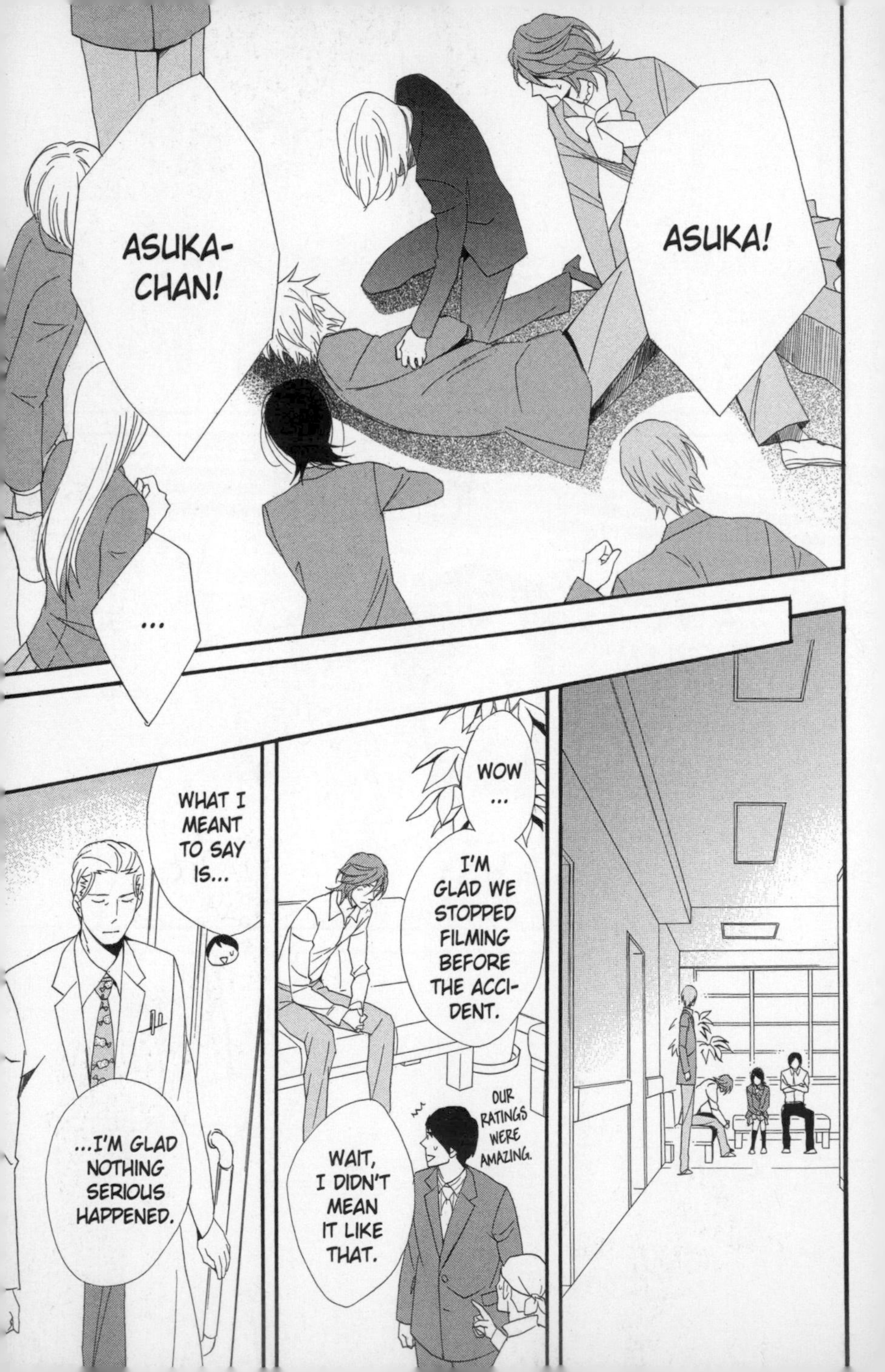
ASUKA!
ASUKA-CHAN!
...
WOW ...
I'M GLAD WE STOPPED FILMING BEFORE THE ACCIDENT.
OUR RATINGS WERE AMAZING.
WAIT, I DIDN'T MEAN IT LIKE THAT.
WHAT I MEANT TO SAY IS...
...I'M GLAD NOTHING SERIOUS HAPPENED.

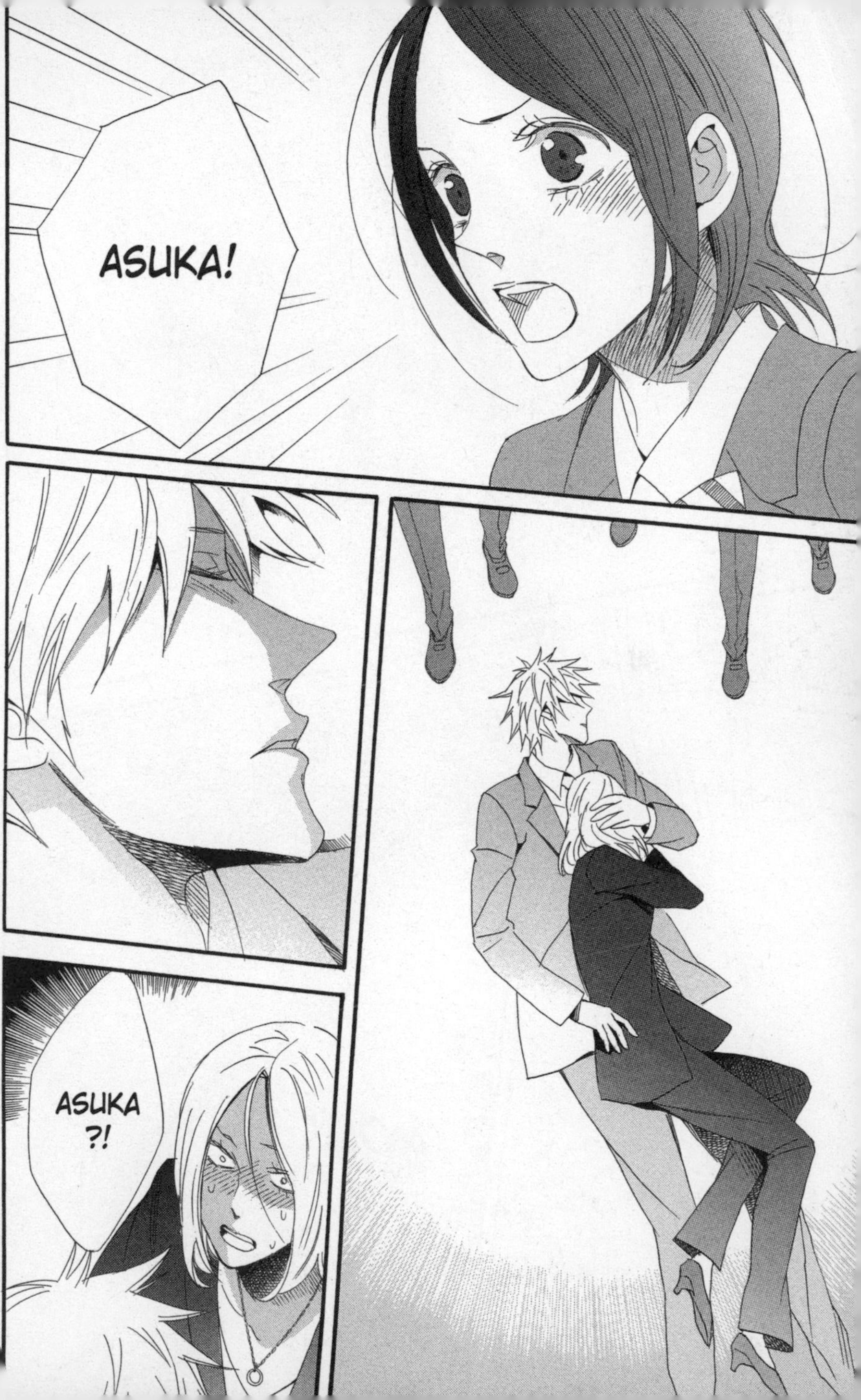
ASUKA!
ASUKA ?!

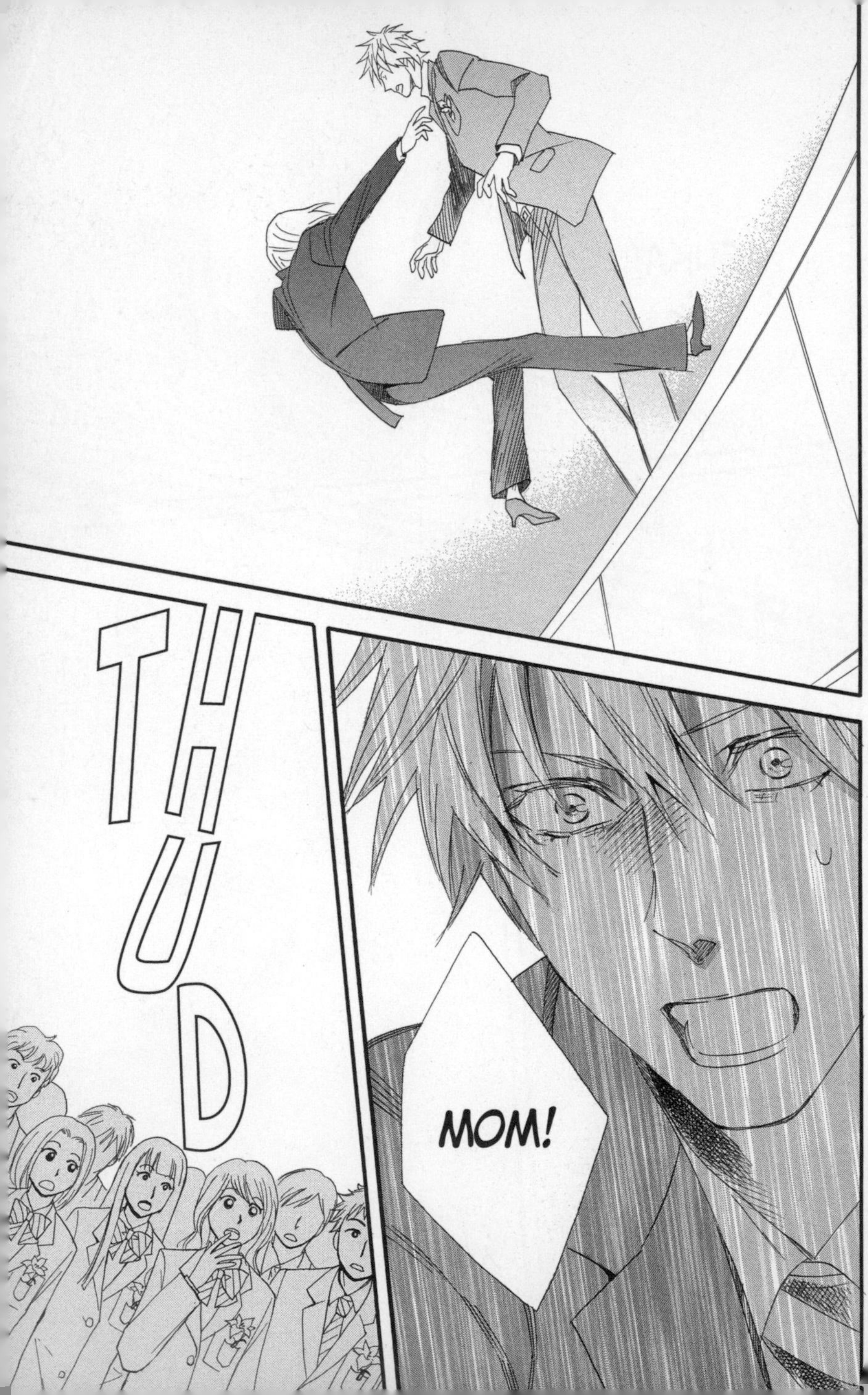
MOM!
THUD

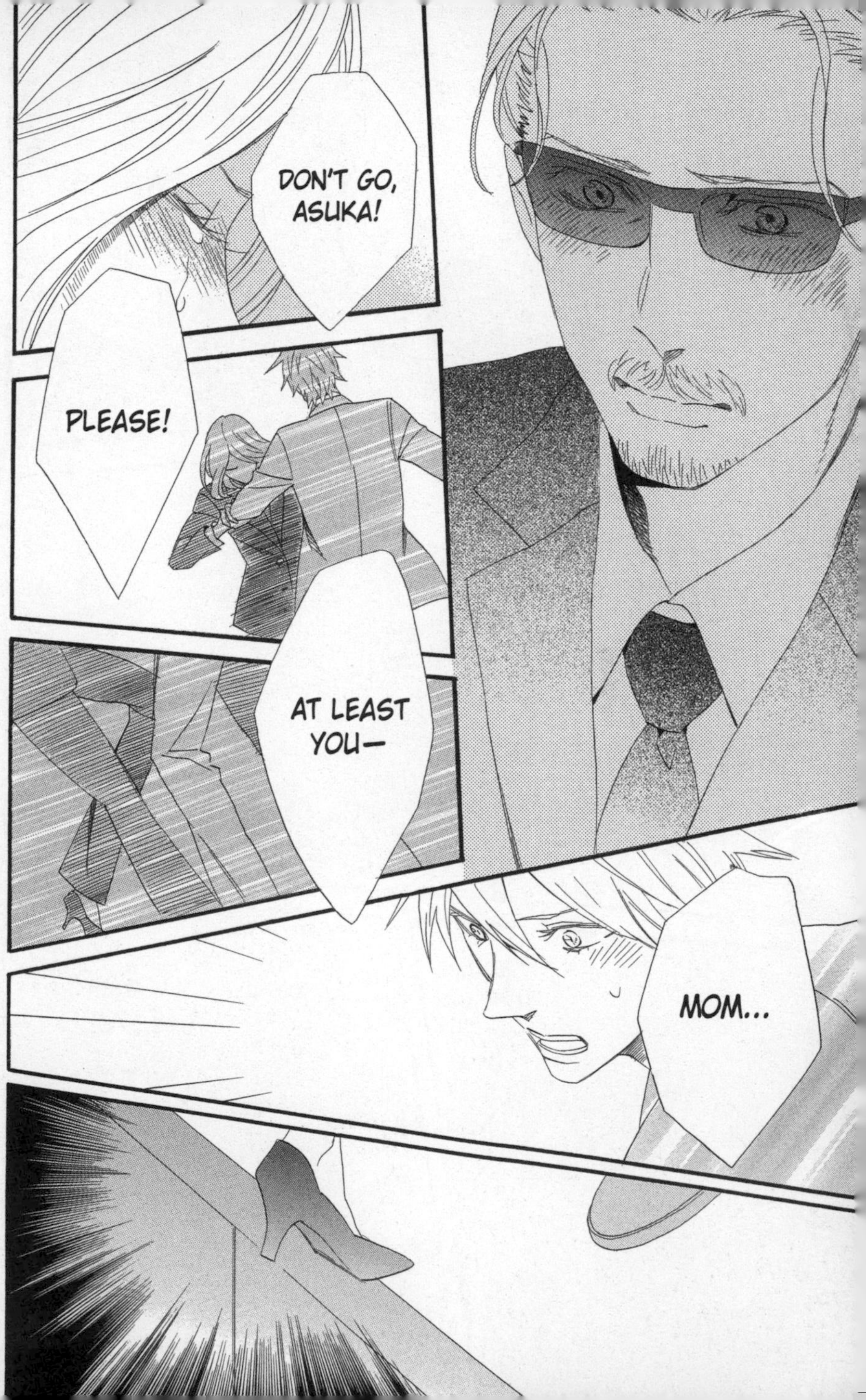
DON'T GO, ASUKA!
PLEASE!
AT LEAST YOU—
MOM...

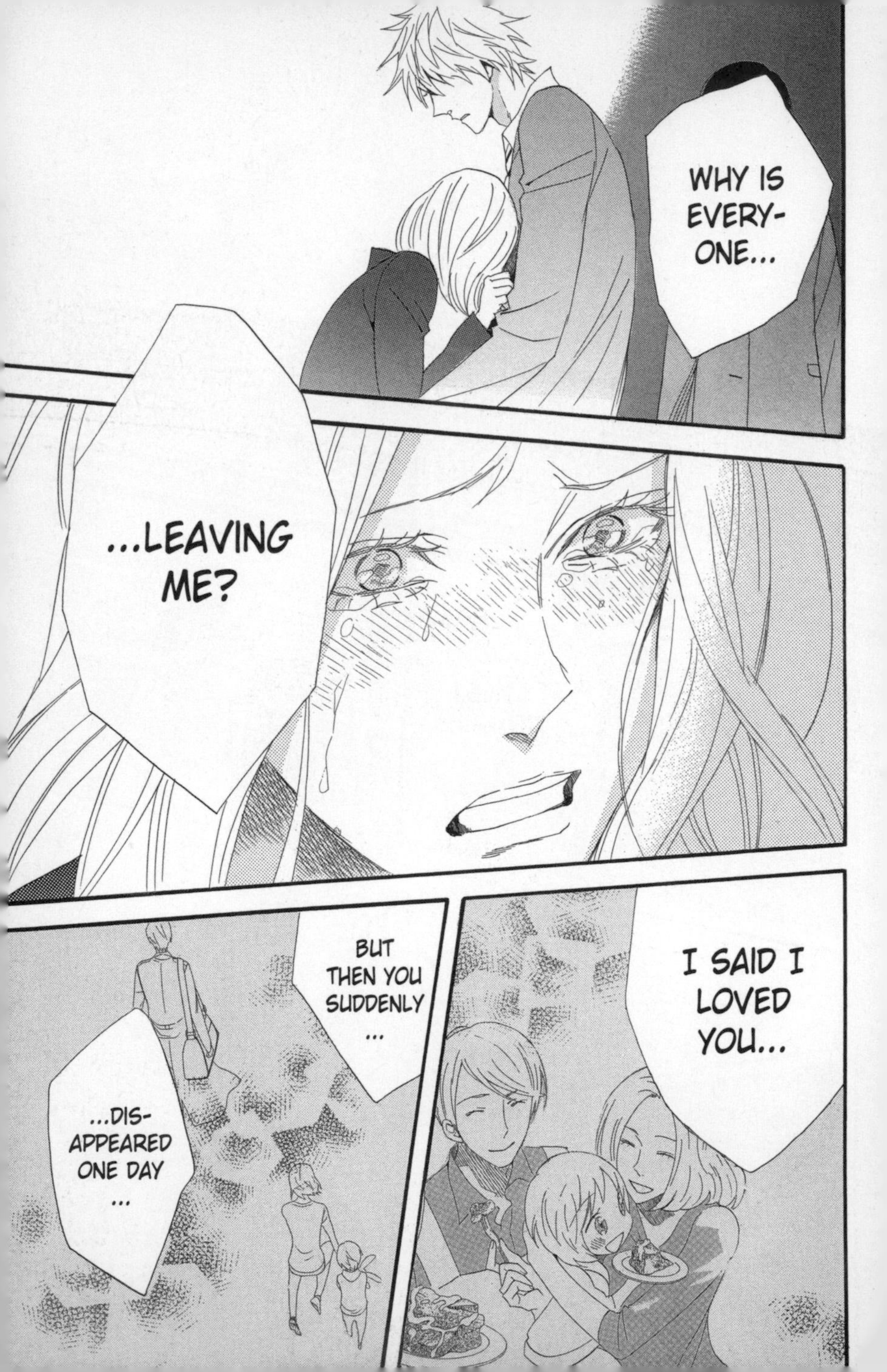
WHY IS EVERY-ONE...
...LEAVING ME?
I SAID I LOVED YOU...
BUT THEN YOU SUDDENLY ...
...DIS-APPEARED ONE DAY ...

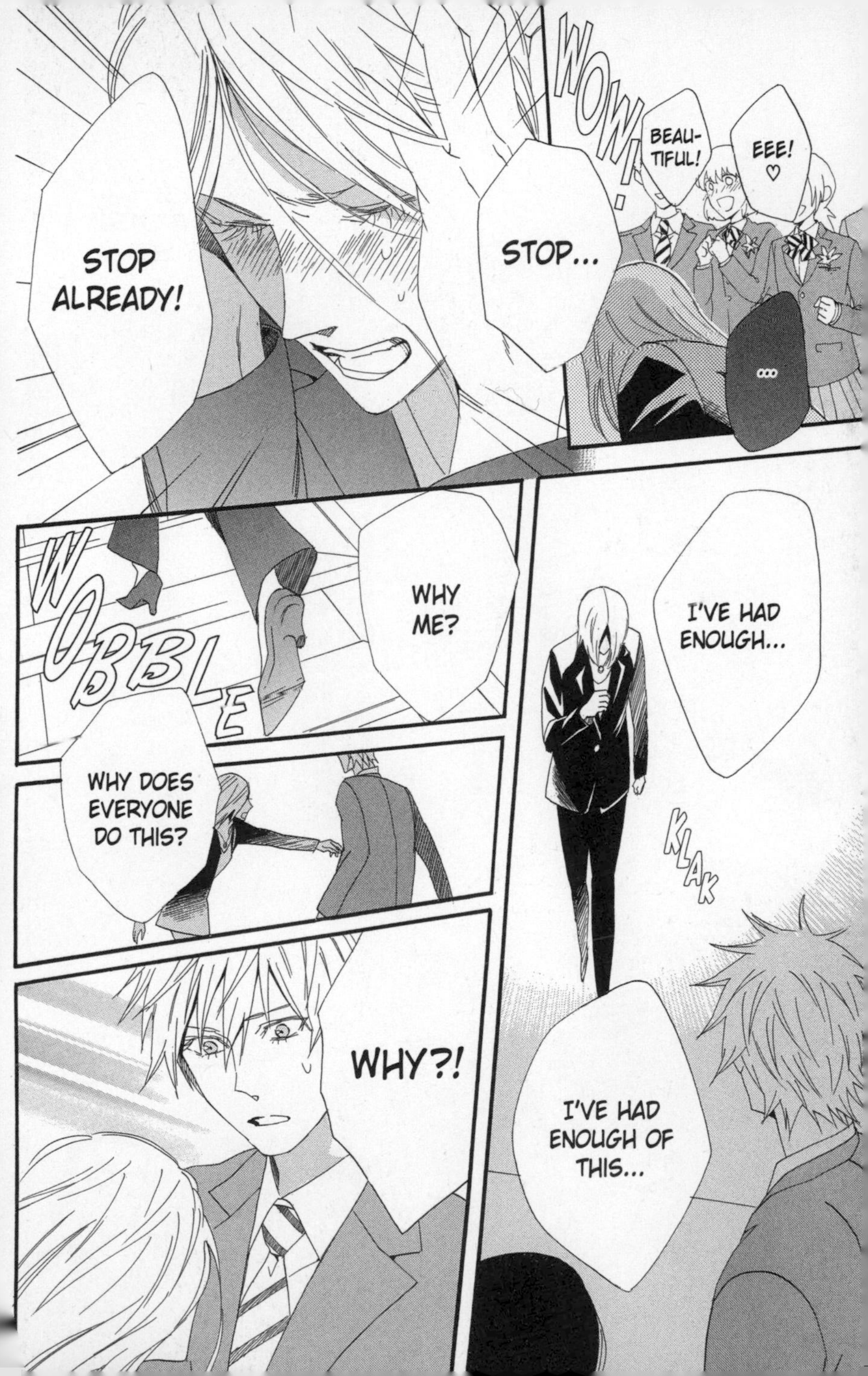
WOW!
BEAU-TIFUL!
EEE! ♡
...
STOP...
STOP ALREADY!
I'VE HAD ENOUGH...
KLAK
I'VE HAD ENOUGH OF THIS...
WHY ME?
WOBBLE
WHY DOES EVERYONE DO THIS?
WHY?!

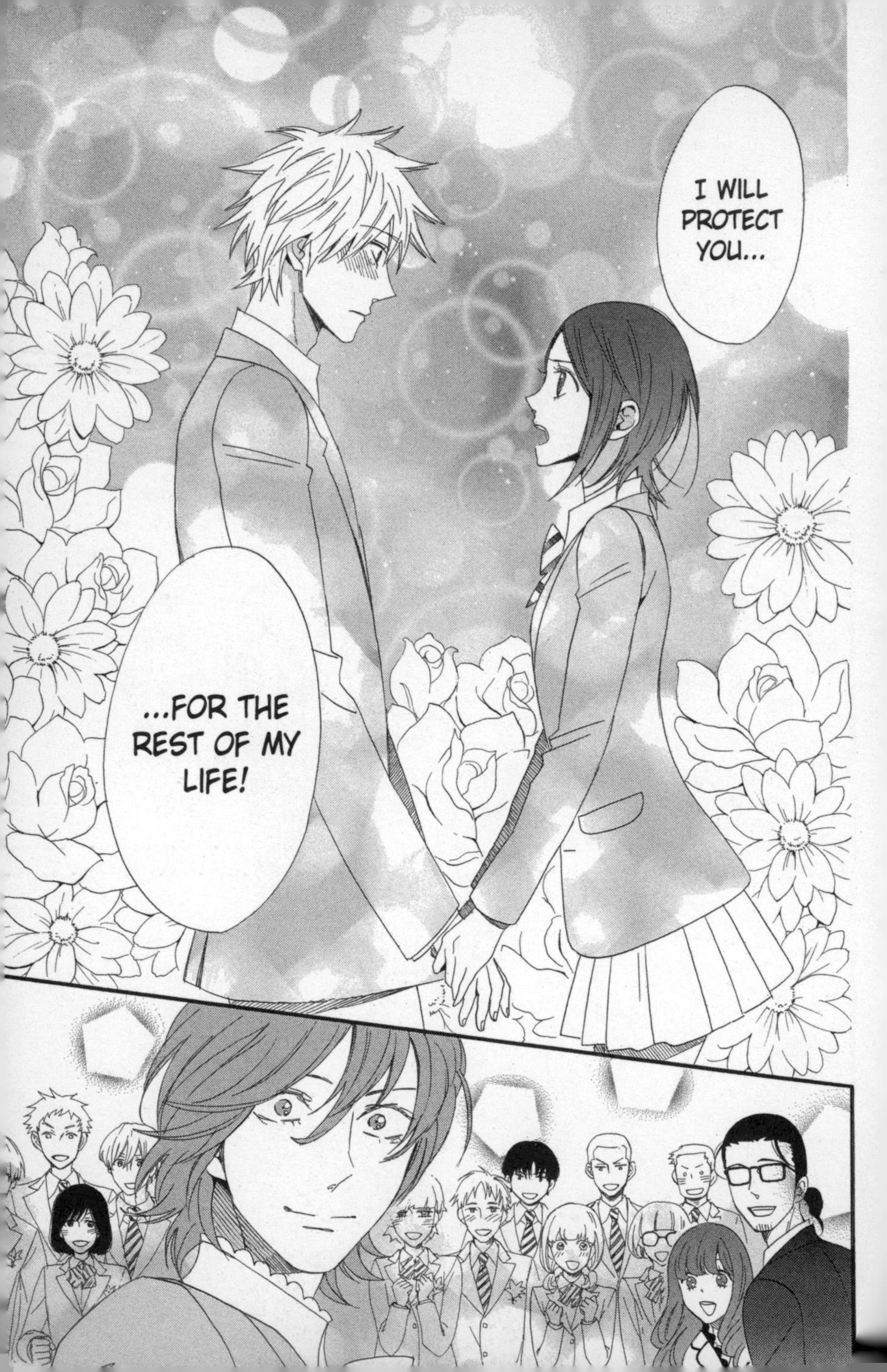
I WILL PROTECT YOU...
...FOR THE REST OF MY LIFE!

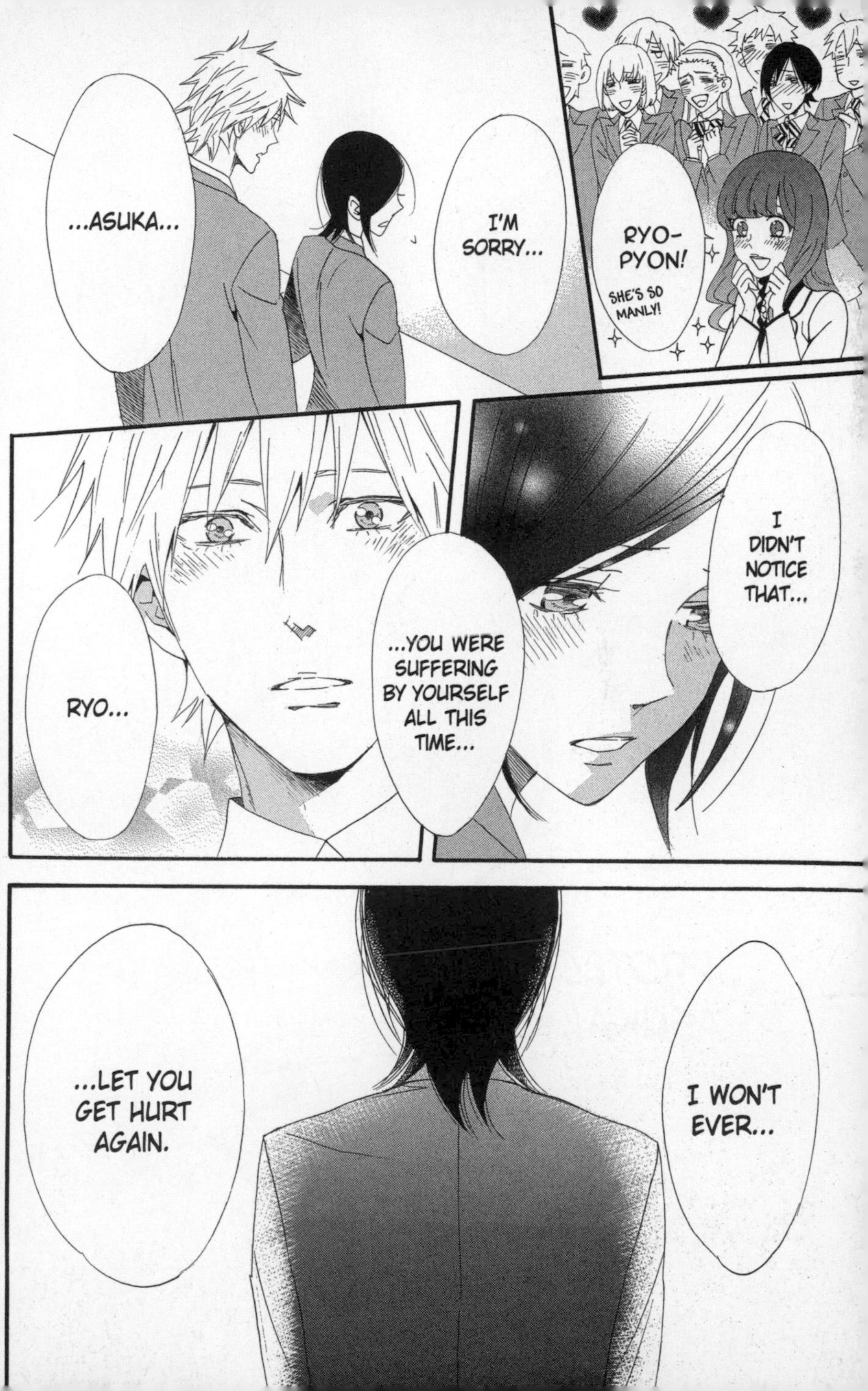
RYO-PYON!
SHE'S SO MANLY!
I'M SORRY...
...ASUKA...
I DIDN'T NOTICE THAT...
...YOU WERE SUFFERING BY YOURSELF ALL THIS TIME...
RYO...
I WON'T EVER...
...LET YOU GET HURT AGAIN.

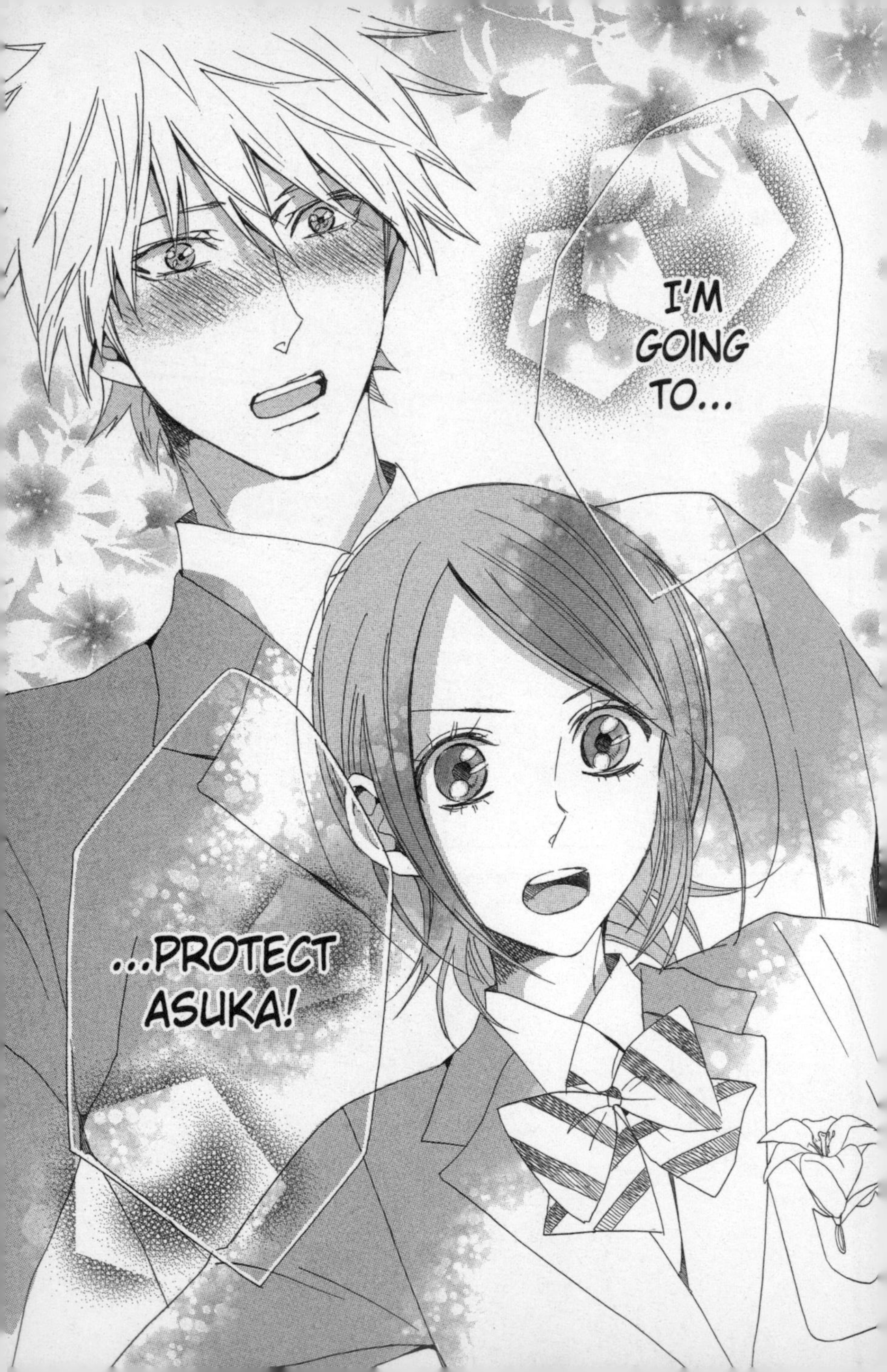
I'M GOING TO...
...PROTECT ASUKA!

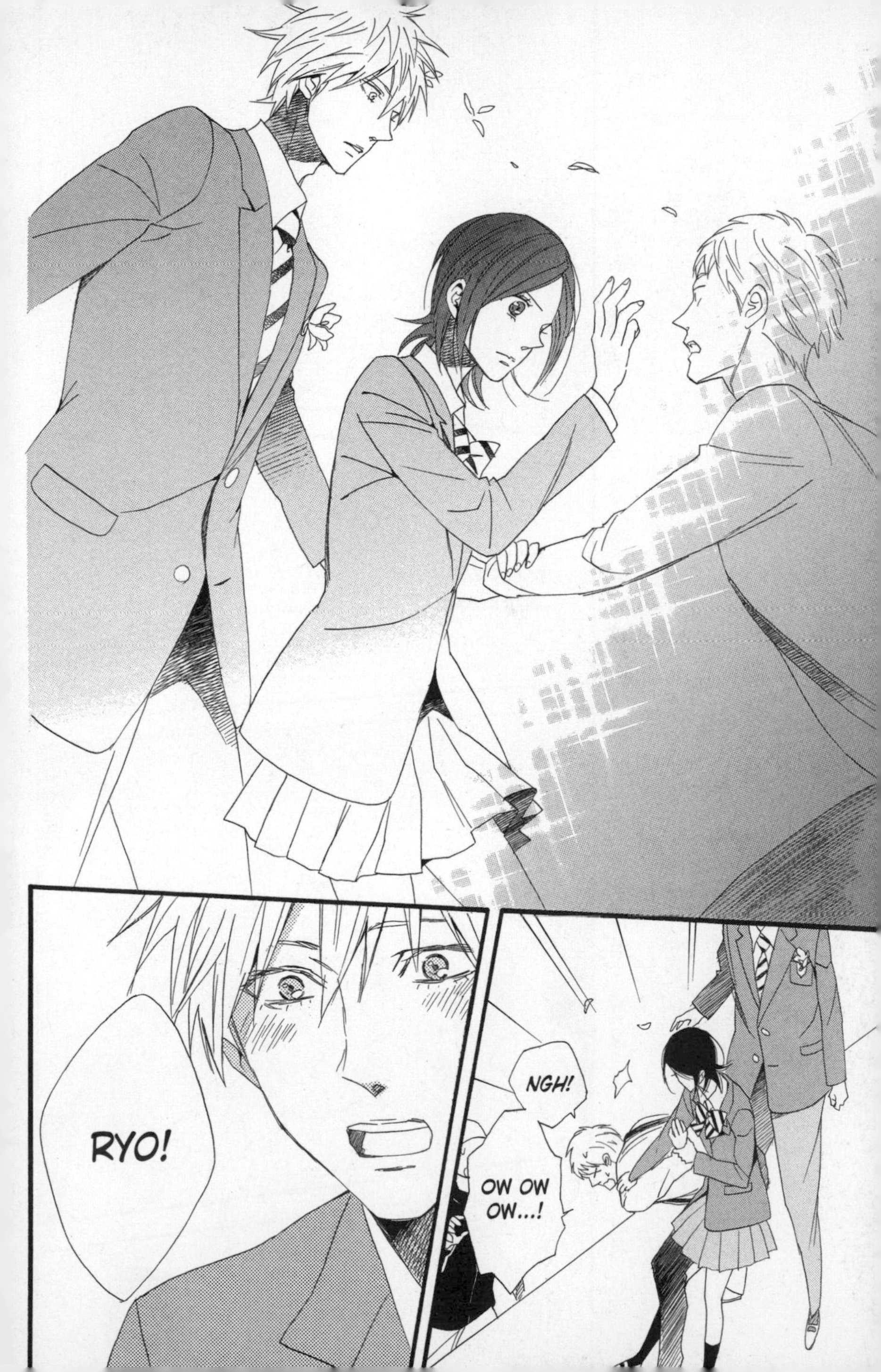
NGH!
OW OW OW...!
RYO!

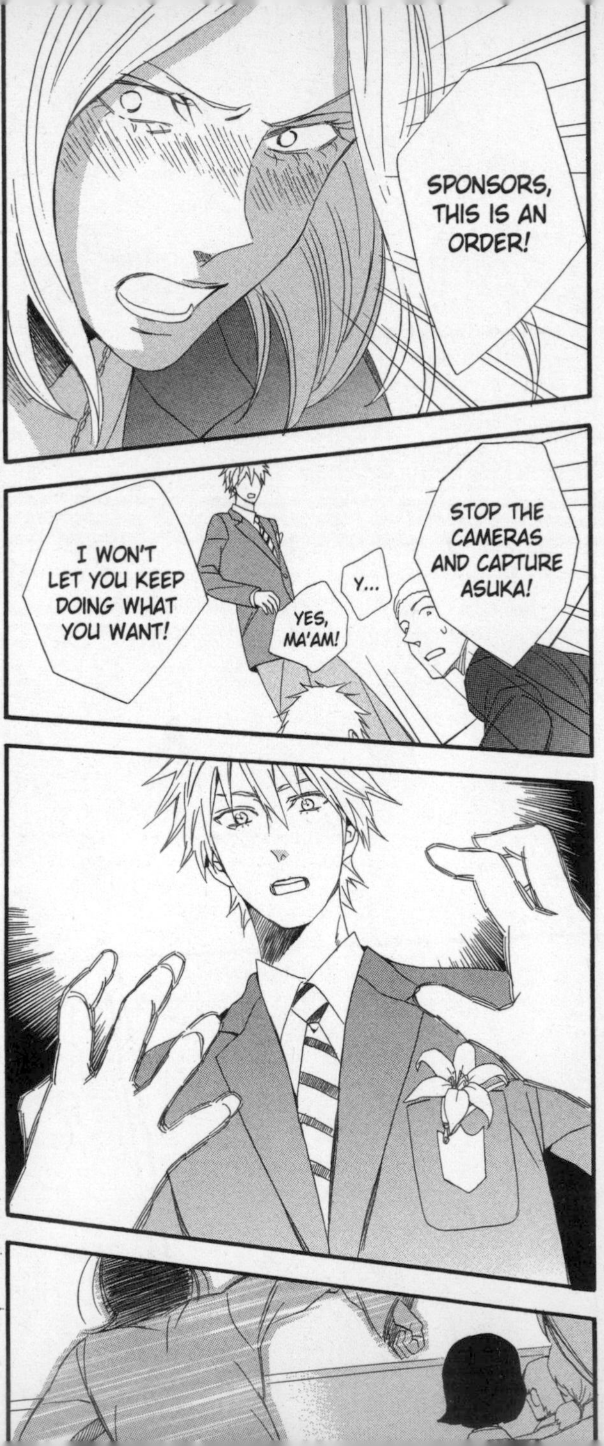
SPONSORS, THIS IS AN ORDER!
STOP THE CAMERAS AND CAPTURE ASUKA!
Y...
YES, MA'AM!
I WON'T LET YOU KEEP DOING WHAT YOU WANT!

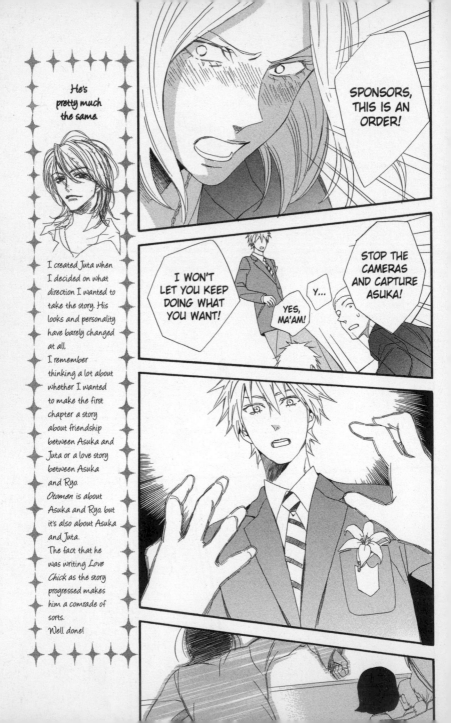

He's pretty much the same.

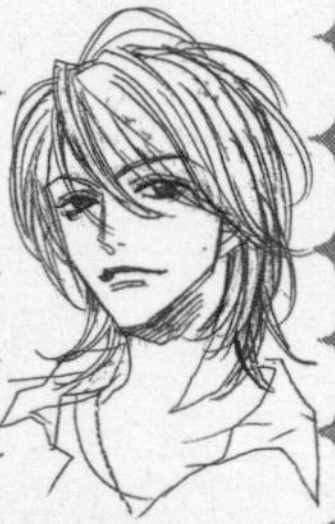

I created Juta when I decided on what direction I wanted to take the story. His looks and personality have barely changed at all.
I remember thinking a lot about whether I wanted to make the first chapter a story about friendship between Asuka and Juta or a love story between Asuka and Ryo.
Otomen is about Asuka and Ryo, but it's also about Asuka and Juta.
The fact that he was writing *Love Chick* as the story progressed makes him a comrade of sorts.
Well done!

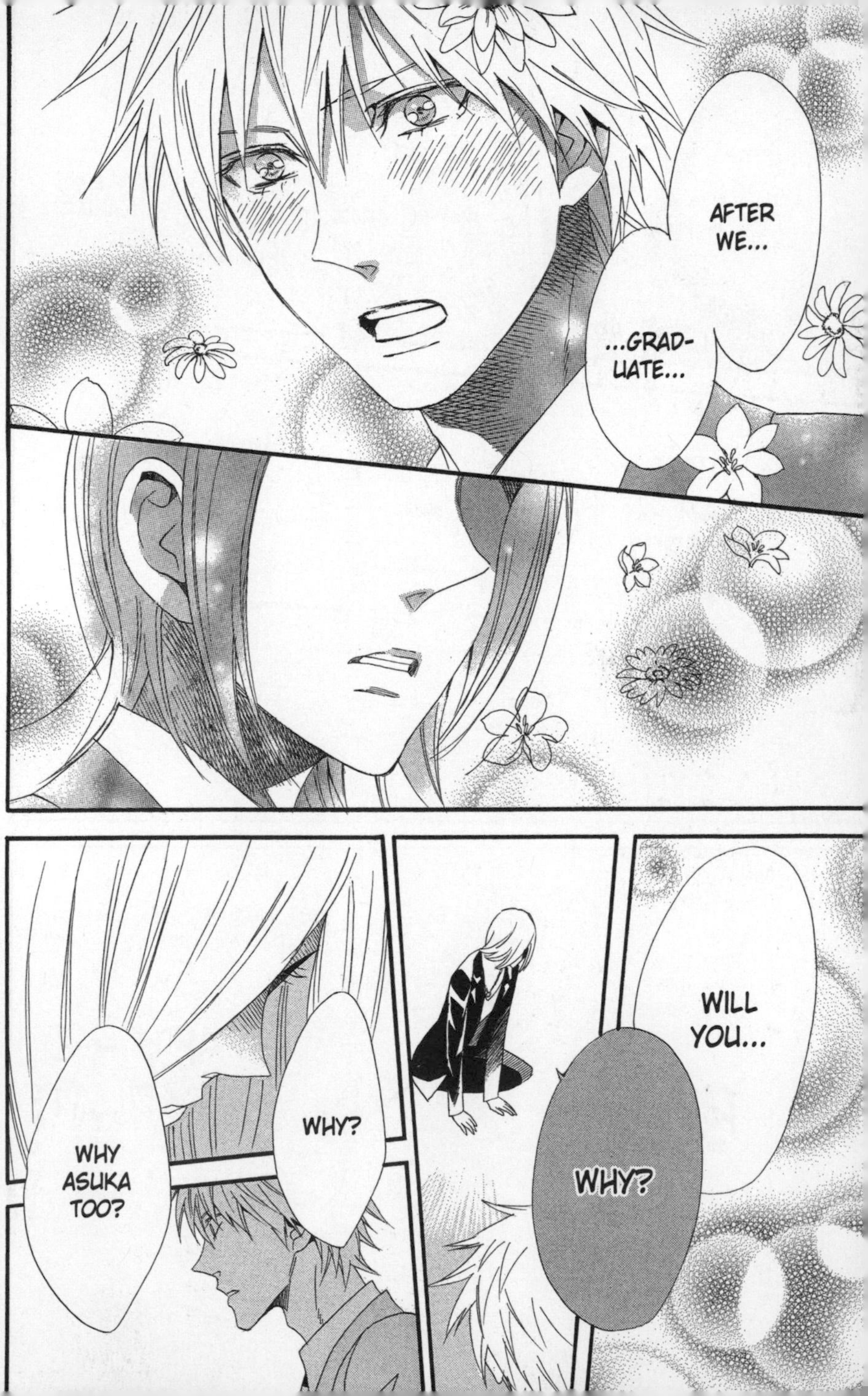
AFTER WE...
...GRAD-UATE...
WILL YOU...
WHY?
WHY?
WHY ASUKA TOO?

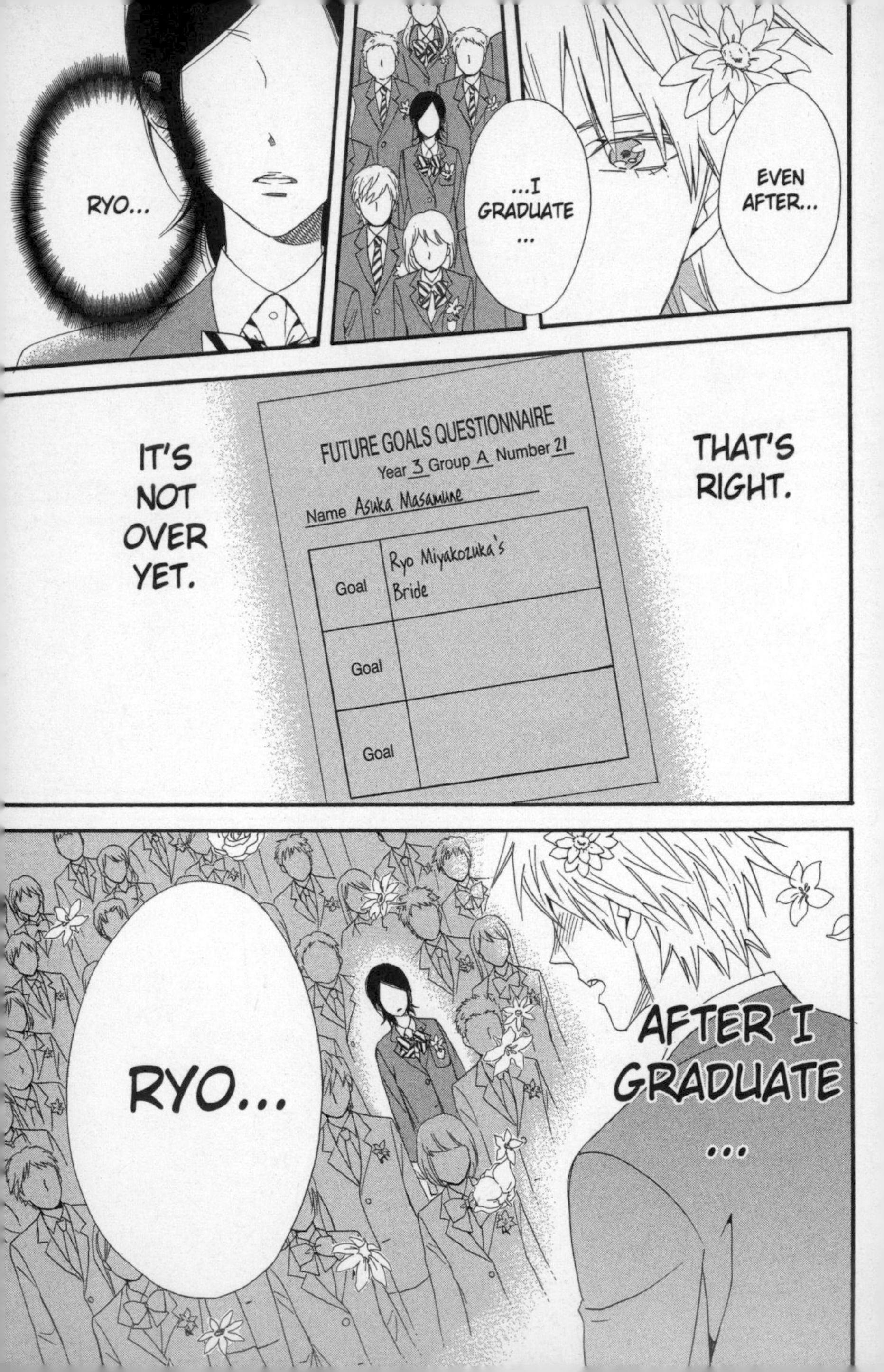
EVEN AFTER...
...I GRADUATE ...
RYO...
THAT'S RIGHT.
FUTURE GOALS QUESTIONNAIRE
Year 3 Group A Number 21
Name Asuka Masamune
Goal Ryo Miyakozuka's Bride
Goal
Goal
IT'S NOT OVER YET.
AFTER I GRADUATE ...
RYO...

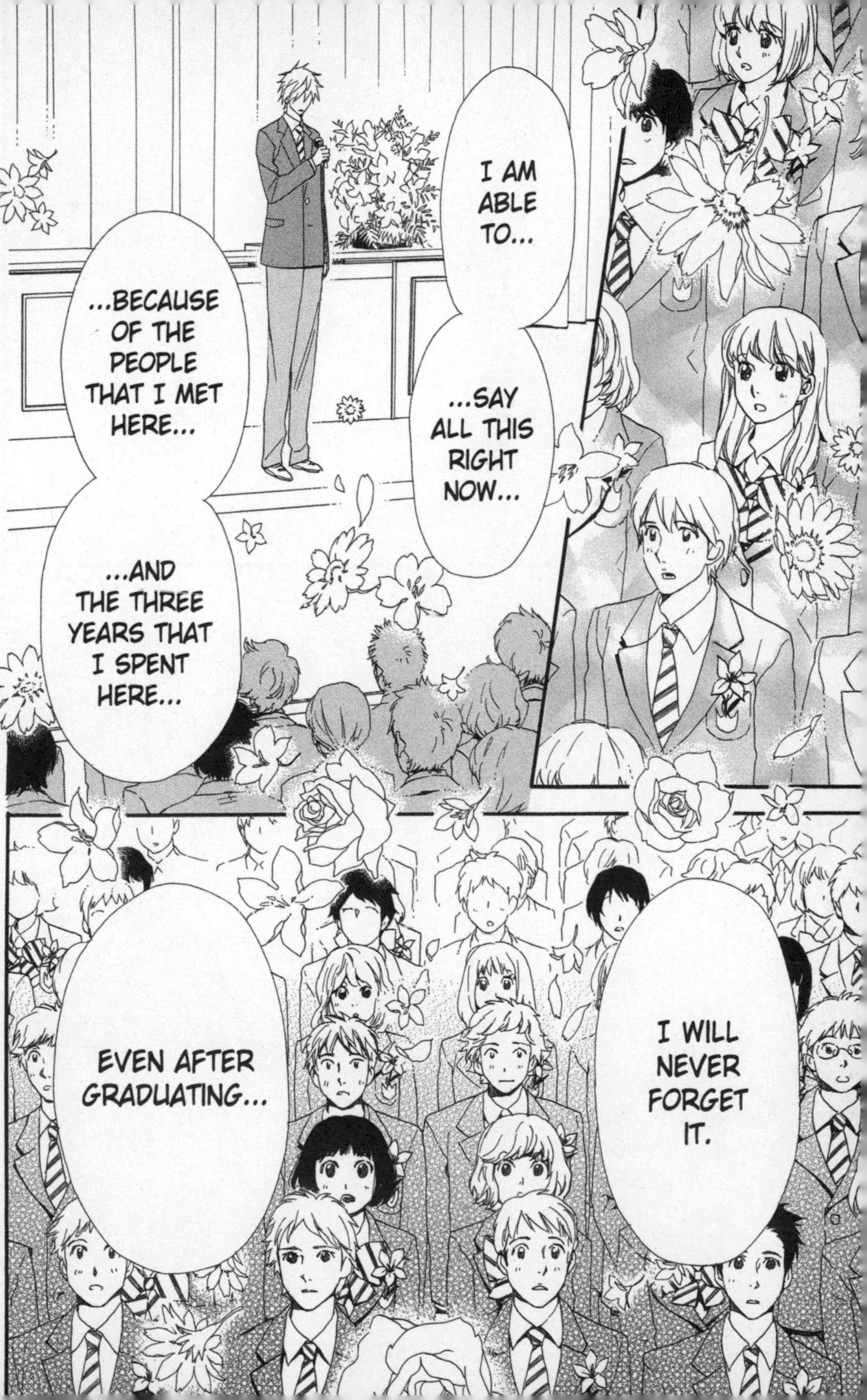
I AM ABLE TO...
...SAY ALL THIS RIGHT NOW...
...BECAUSE OF THE PEOPLE THAT I MET HERE...
...AND THE THREE YEARS THAT I SPENT HERE...
I WILL NEVER FORGET IT.
EVEN AFTER GRADUATING...

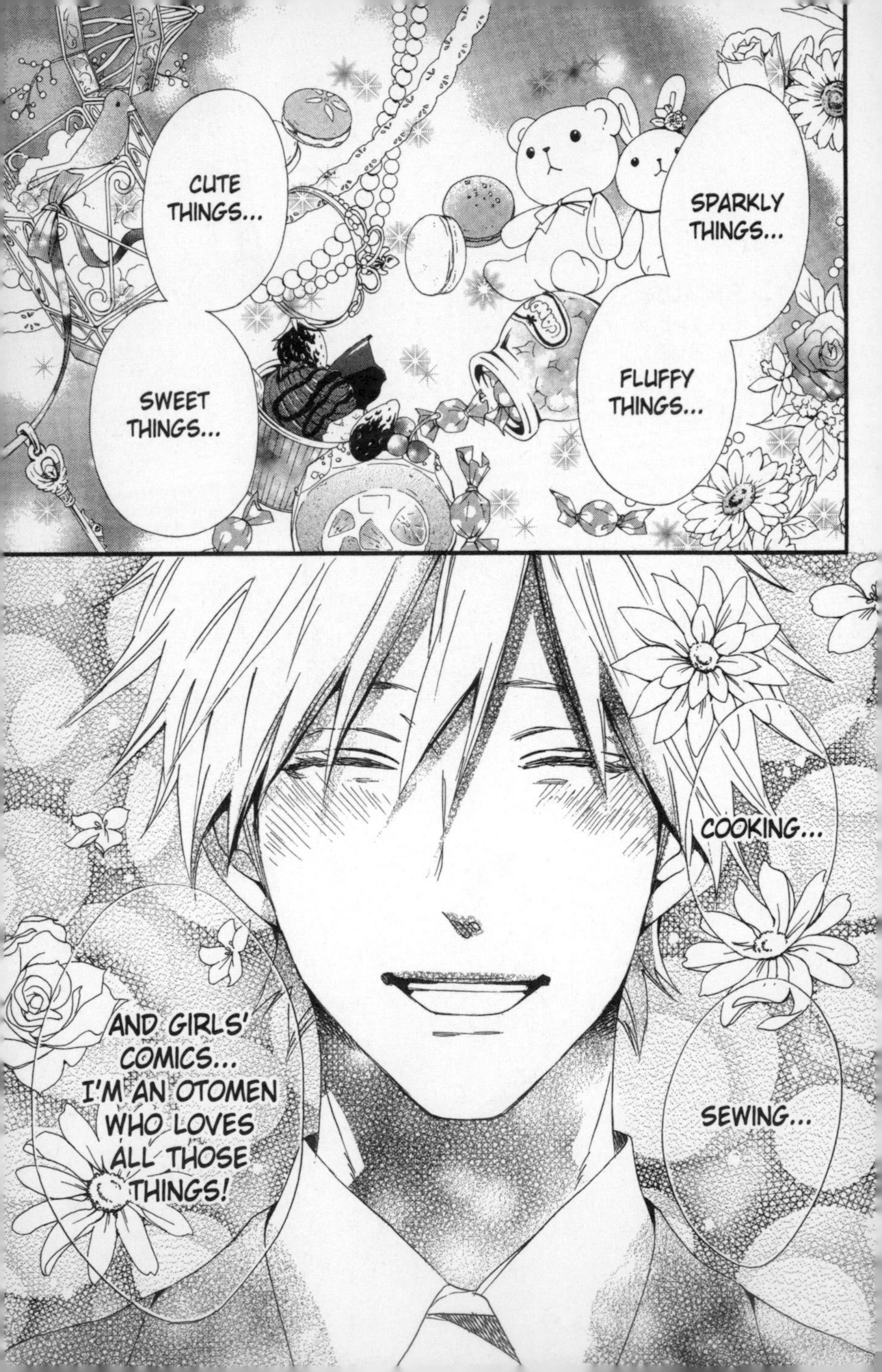
SPARKLY THINGS...
CUTE THINGS...
FLUFFY THINGS...
SWEET THINGS...
COOKING...
SEWING...
AND GIRLS' COMICS... I'M AN OTOMEN WHO LOVES ALL THOSE THINGS!

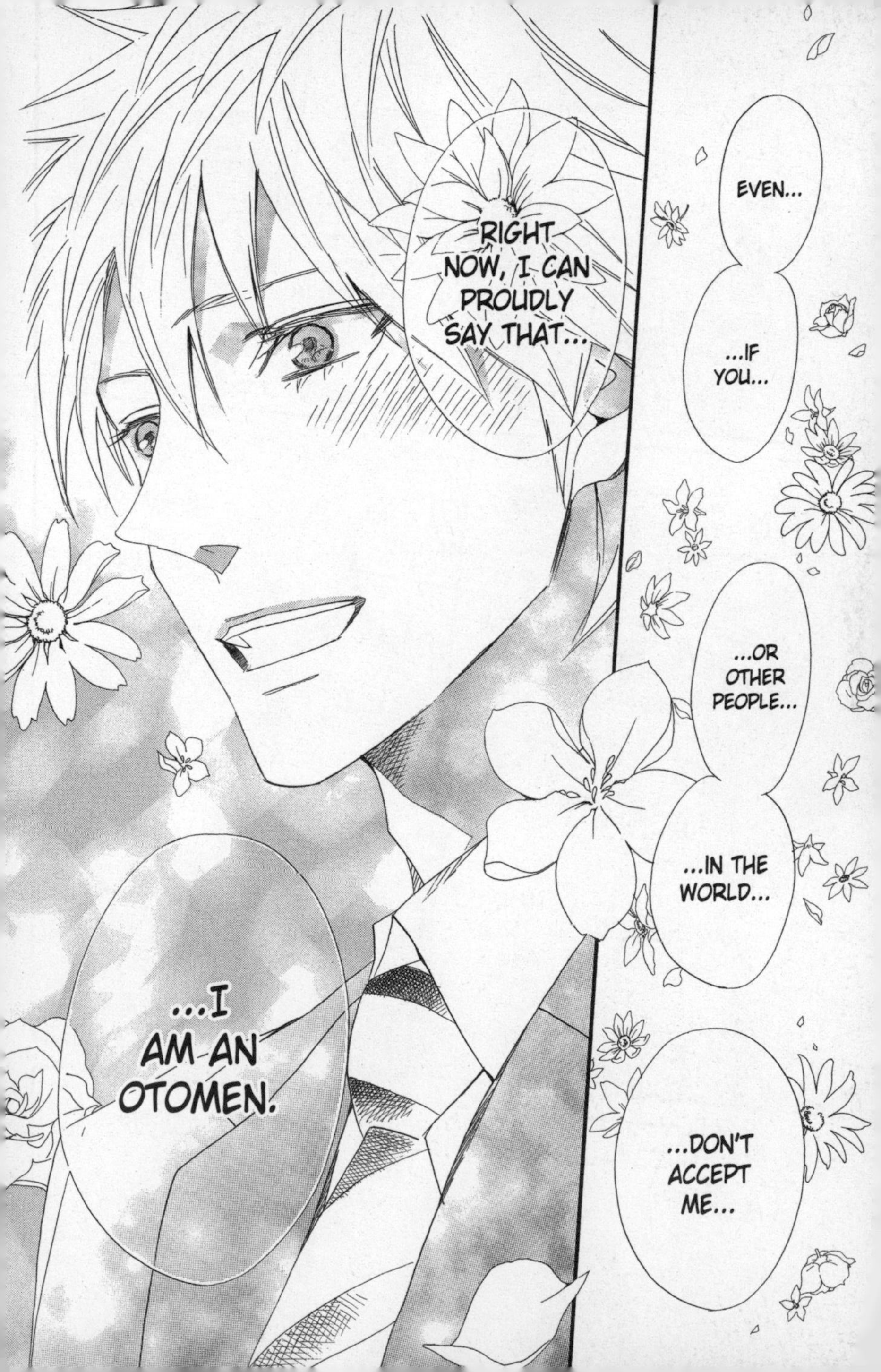
EVEN...
...IF YOU...
...OR OTHER PEOPLE...
...IN THE WORLD...
...DON'T ACCEPT ME...
RIGHT NOW, I CAN PROUDLY SAY THAT...
...I AM AN OTOMEN.

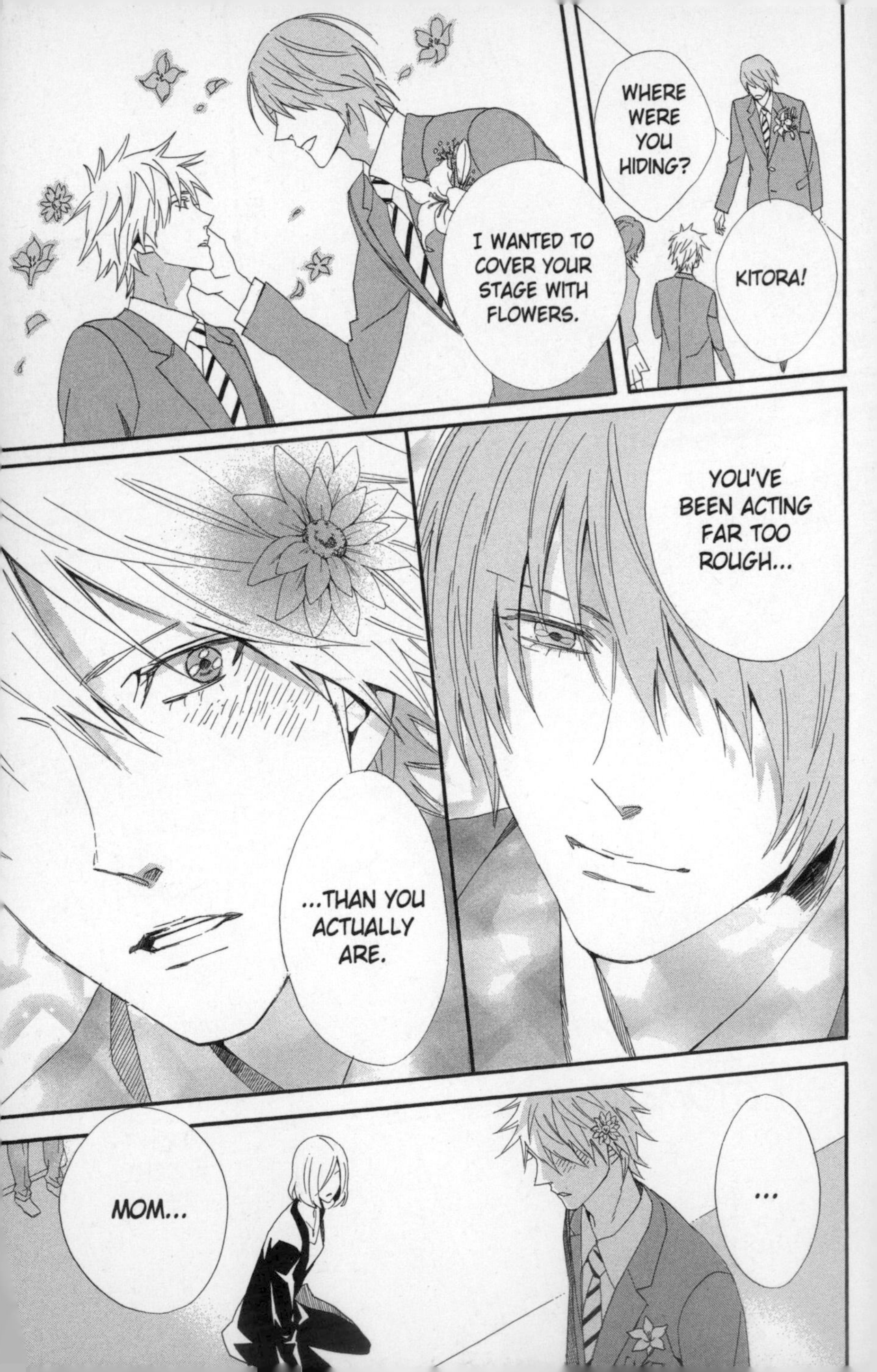
WHERE WERE YOU HIDING?
KITORA!
I WANTED TO COVER YOUR STAGE WITH FLOWERS.
YOU'VE BEEN ACTING FAR TOO ROUGH...
...THAN YOU ACTUALLY ARE.
...
MOM...

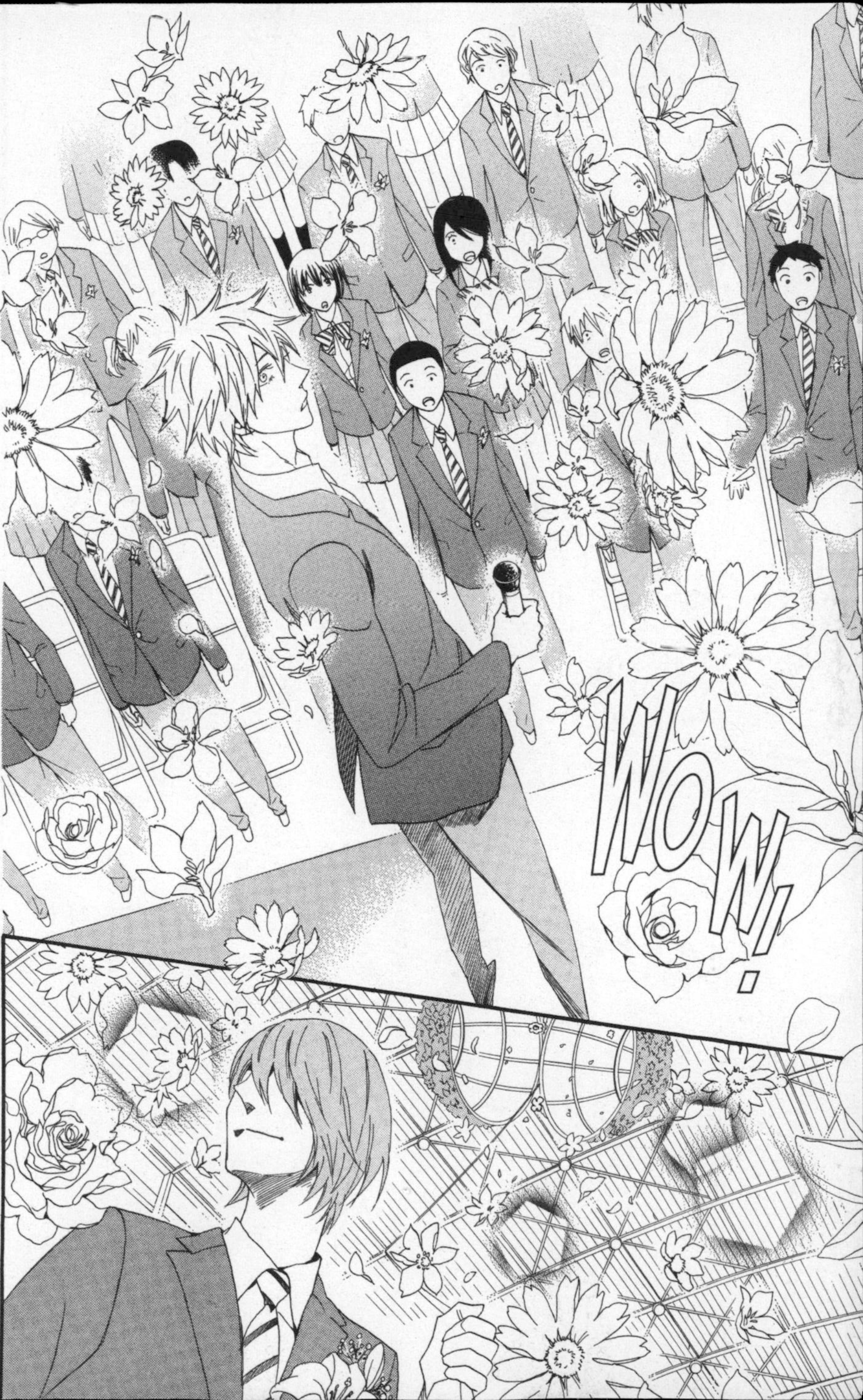
WOW!

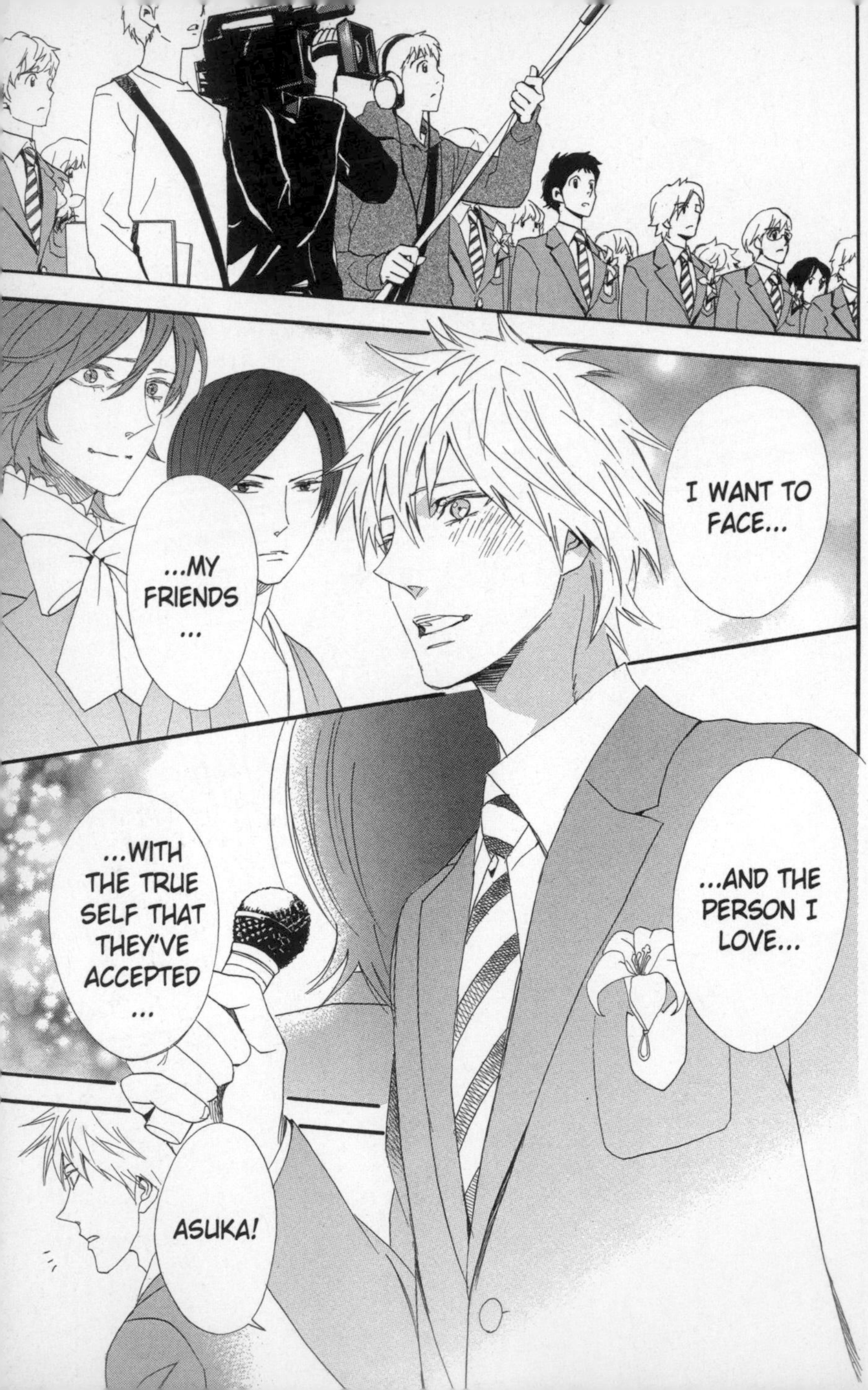
I WANT TO FACE...
...MY FRIENDS ...
...AND THE PERSON I LOVE...
...WITH THE TRUE SELF THAT THEY'VE ACCEPTED ...
ASUKA!

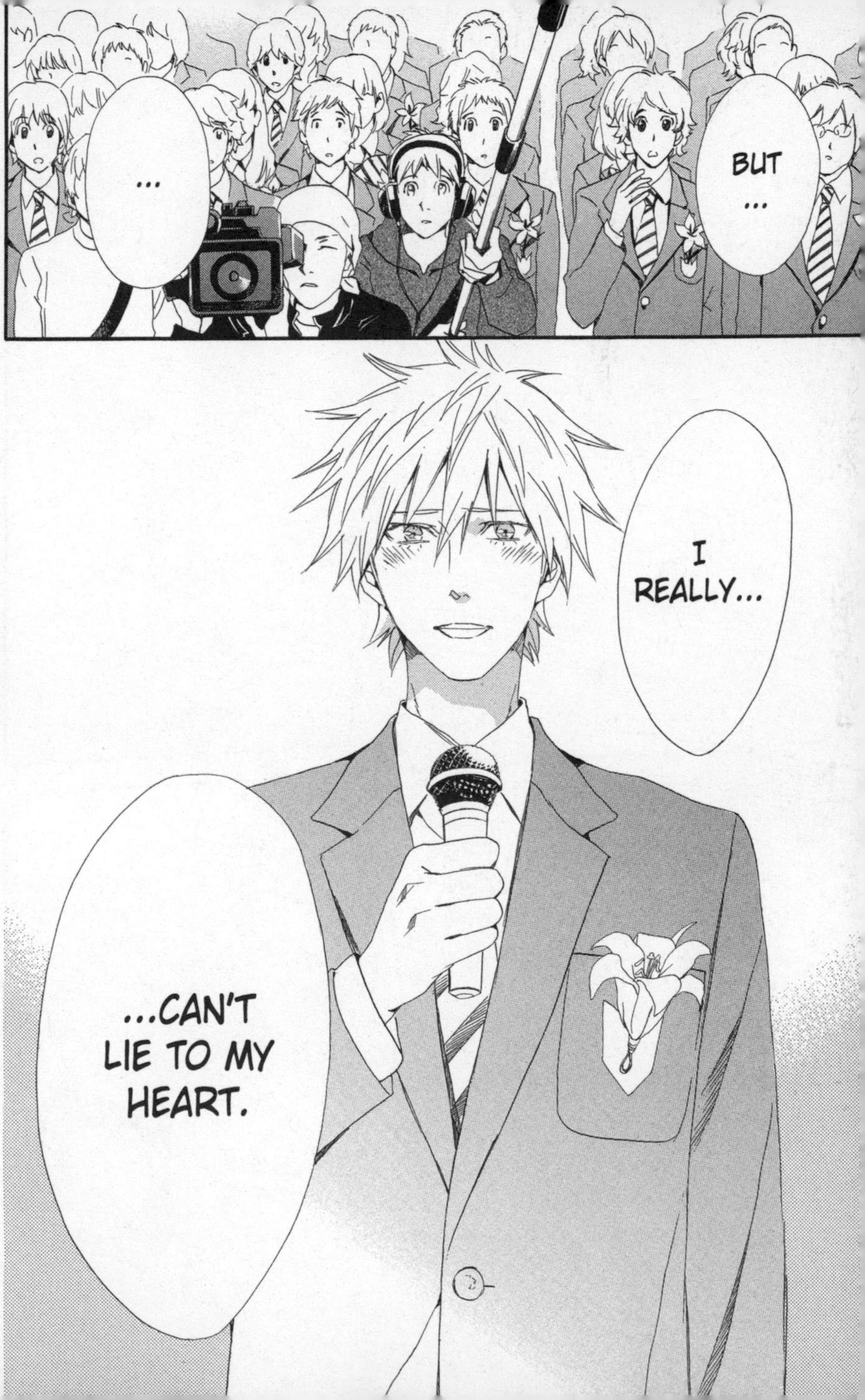
BUT ...
...
I REALLY...
...CAN'T LIE TO MY HEART.

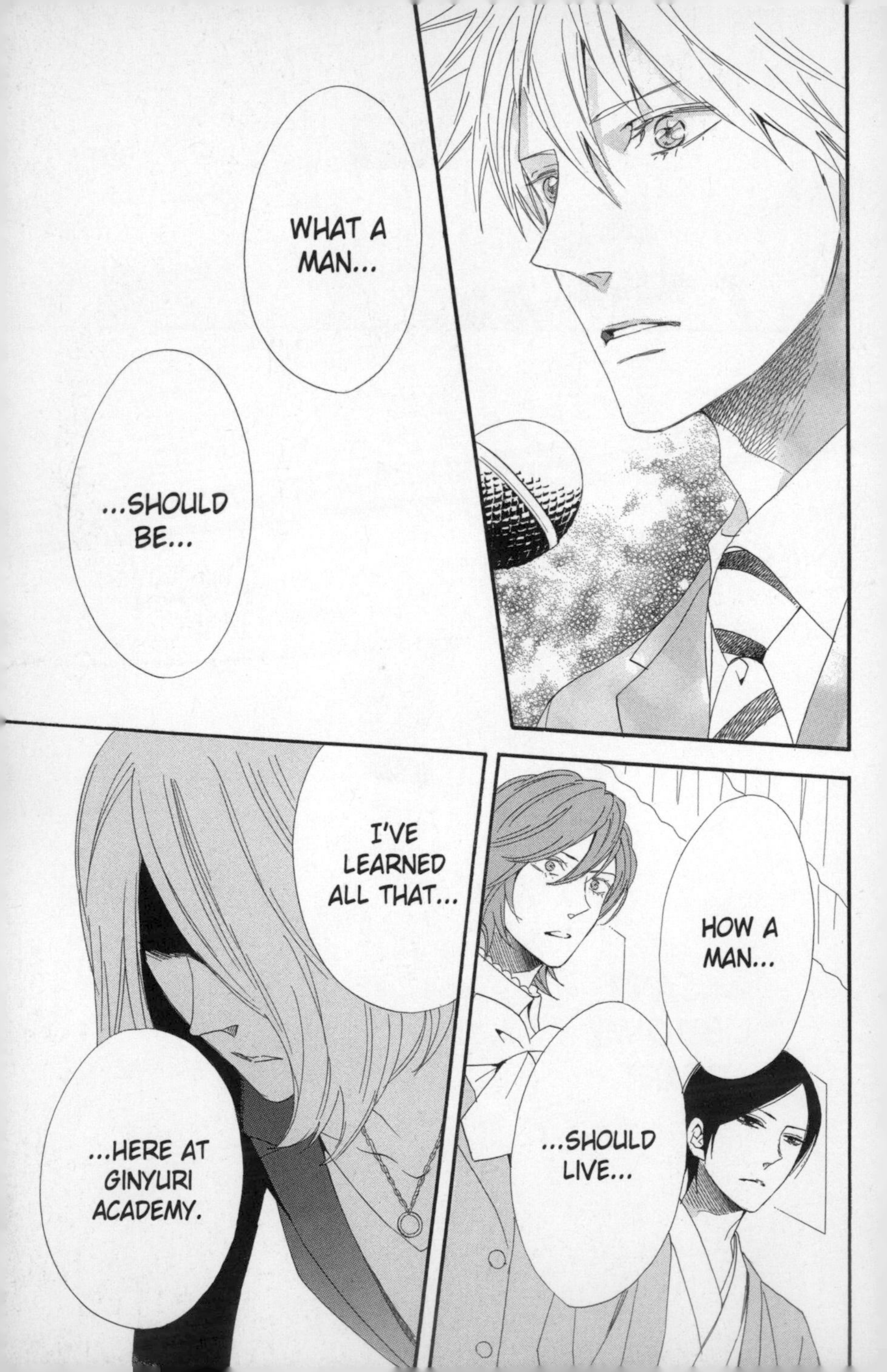
WHAT A MAN...
...SHOULD BE...
HOW A MAN...
...SHOULD LIVE...
I'VE LEARNED ALL THAT...
...HERE AT GINYURI ACADEMY.

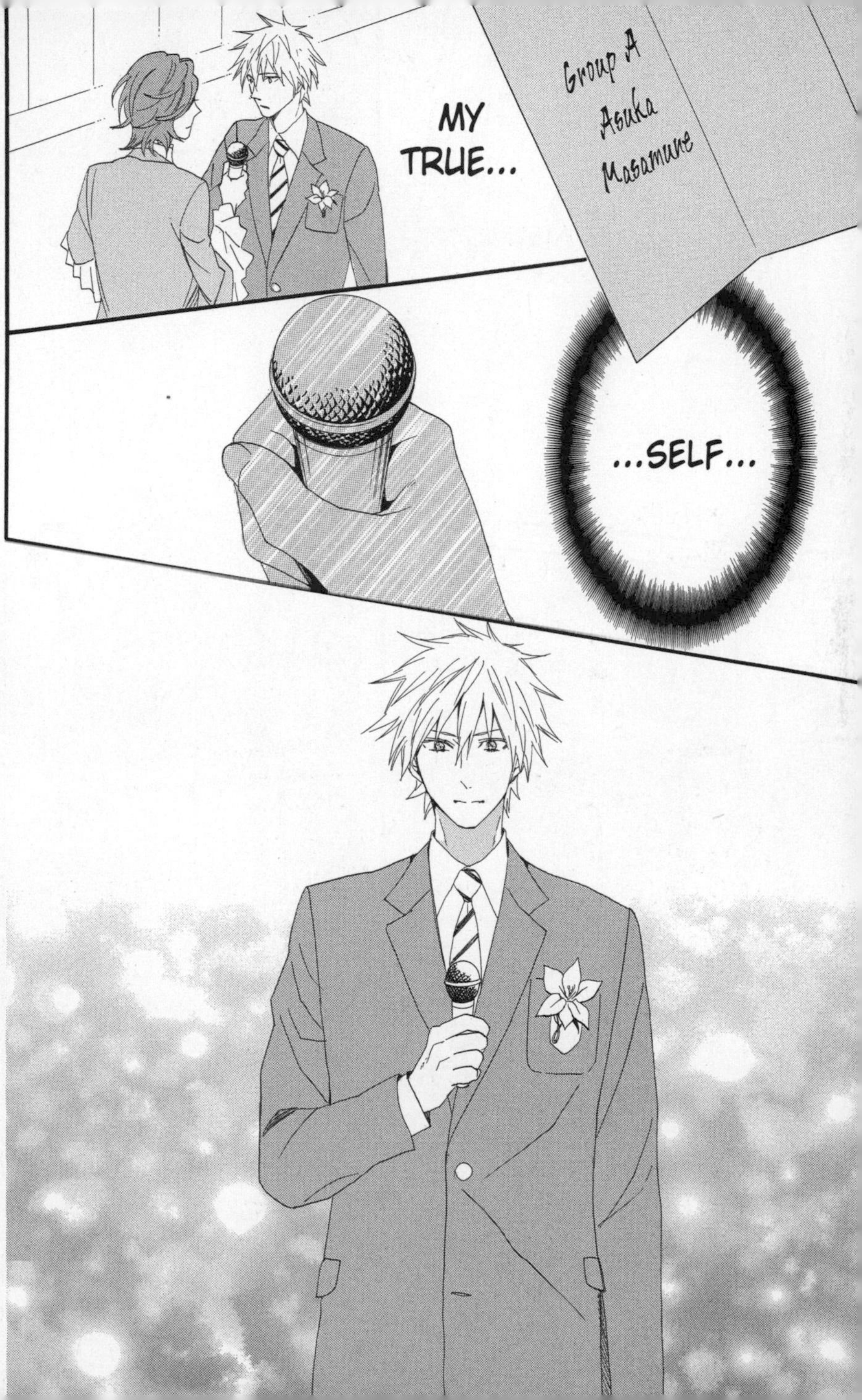
Group A
Asuka
Masamune
MY TRUE...
...SELF...

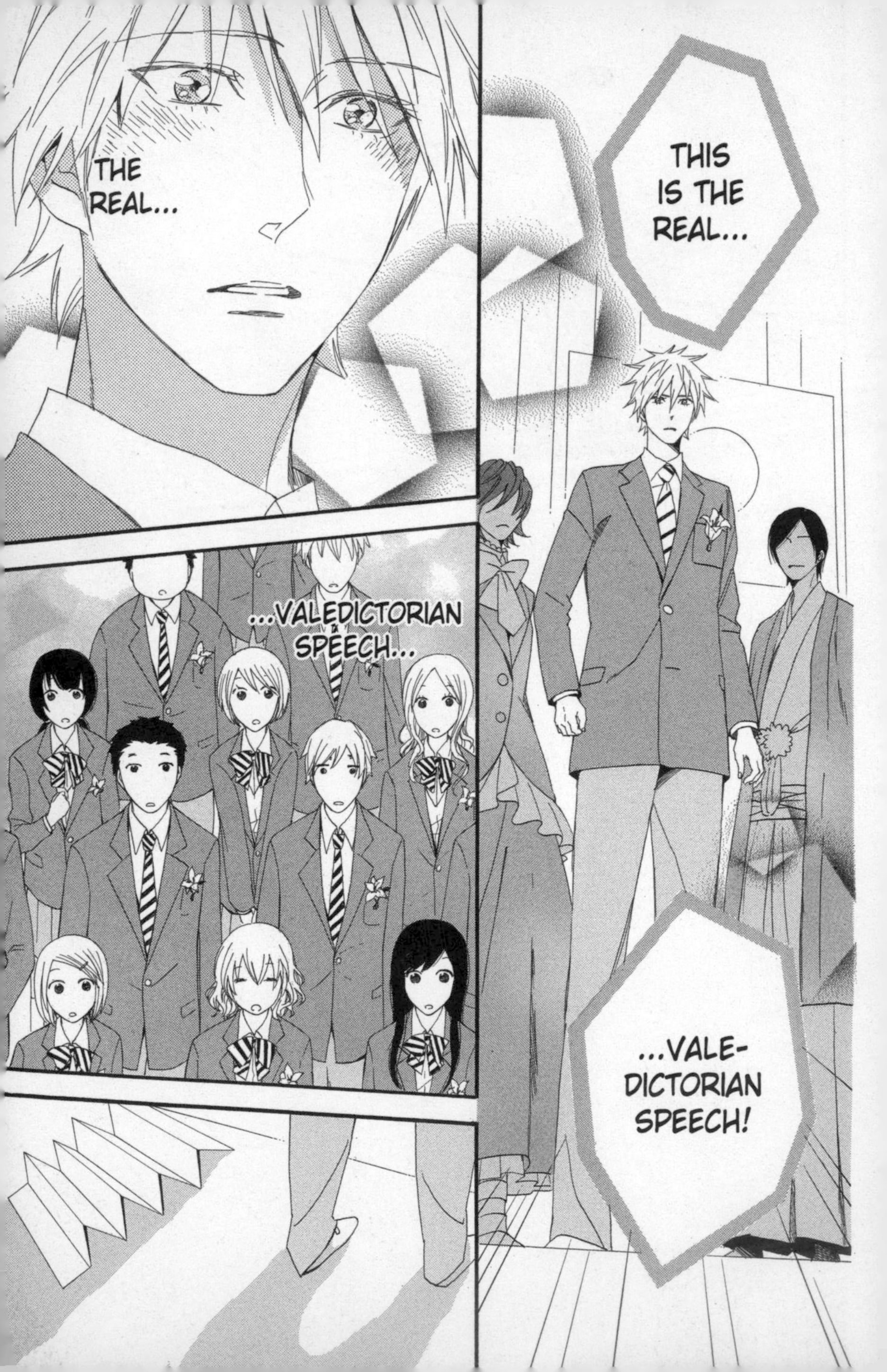
THIS IS THE REAL...
...VALE-DICTORIAN SPEECH!
THE REAL...
...VALEDICTORIAN SPEECH...

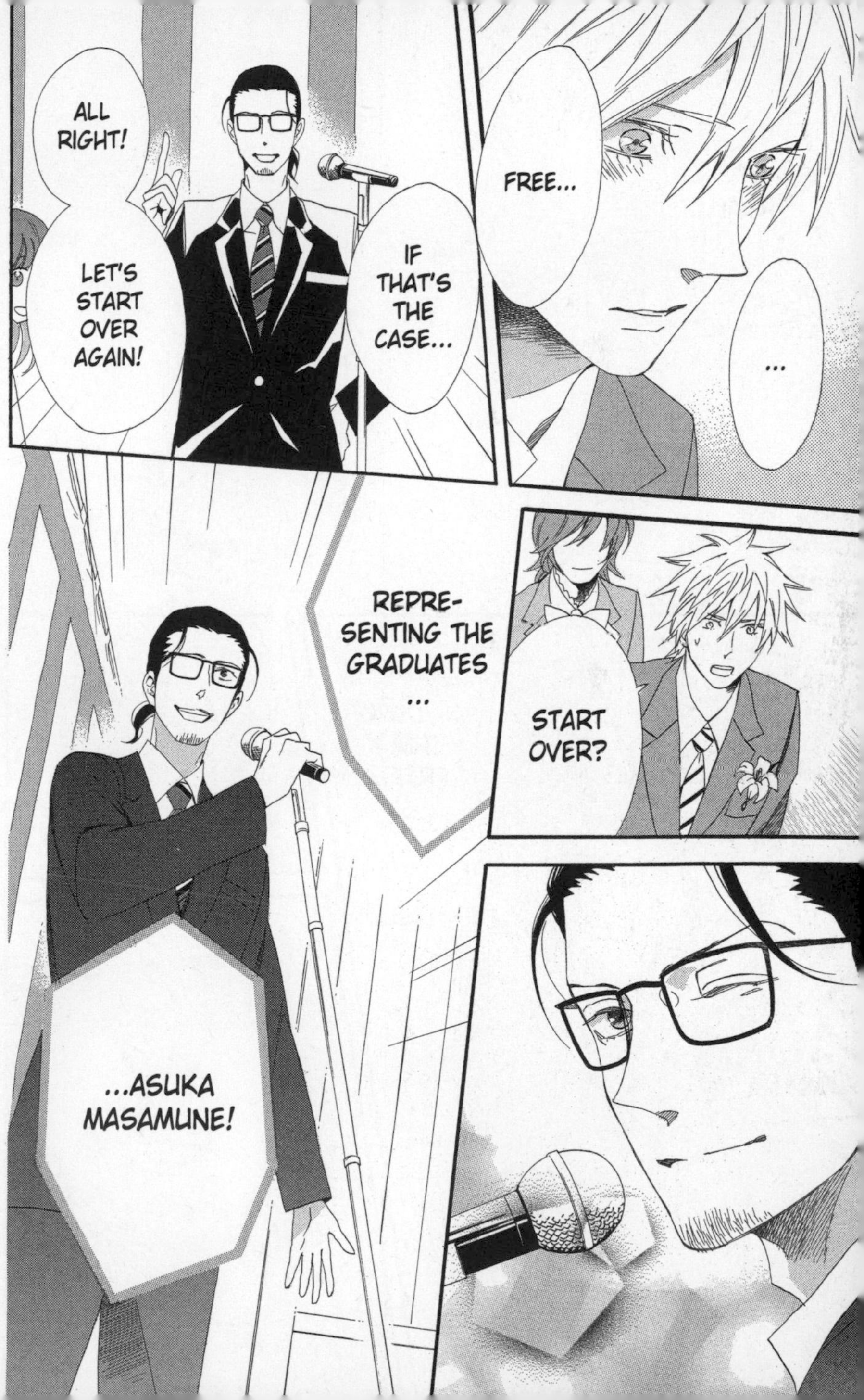
FREE...
...
IF THAT'S THE CASE...
ALL RIGHT!
LET'S START OVER AGAIN!
START OVER?
REPRESENTING THE GRADUATES...
...ASUKA MASAMUNE!

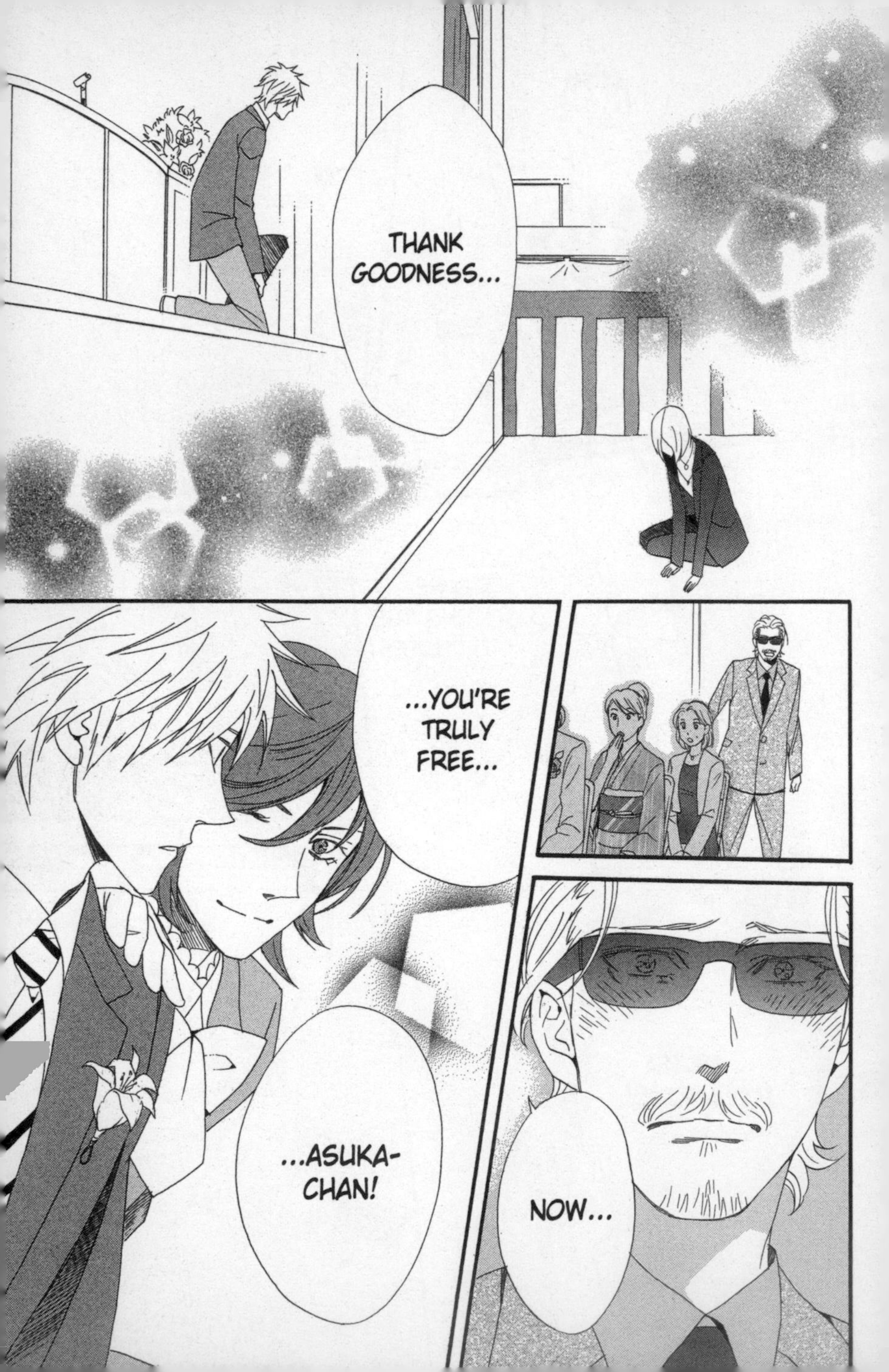
THANK GOODNESS...
NOW...
...YOU'RE TRULY FREE...
...ASUKA-CHAN!

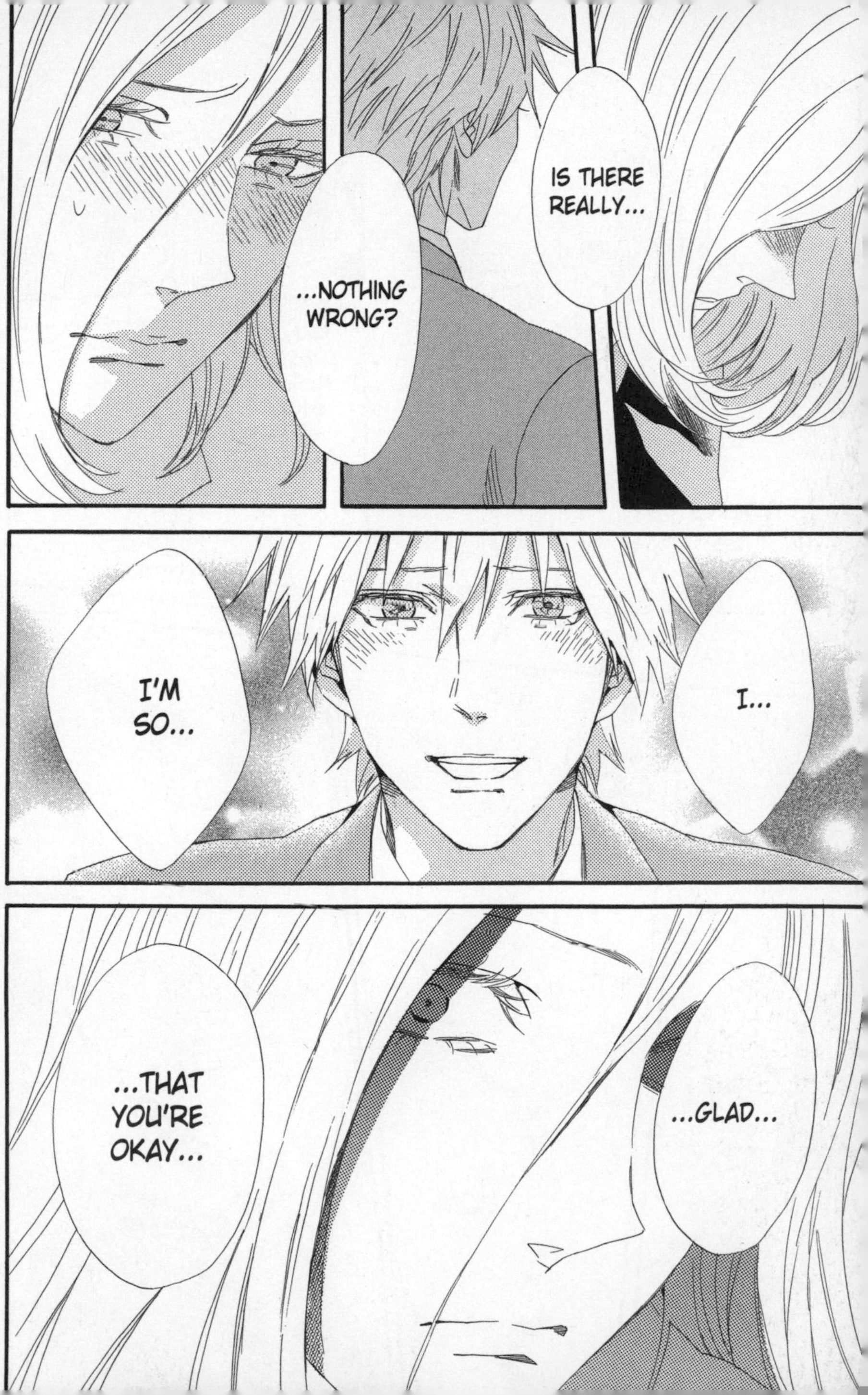
IS THERE REALLY...
...NOTHING WRONG?
I...
I'M SO...
...GLAD...
...THAT YOU'RE OKAY...

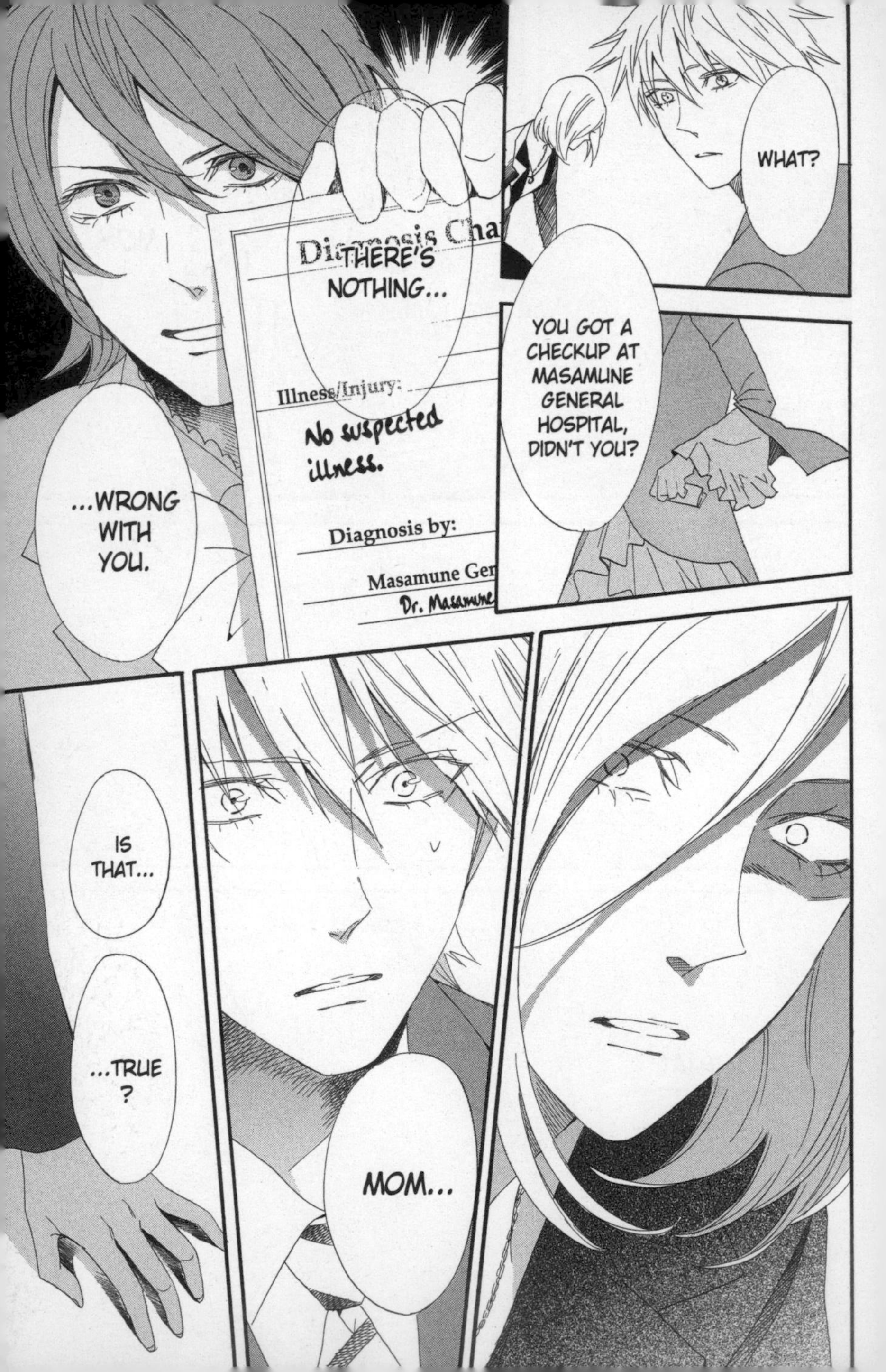
WHAT?
YOU GOT A CHECKUP AT MASAMUNE GENERAL HOSPITAL, DIDN'T YOU?
THERE'S NOTHING...
Illness/Injury:
No suspected illness.
Diagnosis by:
Masamune Gen
Dr. Masamune
...WRONG WITH YOU.
MOM...
IS THAT...
...TRUE?

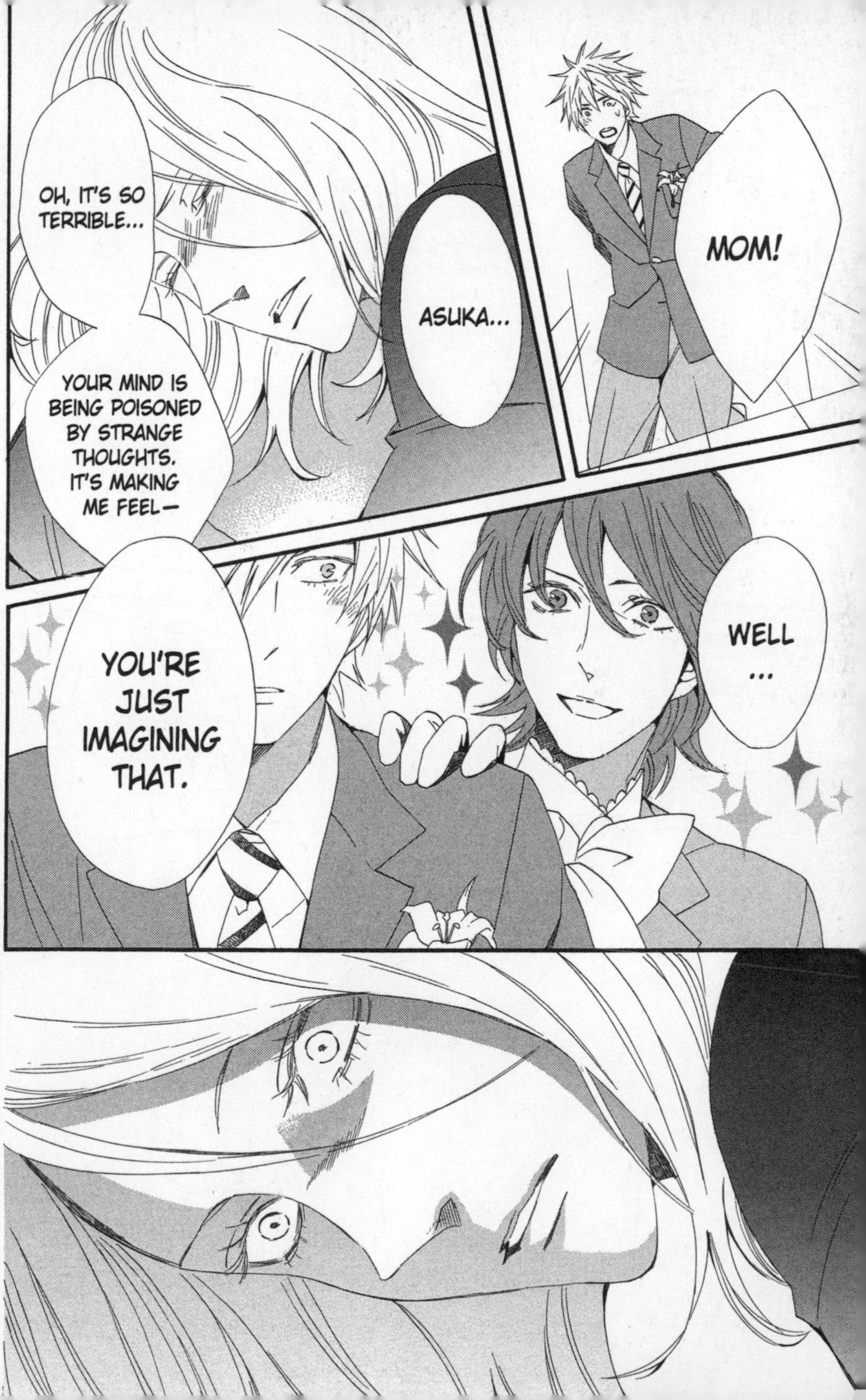
MOM!
ASUKA...
OH, IT'S SO TERRIBLE...
YOUR MIND IS BEING POISONED BY STRANGE THOUGHTS. IT'S MAKING ME FEEL—
WELL ...
YOU'RE JUST IMAGINING THAT.

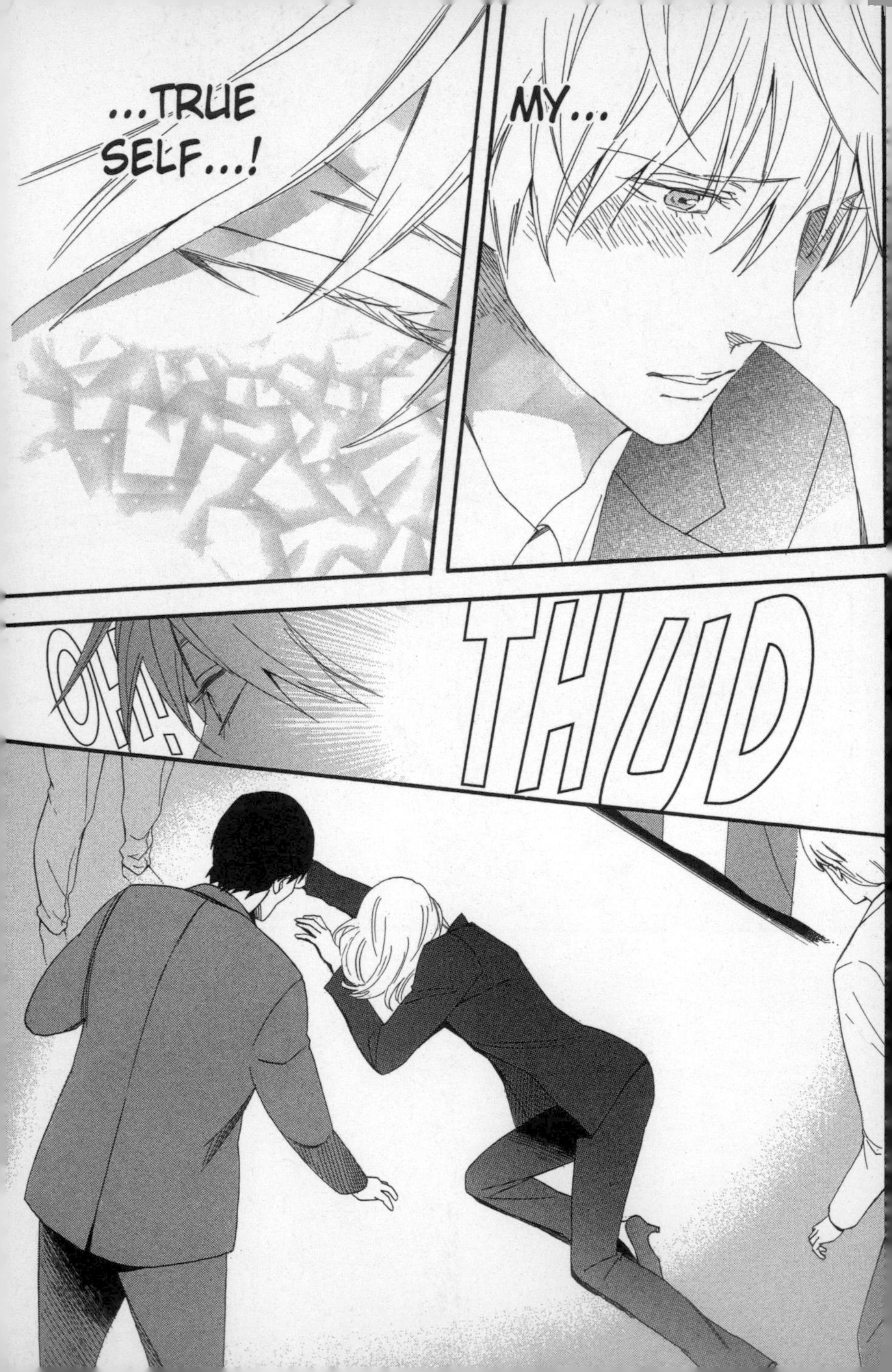
MY...
...TRUE SELF...!
THUD
OH!

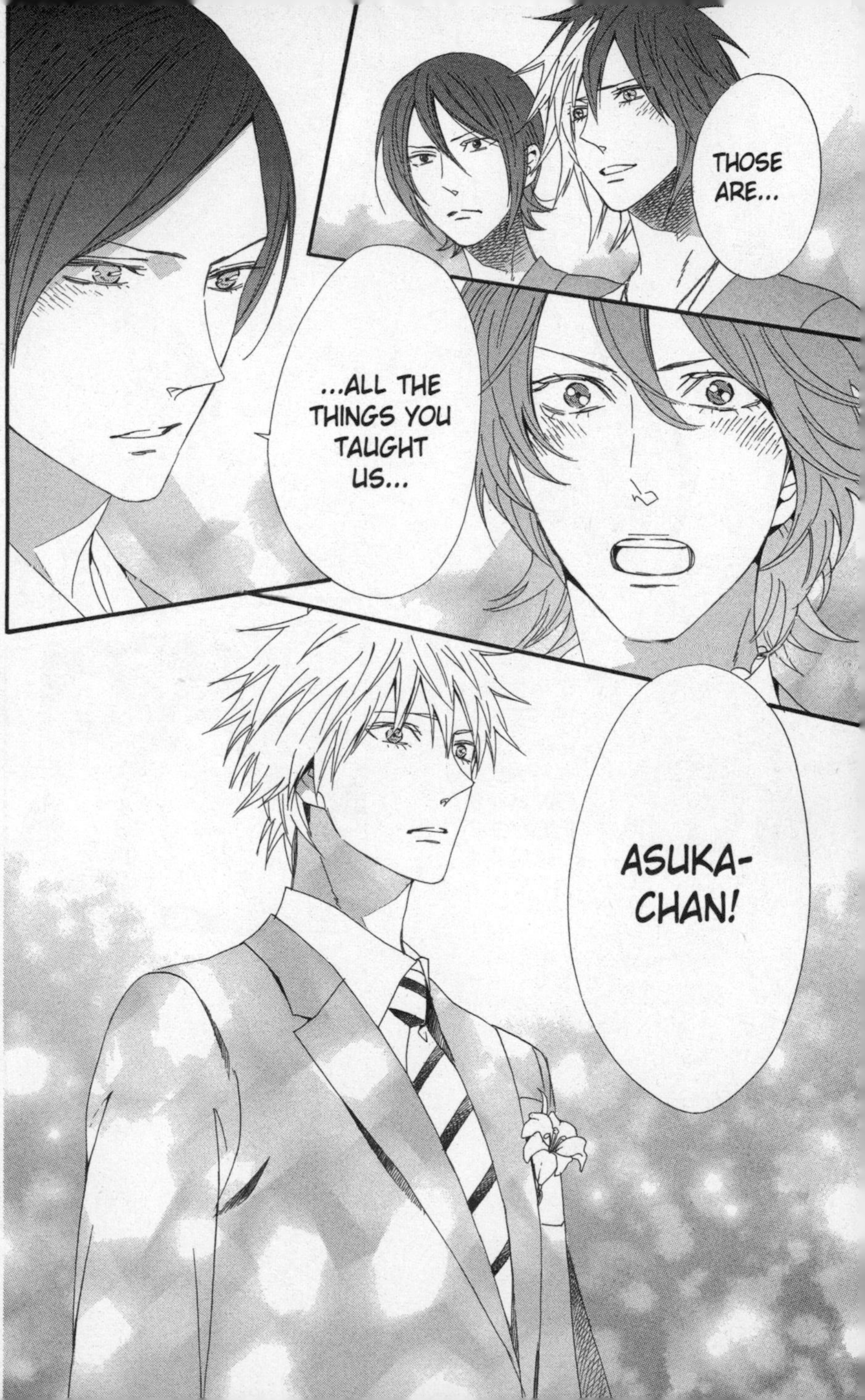
THOSE ARE...
...ALL THE THINGS YOU TAUGHT US...
ASUKA-CHAN!

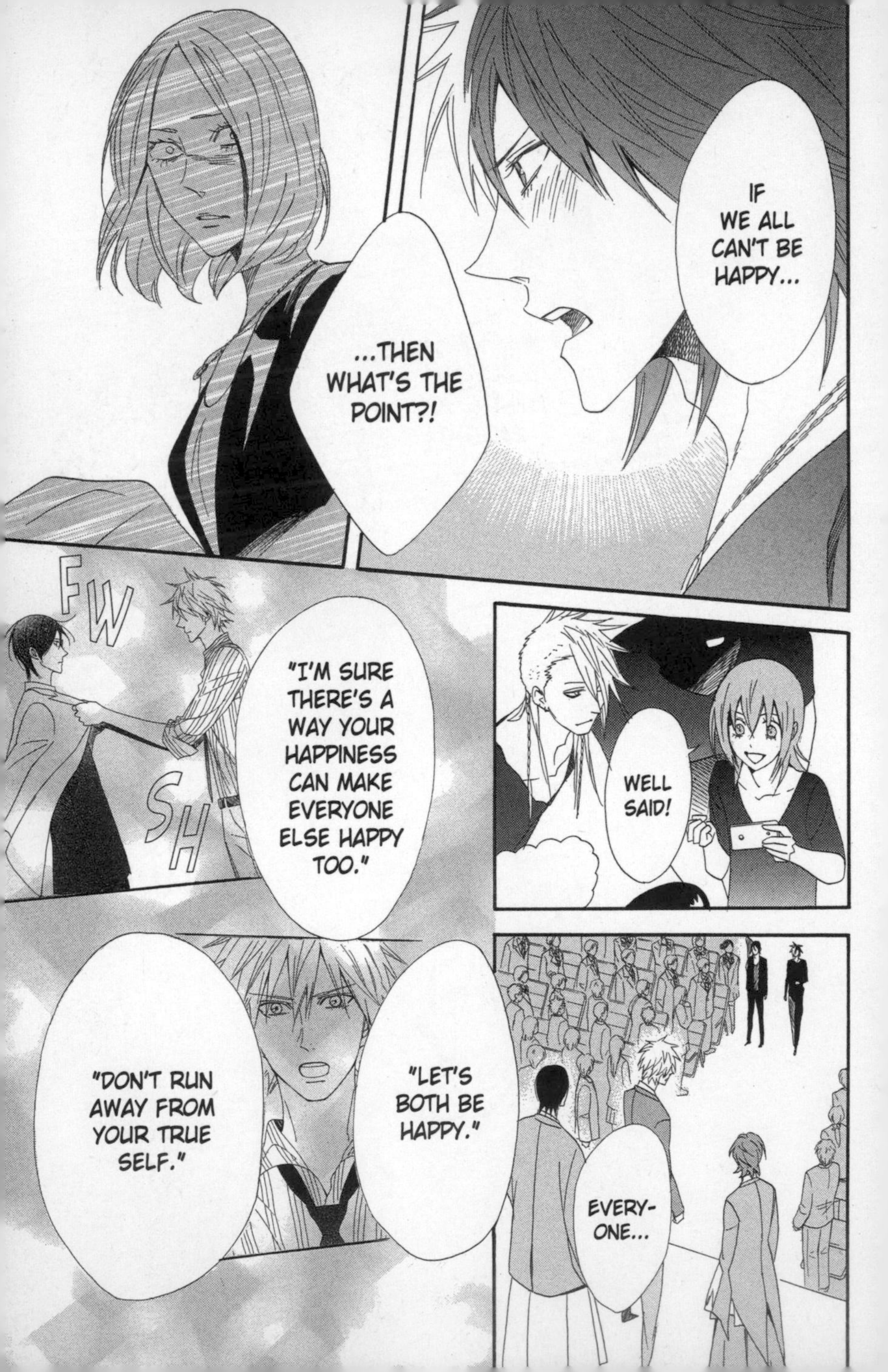
IF WE ALL CAN'T BE HAPPY...
...THEN WHAT'S THE POINT?!
WELL SAID!
FW
SH
"I'M SURE THERE'S A WAY YOUR HAPPINESS CAN MAKE EVERYONE ELSE HAPPY TOO."
EVERY-ONE...
"LET'S BOTH BE HAPPY."
"DON'T RUN AWAY FROM YOUR TRUE SELF."

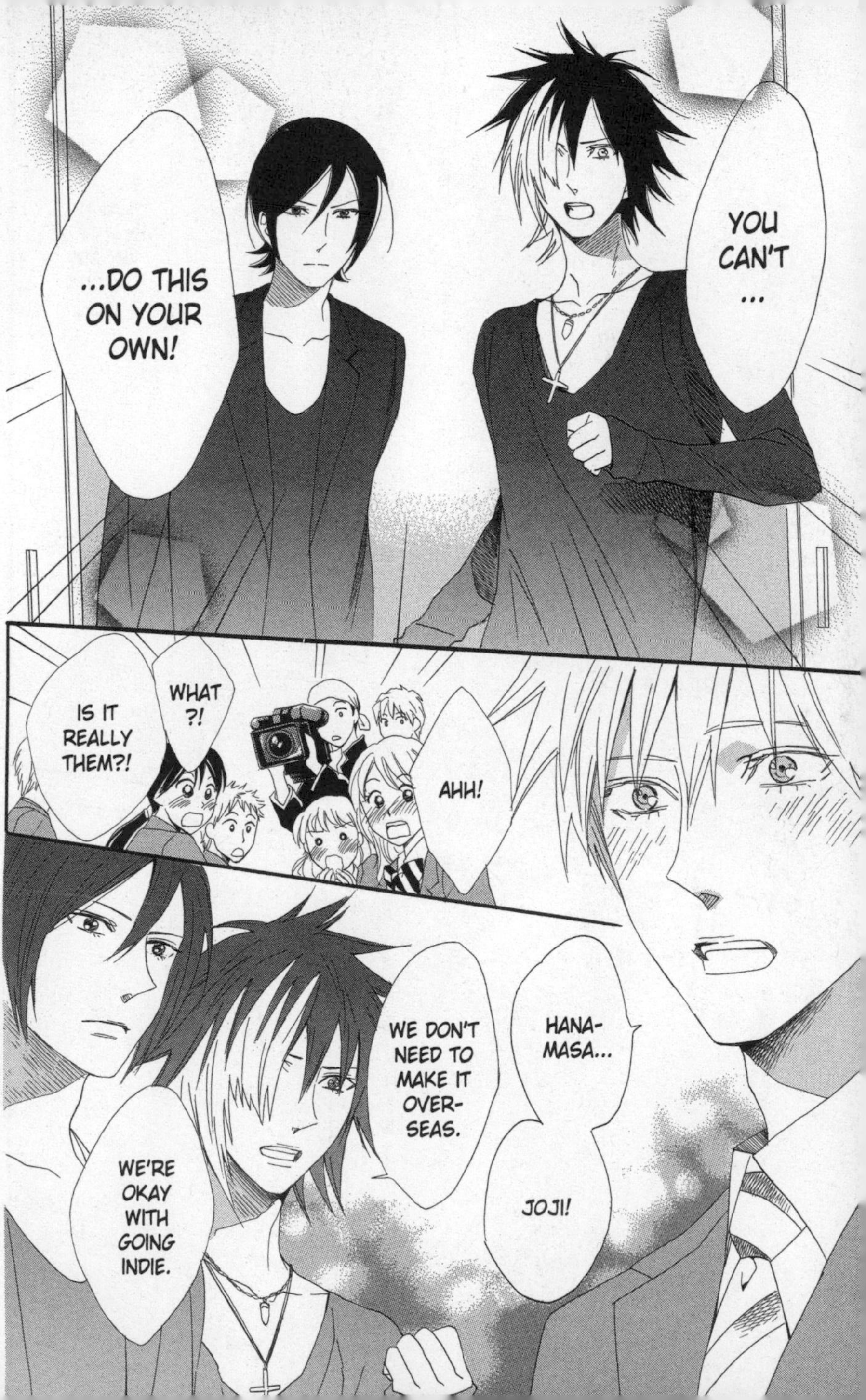
YOU CAN'T ...
...DO THIS ON YOUR OWN!
AHH!
WHAT?!
IS IT REALLY THEM?!
HANA-MASA...
JOJI!
WE DON'T NEED TO MAKE IT OVER-SEAS.
WE'RE OKAY WITH GOING INDIE.

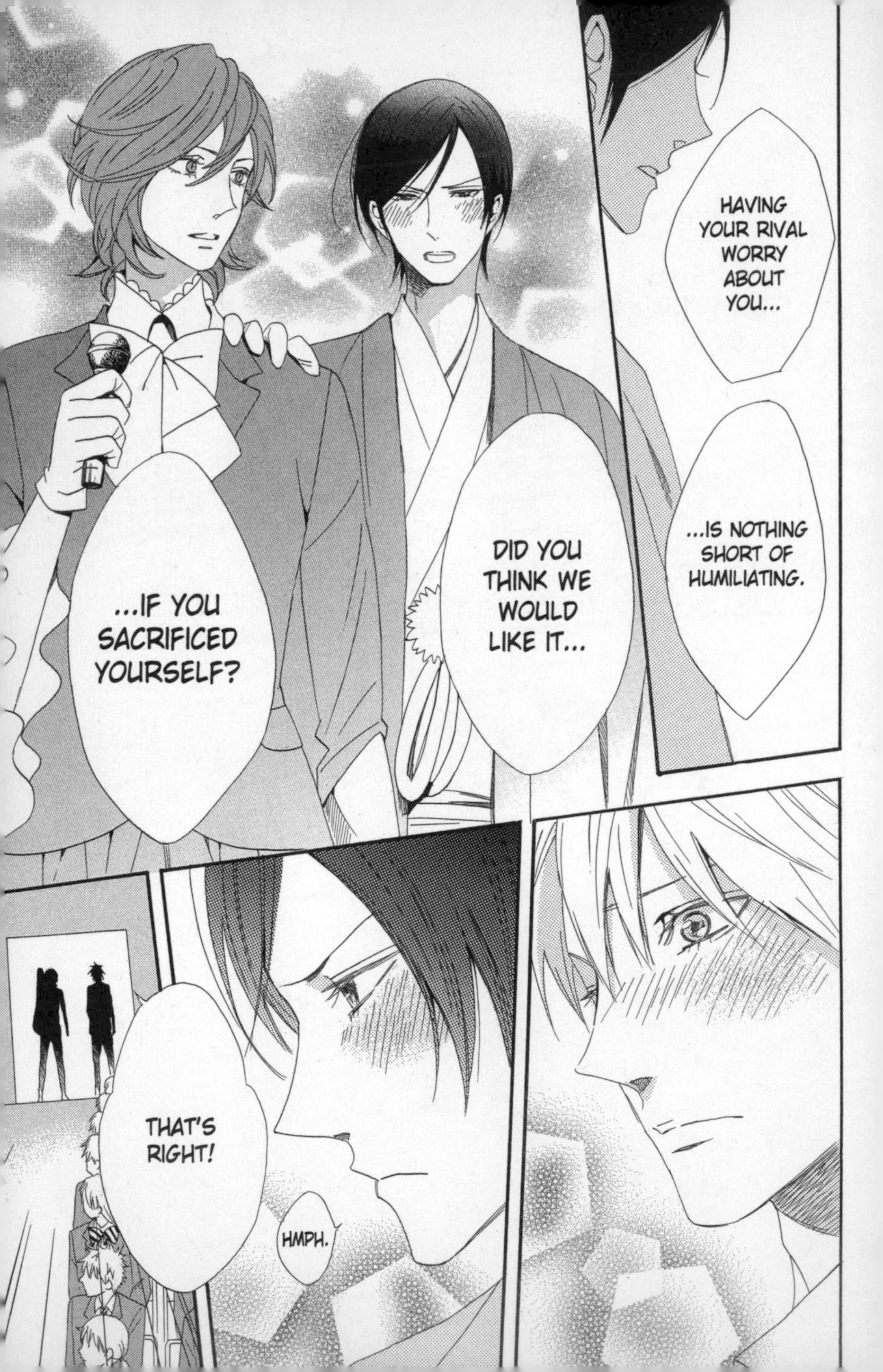
HAVING YOUR RIVAL WORRY ABOUT YOU...
...IS NOTHING SHORT OF HUMILIATING.
DID YOU THINK WE WOULD LIKE IT...
...IF YOU SACRIFICED YOURSELF?
HMPH.
THAT'S RIGHT!

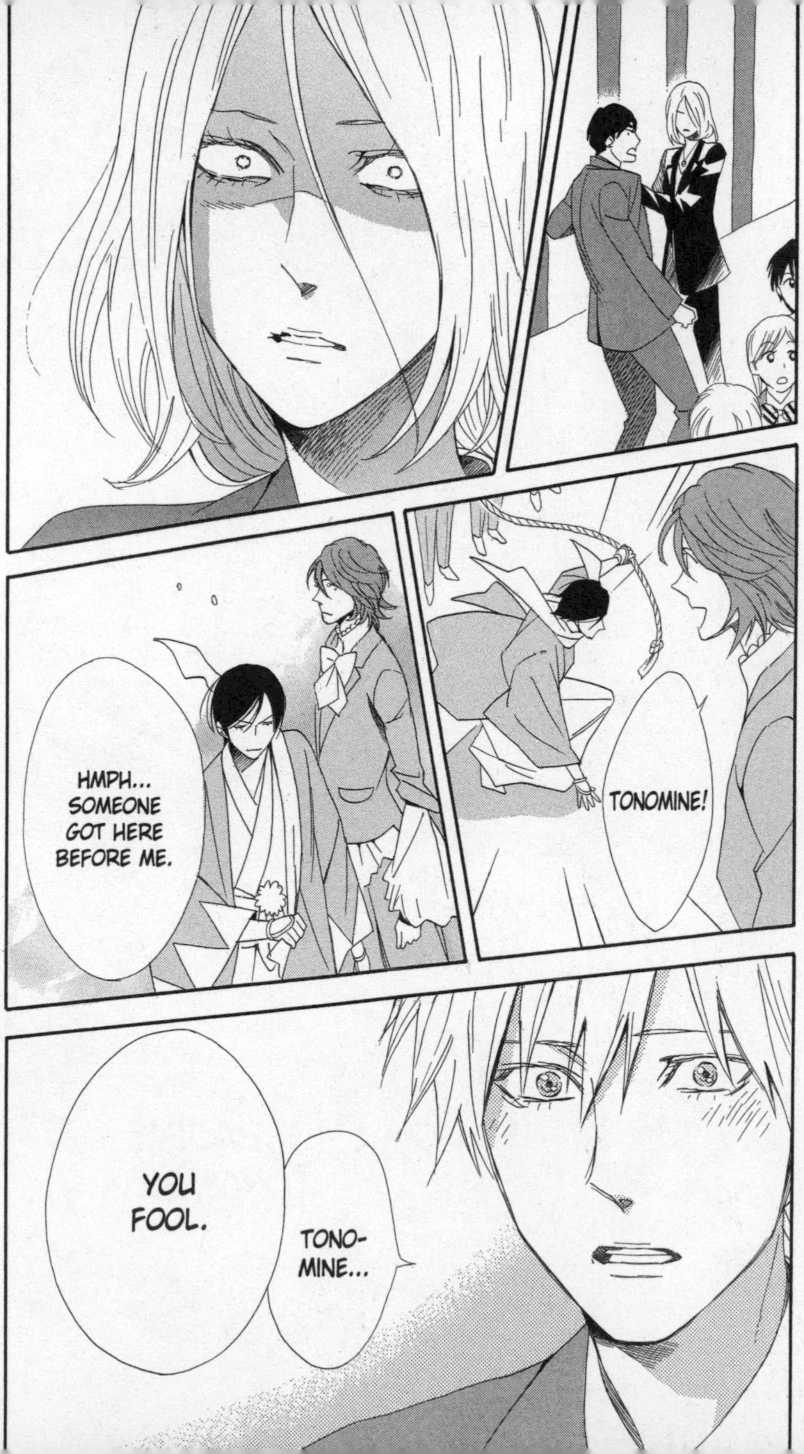
TONOMINE!
HMPH... SOMEONE GOT HERE BEFORE ME.
TONO-MINE...
YOU FOOL.

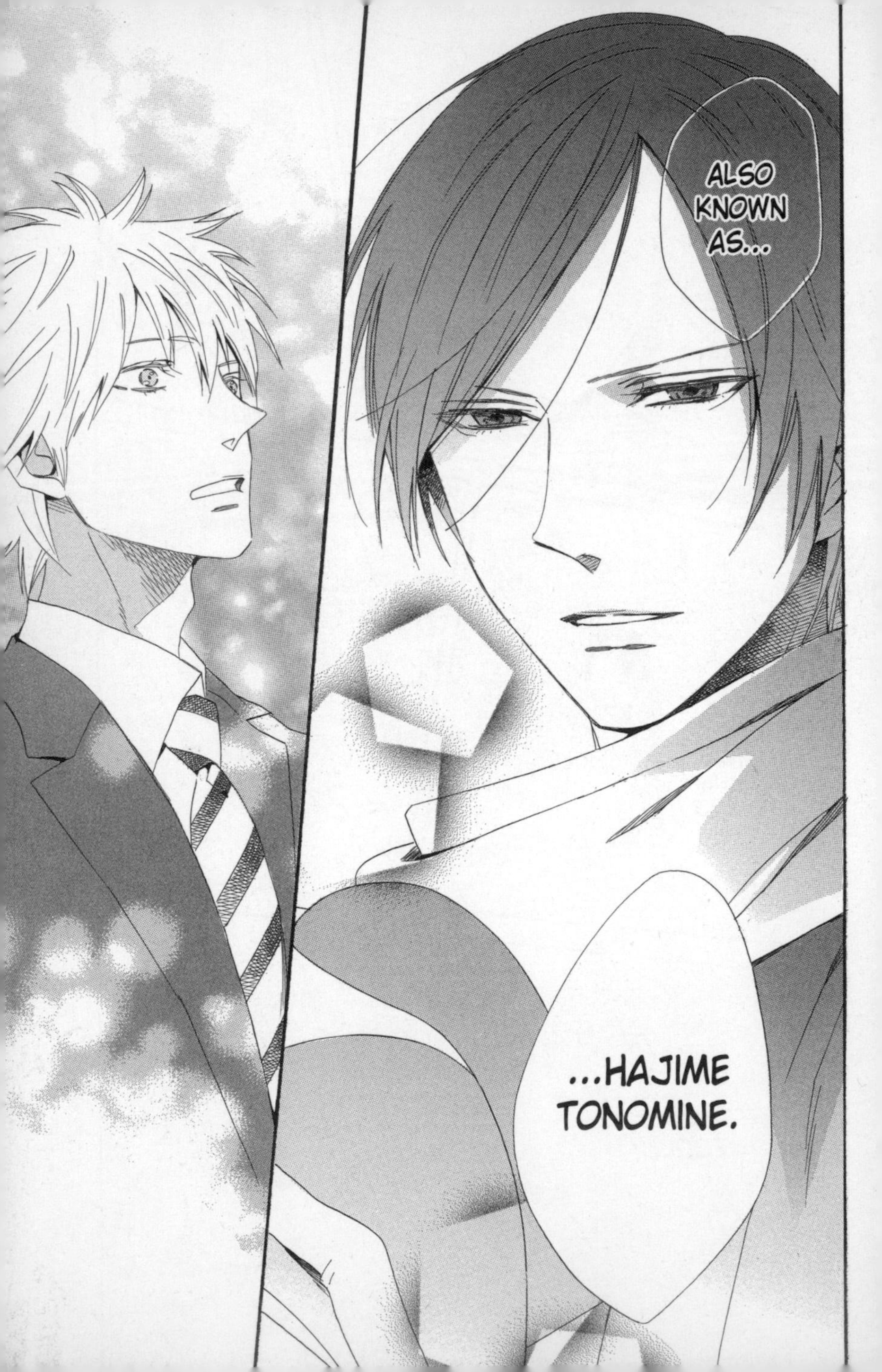
ALSO KNOWN AS...
...HAJIME TONOMINE.

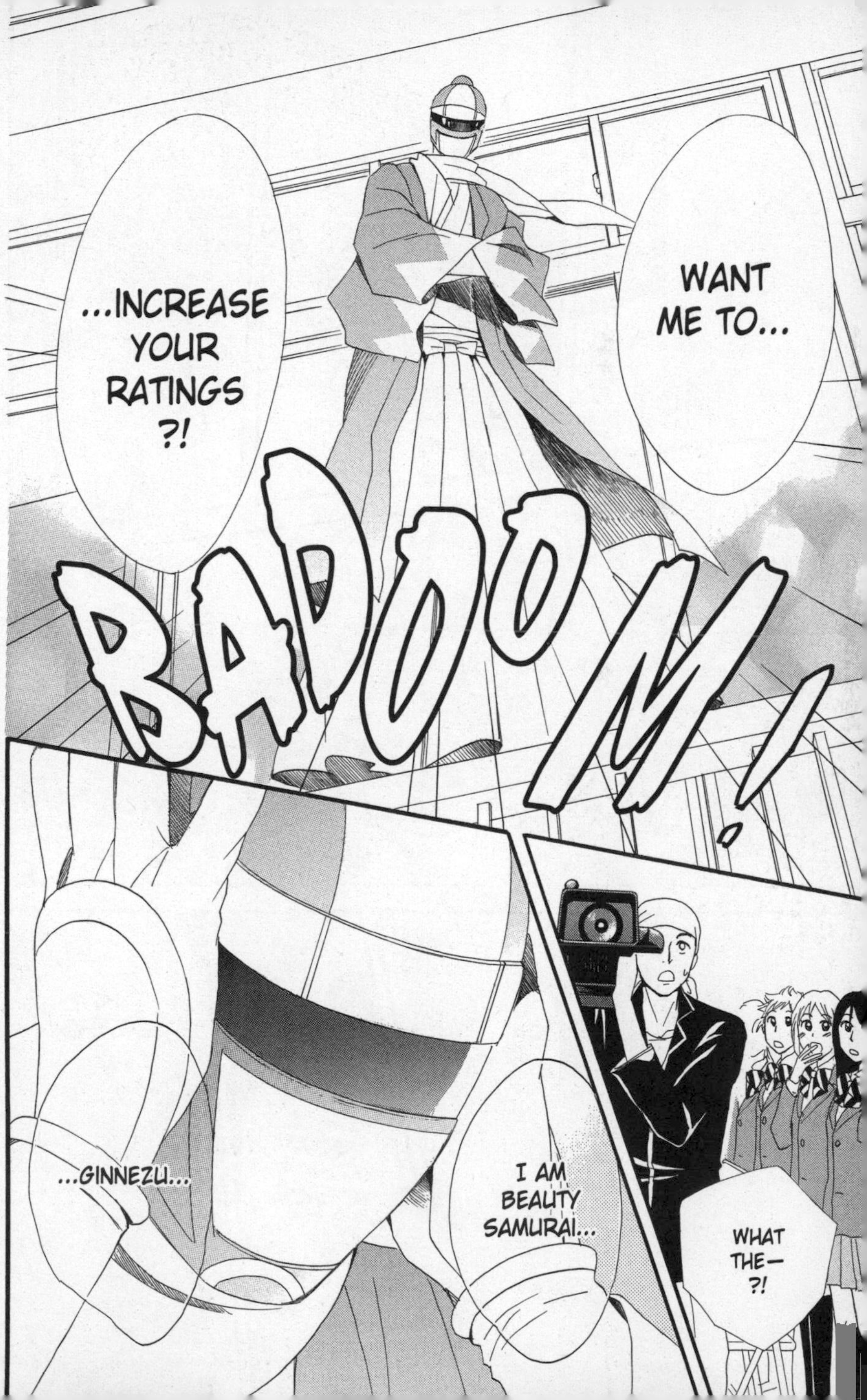
WANT ME TO...
...INCREASE YOUR RATINGS ?!
BADOOM!
WHAT THE— ?!
I AM BEAUTY SAMURAI...
...GINNEZU...

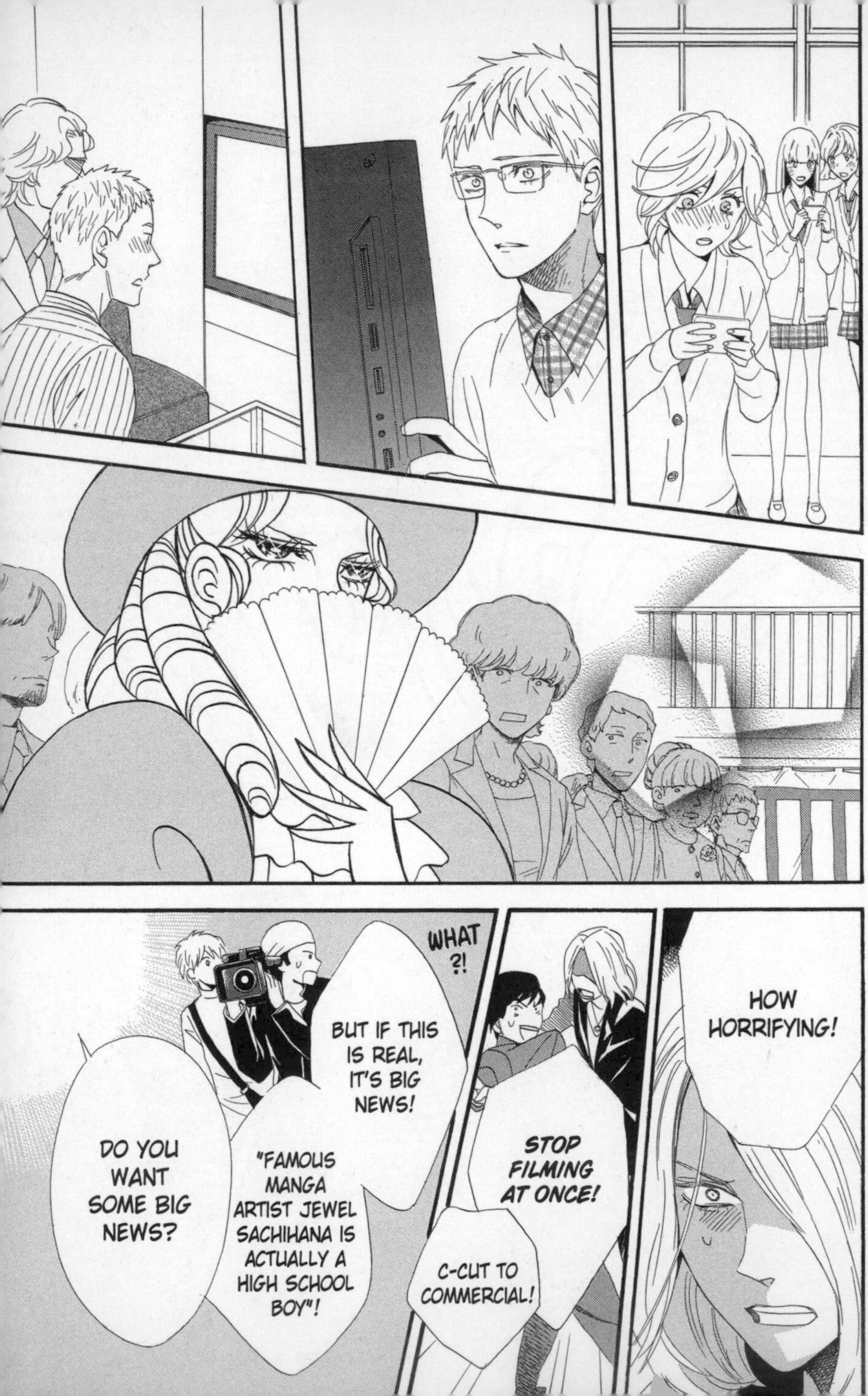
HOW HORRIFYING!
STOP FILMING AT ONCE!
C-CUT TO COMMERCIAL!
WHAT ?!
BUT IF THIS IS REAL, IT'S BIG NEWS!
"FAMOUS MANGA ARTIST JEWEL SACHIHANA IS ACTUALLY A HIGH SCHOOL BOY"!
DO YOU WANT SOME BIG NEWS?

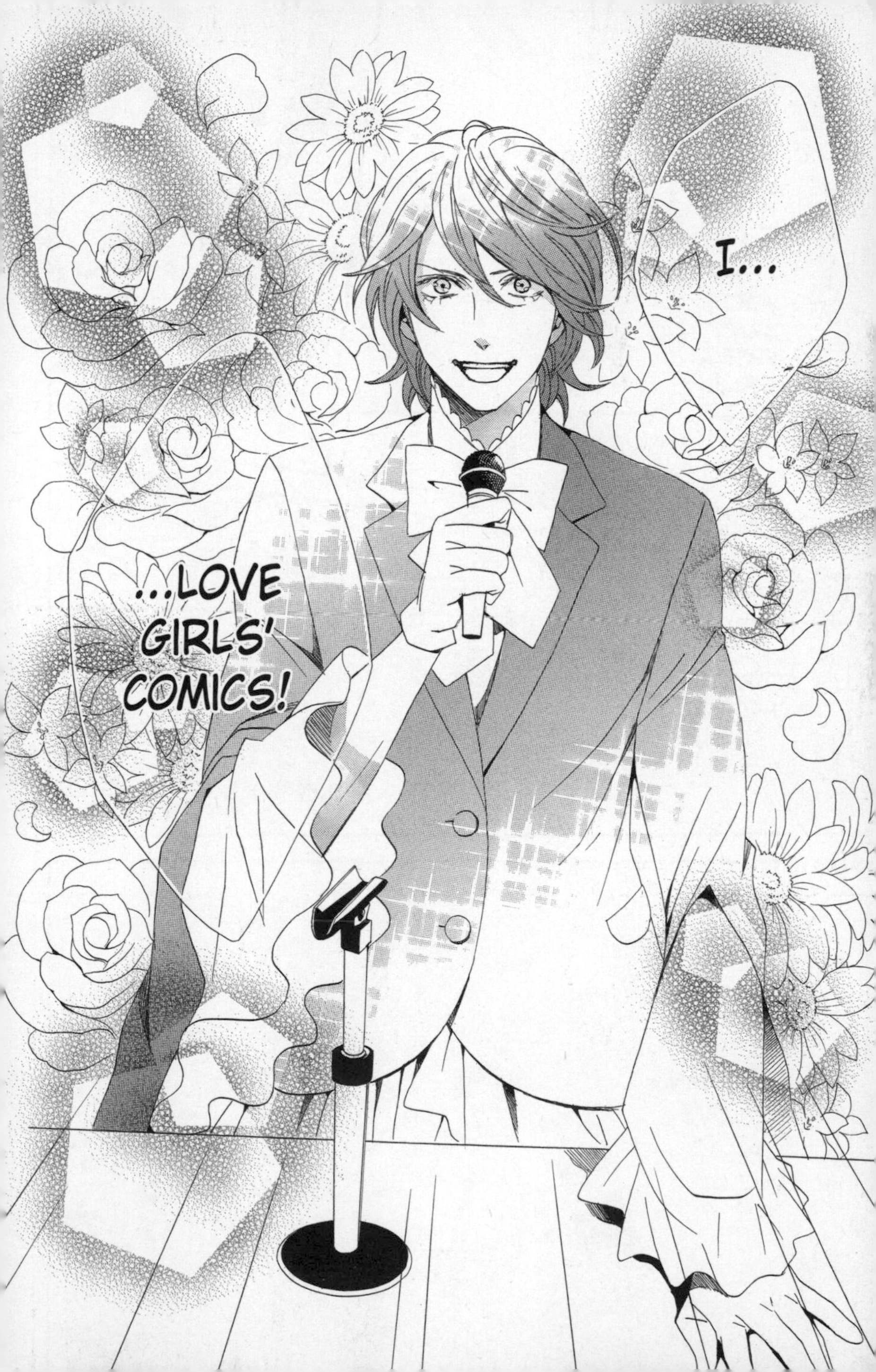
I...
...LOVE GIRLS' COMICS!

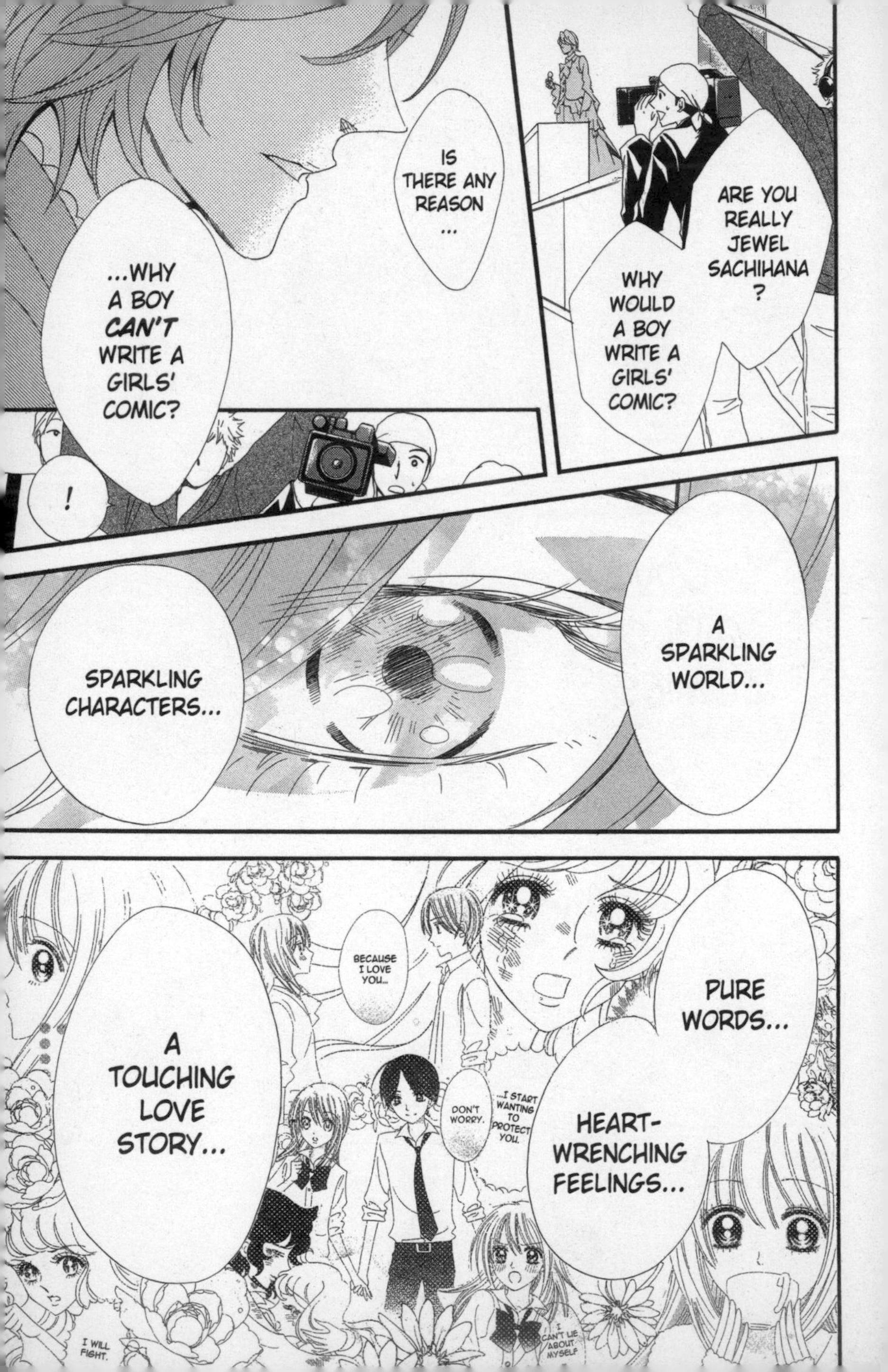
ARE YOU REALLY JEWEL SACHIHANA?
WHY WOULD A BOY WRITE A GIRLS' COMIC?
IS THERE ANY REASON...
...WHY A BOY *CAN'T* WRITE A GIRLS' COMIC?
!
A SPARKLING WORLD...
SPARKLING CHARACTERS...
PURE WORDS...
HEART-WRENCHING FEELINGS...
BECAUSE I LOVE YOU...
...I START WANTING TO PROTECT YOU.
DON'T WORRY.
A TOUCHING LOVE STORY...
I CAN'T LIE ABOUT MYSELF
I WILL FIGHT.

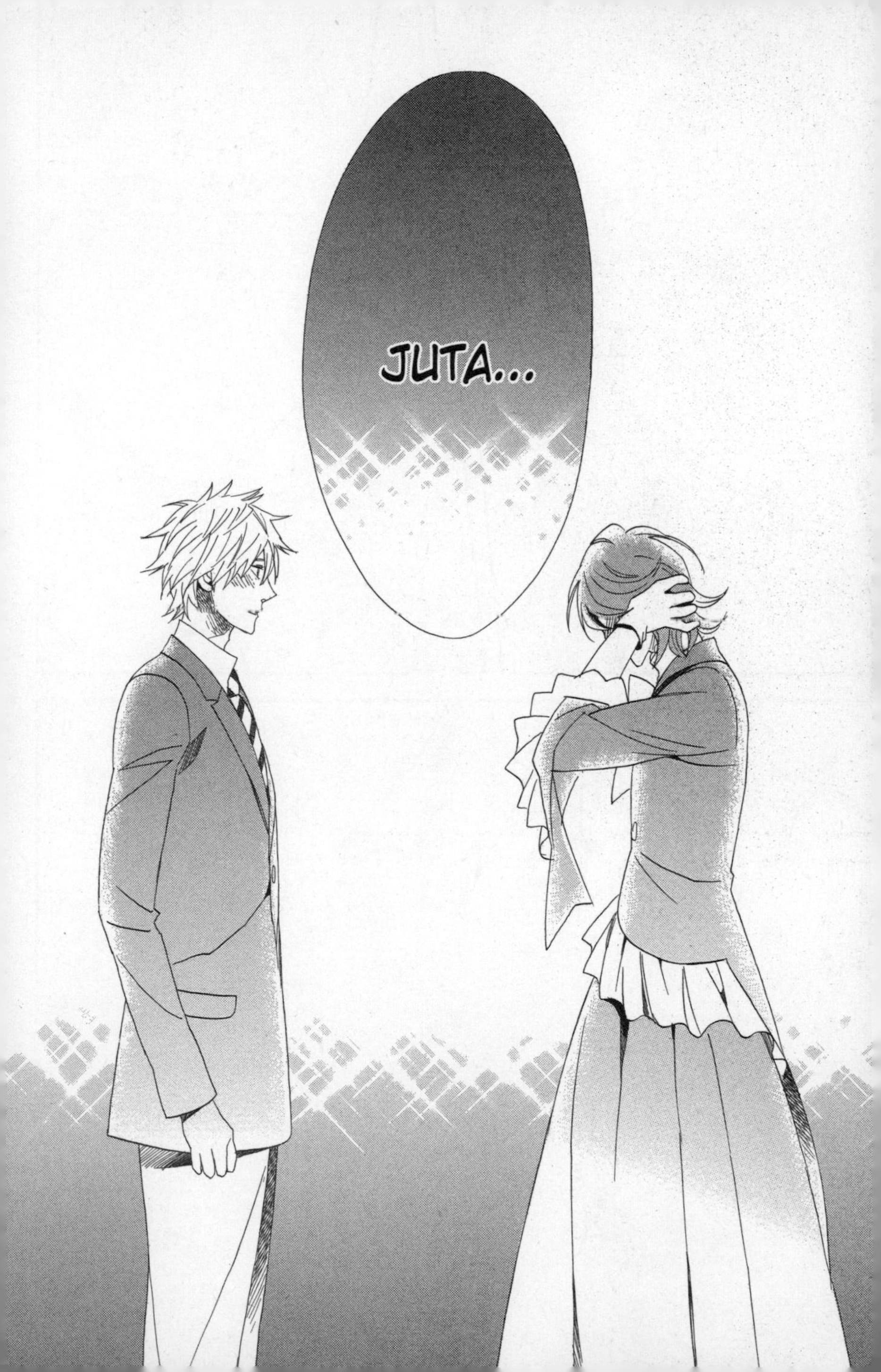
JUTA...

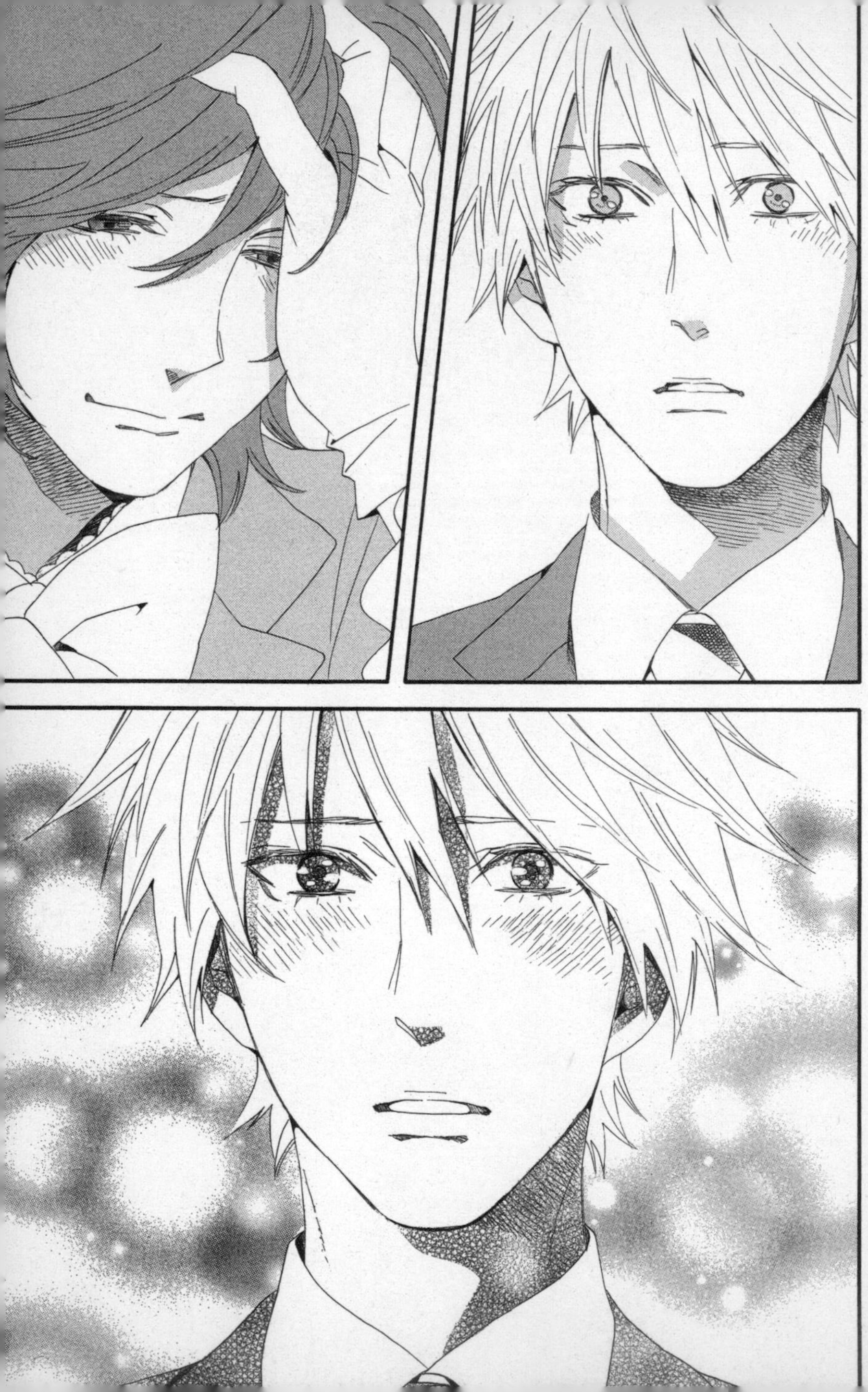

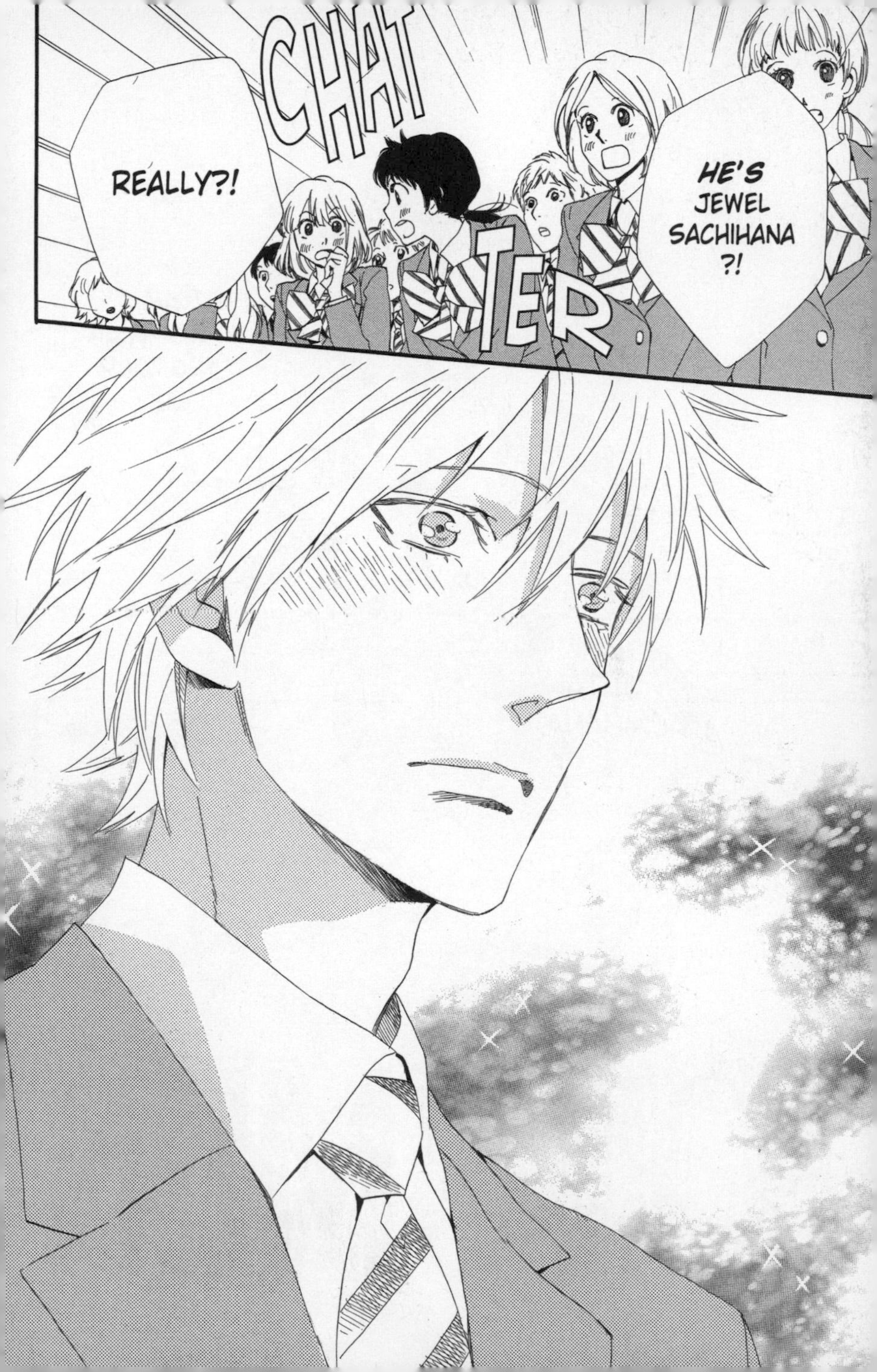
HE'S JEWEL SACHIHANA ?!
CHATTER
REALLY?!

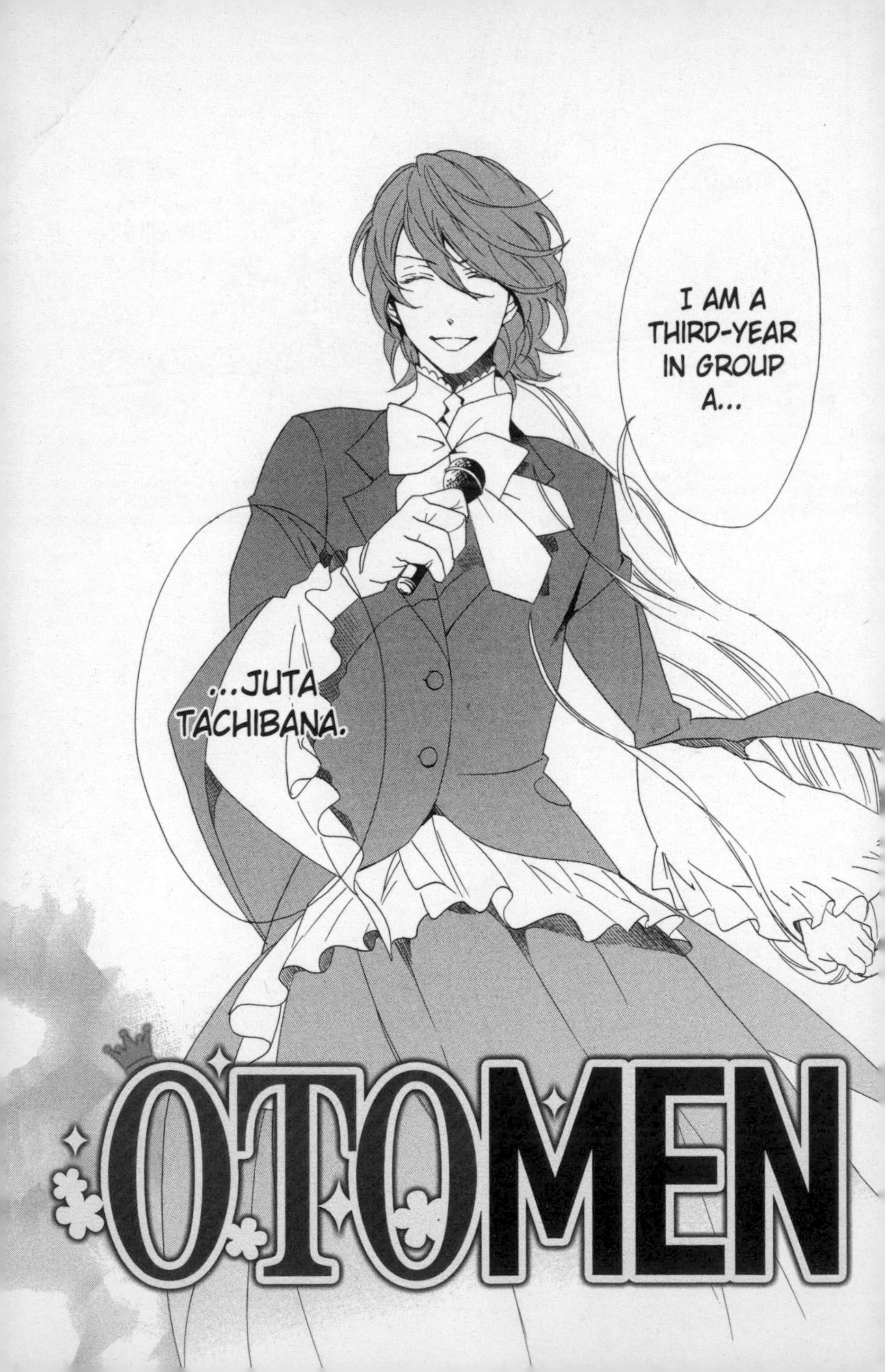
I AM A THIRD-YEAR IN GROUP A...
...JUTA TACHIBANA.
OTOMEN

OTOMEN

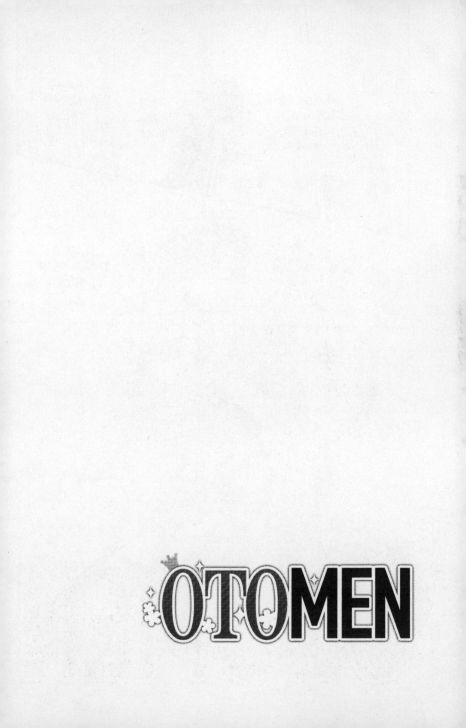

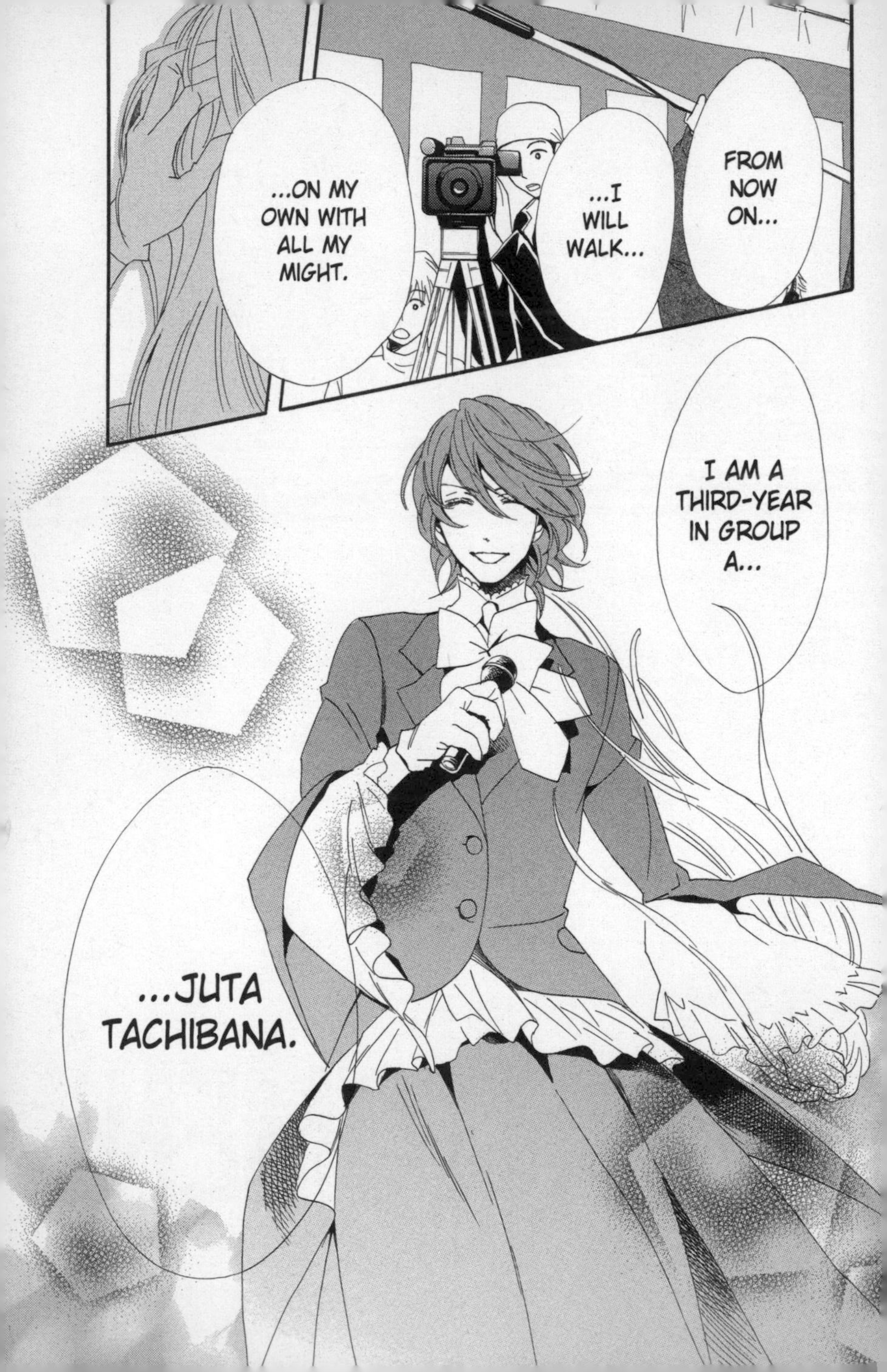
FROM NOW ON...
...I WILL WALK...
...ON MY OWN WITH ALL MY MIGHT.
I AM A THIRD-YEAR IN GROUP A...
...JUTA TACHIBANA.

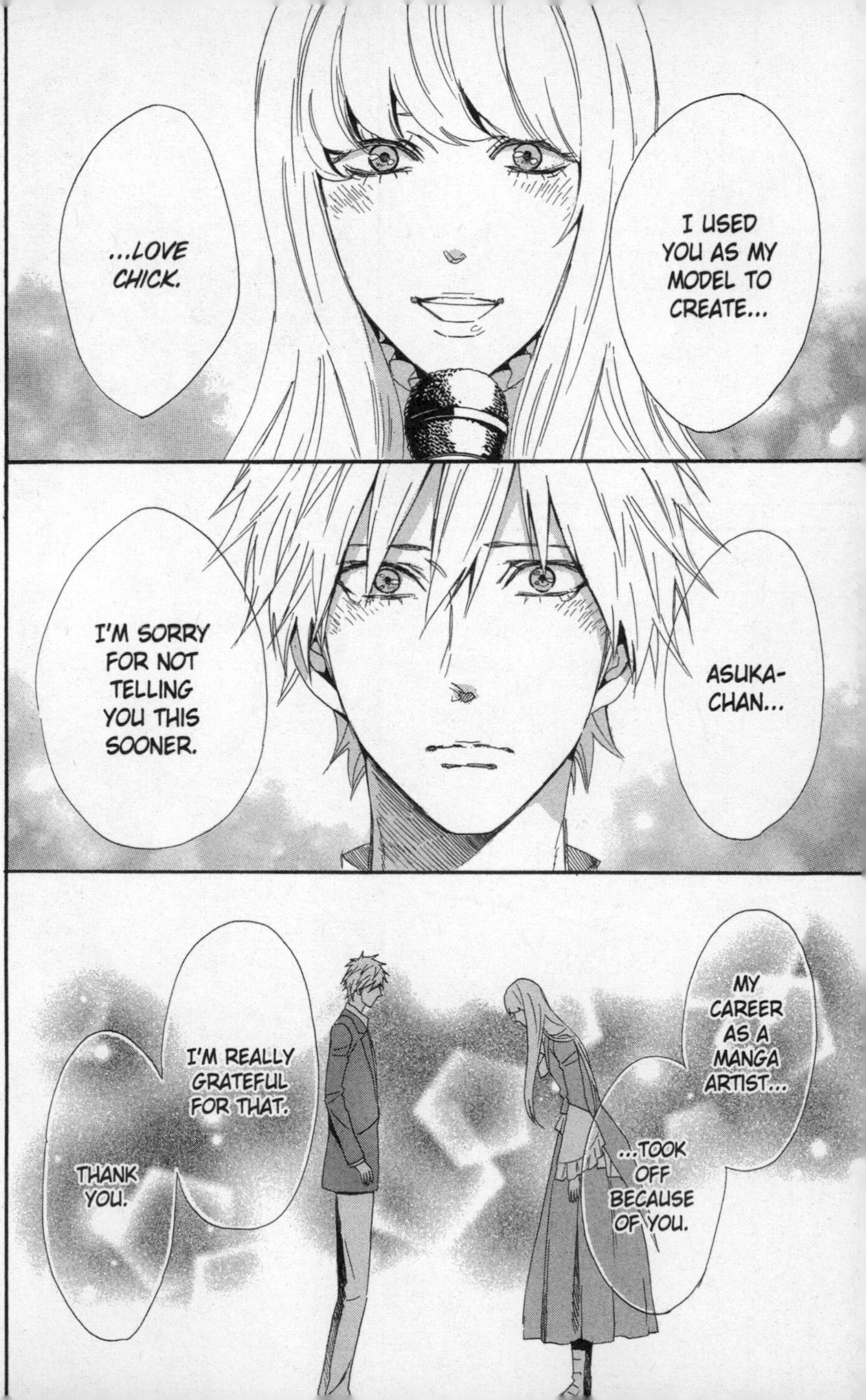
I USED YOU AS MY MODEL TO CREATE...
...LOVE CHICK.
ASUKA-CHAN...
I'M SORRY FOR NOT TELLING YOU THIS SOONER.
MY CAREER AS A MANGA ARTIST...
...TOOK OFF BECAUSE OF YOU.
I'M REALLY GRATEFUL FOR THAT.
THANK YOU.

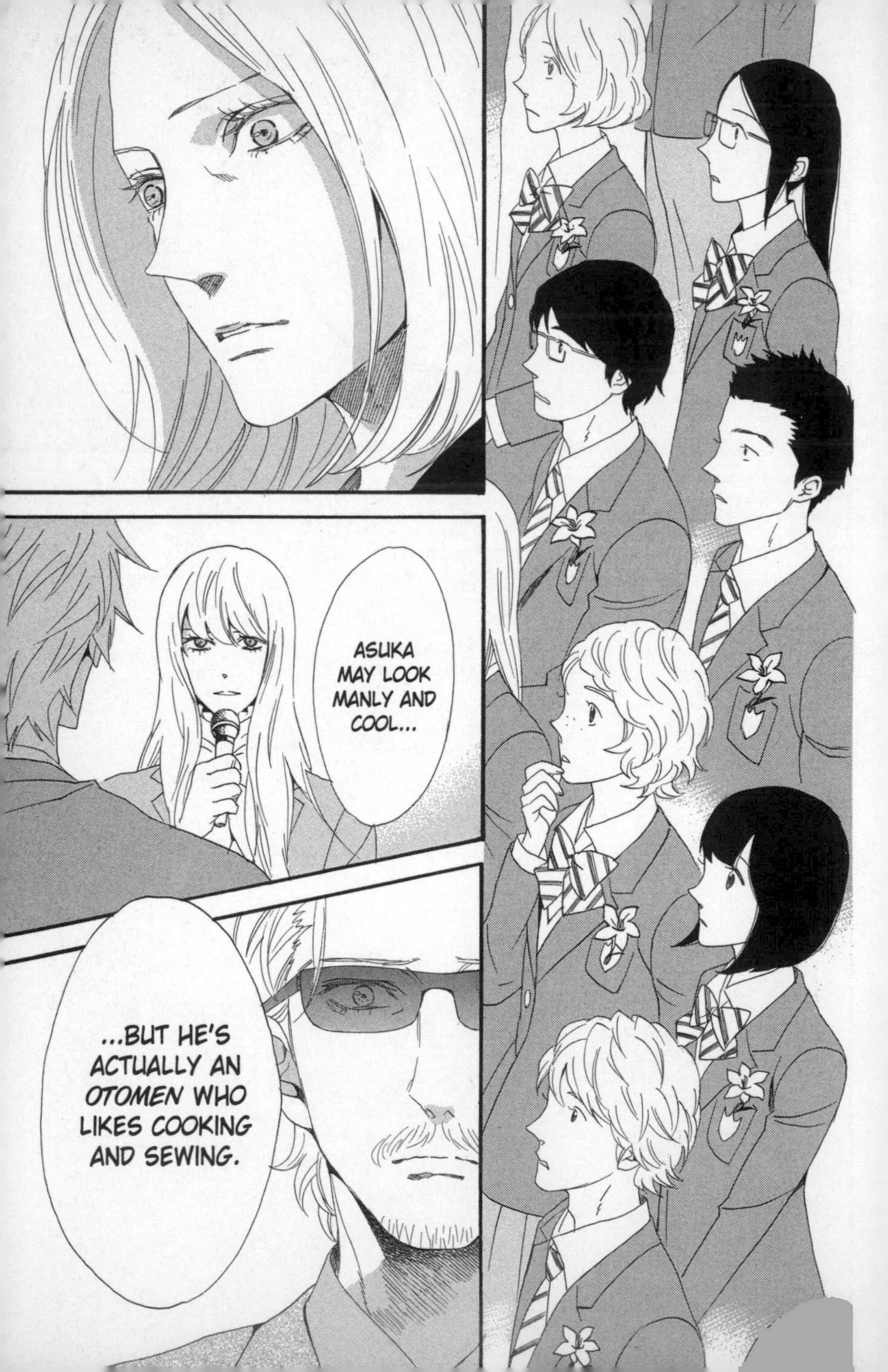
ASUKA MAY LOOK MANLY AND COOL...
...BUT HE'S ACTUALLY AN *OTOMEN* WHO LIKES COOKING AND SEWING.

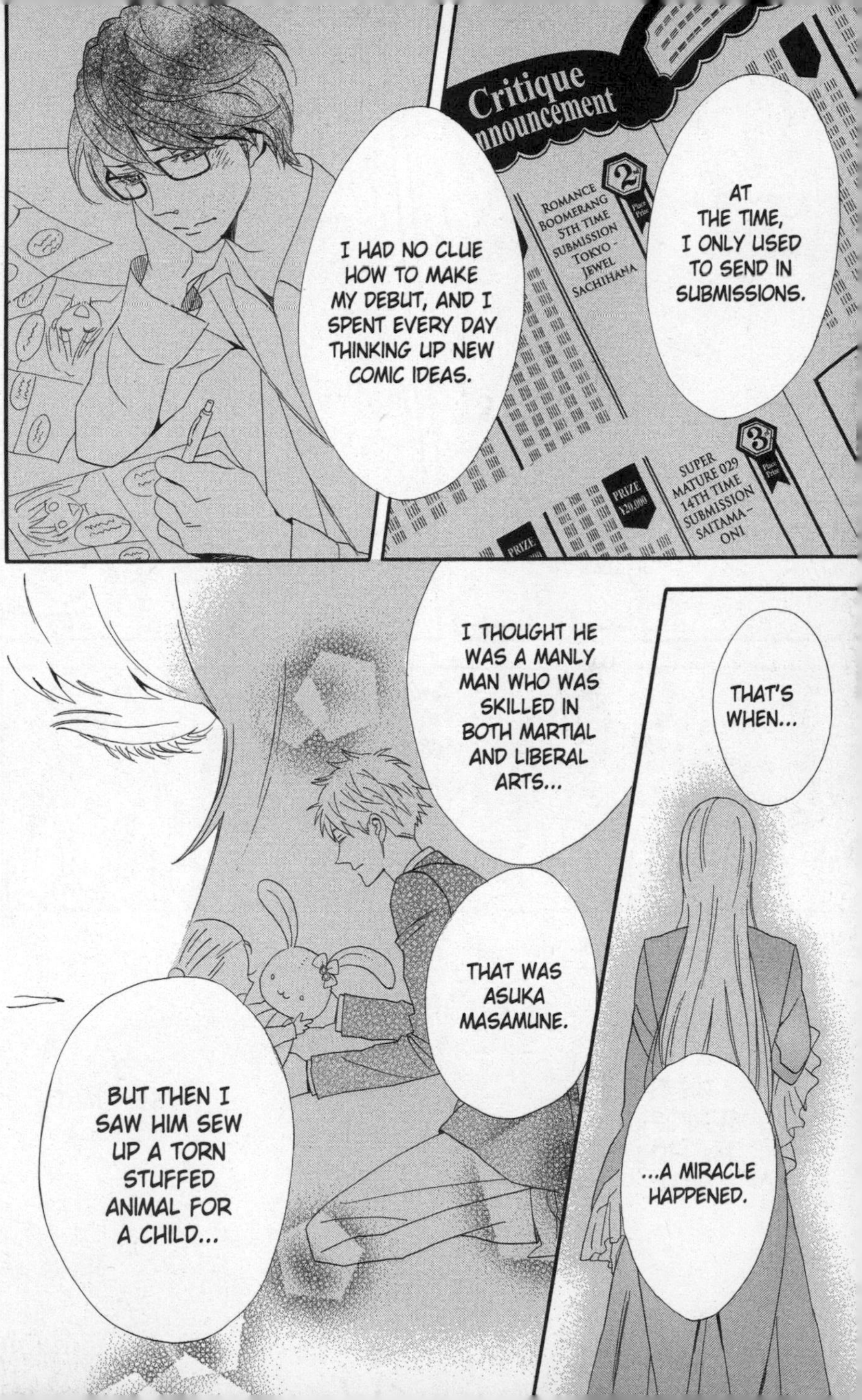
Critique
nnouncement
ROMANCE BOOMERANG 5TH TIME SUBMISSION TOKYO-JEWEL SACHIHANA
PRIZE ¥20,000
SUPER MATURE 029 14TH TIME SUBMISSION SAITAMA-ONI
AT THE TIME, I ONLY USED TO SEND IN SUBMISSIONS.
I HAD NO CLUE HOW TO MAKE MY DEBUT, AND I SPENT EVERY DAY THINKING UP NEW COMIC IDEAS.
THAT'S WHEN...
...A MIRACLE HAPPENED.
I THOUGHT HE WAS A MANLY MAN WHO WAS SKILLED IN BOTH MARTIAL AND LIBERAL ARTS...
THAT WAS ASUKA MASAMUNE.
BUT THEN I SAW HIM SEW UP A TORN STUFFED ANIMAL FOR A CHILD...

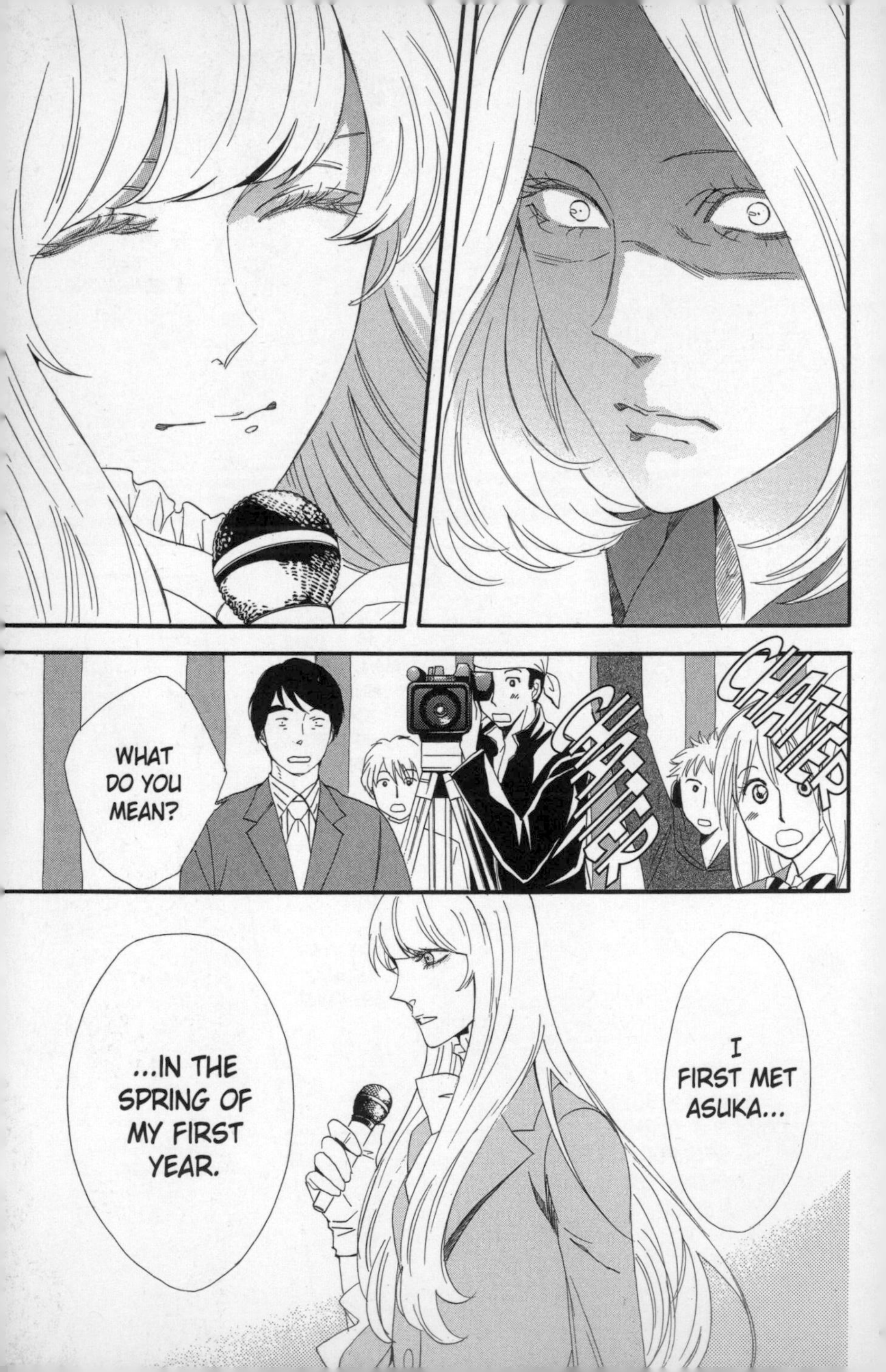
CHATTER
CHATTER
WHAT DO YOU MEAN?
I FIRST MET ASUKA...
...IN THE SPRING OF MY FIRST YEAR.

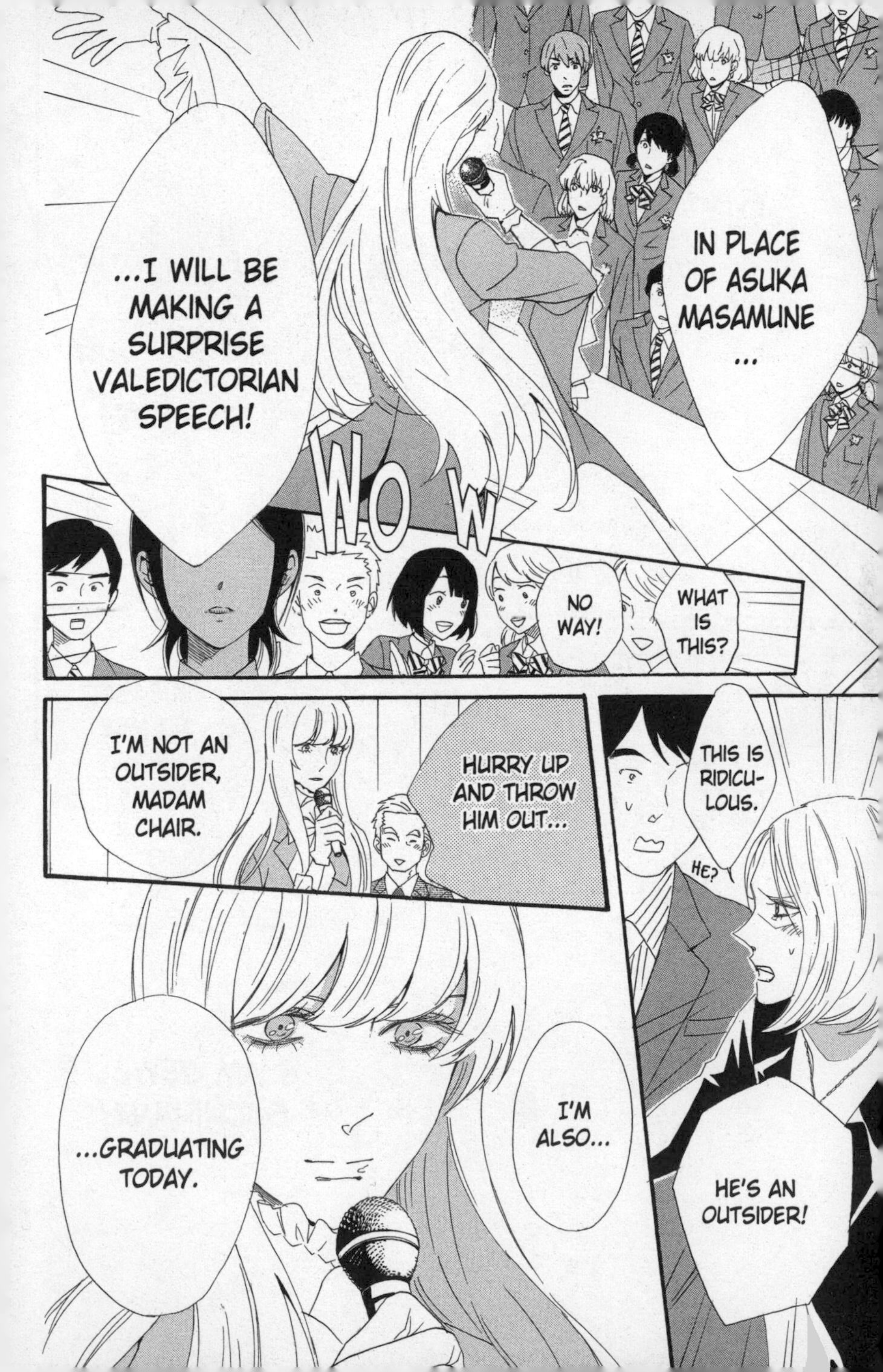
IN PLACE OF ASUKA MASAMUNE ...
...I WILL BE MAKING A SURPRISE VALEDICTORIAN SPEECH!
WOW
WHAT IS THIS?
NO WAY!
THIS IS RIDICU-LOUS.
HE?
HE'S AN OUTSIDER!
HURRY UP AND THROW HIM OUT...
I'M NOT AN OUTSIDER, MADAM CHAIR.
I'M ALSO...
...GRADUATING TODAY.

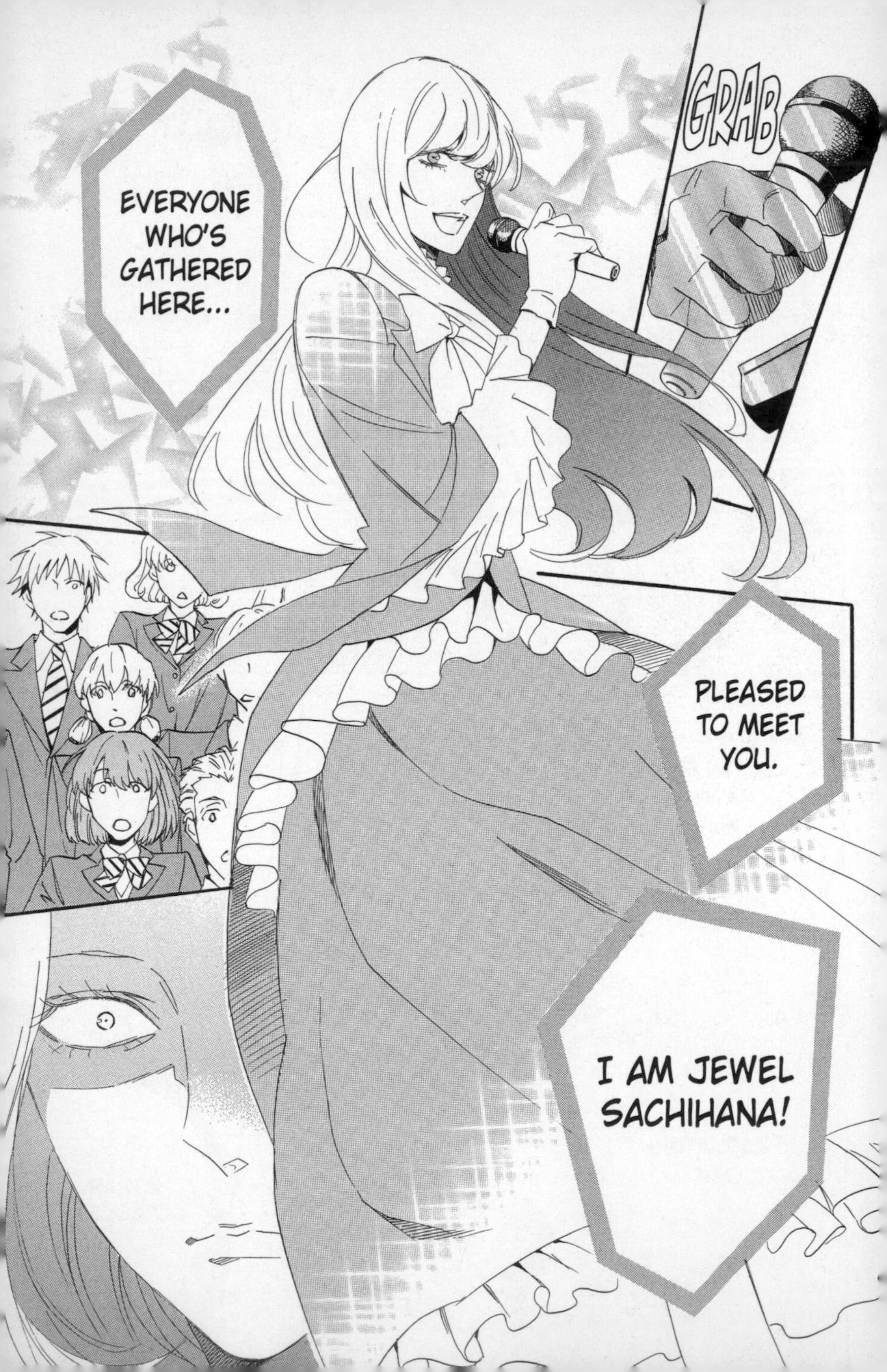
GRAB
EVERYONE WHO'S GATHERED HERE...
PLEASED TO MEET YOU.
I AM JEWEL SACHIHANA!

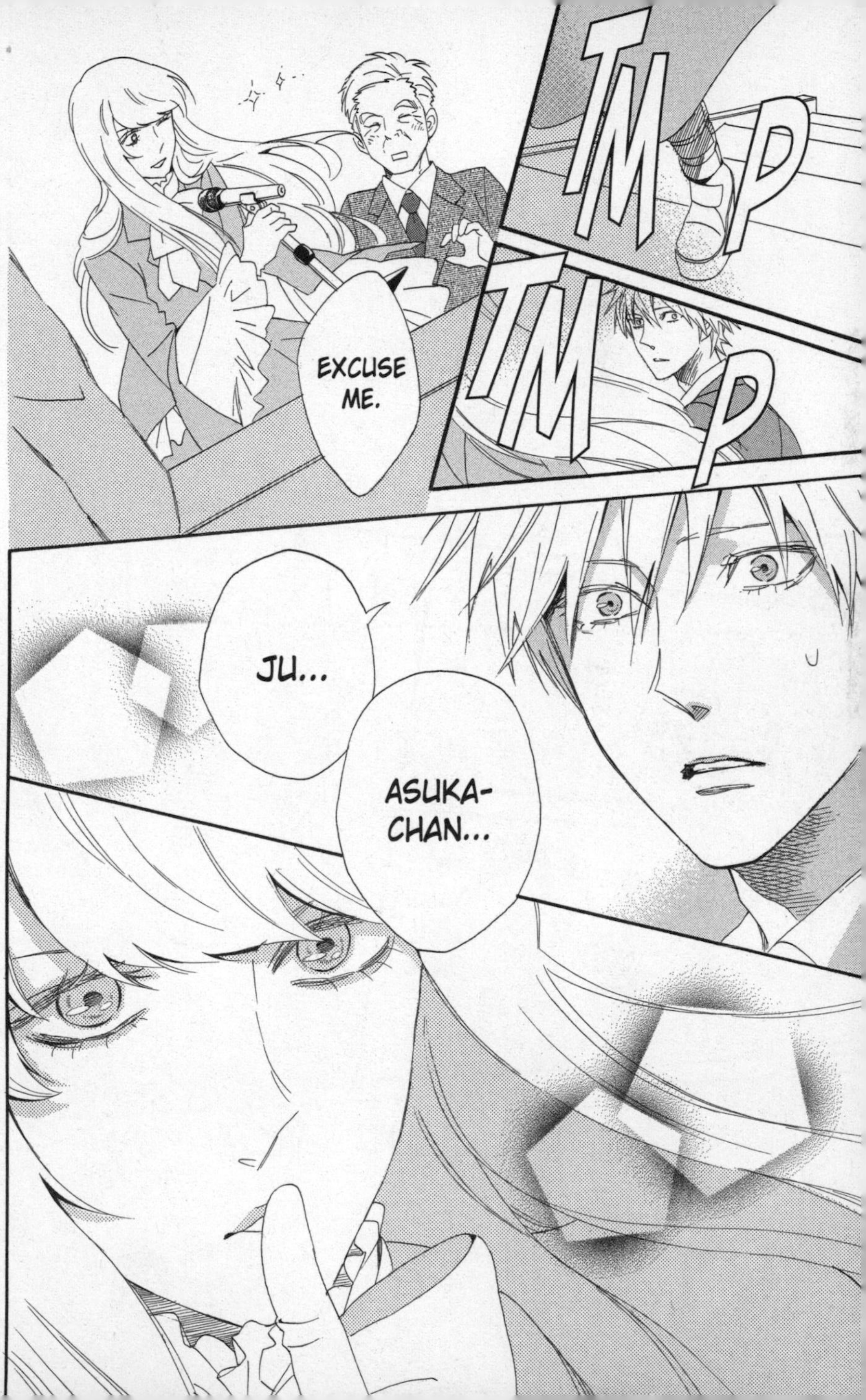
TMP
TMP
EXCUSE ME.
JU...
ASUKA-CHAN...

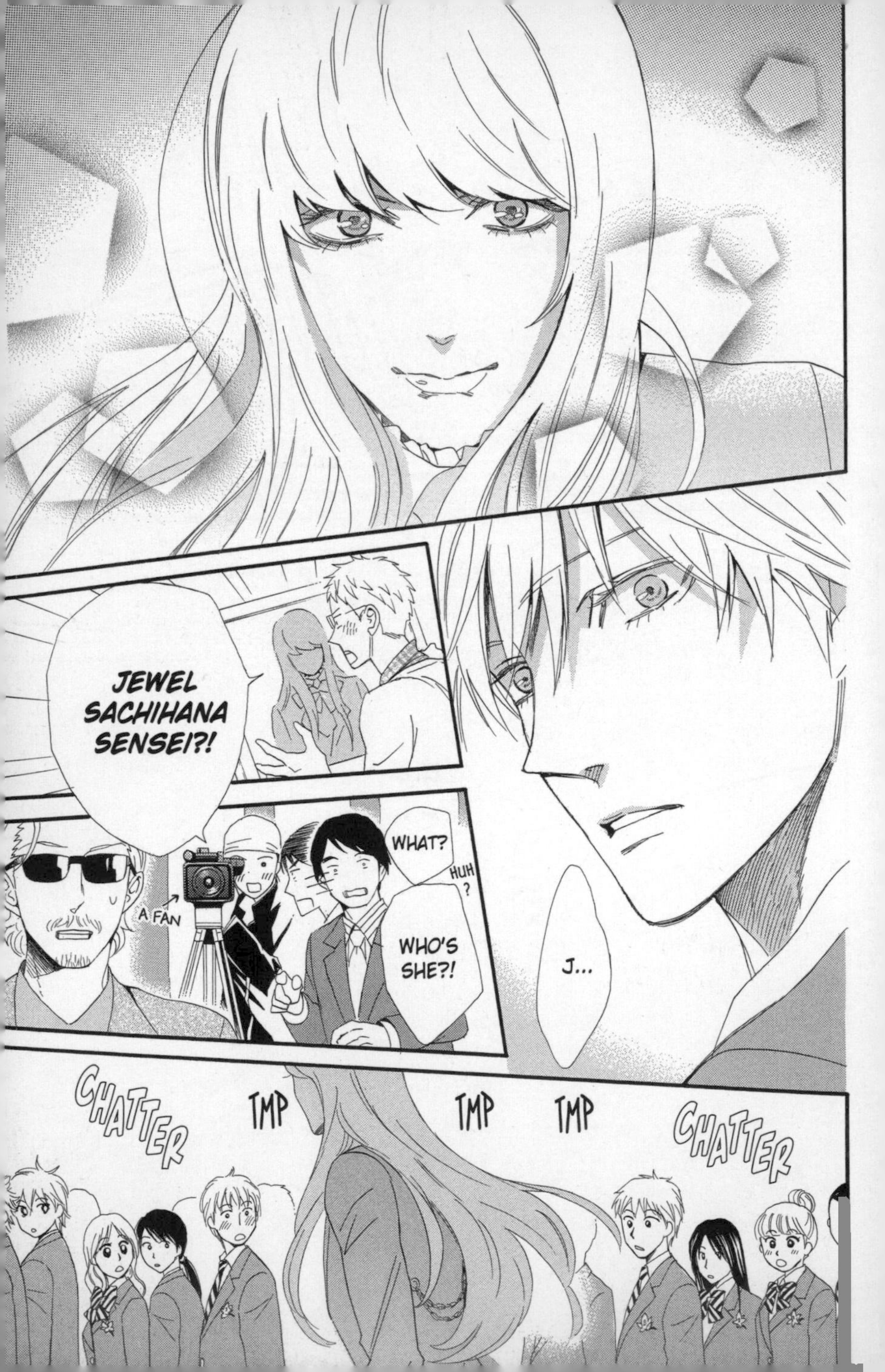
J...
JEWEL SACHIHANA SENSEI?!
WHAT?
HUH?
WHO'S SHE?!
A FAN
CHATTER
TMP
TMP
TMP
CHATTER

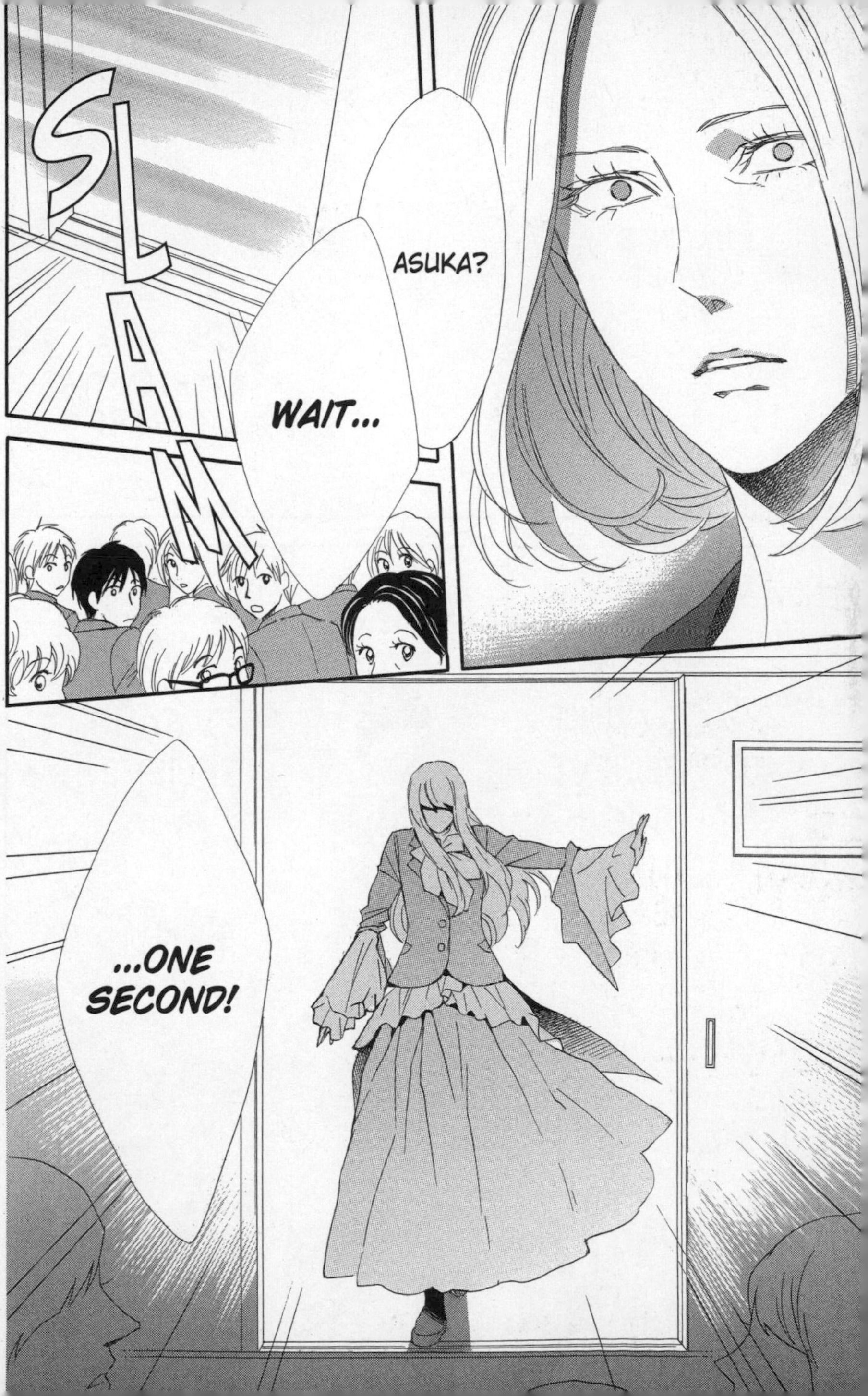
ASUKA?
WAIT...
SLAM
...ONE SECOND!

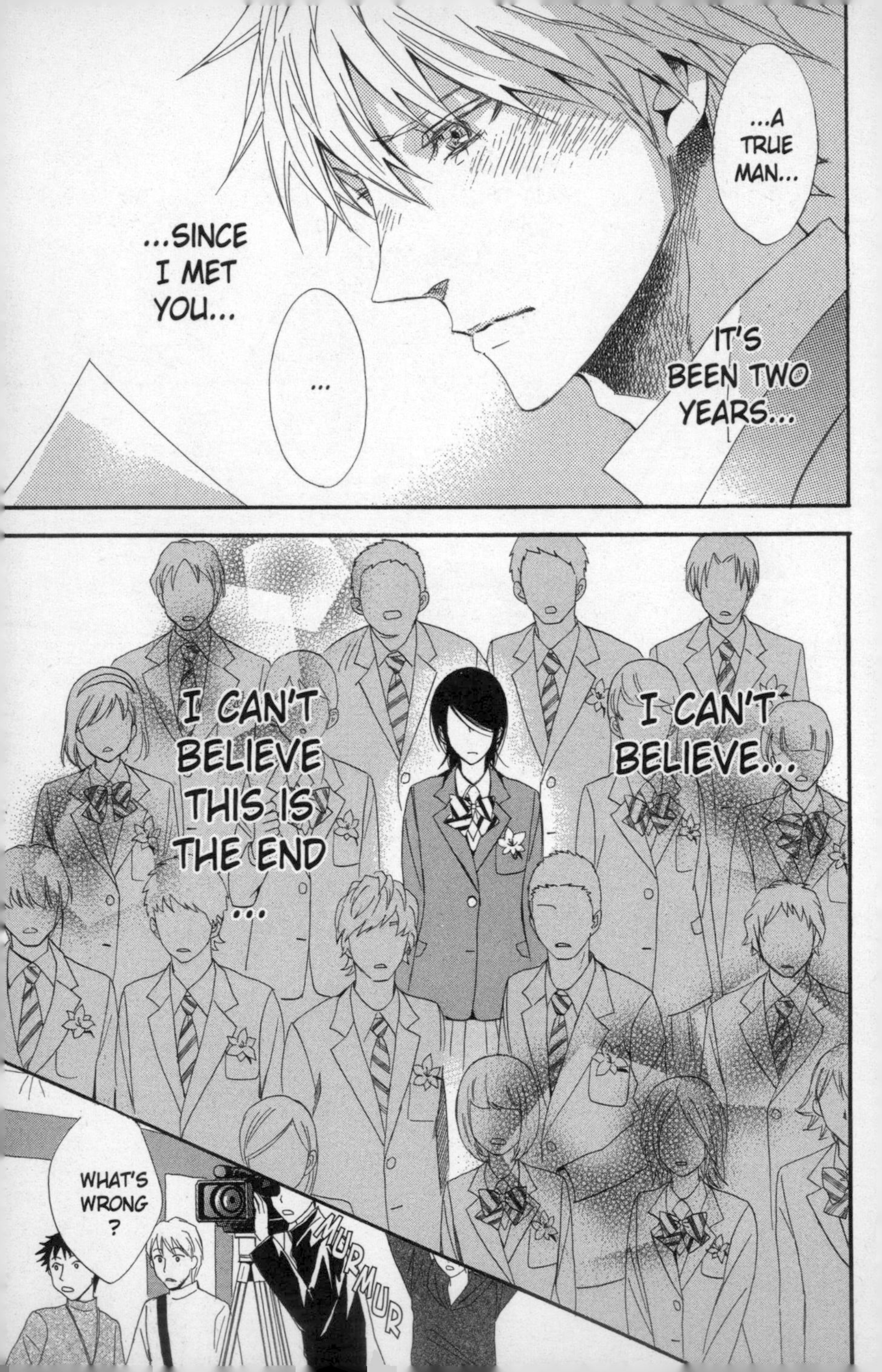
...A TRUE MAN...
IT'S BEEN TWO YEARS...
...SINCE I MET YOU...
...
I CAN'T BELIEVE...
I CAN'T BELIEVE THIS IS THE END...
MURMUR MURMUR
WHAT'S WRONG?

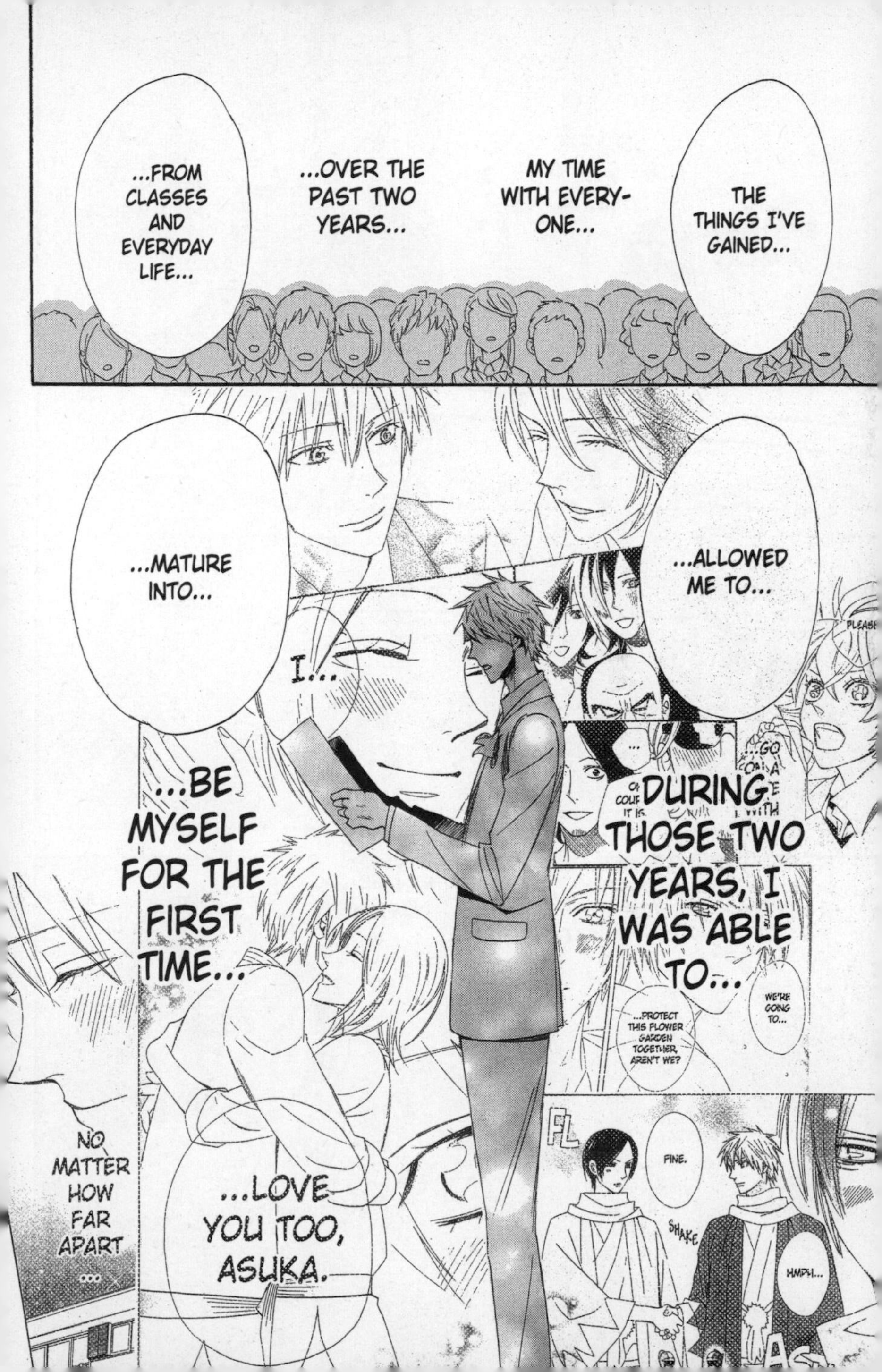
THE THINGS I'VE GAINED...
MY TIME WITH EVERYONE...
...OVER THE PAST TWO YEARS...
...FROM CLASSES AND EVERYDAY LIFE...
...ALLOWED ME TO...
...MATURE INTO...
I...
DURING THOSE TWO YEARS, I WAS ABLE TO...
...BE MYSELF FOR THE FIRST TIME...
WE'RE GOING TO...
...PROTECT THIS FLOWER GARDEN TOGETHER, AREN'T WE?
HMPH...
SHAKE
FINE.
...LOVE YOU TOO, ASUKA.
NO MATTER HOW FAR APART...

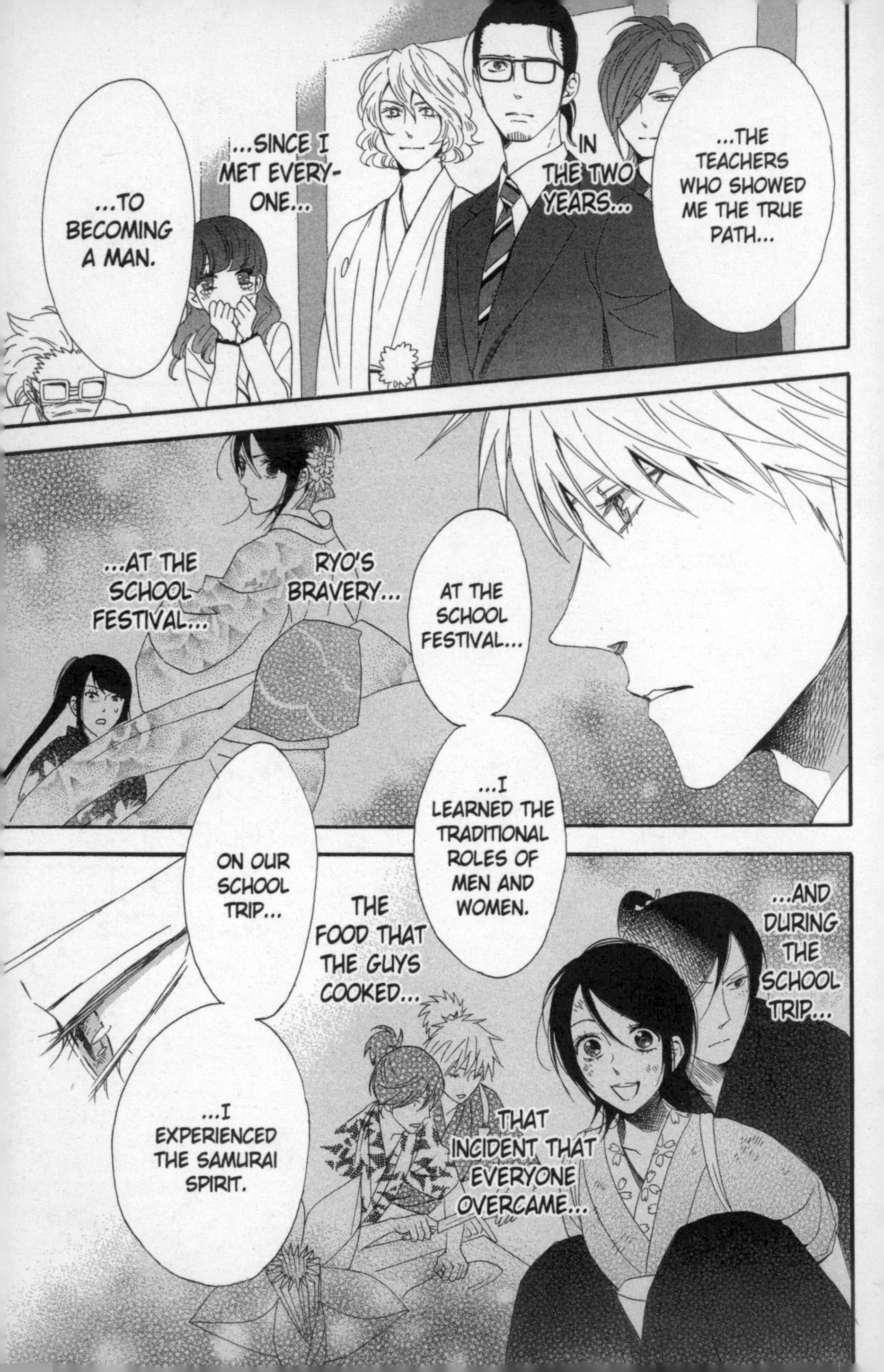
...THE TEACHERS WHO SHOWED ME THE TRUE PATH...
IN THE TWO YEARS...
...SINCE I MET EVERY-ONE...
...TO BECOMING A MAN.
AT THE SCHOOL FESTIVAL...
...I LEARNED THE TRADITIONAL ROLES OF MEN AND WOMEN.
RYO'S BRAVERY...
...AT THE SCHOOL FESTIVAL...
...AND DURING THE SCHOOL TRIP...
THAT INCIDENT THAT EVERYONE OVERCAME...
THE FOOD THAT THE GUYS COOKED...
ON OUR SCHOOL TRIP...
...I EXPERIENCED THE SAMURAI SPIRIT.

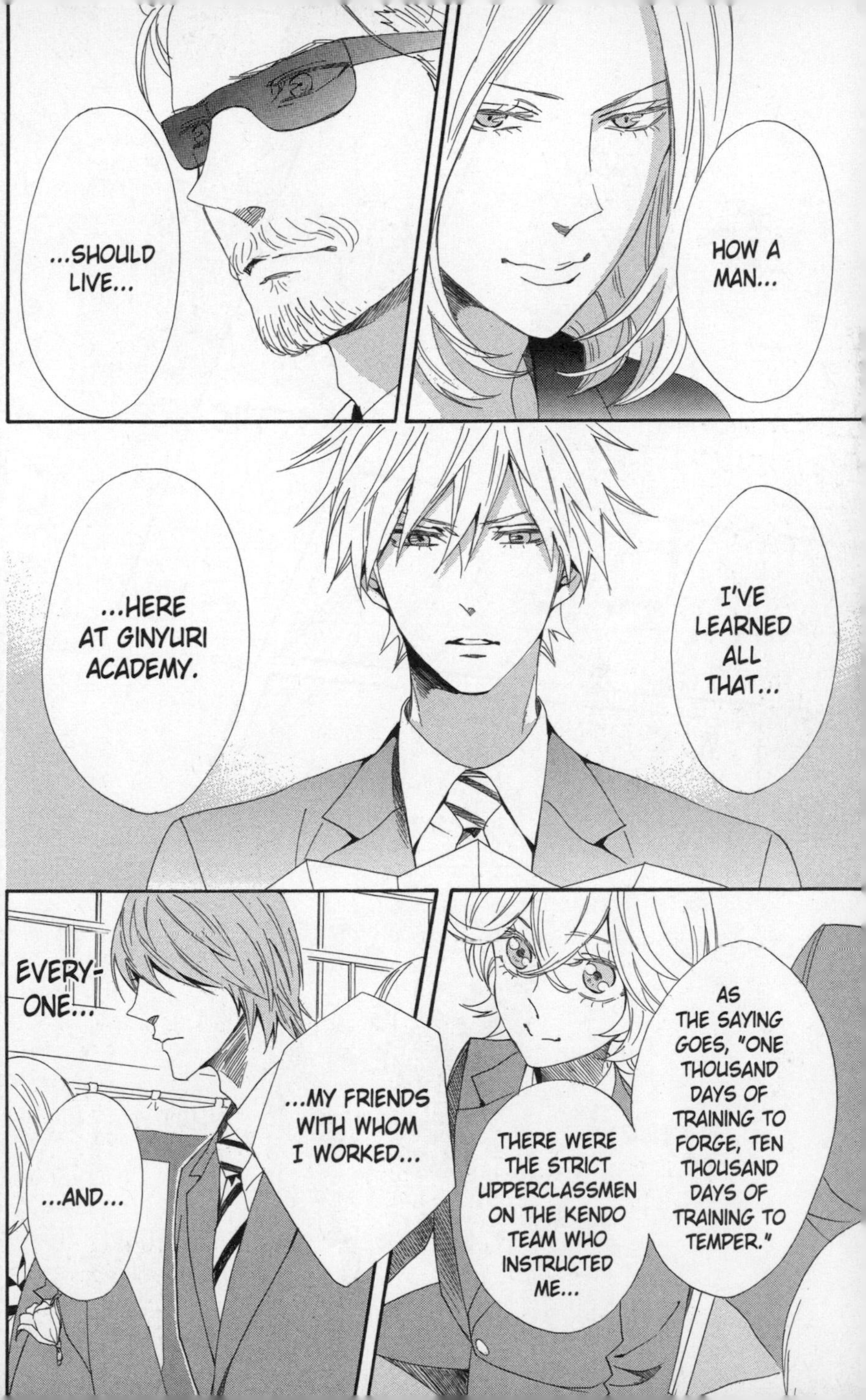
HOW A MAN...
...SHOULD LIVE...
I'VE LEARNED ALL THAT...
...HERE AT GINYURI ACADEMY.
AS THE SAYING GOES, "ONE THOUSAND DAYS OF TRAINING TO FORGE, TEN THOUSAND DAYS OF TRAINING TO TEMPER."
THERE WERE THE STRICT UPPERCLASSMEN ON THE KENDO TEAM WHO INSTRUCTED ME...
EVERY-ONE...
...MY FRIENDS WITH WHOM I WORKED...
...AND...

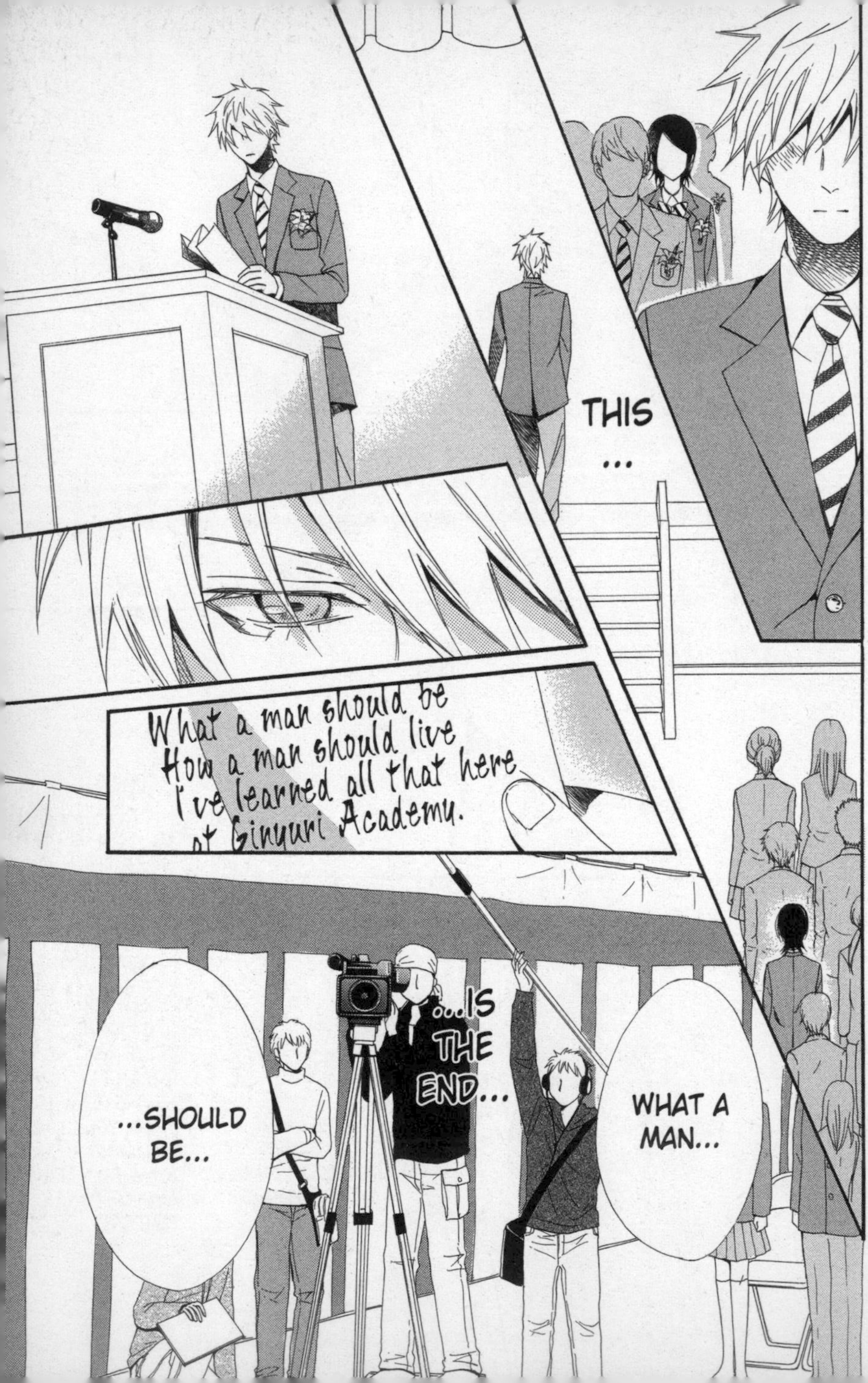
THIS ...
What a man should be
How a man should live
I've learned all that here
at Ginyuri Academy.
WHAT A MAN...
...IS THE END...
...SHOULD BE...

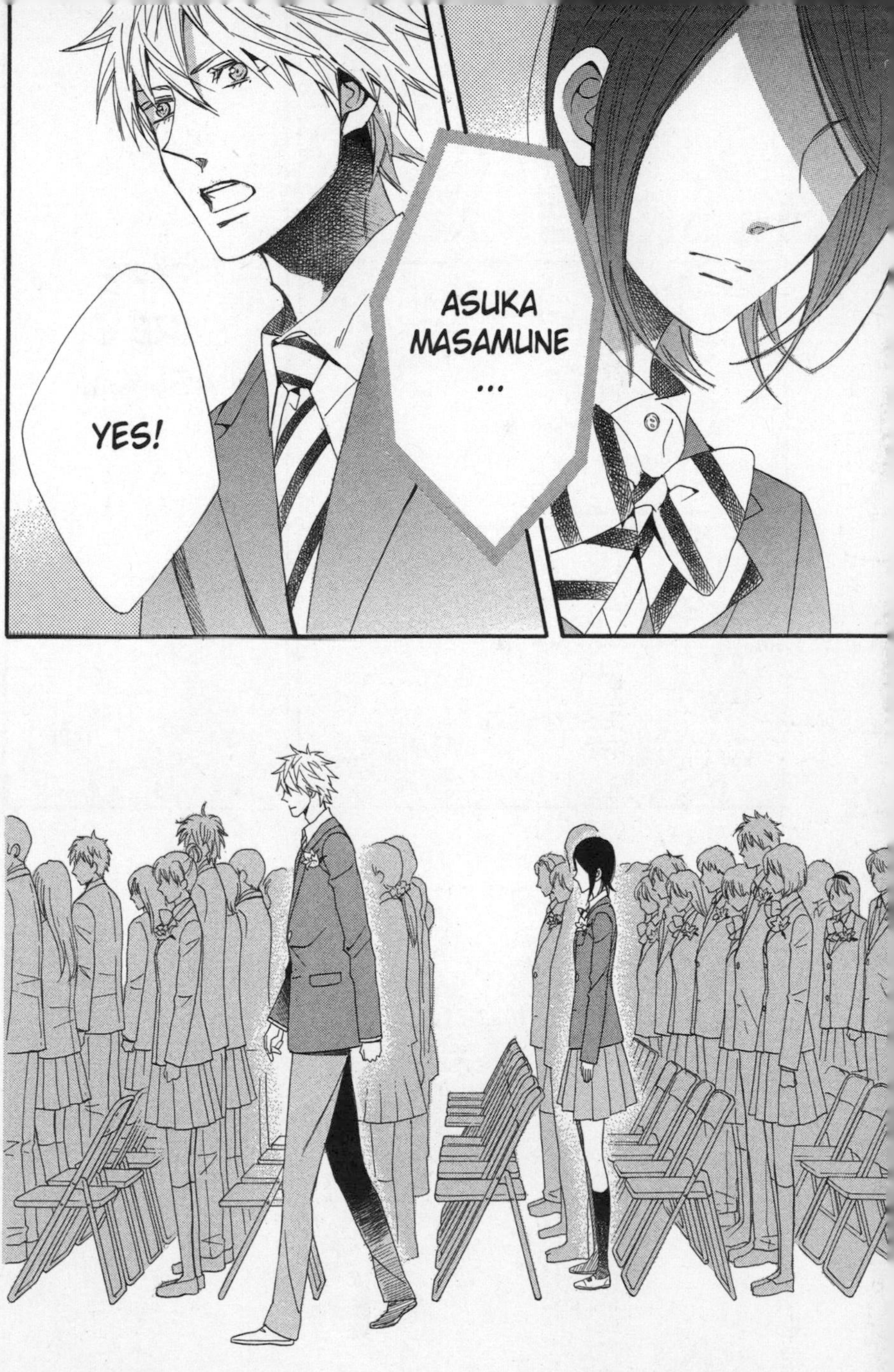
ASUKA MASAMUNE ...
YES!

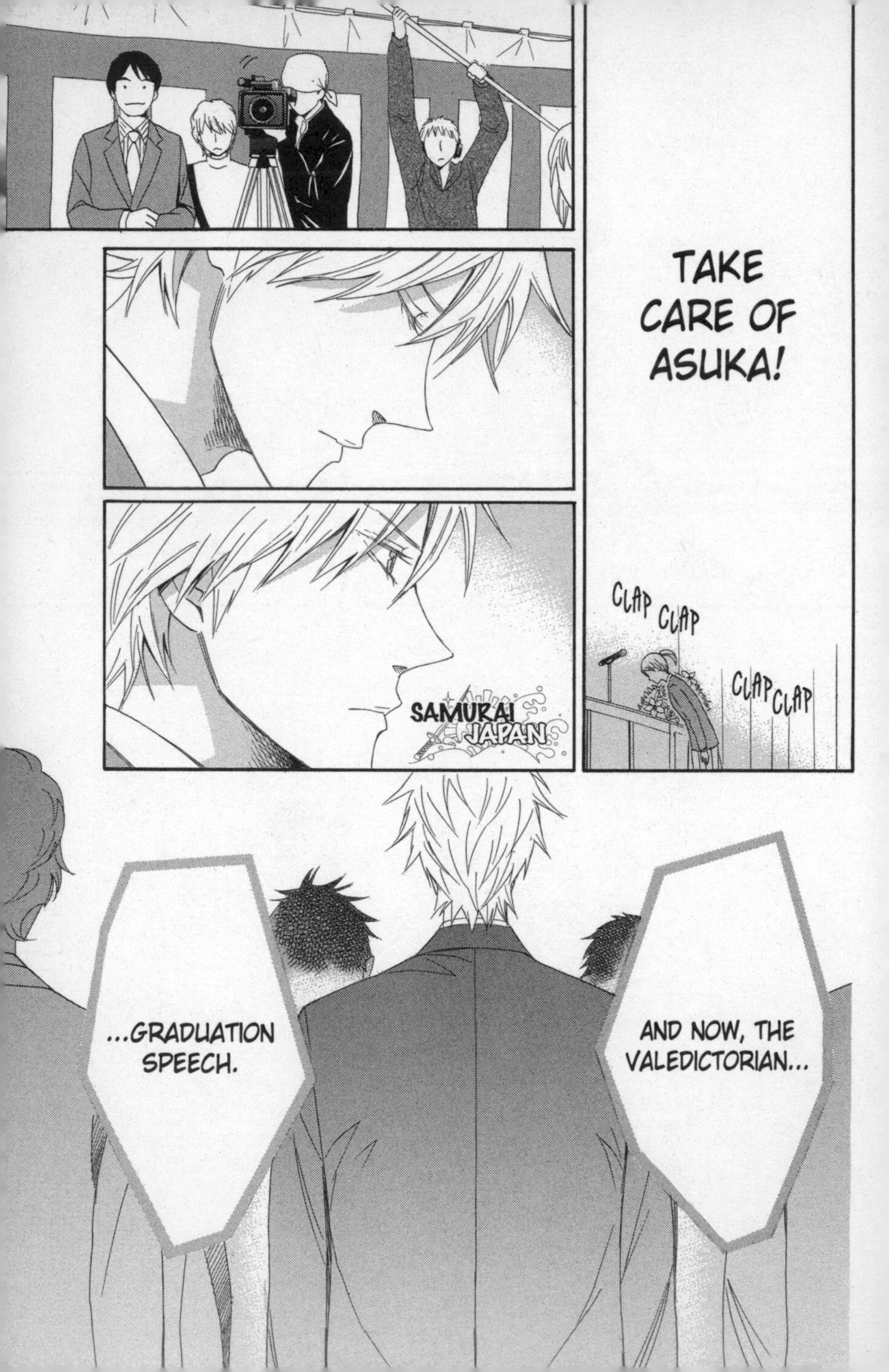
TAKE CARE OF ASUKA!
CLAP CLAP
CLAP CLAP
SAMURAI JAPAN
AND NOW, THE VALEDICTORIAN...
...GRADUATION SPEECH.

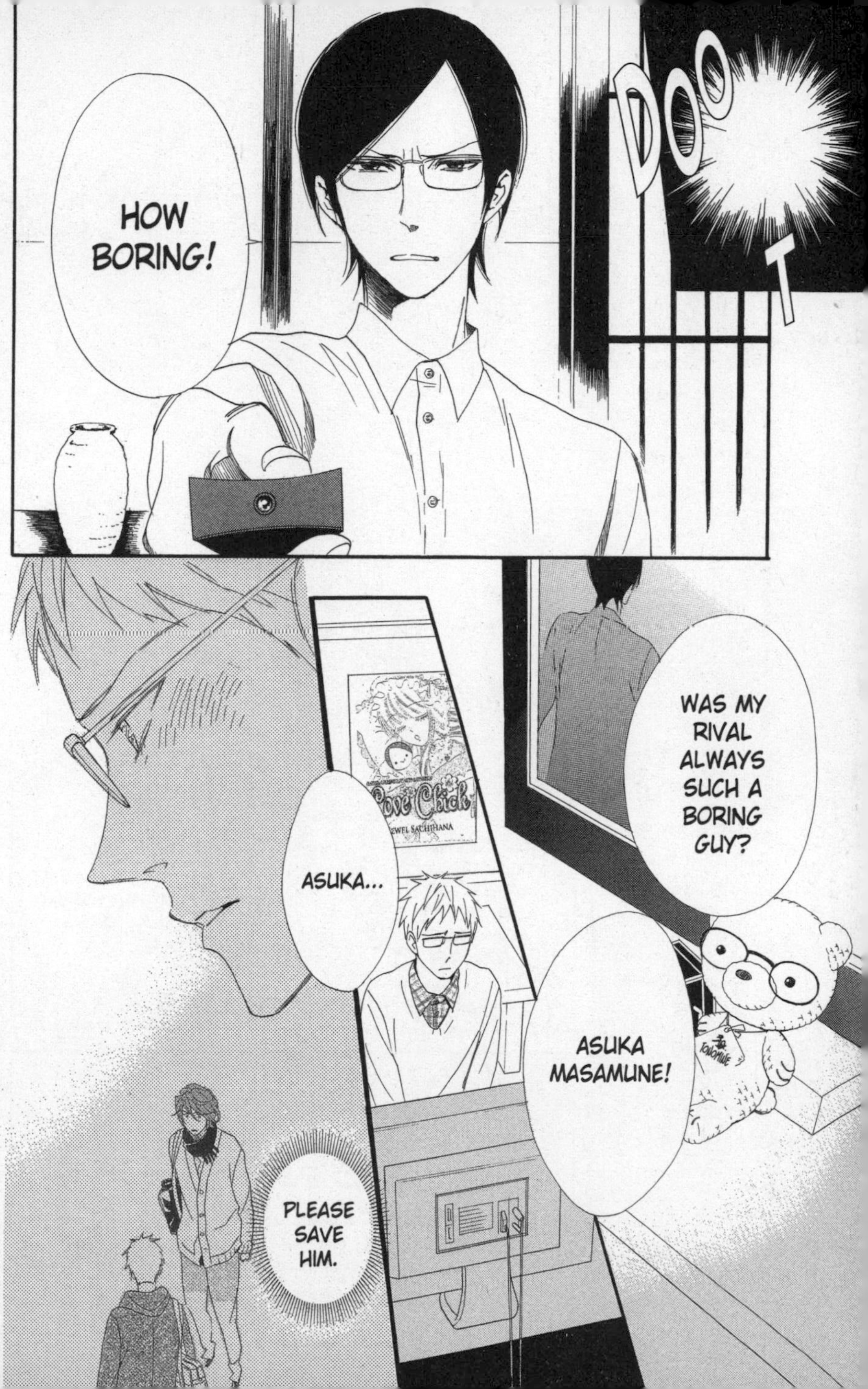
DOOT
HOW BORING!
WAS MY RIVAL ALWAYS SUCH A BORING GUY?
ASUKA...
ASUKA MASAMUNE!
PLEASE SAVE HIM.

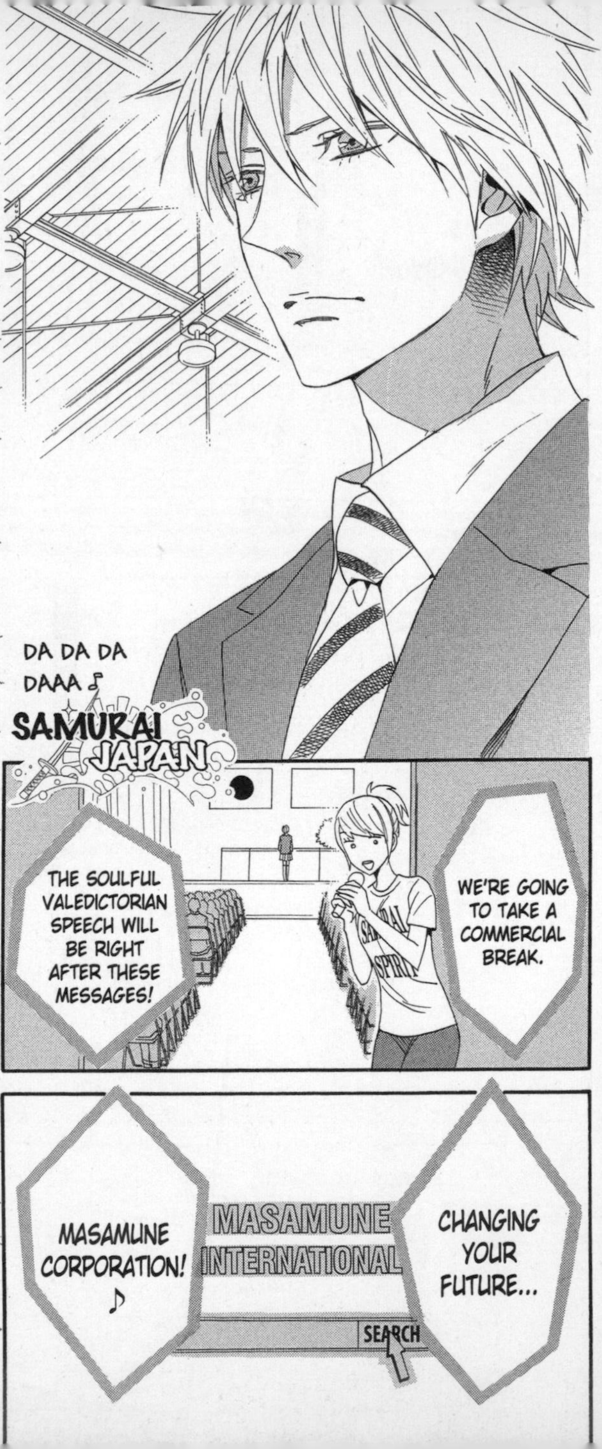
DA DA DA DAAA ♪
SAMURAI JAPAN
WE'RE GOING TO TAKE A COMMERCIAL BREAK.
THE SOULFUL VALEDICTORIAN SPEECH WILL BE RIGHT AFTER THESE MESSAGES!
CHANGING YOUR FUTURE...
MASAMUNE INTERNATIONAL
SEARCH
MASAMUNE CORPORATION! ♪

It's Volume 18!!

We're finally at the final volume. I really want to thank all of my long-time readers for following this series.

I was able to get this far because of all of you readers. *Otomen* is a truly blessed series.

The story of Asuka and his friends has come to an end, but they will continue to live on inside of me.

Someday, I might make that story into a manga.

But until that day, farewell!

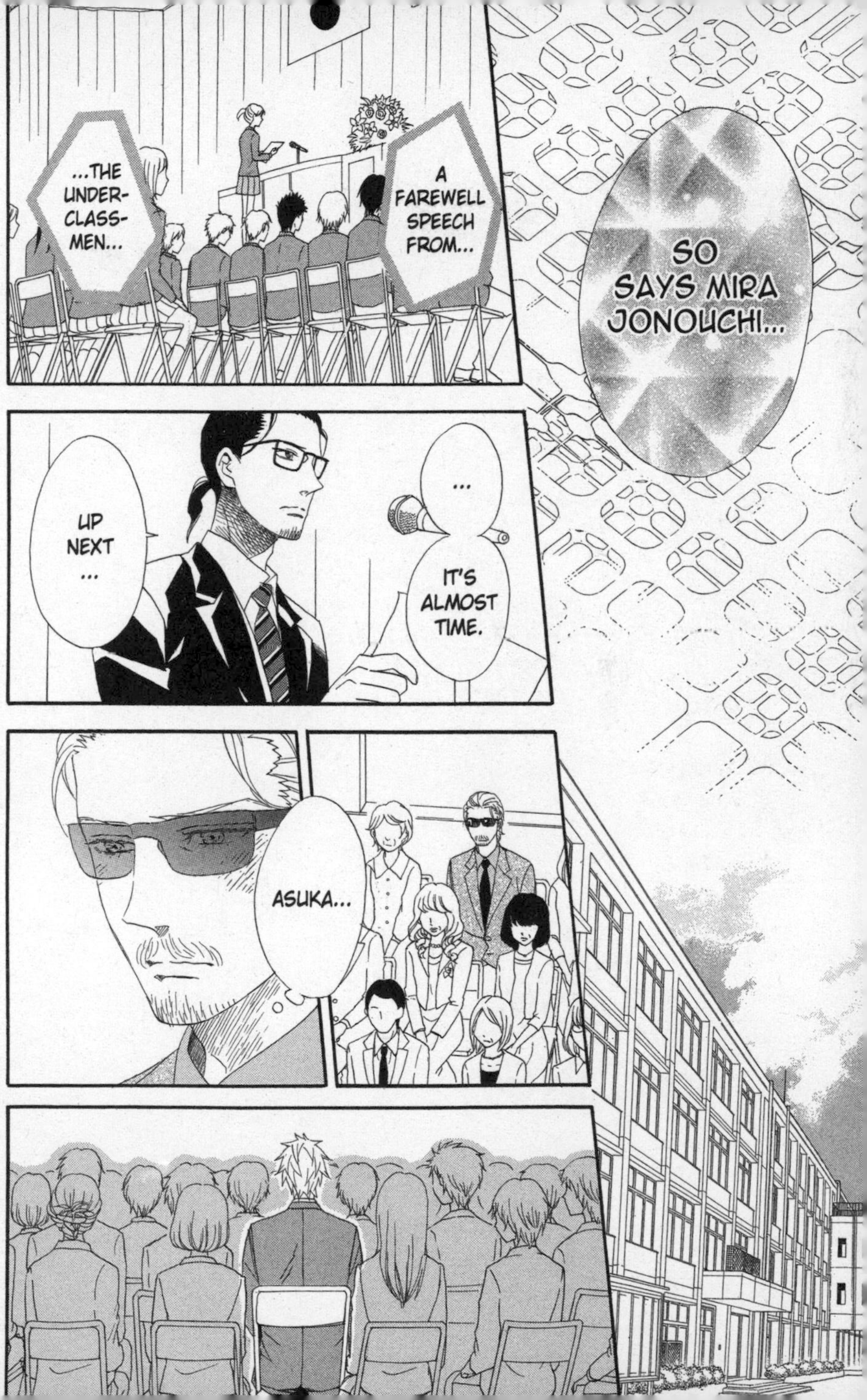
SO SAYS MIRA JONOUCHI...
A FAREWELL SPEECH FROM...
...THE UNDER-CLASS-MEN...
...
IT'S ALMOST TIME.
UP NEXT ...
ASUKA...

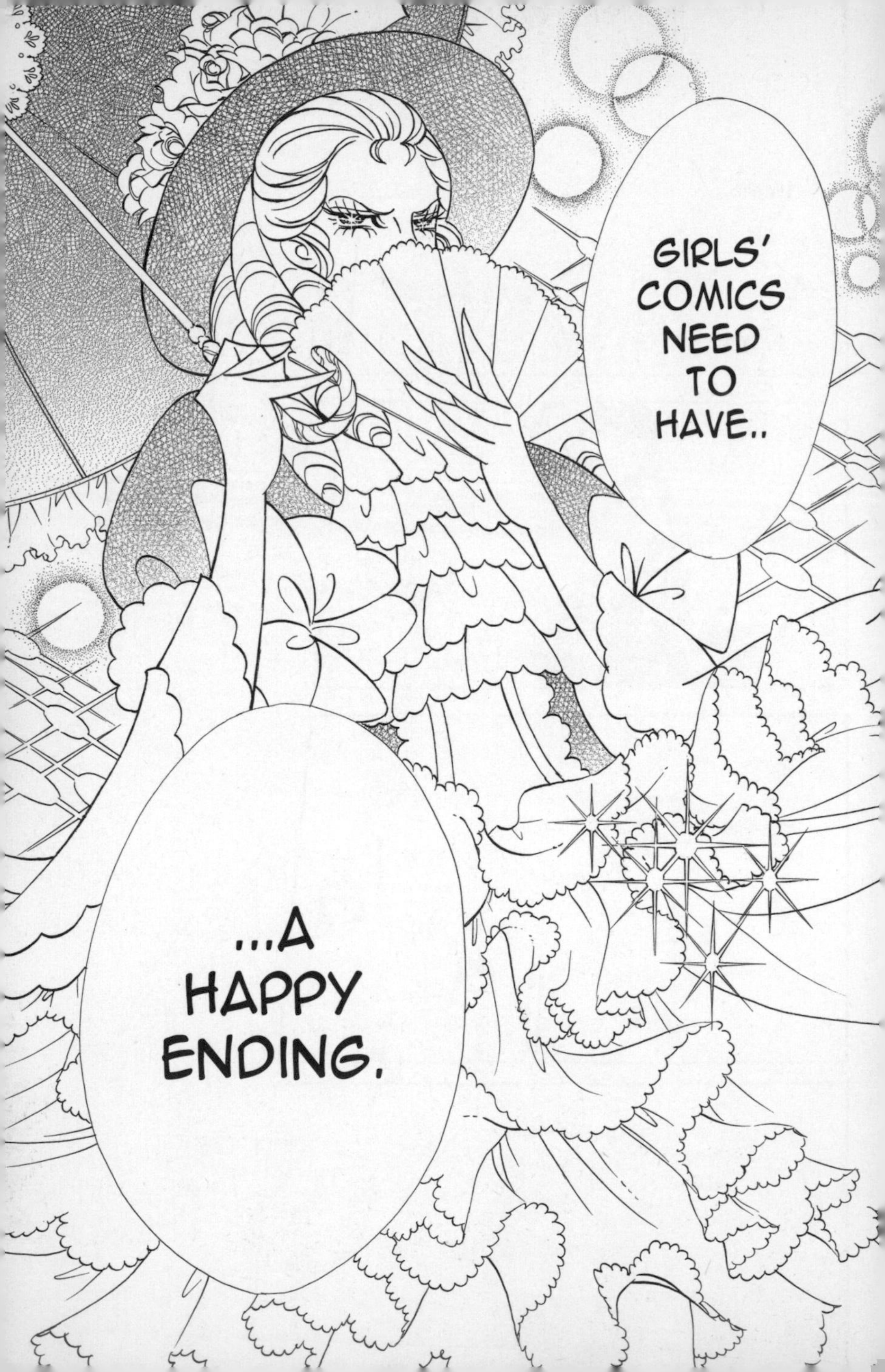
GIRLS' COMICS NEED TO HAVE..
...A HAPPY ENDING.

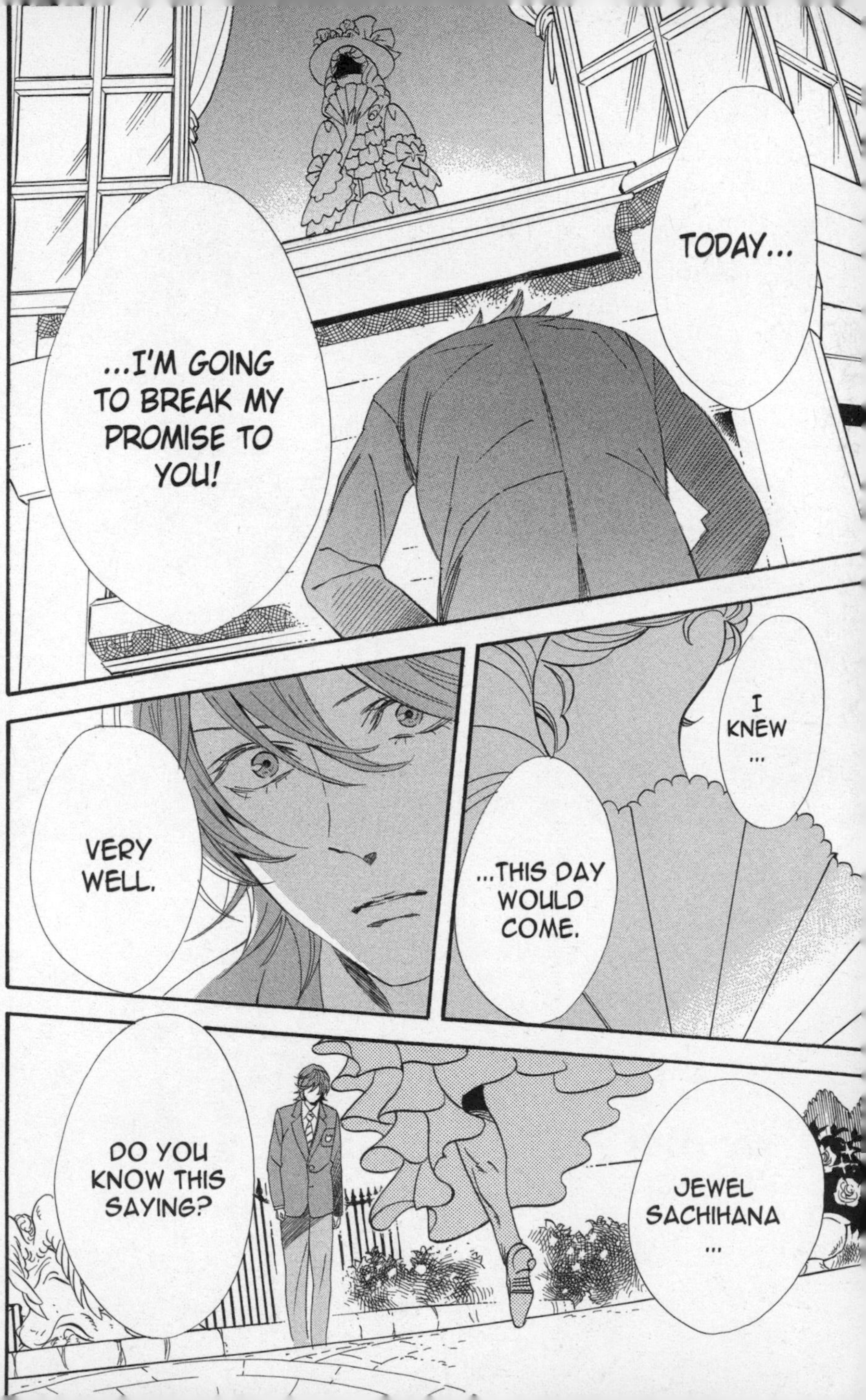
TODAY...
...I'M GOING TO BREAK MY PROMISE TO YOU!
I KNEW ...
...THIS DAY WOULD COME.
VERY WELL.
JEWEL SACHIHANA ...
DO YOU KNOW THIS SAYING?

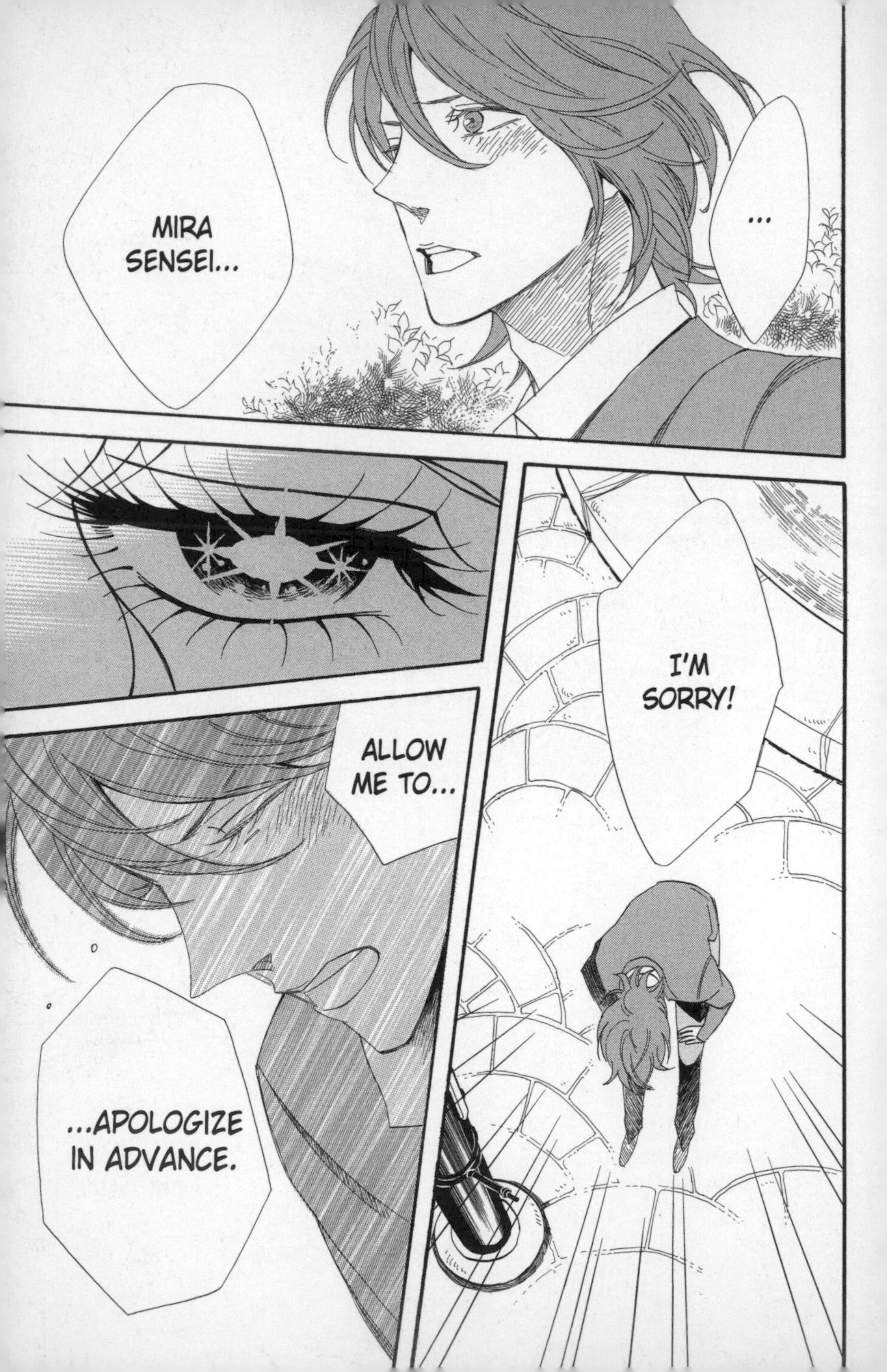
...
MIRA SENSEI...
I'M SORRY!
ALLOW ME TO...
...APOLOGIZE IN ADVANCE.

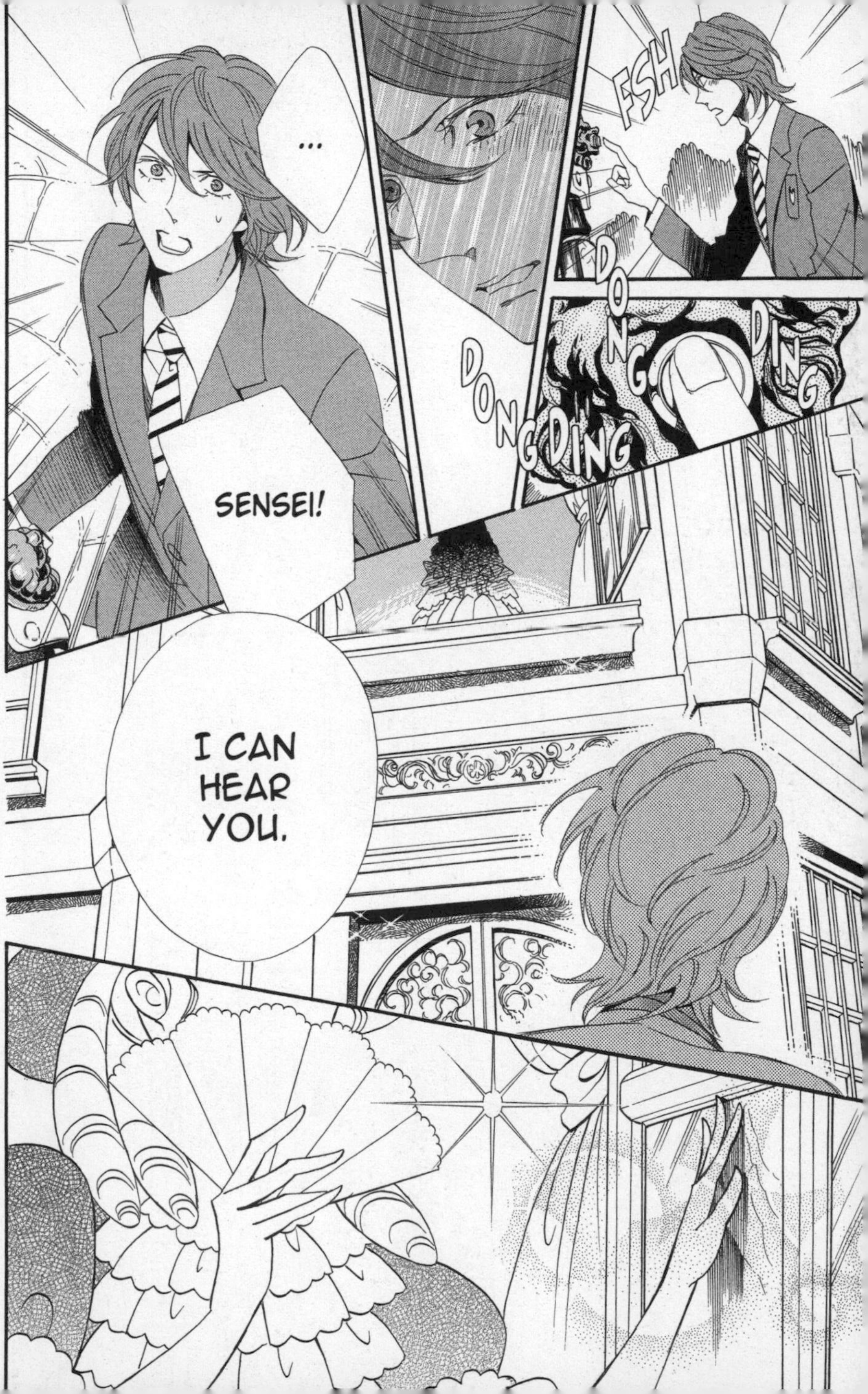
FSH
DING
DING
DONG
DONG
...
SENSEI!
I CAN HEAR YOU.

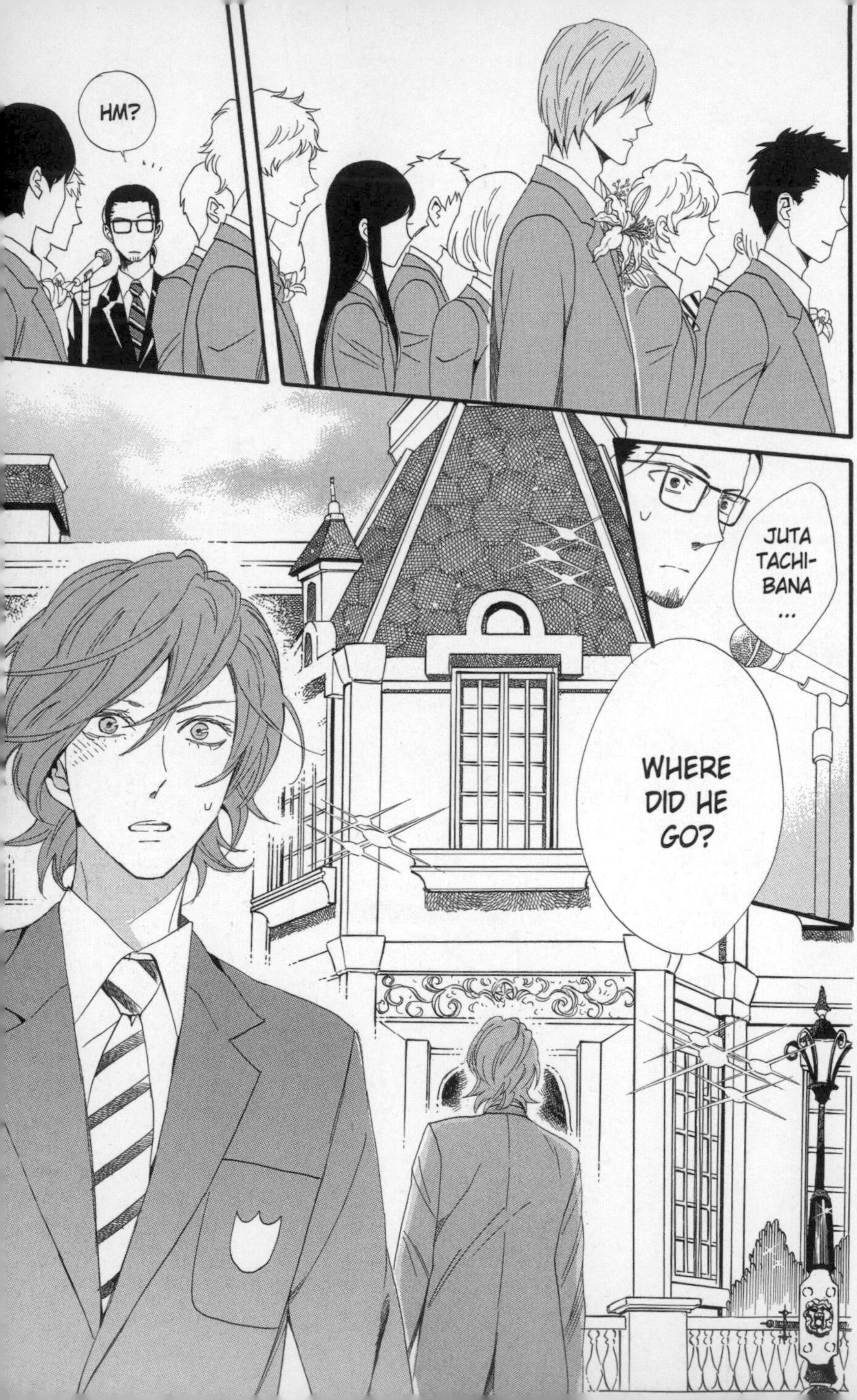
HM?
JUTA TACHI-BANA ...
WHERE DID HE GO?

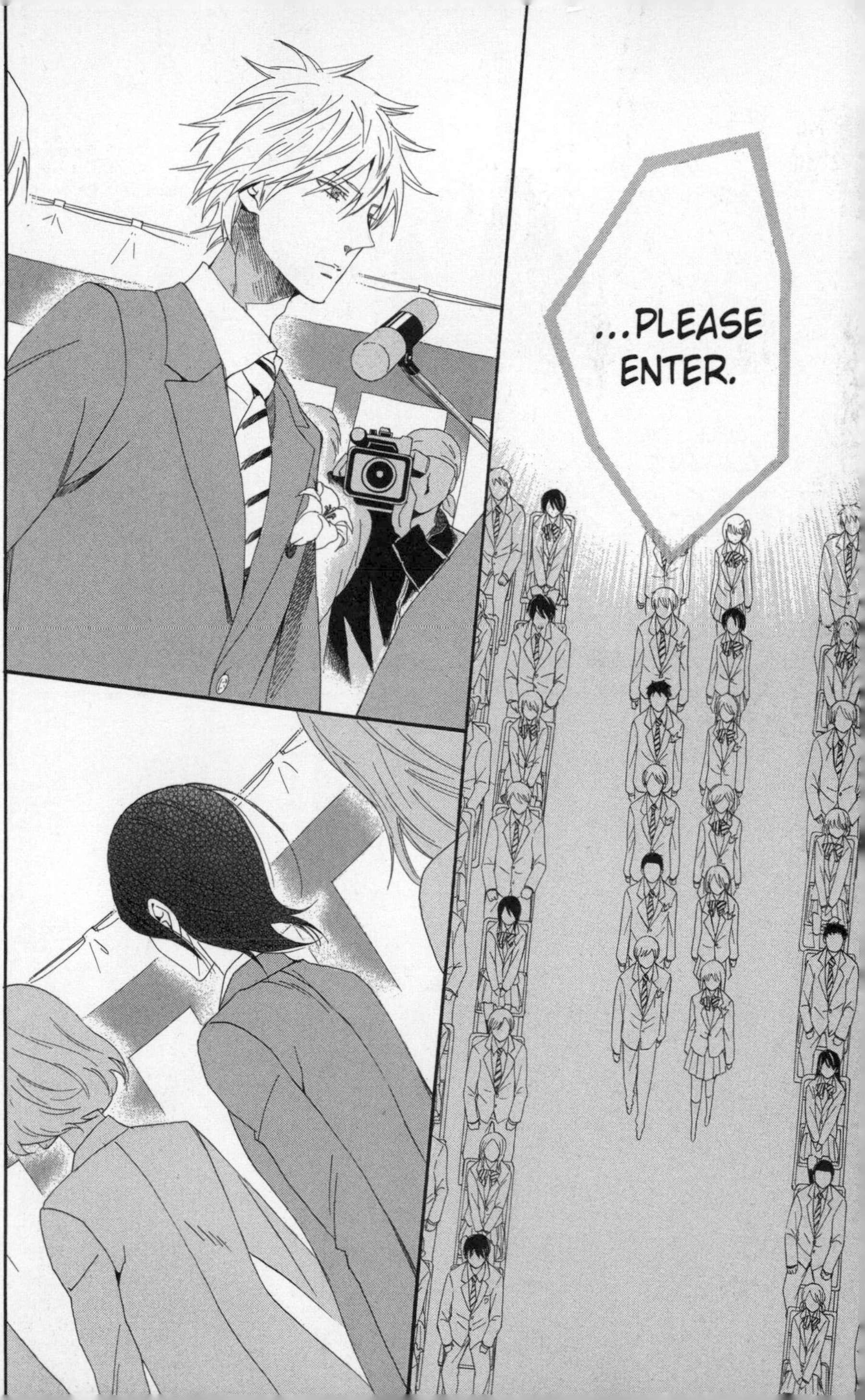
...PLEASE ENTER.

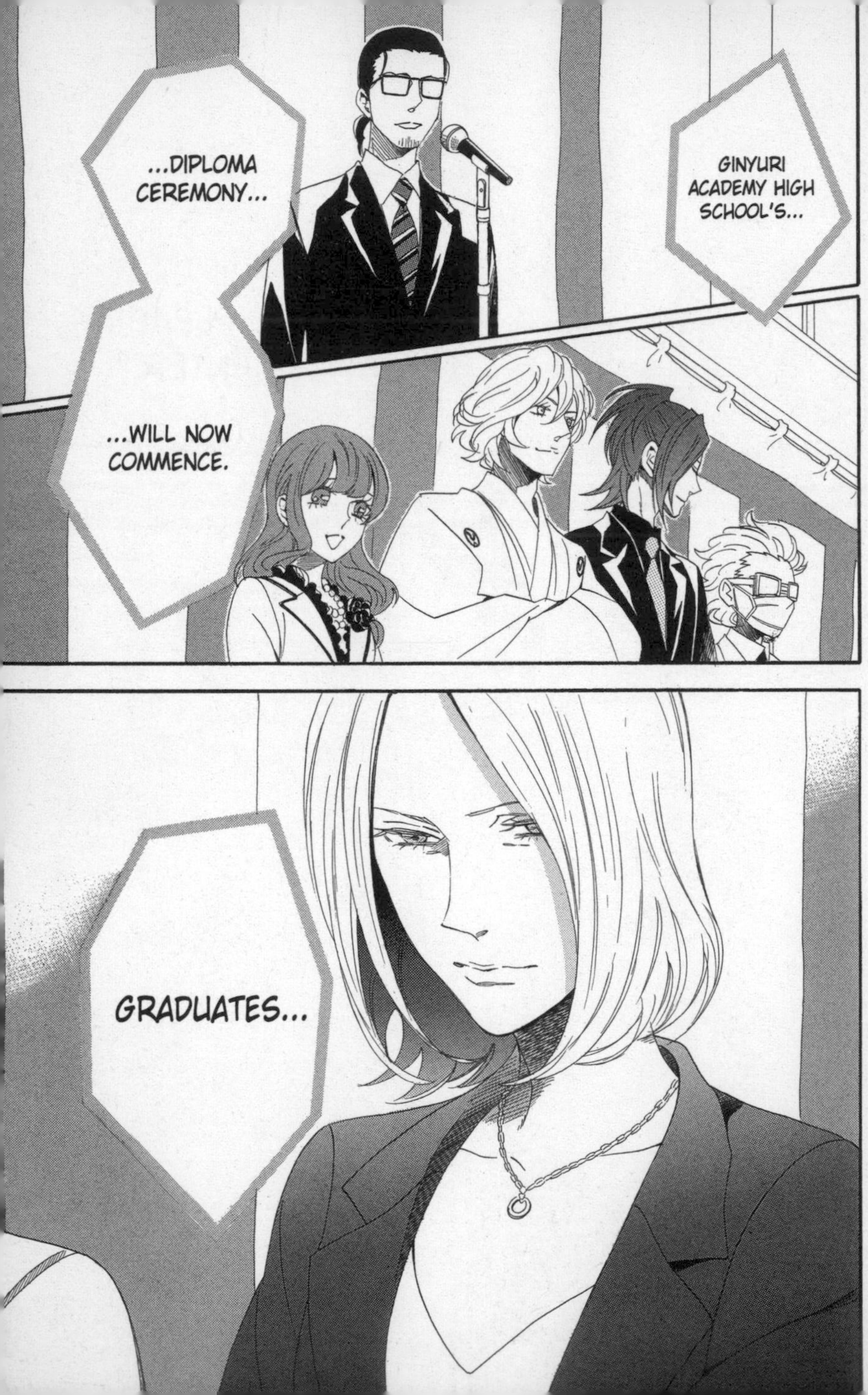
GINYURI ACADEMY HIGH SCHOOL'S...
...DIPLOMA CEREMONY...
...WILL NOW COMMENCE.
GRADUATES...

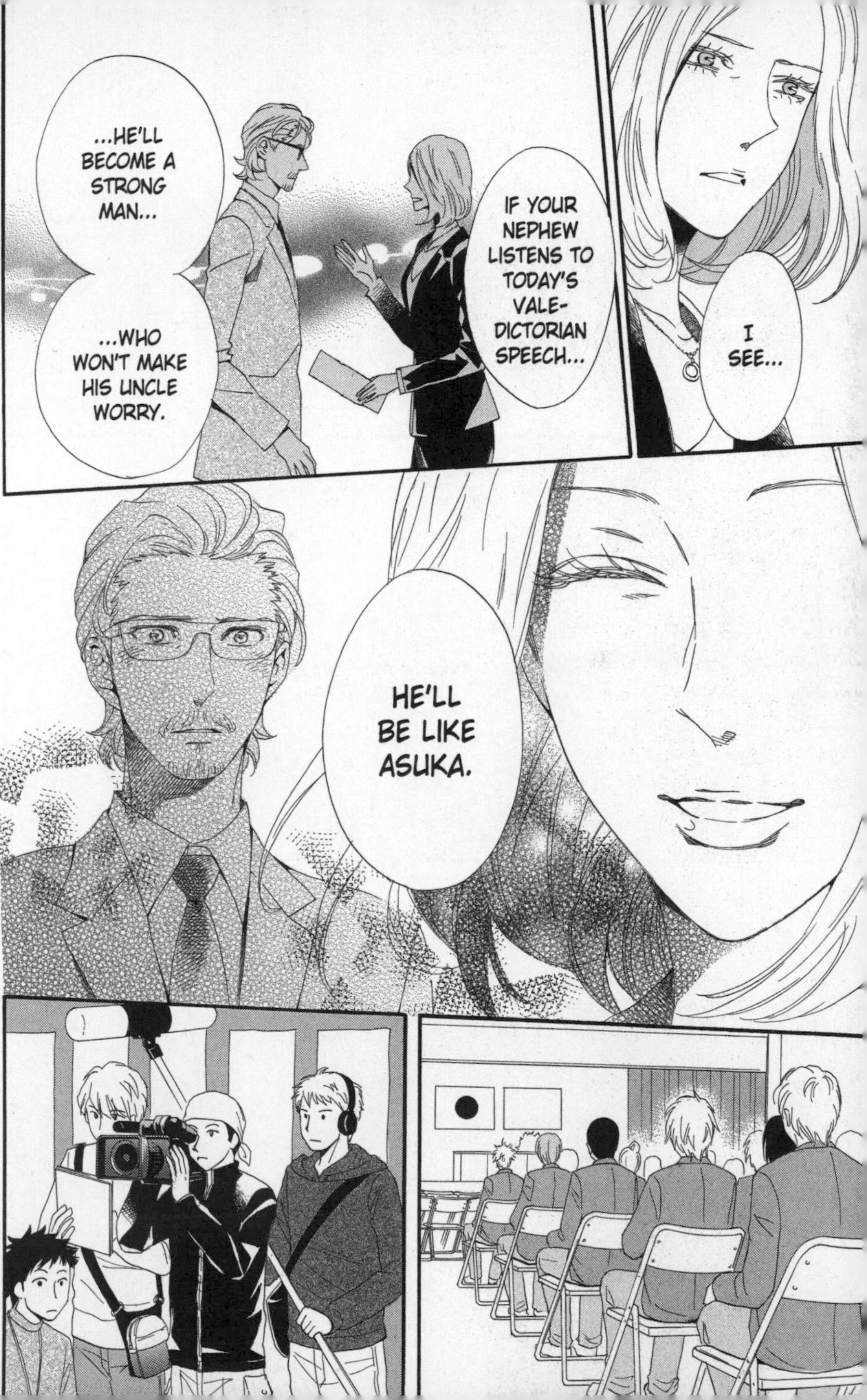
I SEE...
IF YOUR NEPHEW LISTENS TO TODAY'S VALE-DICTORIAN SPEECH...
...HE'LL BECOME A STRONG MAN...
...WHO WON'T MAKE HIS UNCLE WORRY.
HE'LL BE LIKE ASUKA.

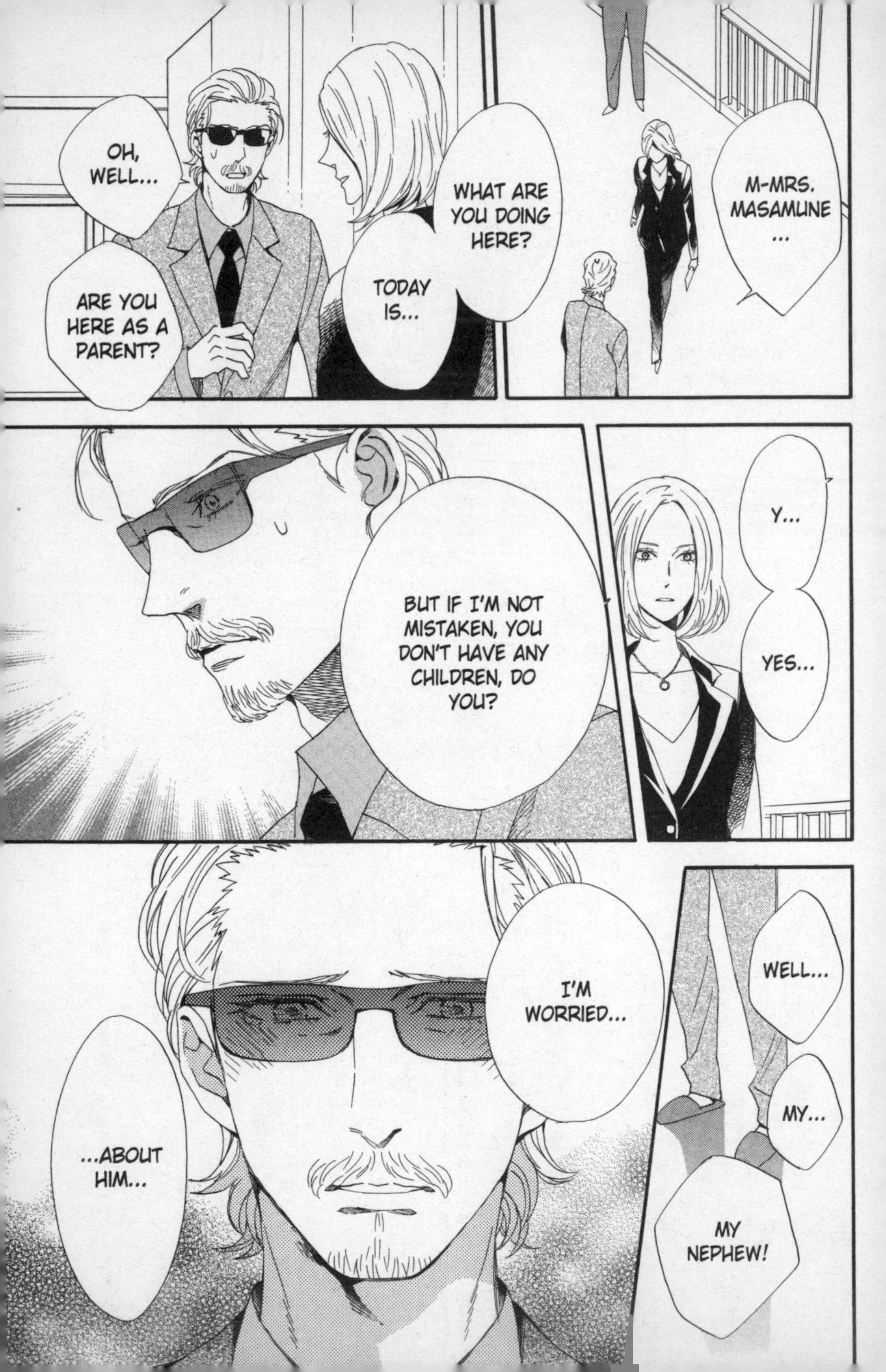
M-MRS. MASAMUNE...
WHAT ARE YOU DOING HERE?
TODAY IS...
OH, WELL...
ARE YOU HERE AS A PARENT?
Y...
YES...
BUT IF I'M NOT MISTAKEN, YOU DON'T HAVE ANY CHILDREN, DO YOU?
WELL...
MY...
MY NEPHEW!
I'M WORRIED...
...ABOUT HIM...

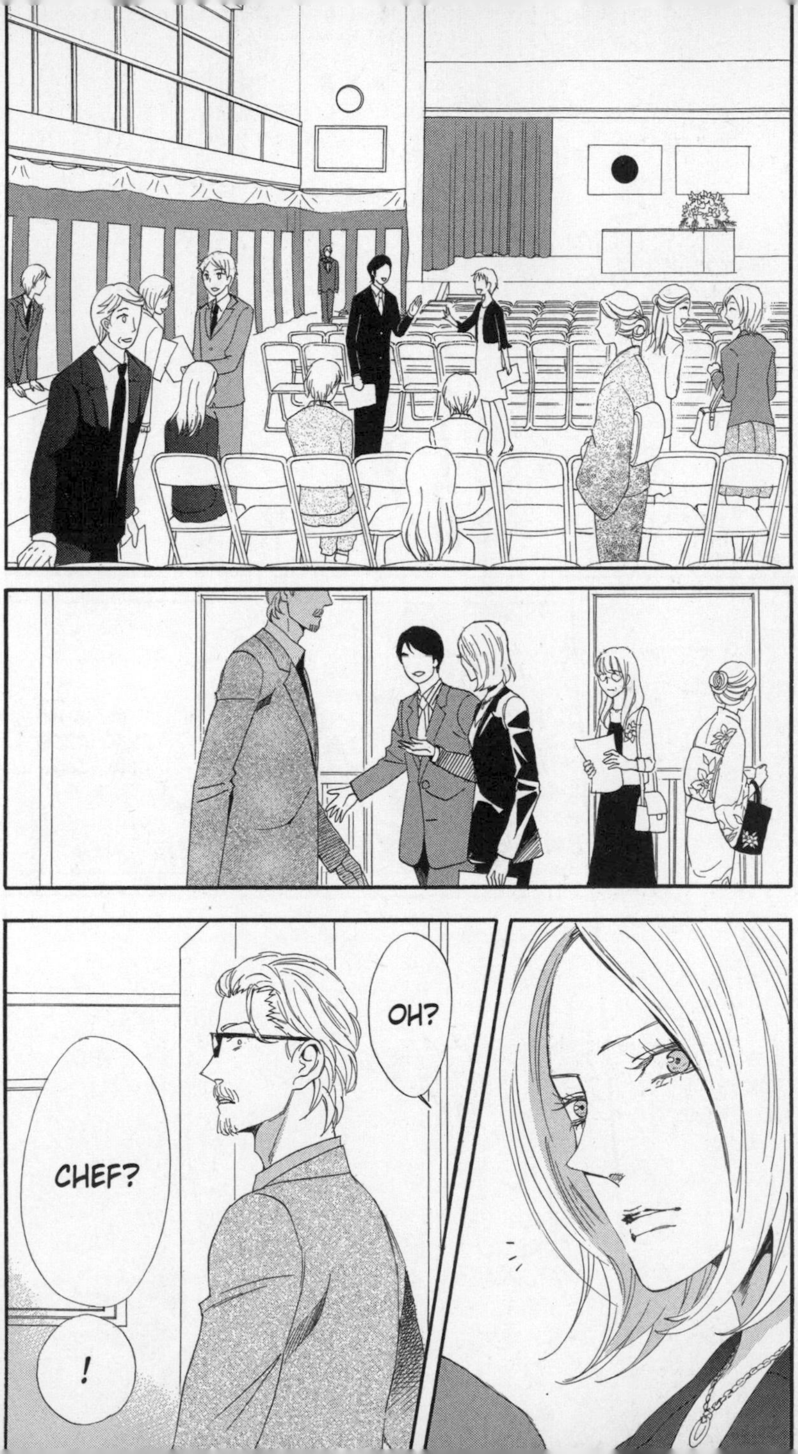
OH?
CHEF?
!

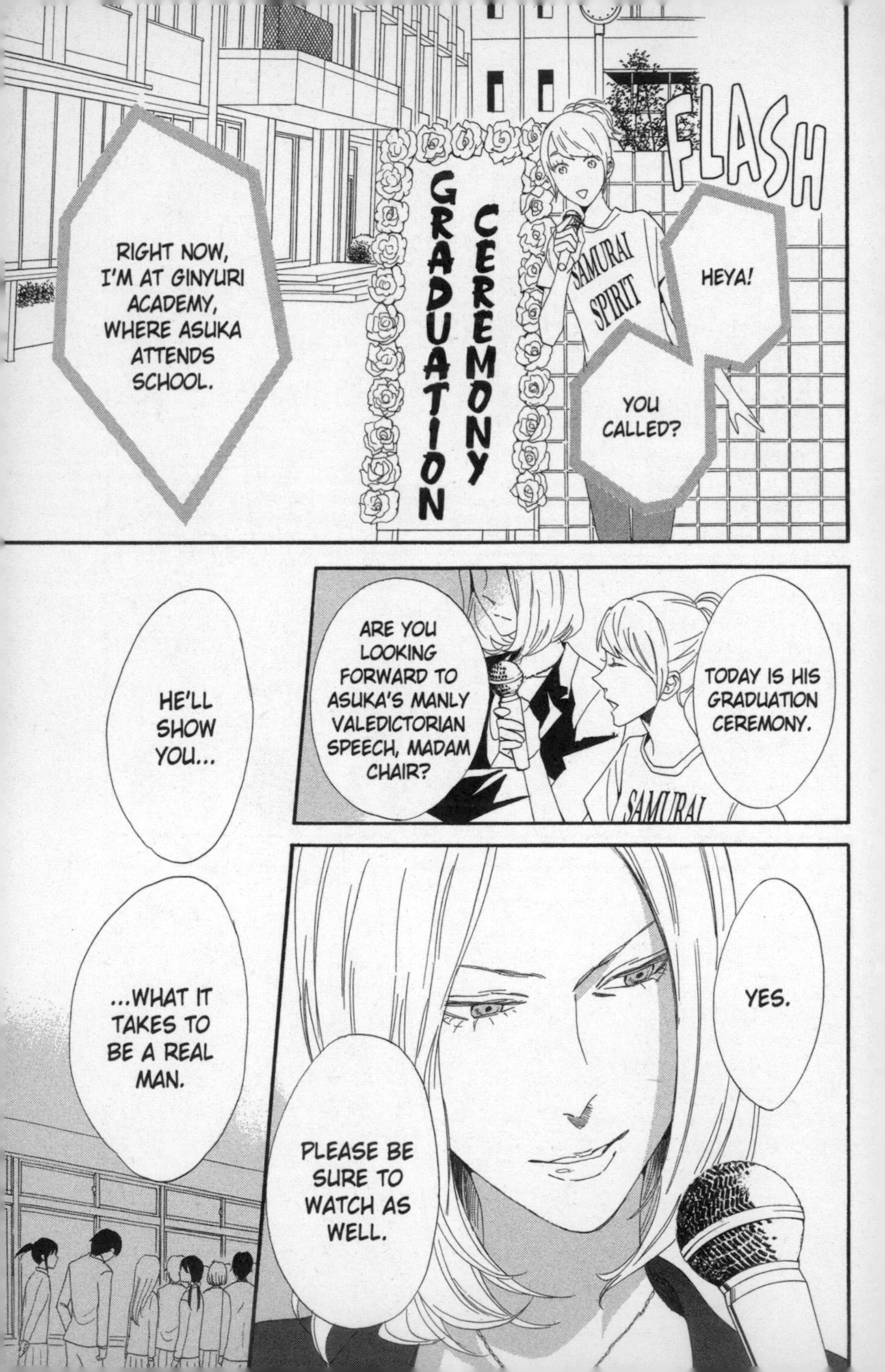
FLASH
HEYA!
YOU CALLED?
GRADUATION CEREMONY
RIGHT NOW, I'M AT GINYURI ACADEMY, WHERE ASUKA ATTENDS SCHOOL.
SAMURAI SPIRIT
TODAY IS HIS GRADUATION CEREMONY.
ARE YOU LOOKING FORWARD TO ASUKA'S MANLY VALEDICTORIAN SPEECH, MADAM CHAIR?
SAMURAI
YES.
PLEASE BE SURE TO WATCH AS WELL.
HE'LL SHOW YOU...
...WHAT IT TAKES TO BE A REAL MAN.

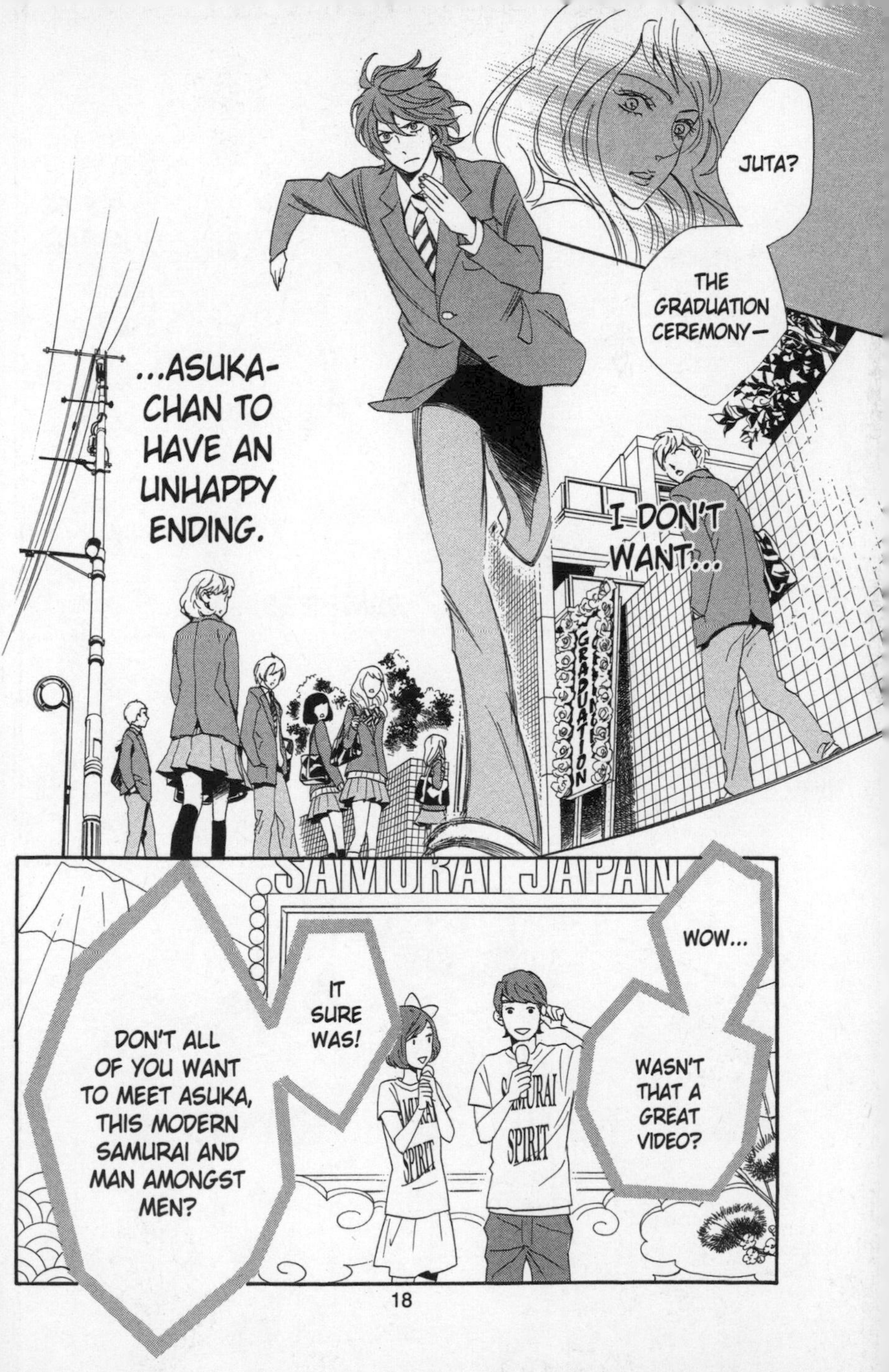
JUTA?
THE GRADUATION CEREMONY—
I DON'T WANT...
...ASUKA-CHAN TO HAVE AN UNHAPPY ENDING.
GRADUATION
SAMURAI JAPAN
WOW...
WASN'T THAT A GREAT VIDEO?
IT SURE WAS!
DON'T ALL OF YOU WANT TO MEET ASUKA, THIS MODERN SAMURAI AND MAN AMONGST MEN?
SAMURAI SPIRIT
SAMURAI SPIRIT

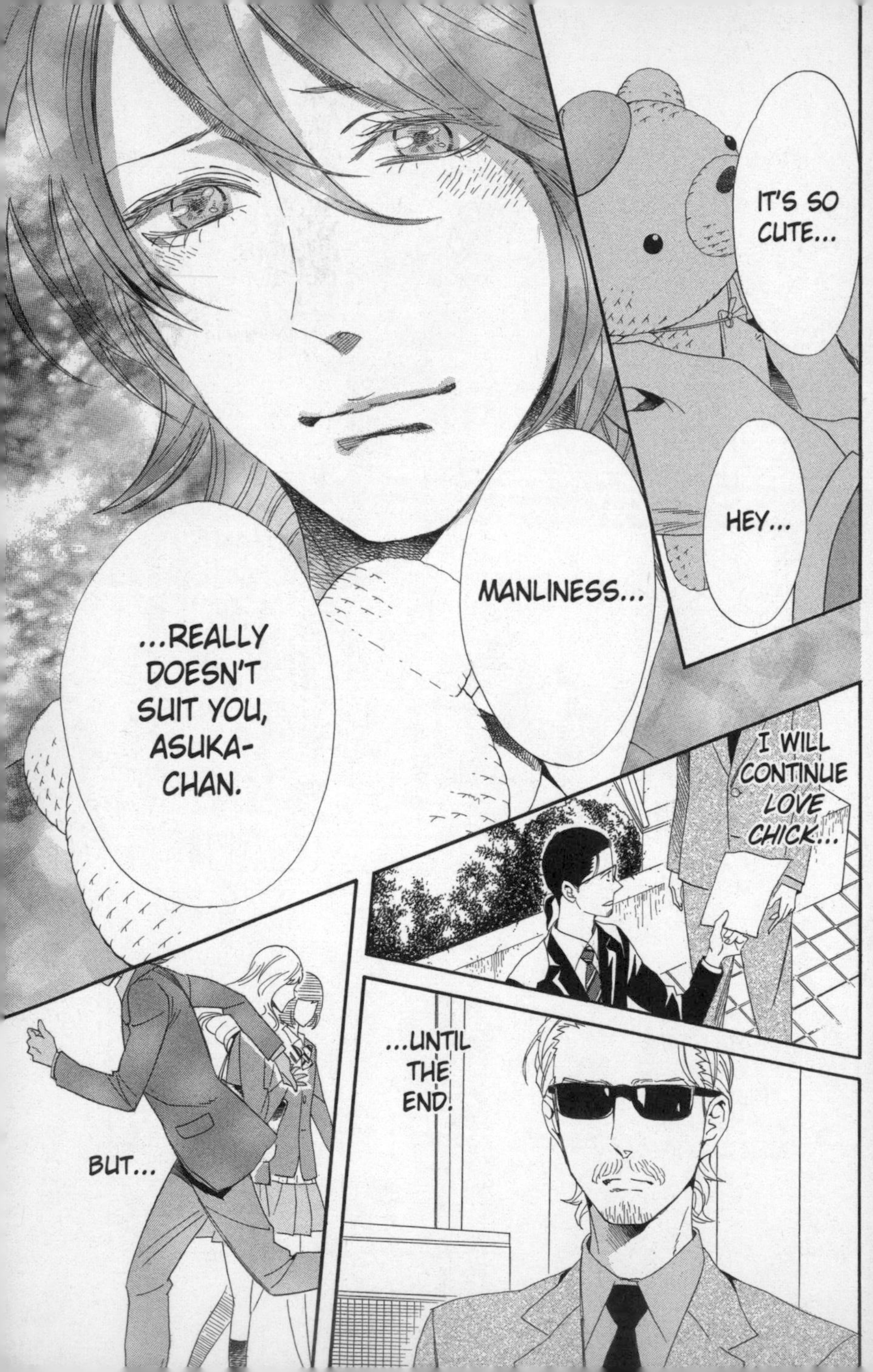
IT'S SO CUTE...
HEY...
MANLINESS...
...REALLY DOESN'T SUIT YOU, ASUKA-CHAN.
I WILL CONTINUE LOVE CHICK...
...UNTIL THE END.
BUT...

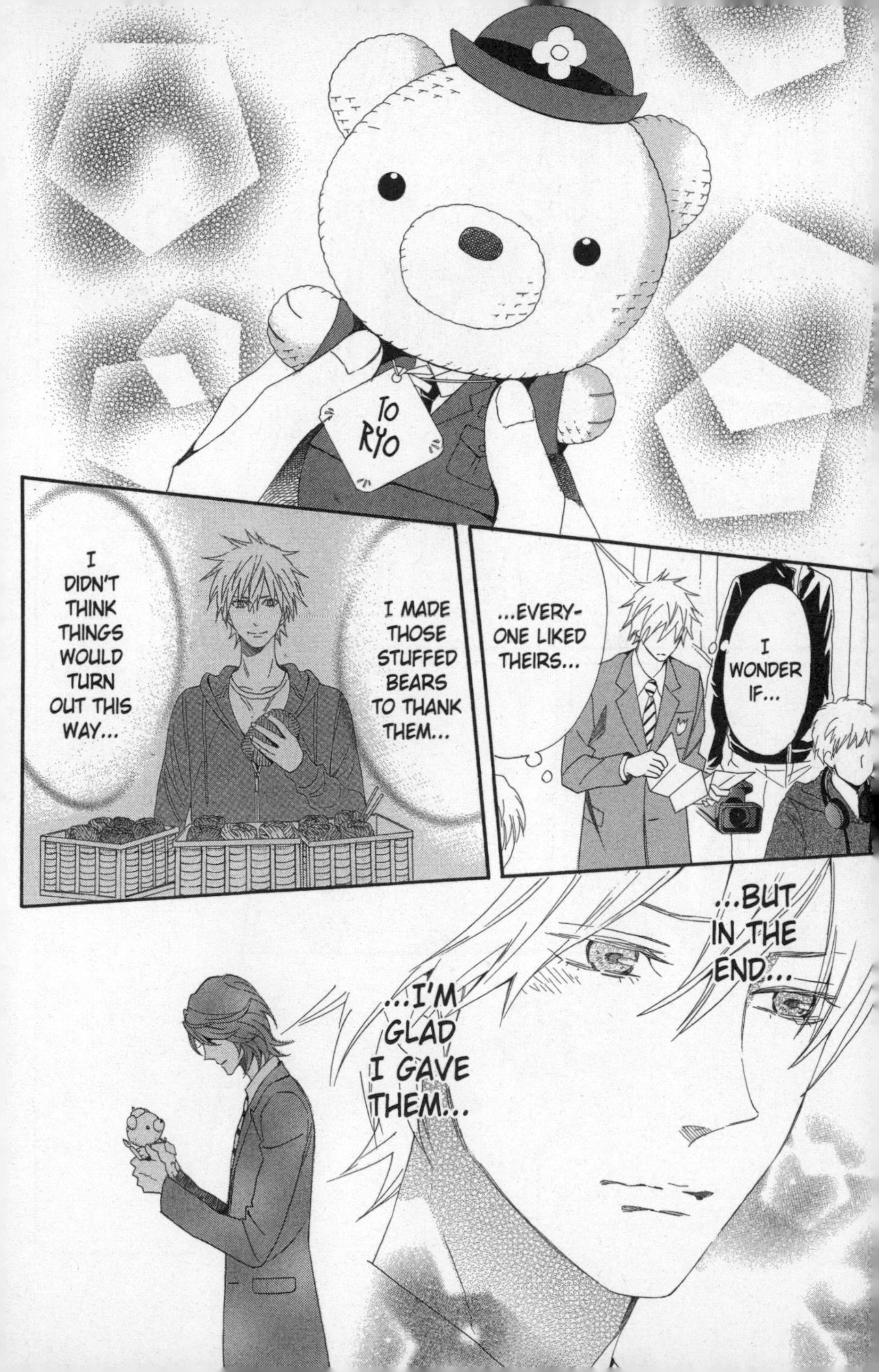
TO RYO
I WONDER IF...
...EVERYONE LIKED THEIRS...
I MADE THOSE STUFFED BEARS TO THANK THEM...
I DIDN'T THINK THINGS WOULD TURN OUT THIS WAY...
...BUT IN THE END...
...I'M GLAD I GAVE THEM...

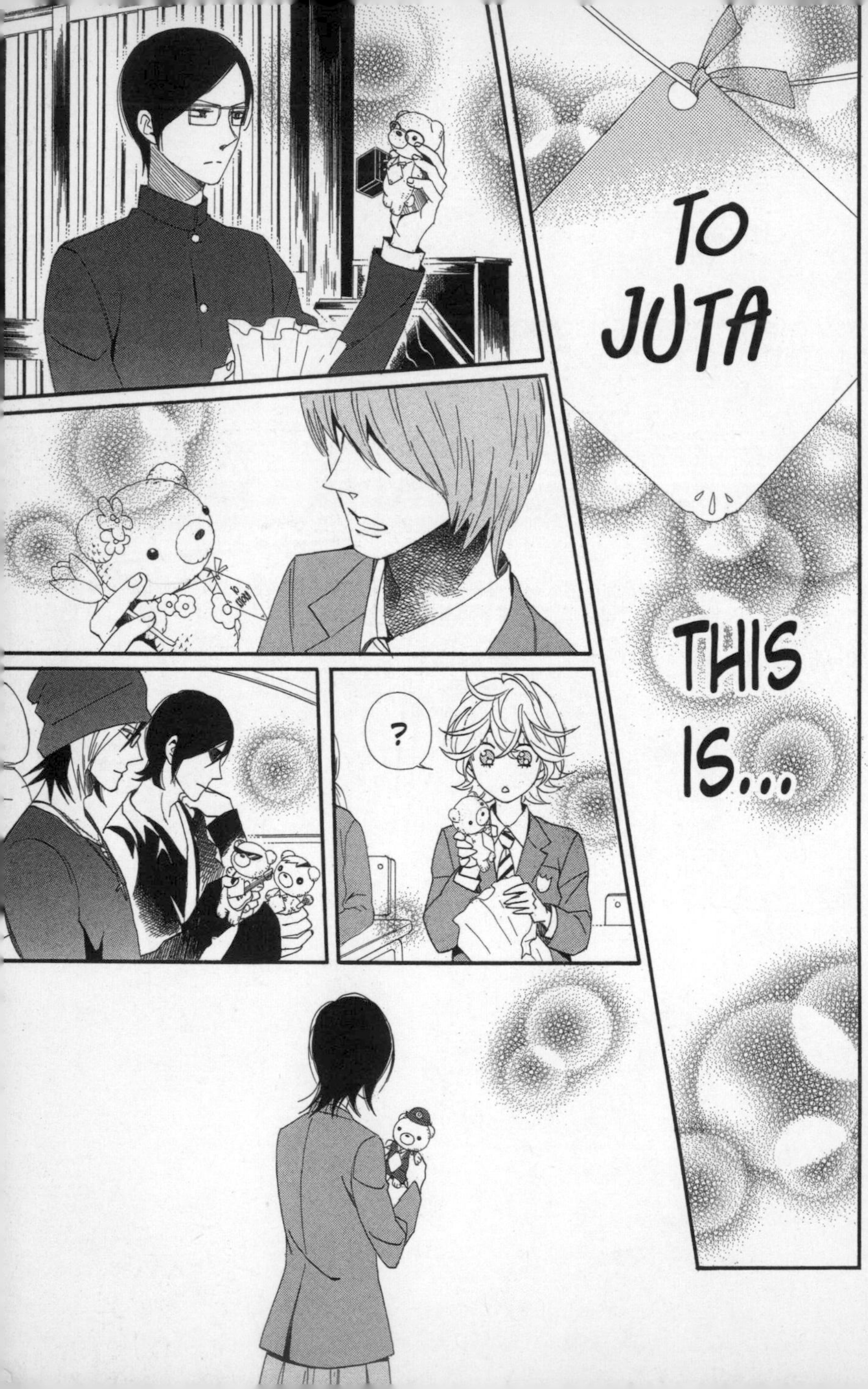
TO JUTA
THIS IS...
?

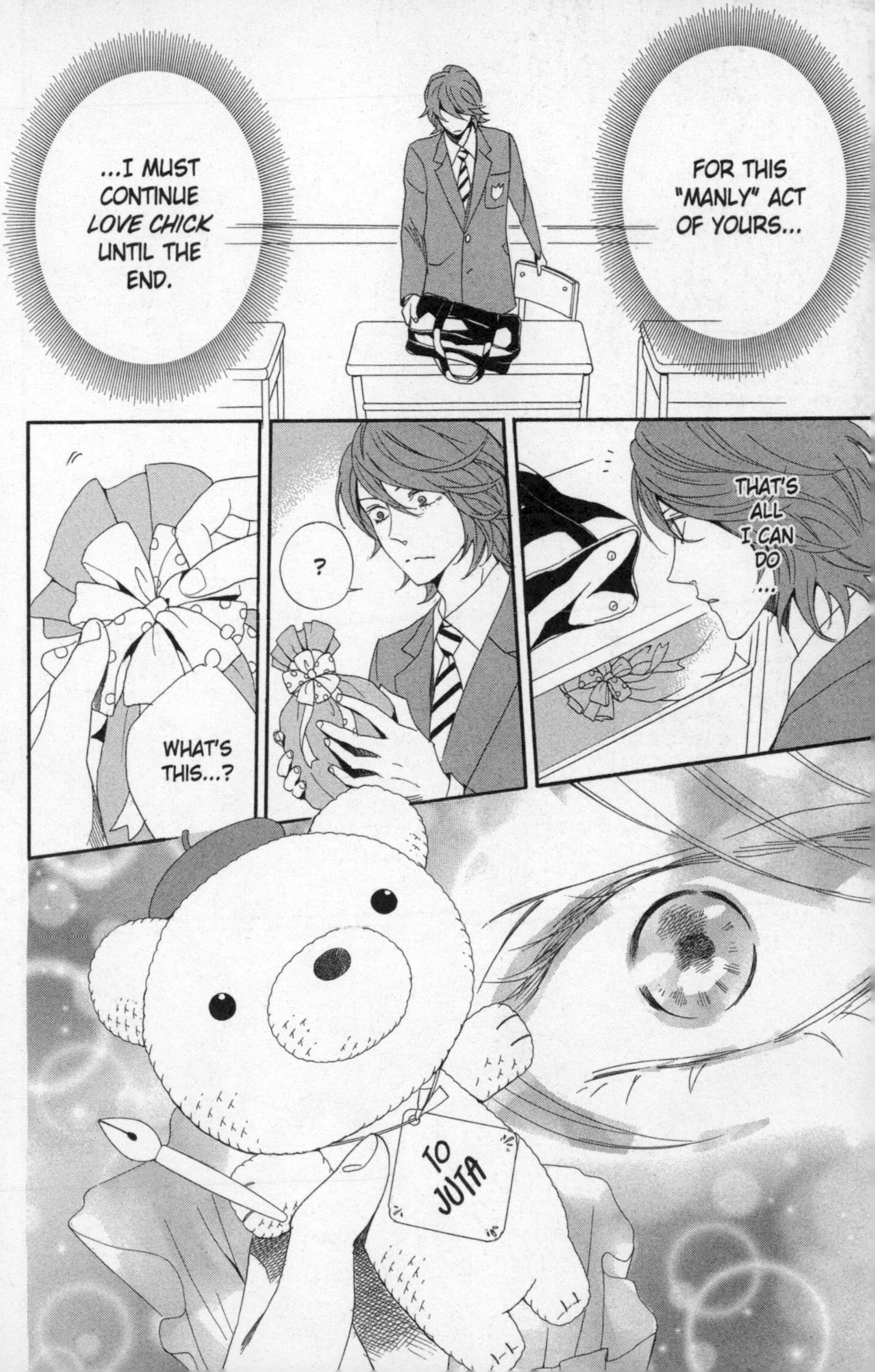
FOR THIS "MANLY" ACT OF YOURS...
...I MUST CONTINUE *LOVE CHICK* UNTIL THE END.
THAT'S ALL I CAN DO...
?
WHAT'S THIS...?
TO JUTA

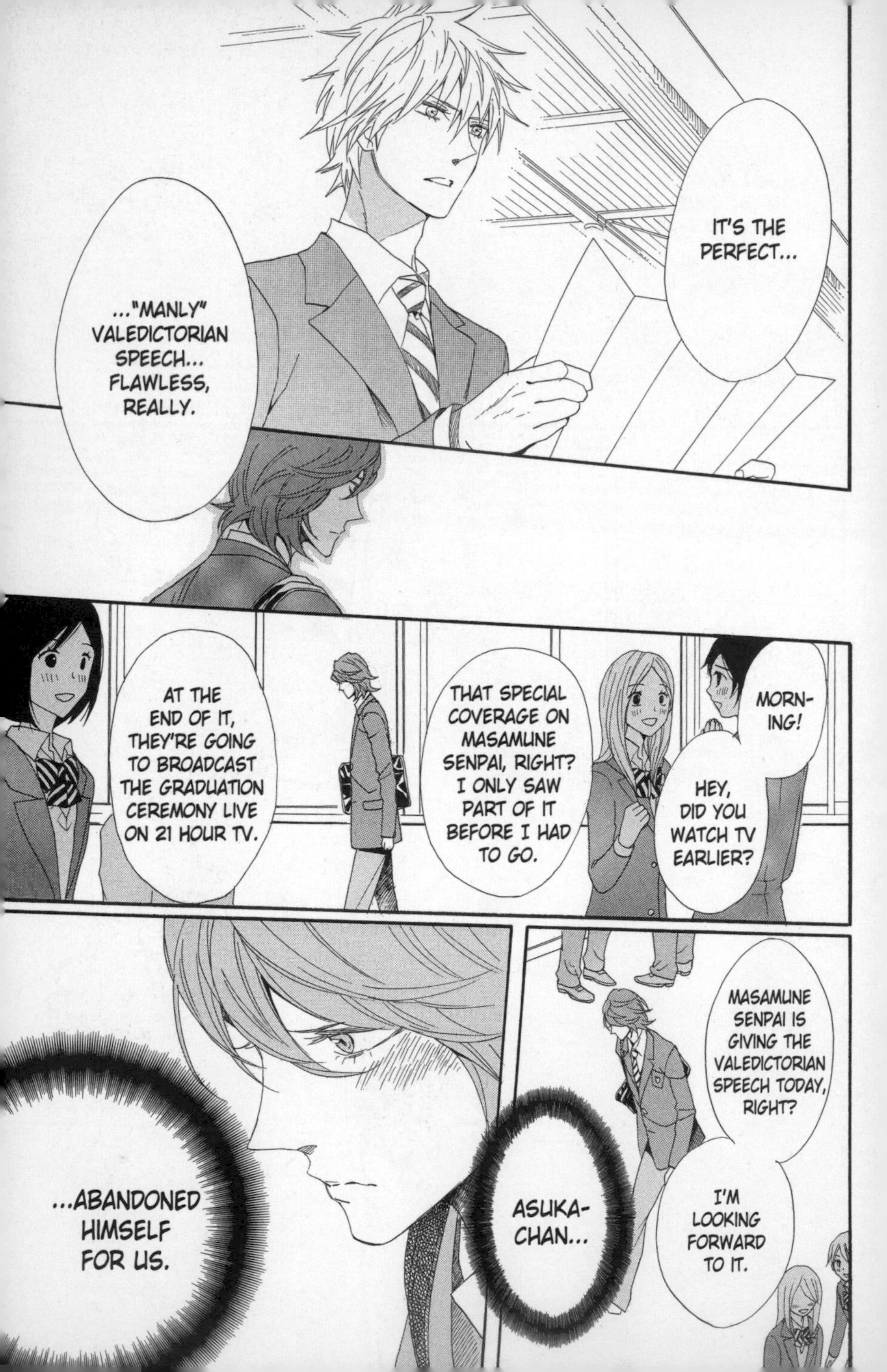
IT'S THE PERFECT...
..."MANLY" VALEDICTORIAN SPEECH... FLAWLESS, REALLY.
MORN-ING!
HEY, DID YOU WATCH TV EARLIER?
THAT SPECIAL COVERAGE ON MASAMUNE SENPAI, RIGHT? I ONLY SAW PART OF IT BEFORE I HAD TO GO.
AT THE END OF IT, THEY'RE GOING TO BROADCAST THE GRADUATION CEREMONY LIVE ON 21 HOUR TV.
MASAMUNE SENPAI IS GIVING THE VALEDICTORIAN SPEECH TODAY, RIGHT?
I'M LOOKING FORWARD TO IT.
ASUKA-CHAN...
...ABANDONED HIMSELF FOR US.

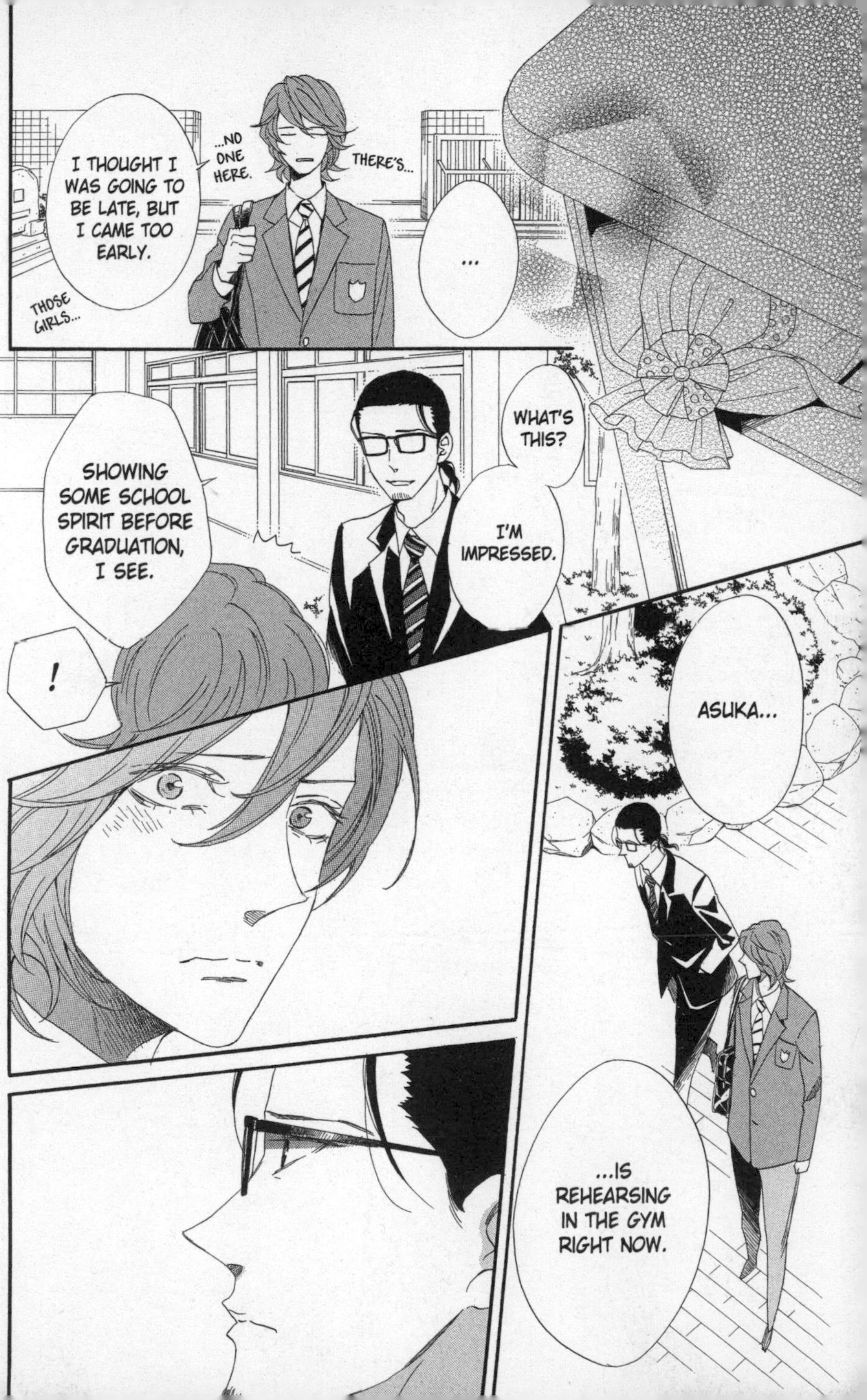
...
THERE'S...
...NO ONE HERE.
I THOUGHT I WAS GOING TO BE LATE, BUT I CAME TOO EARLY.
THOSE GIRLS...
WHAT'S THIS?
I'M IMPRESSED.
SHOWING SOME SCHOOL SPIRIT BEFORE GRADUATION, I SEE.
!
ASUKA...
...IS REHEARSING IN THE GYM RIGHT NOW.

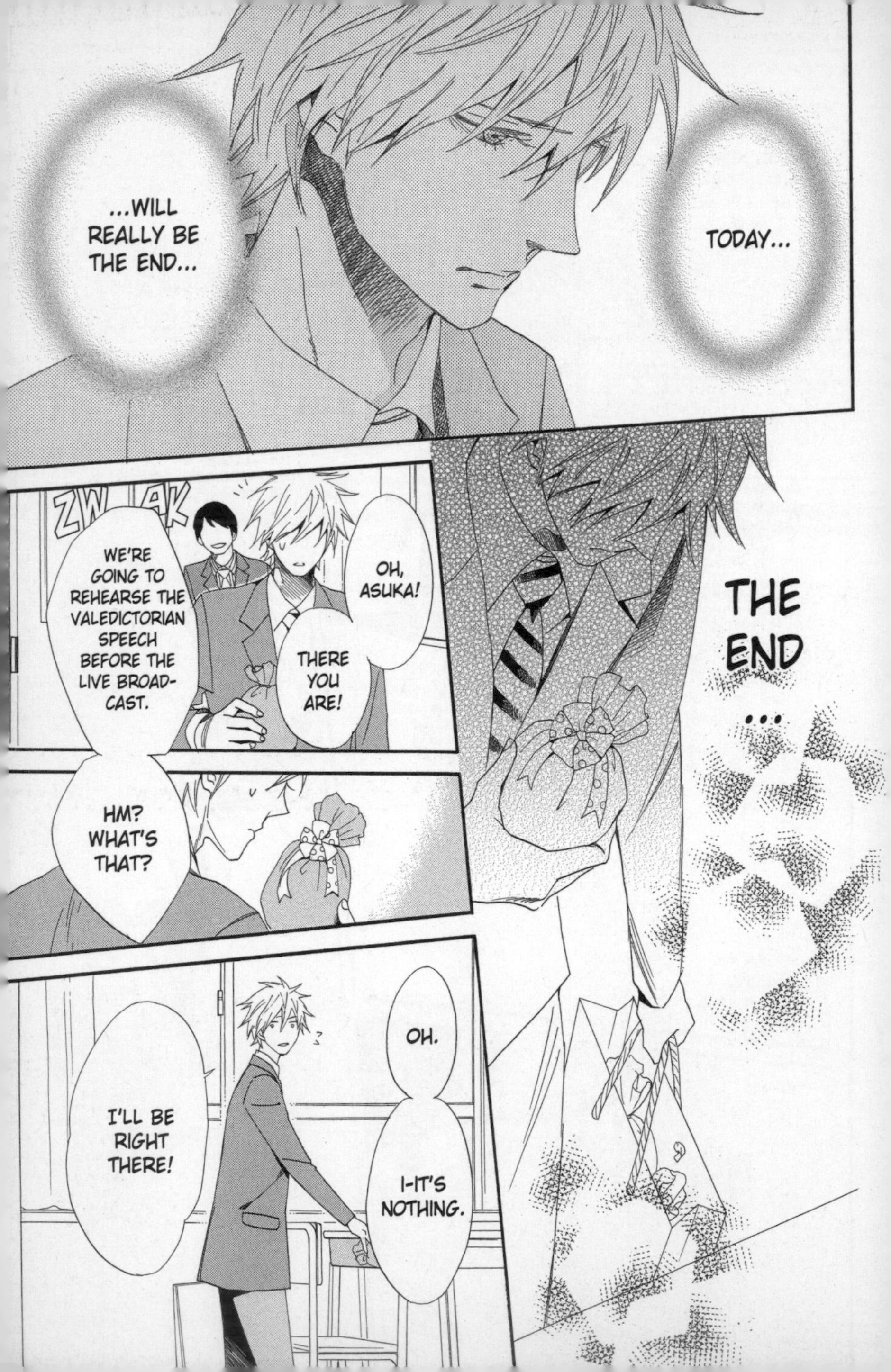
TODAY...
...WILL REALLY BE THE END...
THE END ...
ZWAK
OH, ASUKA!
THERE YOU ARE!
WE'RE GOING TO REHEARSE THE VALEDICTORIAN SPEECH BEFORE THE LIVE BROAD-CAST.
HM? WHAT'S THAT?
OH.
I-IT'S NOTHING.
I'LL BE RIGHT THERE!

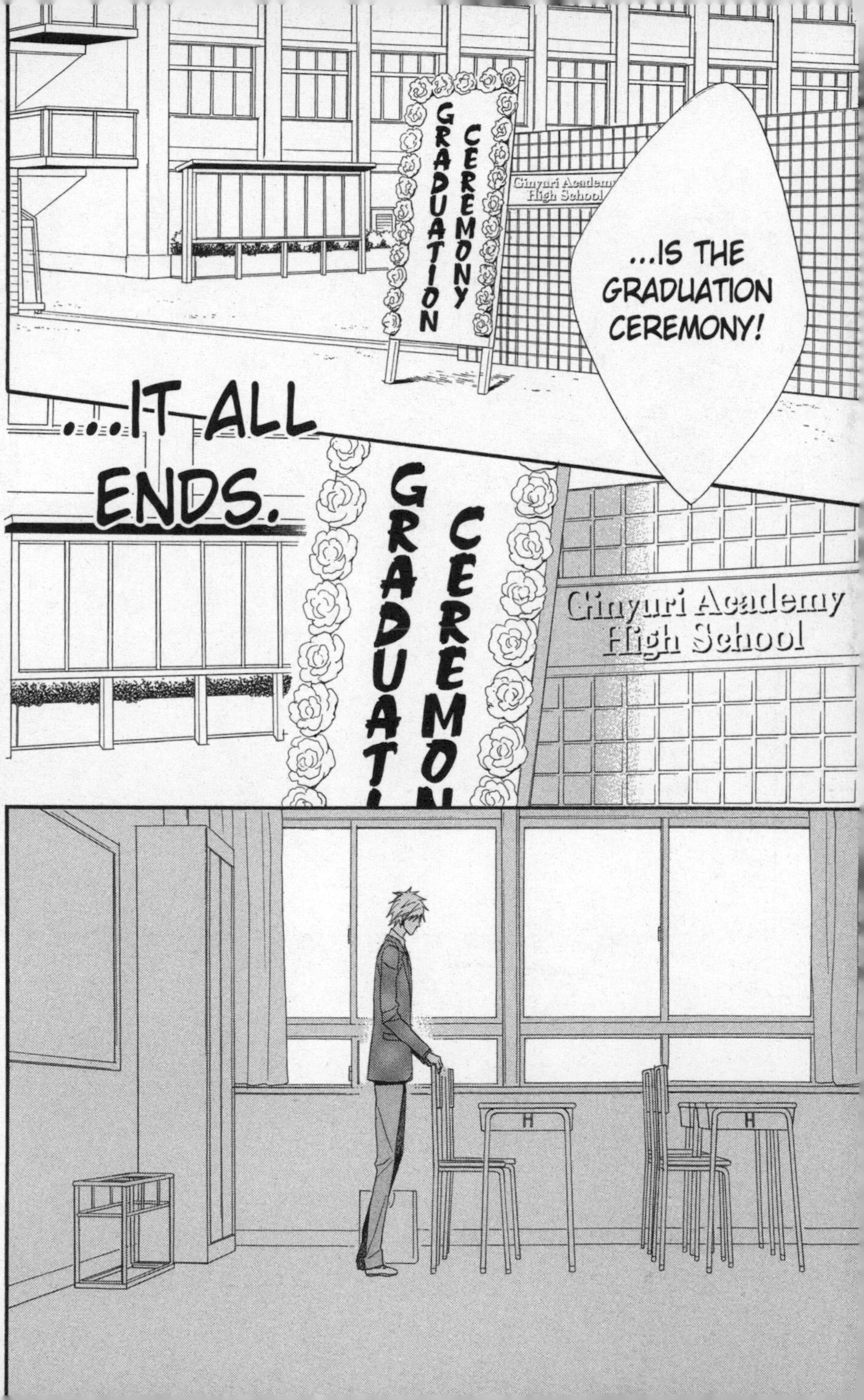
...IS THE GRADUATION CEREMONY!
GRADUATION CEREMONY
Ginyuri Academy High School
...IT ALL ENDS.
Ginyuri Academy High School

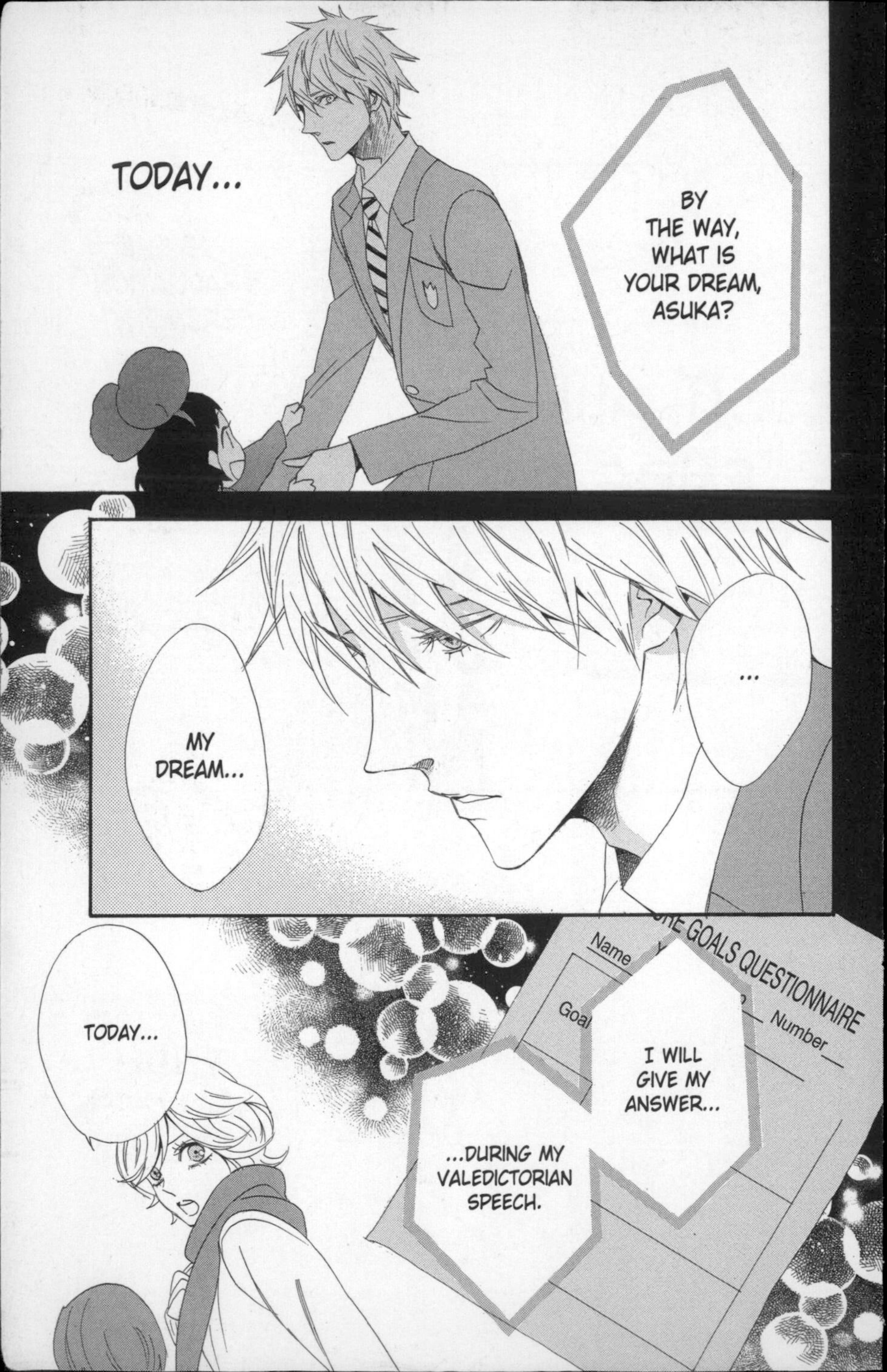
BY THE WAY, WHAT IS YOUR DREAM, ASUKA?
TODAY...
...
MY DREAM...
GOALS QUESTIONNAIRE
Name
Number
I WILL GIVE MY ANSWER...
...DURING MY VALEDICTORIAN SPEECH.
TODAY...

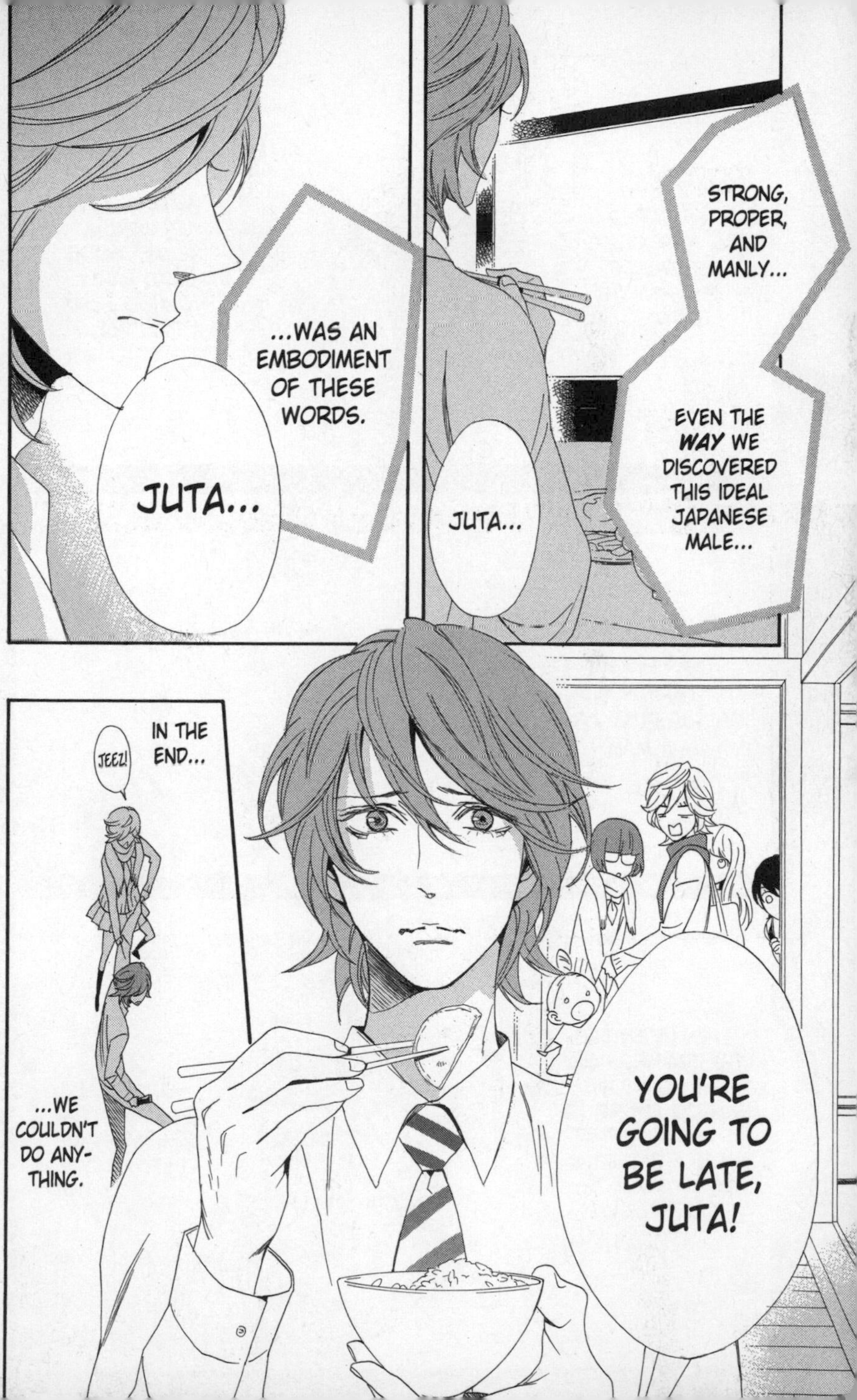
STRONG, PROPER, AND MANLY...
EVEN THE WAY WE DISCOVERED THIS IDEAL JAPANESE MALE...
JUTA...
...WAS AN EMBODIMENT OF THESE WORDS.
JUTA...
YOU'RE GOING TO BE LATE, JUTA!
IN THE END...
JEEZ!
...WE COULDN'T DO ANYTHING.

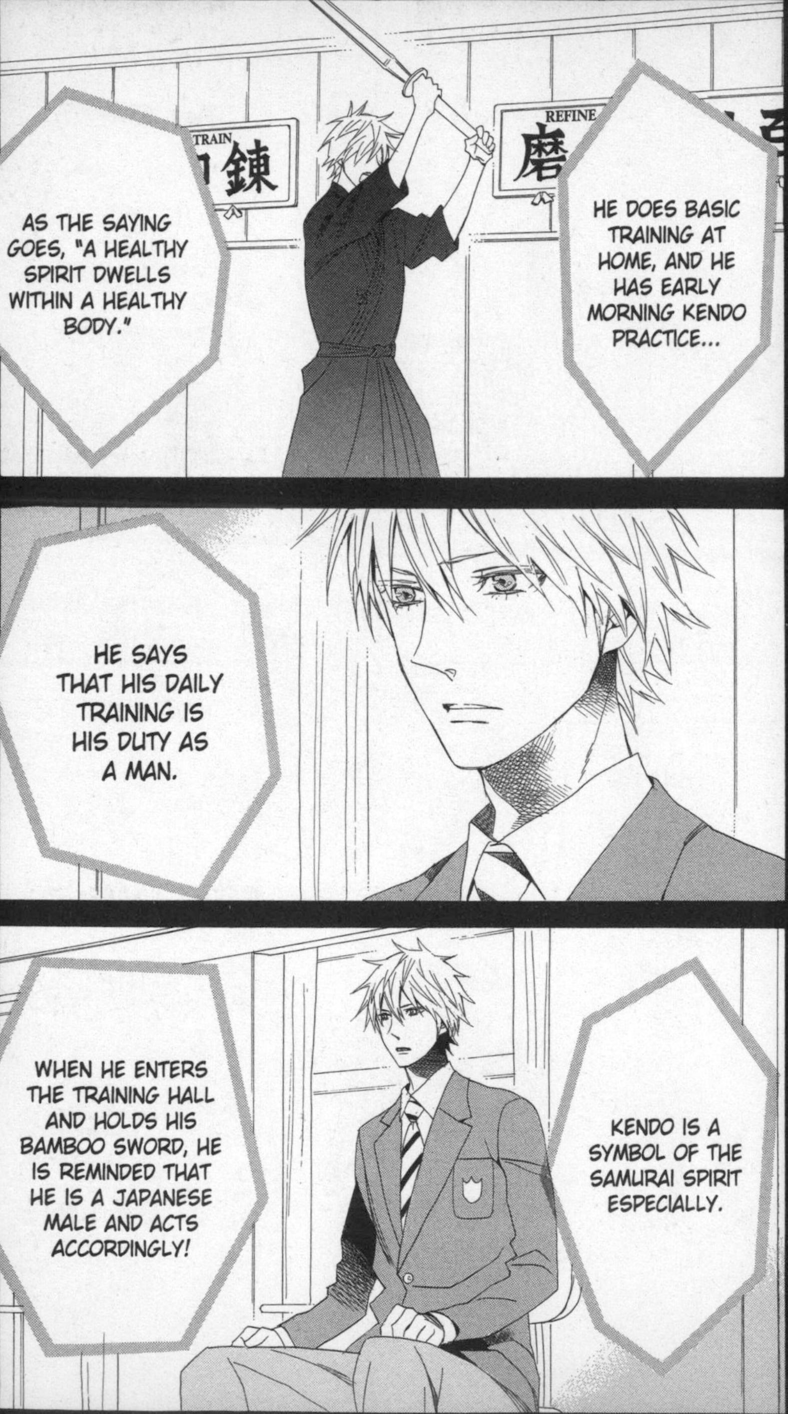
REFINE
磨
TRAIN
錬
HE DOES BASIC TRAINING AT HOME, AND HE HAS EARLY MORNING KENDO PRACTICE...
AS THE SAYING GOES, "A HEALTHY SPIRIT DWELLS WITHIN A HEALTHY BODY."
HE SAYS THAT HIS DAILY TRAINING IS HIS DUTY AS A MAN.
KENDO IS A SYMBOL OF THE SAMURAI SPIRIT ESPECIALLY.
WHEN HE ENTERS THE TRAINING HALL AND HOLDS HIS BAMBOO SWORD, HE IS REMINDED THAT HE IS A JAPANESE MALE AND ACTS ACCORDINGLY!

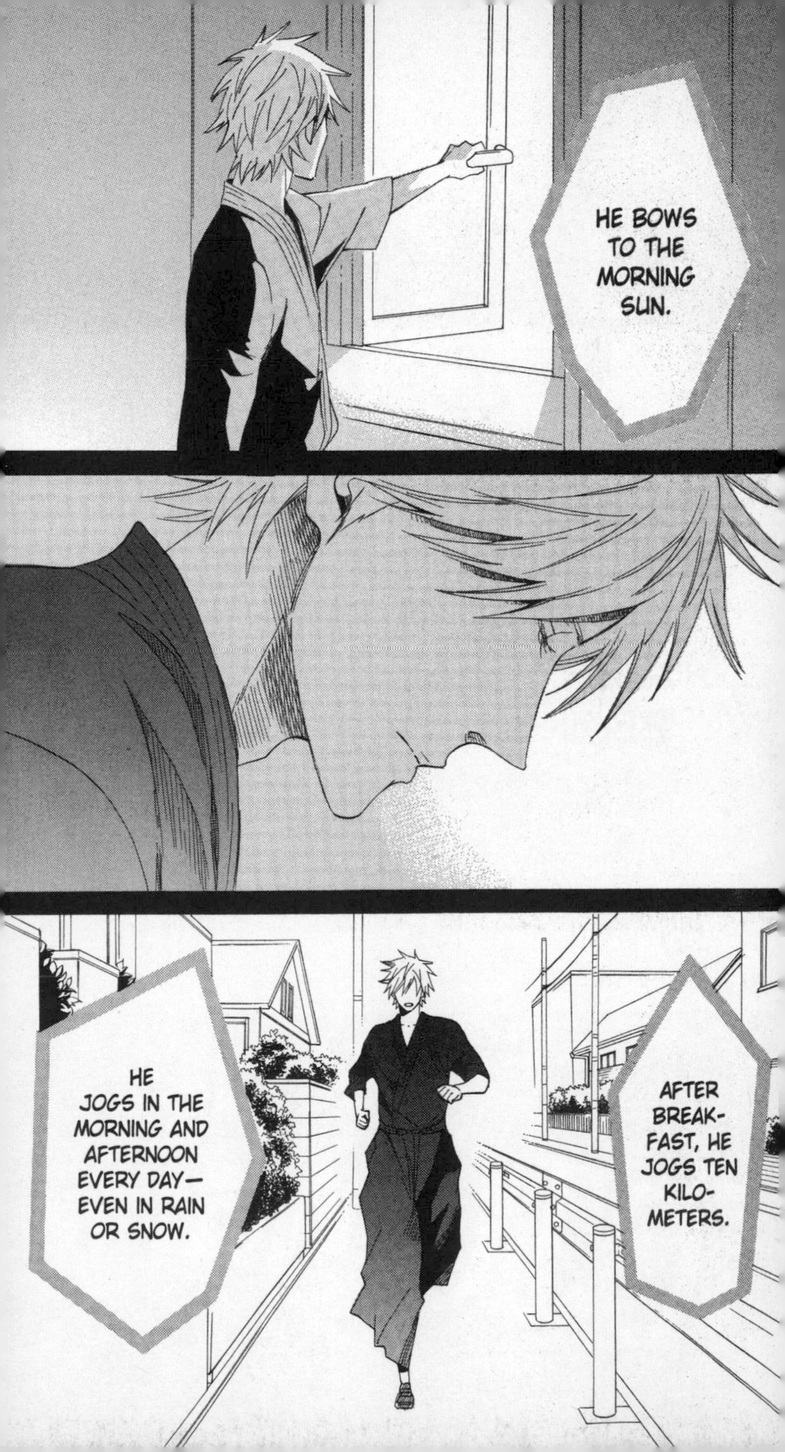
HE BOWS TO THE MORNING SUN.
AFTER BREAK-FAST, HE JOGS TEN KILO-METERS.
HE JOGS IN THE MORNING AND AFTERNOON EVERY DAY—EVEN IN RAIN OR SNOW.

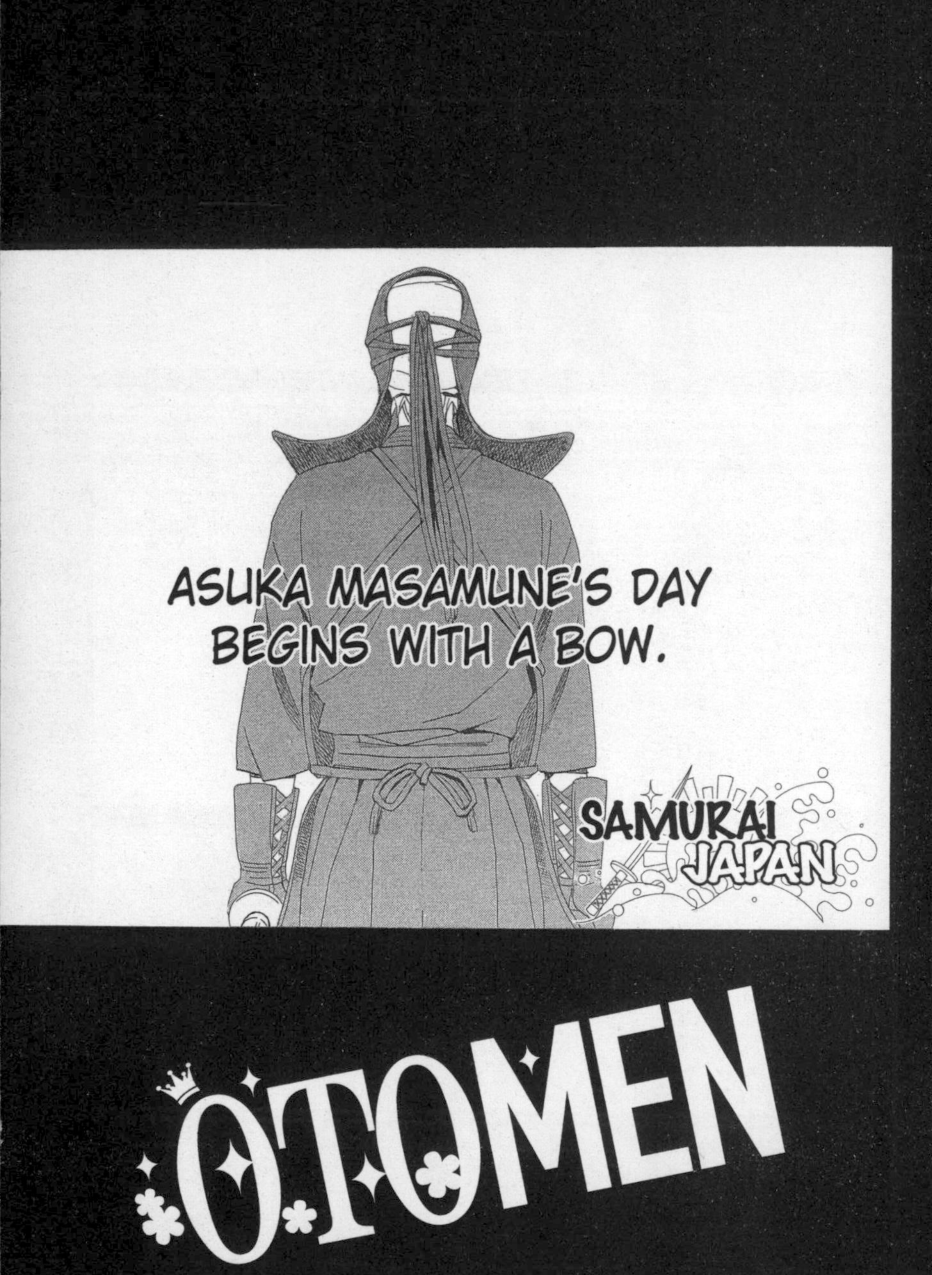
ASUKA MASAMUNE'S DAY BEGINS WITH A BOW.
SAMURAI JAPAN
OTOMEN

OTOMEN
volume 18
CONTENTS

STORY

Asuka learns that his mother Kiyomi has been tormenting Ryo and his friends. He breaks up with Ryo and distances himself from everyone. While fulfilling his mother's wish for him to become a true man, he catches the eye of a television studio executive. Meanwhile, Ryo is in a daze after losing Asuka and becomes an entirely different person. Eventually, she regains her former self, but graduation day is approaching, and she still hasn't reunited with Asuka…

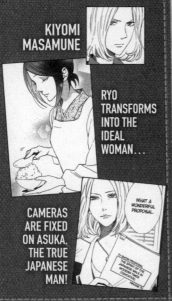

KIYOMI MASAMUNE

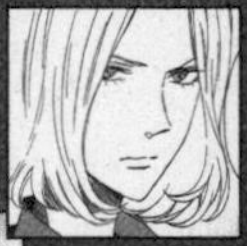

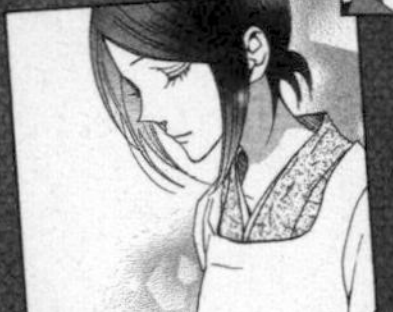

RYO TRANSFORMS INTO THE IDEAL WOMAN…

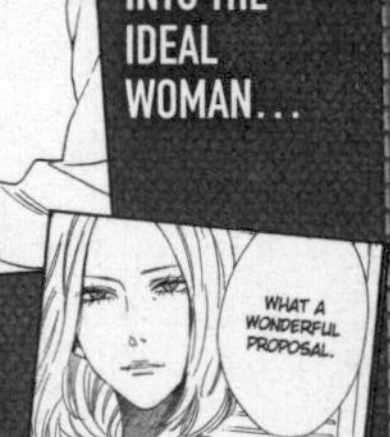
WHAT A WONDERFUL PROPOSAL.
TV SHOW PROPOSAL THE SPIRIT OF THE JAPANESE MALE IN MODERN TIMES (TENTATIVE)
HINODE TV

CAMERAS ARE FIXED ON ASUKA, THE TRUE JAPANESE MAN!

OTHER OTOMEN

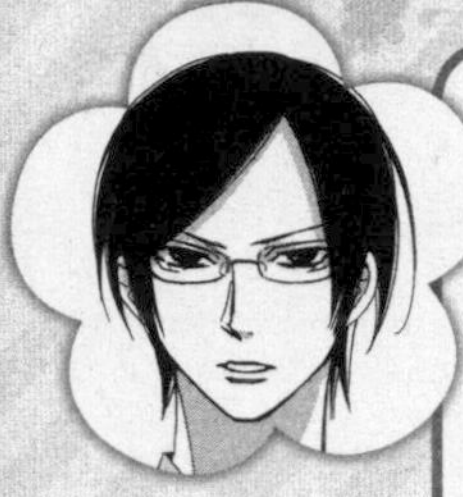

Hajime Tonomine

The captain of the Kinbara High School kendo team, he considers Asuka his sworn rival. He is actually an *otomen* who is good with cosmetics.

Yamato Ariake

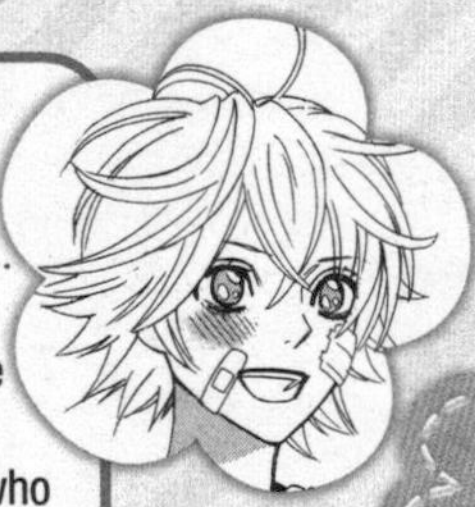

He is younger than Asuka and looks like a cute girl. He is a delusional *otomen* who admires manliness.

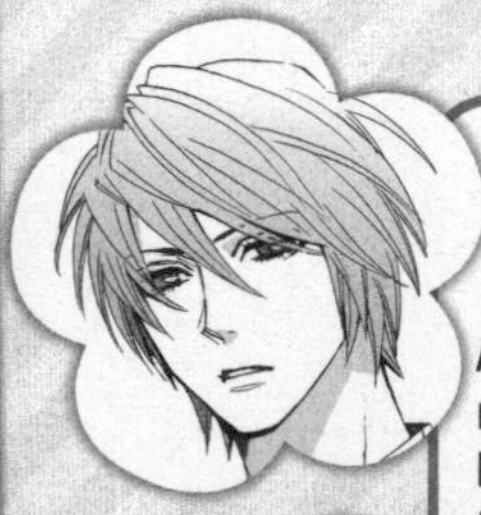

Kitora Kurokawa

Asuka's classmate. A man who is captivated by the beauty of flowers. He is an obsessed *otomen* who wants to cover the world in flowers.

O.T.OMEN Characters & Story

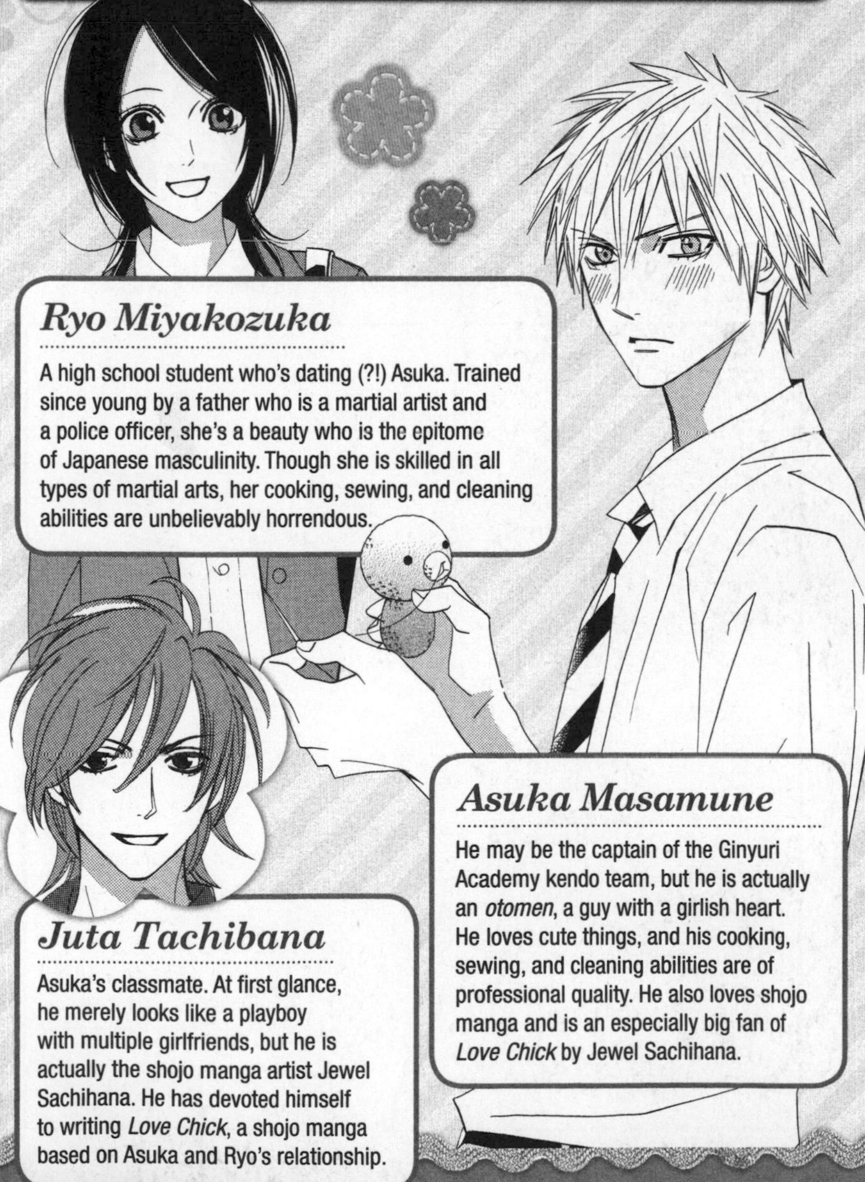

Ryo Miyakozuka

A high school student who's dating (?!) Asuka. Trained since young by a father who is a martial artist and a police officer, she's a beauty who is the epitome of Japanese masculinity. Though she is skilled in all types of martial arts, her cooking, sewing, and cleaning abilities are unbelievably horrendous.

Asuka Masamune

He may be the captain of the Ginyuri Academy kendo team, but he is actually an *otomen*, a guy with a girlish heart. He loves cute things, and his cooking, sewing, and cleaning abilities are of professional quality. He also loves shojo manga and is an especially big fan of *Love Chick* by Jewel Sachihana.

Juta Tachibana

Asuka's classmate. At first glance, he merely looks like a playboy with multiple girlfriends, but he is actually the shojo manga artist Jewel Sachihana. He has devoted himself to writing *Love Chick*, a shojo manga based on Asuka and Ryo's relationship.

Shojo Beat

OTOMEN

Story & Art by
Aya Kanno

Volume
EIGHTEEN

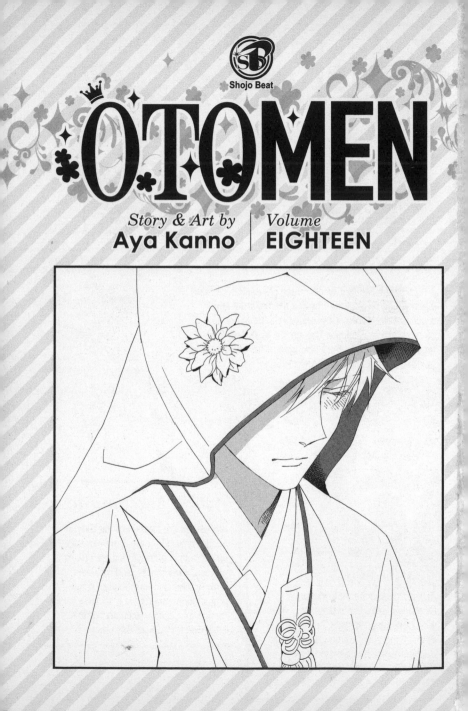